T0407013

Authenticity and Teacher-Student Motivational Synergy

Despite the common association between authenticity and motivation in language learning, there does not currently exist a single volume exploring these connections. This book looks at the relationship between authenticity and motivation by specifically viewing the process of mutually validating the act of learning as *social authentication*, which in turn can often lead to positive motivational synergy between students and teacher(s). The study at the centre of this book uses autoethnography and practitioner research to examine the complex relationship between authenticity and motivation in the foreign language learning classroom. In particular, it traces the links between student and teacher motivation, and proposes that authenticity can act as a bridge to connect learners to the classroom environment and engage with the activity of learning.

Richard Pinner is a language teacher and associate professor at Sophia University in Tokyo. He holds a PhD in ELT and Applied Linguistics and has published several articles on language teaching, most recently in *Language Teaching Research*, *English Today*, and *Applied Linguistics Review*.

Authenticity and Teacher-Student Motivational Synergy

A Narrative of Language Teaching

Richard Pinner

Routledge
Taylor & Francis Group

LONDON AND NEW YORK

First published 2019
by Routledge
2 Park Square, Milton Park, Abingdon, Oxon OX14 4RN

and by Routledge
52 Vanderbilt Avenue, New York, NY 10017

Routledge is an imprint of the Taylor & Francis Group, an informa business

British Library Cataloguing in Publication Data
A catalogue record for this book is available from the British Library

Library of Congress Cataloging in Publication Data
Names: Pinner, Richard S., author.
Title: Authenticity and teacher-student motivational synergy :
a narrative of language teaching / by Richard Pinner.
Description: Abingdon, Oxon ; New York, NY : Routledge, 2019. |
Includes bibliographical references and index.
Identifiers: LCCN 2018058361 | ISBN 9780815395188 (hardback) |
ISBN 9781351184298 (ebook)
Subjects: LCSH: Language and languages–Study and teaching (Higher) |
Second language acquisition. | Teacher-student relationships. |
Authenticity (Philosophy) | Motivation in education.
Classification: LCC P51 .P466 2019 | DDC 407.1/1–dc23
LC record available at https://lccn.loc.gov/2018058361

ISBN: 978-0-8153-9518-8 (hbk)
ISBN: 978-1-351-18429-8 (ebk)

Typeset in Galliard
by Newgen Publishing UK

Contents

Figures

Tables

Ad-hoc interviews

Acknowledgements

I wish to acknowledge my sincere gratitude to Ema Ushioda for her patience, dedication, support, and friendship in writing this book. She has given me the autonomy I needed, the scaffolding necessary to be autonomous, and helped me keep my motivation throughout the process.

Many sincere thanks also to Richard Smith for his comments and other supportive acts of kindness. I would also like to thank everyone at the University of Warwick's Centre for Applied Linguistics, where I was always warmly welcomed on my infrequent visits. I would especially like to thank Erkan Külekçi, Gosia Sky, and Darío Banegas, as well as Sal Consoli and Takumi Aoyama.

I also wish to thank colleagues in Japan who have supported me. Makoto Ikeda for constant, never-ending support and friendship; Rob Lowe for philosophy and craft beer; Dave Rear for critical thinking and post-Brexit woes; and Neale Cunningham for curries and shoulders. Many thanks to Satomi Fuji for kindly checking my transcripts. I also thank Dave Allen, Alex Gilmore, Satoru Uchida, Chantal Hemmi, Mikio Iguchi, Stephen Ryan, Ryo Nitta, Richard Sampson, Dominic Cheetham, and many others whom I could mention, all of whom have helped me in some way as I prepared this manuscript. I also thank Steve Mann and Judith Hanks for their insightful comments and help in arriving at the final version.

Of course, this inquiry would not have been possible without the wonderful students who lend me their ears each semester, but especially those 25 wonderful people who made up the CLERAC course in 2014. Thank you all for your hard work and for your consent to conduct this inquiry. I hope you know how much it means to me.

This has been a very personal inquiry, and at times it has kept me away from my family, so I would like to thank Oscar and Kimie for their love and support as always, and for helping me be the best version of myself. Oscar may not know it, but he and my family are key motivators in why I have worked so hard in order to put together this study.

Finally, I would like to acknowledge anyone who reads this. It is a long inquiry with many twists and turns. I hope it takes you somewhere interesting.

Glossary of abbreviations and specialist terms

attractor state	In dynamic systems theory, attractor states are the usual or ordinary patterns of behaviour that systems gravitate towards.
CaLabo	CALL-Room proprietary software used by the university which enables teachers to monitor and control students' networked PCs.
CALL	Computer-aided language learning.
CLER	Centre for Language Education and Research, which is responsible for university-wide compulsory and elective foreign language courses.
CLERAC	The compulsory course for first-year students in the university called Academic Communication, which was the focus of the current inquiry and where the majority of data was collected in 2014.
Coffee Room	An online discussion forum often used for homework tasks on the university Moodle-based VLE.
complexity	Behaviour is dependent on so many variables that it is hard to predict and needs to be understood in relation to the other processes that influence it.
DCT	Discussion on Contemporary Topics. A class taught in 2012 and one of the starting points for this inquiry.
EROI	Energy return on investment.
EP	Exploratory Practice.
Indicator of synergy	A way of observing or theorising the existence of synergy. Indicators are conceptualised as being retrospective, based on signs left by the creation of synaptic crossings.
Initial Conditions	The starting conditions at the time when measuring or observation begins.
INT	A class entitled Intermediate also taught at CLER in 2013.
Moodle	Modular Object Oriented Dynamic Learning Environment, a free VLE widely used in education.

motivational synergy	When teacher and student motivation works in a harmonious or reciprocal way, which can have either positive or negative valence.
NI	Narrative inquiry.
RED	Relationship to English Diagram, a task used in the first and last classes to collect multimodal data.
social authentication	The process of groups mutually authenticating and validating learning.
strange attractor	An attractor state that is never quite fully reached although systems tend to gravitate towards it.
synaptic crossing	A way of facilitating motivational synergy. Synaptic crossings are the myriad moments in which synergy is attained.
VLE	Virtual learning environment.

1 Introduction

> If you seek authenticity for authenticity's sake, you are no longer authentic.
>
> Jean-Paul Sartre (1992, p. 4)

This book examines the connections between authenticity and motivation in language teaching and learning, two often cited yet highly elusive constructs. Despite this elusiveness, authenticity and motivation are high-frequency collocates in discussions around language teaching, and both are seen as having an important position in the process of second-language acquisition (SLA) (Dörnyei & Ushioda, 2011; Gilmore, 2011; Mishan, 2005). For example, in the collection of papers entitled *International Perspectives on Motivation* edited by Ushioda (2013c), authenticity is mentioned almost as frequently as autonomy, as can be confirmed with reference to the index. In a typical example, Banegas (2013, p. 86) directly equates authentic content with increased student and teacher motivation. In the same volume, Henry (2013) dedicates an entire chapter to bridging the authenticity gap between students' personal lives and the type of instruction they receive. Mishan (2005) points out that the 'motivation factor is one of the key justifications for the use of authentic texts for language learning' (p. 26), and Gilmore (2007a, 2011) has also examined the links between authenticity and motivation in some detail.

The most pervasive definition of authenticity usually refers to materials, and is often reduced to some kind of inherent trait based largely on the original intention of the materials not having been for language teaching. In other words, authenticity in language teaching tends to mean materials designed for anything *but* language teaching, which somehow implies that the very act of language teaching is also somehow *inauthentic*. I refer to this as the 'classic' definition of authenticity. However, authenticity is not necessarily something merely attributed to learning materials and content, and is more usefully seen as something connected with identity, society, and Self.

Despite being a central and familiar concept in the field of applied linguistics, the theme of authenticity is one which is fraught with much debate and confusion. This is perhaps because authenticity is a deeply personal concept, unique to each individual and yet relevant to the way she or he interacts in society. It is also perhaps due to the way the concept of 'authentic language' is tied up with other issues, such as native-speakerism, linguistic imperialism, social class, and academic gatekeeping. Textbook publishers, language test makers, academic institutions, teachers, and students all regularly interact with the concept of authenticity in language at both the personal and the professional level, yet because of the complexity and controversy surrounding this theme, its importance is rarely discussed head-on. Instead, the outdated 'classic' definitions of authenticity are still implicit in many of the materials which are branded 'authentic', and either feature an embedded culturism or tend to gravitate unfairly towards so-called 'standard' or 'native-speaker' varieties of the target language (Lowe & Pinner, 2016; Pinner, 2016b). These definitions approach authenticity as a static or inherent trait rather than as a dynamic process. Researching the issue of authenticity is not merely marred by these problems but also has more or less been ground to a halt by them. In the past 20 years there have been very few papers which feature an inquiry into authenticity as their main focus. Those papers which have attempted to research the issue of authenticity in language teaching have tended to fall short by defaulting back to the aforementioned 'classic' definitions which do not reflect the reality of English as an international language. Widdowson (1978) wrote about the inherent fallacy of what I refer to as the 'classic' definition of authenticity when he discussed the difference between *genuineness* and *authenticity*.

> We read what is relevant to our affairs or what appeals to our interests; and what is remote from our particular world we do not bother to read at all. To present someone with a set of extracts and to require him to read them not in order to learn something interesting and relevant about the world but in order to learn something about the language being used is to misrepresent normal language use to some degree. The extracts are, by definition, genuine instances of language use, but if the learner is required to deal with them in a way which does not correspond to his normal communicative activities, then they cannot be said to be authentic instances of use. Genuineness is a characteristic of the passage itself and is an absolute quality. Authenticity is a characteristic of the relationship between the passage and the reader and it has to do with appropriate response.
>
> (p. 80)

In other words, authenticity is *created* through interactions. Authenticity is something socially constructed, in the moment, and to label a text as inherently authentic is to oversimplify the construct.

Language is centrally tied up with identity, not just because language is how we construct our social identities but also because language is how we make sense of and codify our experience of the world. One of the main ways we do this is by telling stories, and narratives are 'considered by many to be the *prototypical* or *core* genre' of discourse (McCarthy & Carter, 1994, p. 33; original emphasis). Language can be viewed as not only what makes us innately human but also what makes us ourselves. However, it is rather unusual for a person to know only a single language (Fabbro, 2001), and many education systems around the world require learners to practise and undertake high-stakes tests in foreign language proficiency. For others living in multicultural societies, the second language is even more integrated, and in such cases just as much a part of a person's social and individual Self as is their first language. As the world moves towards super-diversity (Blommaert & Rampton, 2012; Blommaert & Varis, 2011; Vertovec, 2007) and a period of 'transnational connectedness, which scholars have labelled *modernist globalisation*' (Canagarajah, 2013, p. 25; emphasis in original), more and more emphasis is being put on the social aspects of SLA (Atkinson, 2011; Block, 2003).

However, even if the foreign language is merely something learned at school or university, as Williams and Burden (1997) point out, 'it involves an alteration in self-image, the adoption of new social and cultural behaviours and ways of being, and therefore has a significant impact on the social nature of the learner' (p. 115). Even though Williams and Burden do not use the word directly, essentially they could be talking about the *authentic self* here, in the existentialist sense, as it relates to identity. By extension, this means that as language teachers one of our jobs is perhaps to enable our students to learn how to express their authentic self through the target language. Therefore, finding authenticity may also entail the creation of a foreign language (L2) identity, and this L2 identity may or may not be the same as the first language (L1) identity (Block, 2007). Identity in the language classroom is strongly connected to motivation, and recent theories of L2 motivation have begun to draw heavily on self-concepts (Csizér & Magid, 2014; Dörnyei, 2009; Dörnyei & Ushioda, 2009, 2011; Gregersen & MacIntyre, 2015; Mercer, 2015a; Nitta & Baba, 2015; Ryan & Irie, 2014). Again, the connection between authenticity and motivation is hinged on the idea that language is about expressing the authentic self, and that good teaching therefore allows learners the chance to express themselves in an authentic way.

> [L]anguage is a medium of self-expression and a means of communicating, constructing and negotiating who we are and how we relate to the world around us – that is, of giving ourselves voice and identity. A foreign language is not simply something to add to our repertoire of skills, but a personalized tool that enables us to expand and express our identity or sense of self in new and interesting ways and with new kinds of people; to participate in a more diverse range of contexts and communities and so broaden our experiences and horizons; and to access and share new and alternative sources of information, entertainment or material that we need, value or enjoy.
>
> (Ushioda, 2011a, pp. 203–204)

Indirectly again, Ushioda seems to be talking about authenticity in the existential sense, and here situating the use of language as being innately authentic and individual. As Mishan (2005) points out in her seminal work on authenticity, 'language learning is a natural – an *authentic* – activity' (p. ix; emphasis in original).

However, learning a foreign language is both a face-threatening and a daunting task (van Dam, 2002). In learning to speak a foreign language, learners inevitably have to struggle through situations in which they do not have the linguistic repertoire to easily and successfully convey meaning. They may find themselves in unfamiliar cultural territory as well, even if they are learning in their own country where the target language is a foreign language. In particular, English is a very high-stakes language; proficiency in English is often linked with educational and social success, as demonstrated by Seargeant's (2009, 2011) work which focused on Japan. Despite this, the fact that English is an international, global, or even 'hyper-centralised' language (de Swaan, 2001) means that it could also become a disembodied language – in other words, it is very far removed from a discernible cultural base. In other words, English is 'divorced' from its use contexts and 'just another school subject' where the learners' true selves are often left at the classroom door (Lamb, 2013, p. 19). The hyper-centralising of English simultaneously makes it more and less real, especially for English as a foreign language (EFL) learners. This can have a very depersonalising effect on the way English is both taught and learned.

Teaching is a deeply personal endeavour. Several studies have shown that, contrary to the adage 'those who can, do; those who can't, teach', most teachers become teachers because they are intrinsically motivated to do so, and usually because they are passionate about their subject and wish to communicate this to other generations (Dinham & Scott, 2000; Dörnyei & Ushioda, 2011; Richardson & Watt, 2006). Furthermore, there is a 'synergistic' relationship between student and teacher motivation (Deci, Kasser, & Ryan, 1997, p. 68; Dörnyei & Ushioda, 2011), and so this seems to be a matter of central importance to language learning and teaching.

This book presents a narrative of my attempt to make sense of these elusive yet vital components of language learning. At the heart of this book is a narrative of my own practitioner research, which was conducted at a Japanese university in Tokyo, with a group of first-year non-English majors taking compulsory courses as part of their Bachelor's degree. Because I have come to approach authenticity as a deeply personal, contextually dependent, and socially constructed phenomenon, I have adopted an exploratory and reflective approach to this inquiry. The methodology I have adopted has grown out of the puzzle at the heart of the inquiry, which is an investigation of the nature of authenticity and motivation in language teaching, specifically related to English teaching in EFL contexts. This puzzle acts as the central research question, which aims to gain a deeper understanding of the process of social authentication and examines how this relates to teacher-student motivational synergy. Because this relates to my own working environment and teaching persona, the inquiry has also grown somewhat to include aspects of my own professional development as I mature as a teacher and researcher. In this way, this book charts a pivotal moment in my own development by focusing on my evolving and emergent professional identity. In order to further extend upon this narrative, I have also collected nine vignettes from other practitioning teachers from around the world. These are presented alongside certain of my own observations, in order to provide other points of view. These vignettes also have in common that they share insights into the reasons why teachers teach, and how their motivations are linked to those of their students.

This development in the inquiry, focusing on my own emerging identity, is a result of my attempt to focus in particular on the 'synergistic' relationship between student and teacher motivation (Deci et al., 1997). This relationship, I have come to believe, is based to a large extent on authenticity, as conceptualised as a process of validating the act of learning/teaching and shared social sense of investment in the process. When this process happens en masse within a classroom environment, I refer to it as *social authentication*. Through this inquiry, I have come to see authenticity as a powerful affective component of perceived validity which bridges the individual and social worlds of both learning and teaching. It is a fluid component of identity and part of the dynamic system of motivation. As such it is both essential to language learning and at the same time highly elusive and hard to define.

The only way to gain genuine insight into such a personal and internalised process was to turn myself into a research subject. Therefore, I have combined autoethnography with Exploratory Practice to attempt to unearth some of the deeper meanings behind my practice as it undergoes an important change in my developmental continuum. This study focuses on my own interpretations of my teaching practice and interactions with students. Reflecting on the way I responded to the students' needs and navigated through the learning process is, I will argue, one of the ways in which I attempted to create a culture of authenticity in the 'small culture' (Holliday, 1994, 1999) of my own classroom and teaching context. This has much in common with ecological approaches to language learning, which refer to the study of organisms in relation to others and their environment (Kramsch, 2002b; Tudor, 2003; van Lier, 1998). Such a view also fits within the paradigm of language as a complex dynamic system (de Bot & Larsen-Freeman, 2011; King, 2016c; Larsen-Freeman, 1997; Larsen-Freeman & Cameron, 2008a; Verspoor, de Bot, & Lowie, 2011).

In order to make sense of this inquiry, I present it as a chronological narrative structured around my observations, analysis, and academic reading on these subjects. As such, in the next section I start at the beginning and explain how I came to this inquiry and what my starting point was.

1.1 Arriving at social authentication

Teaching and learning a foreign language poses many challenges, but perhaps one of the simplest and yet most pressing issues is the question of what to teach and how to teach it, that is, the content of the lessons and the tasks used to facilitate engagement. The choice of materials to use in the foreign language classroom is fundamentally important. No single activity or text will be interesting or engaging for every single learner to the same extent (van Lier, 1996). Materials designed to inspire debate can cause offence; materials designed to be contemporary can age quickly and be expensive both to produce and to replace. Materials designed for large multinational circulation lack the localised relevance and cultural understanding required to avoid being overly generic and thus can be uninteresting for learners (Mishan, 2005). When considering materials, both content and context are of central concern (Copland & Mann, 2012; Mann & Copland, 2015). This has always been the case in my own teaching, and for a long time I have been using almost entirely my own materials, which I have written for specific classes and recycled or adapted in a continuous process of development, which a colleague of mine quite poetically termed *the living textbook*.

I felt these self-made materials to be 'authentic'. Without realising it, I had rejected the materials produced by most EFL textbook publishers, and on reflection I feel that this is due in some way to what I perceived as an inherent culturism and native-speakerism which I now think is rather deeply embedded in many commercial (but not all) textbooks. This led me to question the place of global English in today's materials and how the concept of authenticity might be related to these issues. The connection between authenticity and motivation in language classrooms is often acknowledged from a practitioner's viewpoint (Mishan, 2005), and it seems logical that using authentic materials for language learning would be more motivating for students than 'inauthentic' or contrived materials because they bear a resemblance to the place where the language will actually be used (Widdowson, 1990, p. 44). However, there is a great deal of complexity surrounding this issue, especially as we move deeper into the information age. Immense changes have come over society and language due to the acceleration of information communication technology (ICT). These have long been a feature in the discussions about language teaching, and the heightened importance of the debate about English as a global language has begun to feature heavily in the reconceptualisation of motivation (Ushioda, 2013b; Ushioda & Dörnyei, 2009). However, examinations of the special status of English and its homogeneous 'world-culture' remain scarce in discussions about authentic materials. It is widely acknowledged (Gilmore, 2007a, 2011; Mishan, 2005; Richards, 2001) and even empirically tested (Peacock, 1997) that authentic materials are more motivating for students and expose them to 'real' language. A very common assertion, which Widdowson (1990) labels the means/ends equation, is that authentic language is necessary. It is a means to an end because 'real' language is what learners will need to be able to use and understand since very few learners wish to become unnatural speakers or to learn English in a way which is only adequate for the classroom or to pass exams. However, definitions based around the notion of a single target language culture are problematic. Just as the global position of English has started to change how applied linguists conceptualise motivation, in the same way the traditional or culturally embedded definition of authenticity is in need of reconceptualising. The ideas relating to global English are now also being acknowledged by major EFL publishers, as illustrated by textbooks such as Macmillan's *Global* and Heinle ELT's *World English* series featuring images from *National Geographic*. Although there are heated discussions about what kind of models teachers and materials writers should present to learners of English (Crystal, 2003; Jenkins, 2002, 2006; Nunan, 2003; Seidlhofer, 2005) and the need to reflect English's special status as 'the world's second language' (Krashen, 2003), these discussions have yet to seriously address the potential that within the global context the idea of authenticity becomes more problematic than ever and perhaps even faces extinction. Part of the initial impetus for this study was an attempt to understand the process of *authenticating* the learning of English in an EFL context on both a social and an individual level. Hinting at the key to this inquiry, van Lier (1996) foreshadows my own observations when he notes that

> the people in the setting, each and every one individually for himself or herself, as well as in negotiation with one another, authenticate the setting and the actions in it. When such authentication occurs *en masse*, spontaneously or in an orchestrated fashion (socially constructed authentication, so to speak), we may well have the most authentic setting possible. A good teacher may be able to promote such authenticity. It may be easier to achieve it in some settings than in others.
>
> (p. 128)

This concept of socially co-constructing a climate of authenticity has become the elusive goal at the centre of my 'quest' for authenticity: *social authentication*. Conceptualised in this way authenticity strongly connects with motivation, because when everyone in the class feels connected to each other by feeling congruent, synergistic teacher-student motivation is a natural product of the environment and part of the process of experiencing authenticity (Muir & Dörnyei, 2013).

1.2 Overview

This book is structured around a central narrative which focuses on my own experience of language teaching. For this reason, both data and analysis are entwined. Therefore, in Chapter 2 I present the theoretical framework, which contains a working definition of the constructs under examination in this inquiry, namely authenticity and motivation, and also a brief contextualisation of the current thought on these issues. This chapter brings together current work on L2 identity, L2 motivation, and authenticity in language teaching and learning, all of which are linked together through the paradigm of complexity theory. The second part of this chapter explains the concept of *social authentication* as a dynamic process and lists six indicators of motivational synergy (between teacher and students) which are later used as the basis for empirical observations from practitioner research and autoethnography.

Chapter 3 outlines the research methods, which in itself is a form of narrative. This chapter is given an in-depth treatment as one of the justifications for this study is the research method itself, which it is hoped will be of interest and value to other practitioners. This is not a traditional research methods chapter as it focuses on the *evolution of the design*, presenting a hybrid methodology for practitioner research grounded in evidence-based Reflective Practice, Exploratory Practice, and autoethnography. The overarching methodology is Narrative Inquiry, and as such this chapter is presented in a narrative style.

Chapters 4 and 5 present the main narrative (data and analysis) of a year-long class I taught to first-year students at a Japanese university in Tokyo entitled Academic Communication (CLERAC), which became the main investigative ground for this inquiry into social authentication and motivational synergy. This narrative acts as data for both the study and the first-layer analysis. The narrative centres around class activities and the techniques used to gauge, reflect on, and maintain motivation to learn English in an EFL context where English is a compulsory subject taught to non-English majors. Certain key learners from the study are given additional focus in the narrative and treated as Focal Participants, and data such as classroom dialogue transcripts, screenshots from online discussions, reflection papers, and classroom observations are presented. Chapter 6 discusses the way that these observations might be usefully seen as attempts at praxis, and thus it forms a second-layer analysis as well as offers practical suggestions where appropriate. This chapter takes a step back from the narrative and, applying the theoretical framework from Chapter 2, provides a second layer of analysis. In particular, this chapter looks more holistically at the core concepts of social authentication and motivational synergy.

Following this analysis, an additional layer of data is provided in the form of a collection of nine vignettes in Chapter 7. These vignettes were elicited by posting a call for contributions on various websites and online forums frequently used by teacher-researchers (such as the International Association for Teachers of English as a Foreign Language Research Special Interest Group). Some vignettes were also solicited through personal contact with teachers whom I know personally and felt would have something to contribute. All these teacher-researchers were asked to write a reflective narrative demonstrating how their motivation as teachers is influenced and synergistic with their perceptions of their learners' motivation. These vignettes are not part of my own narrative, and hence they are 'stuck on at the end' in some sense because they do not inform the main work; however, they are intended to help broaden the scope of the book, making it more internationally focused by including reflections from other teachers around the world, as well as by adding examples from other contexts and expanding the concepts to discuss how they might be relevant in a more diverse range of teaching scenarios and cultures. This inquiry focused specifically on Japan, but the issues under examination have a wider relevance to language teaching more broadly, although particularly English language teaching, with a particular focus on Asian and EFL contexts. I feel these vignettes add a variety of voices and views on the issues being discussed.

Finally, Chapter 8 offers a summary and conclusion, making suggestions for further research and answering the 'so what?' question.

Throughout the book, I continually emphasise that the main focus is on the synergistic relationship between teacher and student motivation, and how the concept of authenticity is an aspect of this dynamic process. From these elusive and complex interactions, I have been able to distil what I believe are genuinely practical insights into the nature of classroom interactions at both an individual and a group level, paying particular attention to context. What this means for other practitioners, language teacher educators, and researchers is a deeper understanding of language teacher identity and a rare cross section of a single language course spanning a year of twice-a-week instruction. In that sense, this study is quite unique in that it allows the reader a deep and personal account of these vital processes, which I have argued are central to the authentic experience of language teaching and learning. Fundamentally, autoethnographies are about empowering people, as I have explained throughout this inquiry. The idea that teachers can do research is no longer controversial, but the idea that they can do serious work which will be accepted as good quality research done *by* teachers *for* teachers and yet able to sit alongside more established forms of SLA and applied linguistic research in academic circles is still much contested. In writing a book such as this, which attempts to be both academically rigorous and yet ultimately based on practice and intended to achieve praxis (i.e. to inform practice through theoretical insights), I have attempted to empower such forms of practitioner research, and thus to empower teachers. This study is my attempt to challenge the often-perceived gap between theory and practice.

2 Theoretical framework
Stepping stones

2.1 Introduction

In this section, I will present a summary of my current views on authenticity and trace their development. I will, in doing so, draw on my own previous research and also that which has gone before, looking at the most important work from the research literature at this point. I will discuss motivation as a complex dynamic system and explain how teacher-student motivational synergy emerged as the most salient feature of my exploration into authenticity. This chapter will first introduce the complexity paradigm and then discuss my identity as a developing language teacher. Then I will outline my views on authenticity and the authenticity continuum, narrating how they emerged and took on a larger meaning as a result of this inquiry. I will also discuss motivation and the interdependence of autonomy and authenticity in conceptualising the construct, proposing that these three form a triadic relationship, which I name the Language Impetus Triad. Finally, I will explain how I attempted to look for synergy by explaining briefly about indicators of synergy, which are the main justifiers behind the observations I present in the narrative of Chapters 4 and 5.

2.1.1 Complexity paradigm

We are moving away from 'prescription' and more towards 'description', from 'precision' to 'scattergun', and from 'simplicity' to 'complexity' (Allwright, 2006b). As part of the 'paradigm shift' (Dörnyei, MacIntyre, & Henry, 2015a) and 'social turn' (Atkinson, 2011; Block, 2003) in applied linguistics, complexity theories have been gaining prominence in the research literature, which has also been reflected in the literature on L2 motivation theory and research. Complexity theory is an overarching paradigm that encompasses chaos theory, complex dynamic systems theory and complex adaptive systems, and complements ecological perspectives of language. These theories are themselves interdisciplinary, used widely in fields ranging from meteorology to mathematics, from sociology to SLA.

Complexity is more of a paradigm than an individual theory (Dörnyei et al., 2015a; Larsen-Freeman, 2015), and in terms of applied linguistics and SLA, one essentially grounded in social, sociocultural and ecological perspectives. The emphasis is on qualitative understandings, retrospection and reflection (Larsen-Freeman, 2011; Larsen-Freeman & Cameron, 2008a, 2008b).

The fundamental idea underlying the complexity paradigm is deceptively simple. These theories posit that for many phenomena, the processes that make them what they are and behave as they do are so fixed to specific contexts, so inherently dependent on such a vast number of variables, and so unique in space and time that a full understanding of the process is not possible by looking only at each component part. In other words, we cannot understand a system by looking at the parts in isolation; instead, we must look at the relationships between these parts and how they interact in order to gain a better understanding of the whole.

Cleary, complexity theory has much to offer in terms of understanding classroom behaviour and examining dynamic processes such as motivation (Sampson, 2015, 2016). A learner is not merely 'motivated' or 'demotivated', and the state of experiencing high or low motivation is never constant but permanently in flux (Ushioda, 1996, 2009, 2015). Complexity theory is a useful tool for understanding the reality of the classroom. Within this paradigm, the word 'chaos' means that a system is so complex as to be unpredictable. Although classes are not always unpredictable, I would argue that due to the immense complexity of a classroom setting, chaos is an accurate word often appropriate to these contexts. Of course, this is not to say that our classrooms are chaotic, as the word carries a specialised meaning when used in relation to complexity theory.

There are many specific terms used in complexity theory. In this study I will only examine a small number of these technical terms based on phenomena that were directly observable in the classroom. First, *initial conditions* are recognised as the starting point of the system being observed. These represent an important part in the system's overall nature, and a clear picture of the initial conditions is necessary for measuring changes. Therefore, I dedicate a significant portion of the narrative to examining the first class and the initial conditions of the learners.

Secondly, *attractor states* are broadly defined as the position that a dynamic system most naturally returns to. For example, in his studies examining silence in Japanese university English classrooms, Jim King (2013b) often describes the state of silence as a semi-permanent attractor state, meaning that to 'not orally participate in one's foreign language class is deemed, by both students and teachers alike, to be normal behaviour' (p. 339). In other words, this is the normal state of things. The more powerful the attractor state, the more energy is required to cause a shift in behaviour and move into a different pattern of activity. More simply, applied to the classroom conditions under observation in this inquiry, the attractor state could be the most common affective disposition that the learners take towards the lesson in terms of their motivation to learn. Some classes are perceived as being highly motivated in general, whereas others are less so. There may be more than one attractor state in a non-linear system, and it is possible to alter what the attractor state will be, although, as I stated before, this requires some kind of impetus and the expenditure of energy (see Section 2.6.2 for a discussion of energy return on investment). In this inquiry it is important to be able to say what the most common attractor states were in terms of student motivation and to see how this coincides with my own motivation as I teach the course. Understanding what the attractor states were is something inherently fraught with difficulty, and it is beyond the means of this study to be able to provide a quantifiable measure for the attractor states. As Hiver (2015a) explains, 'in reality, because of the immense complexity of life, systems that only tend to settle into a single fixed-point attractor state are rarer than we might think' (p. 21). However, this is still a very useful term and, utilising the indicators of synergy which I will outline in Section 2.6.3, I will attempt to justify my generalisations of the class' motivation in terms of attractor states in order to make holistic observations about the class. It is also important to point out here that a *strange attractor* is an attractor state that systems gravitate towards but never seem to reach, which has relevance for the CLERAC course as findings from this inquiry seem to suggest that we never quite managed to make high motivation a full attractor state for the classes.

Finally, the word 'context' has a special importance for complexity theory because 'a person is coupled with his or her environment' (Larsen-Freeman, 2015, p. 16) and thus learners both 'shape and are shaped by context' (Ushioda, 2015, p. 48). Indeed, complex systems are in fact context dependent (Larsen-Freeman & Cameron, 2008a, p. 69). This has led Kramsch (2002a) to apply a metaphor from Yeats in asking, 'how can we tell the dancer from the dance?'. Ema Ushioda's (2015) solution is 'to think big and small at the same time' (p. 53). She applies the metaphor of an analytical lens that focuses in and out of contexts surrounding the learners. This has become a guiding principle in the way I present the narrative data in Chapters 4 and 5.

Although complexity theory has many more aspects than I have covered in this brief section, these are the main analytical tools that I have taken from complexity theory and applied to this inquiry. Complexity will be discussed in more detail in the narrative and the praxis sections of this book in Chapters 4, 5 and 6.

2.2 Identity

This inquiry is not about authentic materials or motivation as a trait that can be plotted onto a graph. This inquiry is a personal journey into my own practice which has led me to make evidence-based conclusions about how my professional development has aligned with my teaching behaviour in an attempt to create more authentic and motivating lessons for my learners, as I develop my own philosophy of teaching. Ushioda (2011b) observes that 'the notion of engaging our students' identities is something many experienced language teachers have intuitively recognised as important' (p. 17). In breaking down and analysing what it is that 'good teachers' do to motivate their students, it might be possible to use this information in teacher training programmes and perhaps also to inform materials design. As Glatthorn (1975) states, being an authentic teacher means achieving self-knowledge. Perhaps encouraging reflexivity in teacher education programmes might help connect teachers with their students through an authentic process of engagement. For this reason, reflection became one of the main sources of data and methods of analysis in this inquiry. My own developing identity as a practitioner is therefore a central theme in the narrative.

Zimmerman (1998) differentiates between the identities speakers invoke during discourse. These are

- situated identities, which are explicitly conferred by the context of communication, such as doctor/patient identities in the context of a health clinic or teacher/student identities in the context of a classroom;
- discourse identities, as participants orient themselves to particular discourse roles in the unfolding organisation of the interaction (e.g. initiator, listener and questioner); and
- transportable identities, which are latent or implicit but can be invoked during the interaction, such as when a teacher alludes to her identity as a mother or as a keen gardener during a language lesson (see also K. Richards, 2006 and Ushioda, 2011b for expansion).

When people interact in different social contexts, they might often invoke transportable identities as a way of showing that they are not merely the sum of their situational identity. Teachers are not merely teachers, nor students merely students; we each have various identities that both complement and contradict our professional or situated identities. Good teachers in any discipline encourage their students to engage with learning content through a process of personal meaning-making. When speakers use languages which they have learned as either foreign or second languages, however, it can be difficult to render a satisfactory presentation of the Self using a limited or less familiar linguistic repertoire (Csizér & Magid, 2014). This is particularly important in language learning and teaching, where people are constructing their identities using limited linguistic resources, whilst simultaneously having to learn new discourse strategies and sociocultural modes of behaviour. Added to this is the additional factor that, in terms of teaching, all of these identity negotiations are often happening in a language classroom, which is an 'intrinsically face-threatening situation' (van Dam, 2002, p. 238). However, teachers can alleviate some of this by personalising the class and making 'self-disclosures', which have been shown to be effective in creating a positive teacher-student relationship (Henry & Thorsen, 2018).

When we speak to students at school or on campus, our situational identity is very strong; this is the identity which is explicitly imposed by the context of the discourse. Teachers may often invoke aspects of their transportable identities in order to personalise the content of language classes (K. Richards, 2006; Ushioda, 2011b). Because of the power imbalance of the teacher/student relationship, it is essential to retain a professional distance between teacher and student, and to retain the ability to be objective towards the students' achievement, for their own sake and as a duty of the teacher role. However, K. Richards (2006) notes that it would be 'perverse' to insist that the personal self should be left at the classroom door (p. 74).

Table 2.1 Early and developing teaching persona identities

	My early teaching persona – London	My developing teaching persona – Tokyo
Situated Identity	Local/British 'native speaker'– in home country, part of majority. Fluent in English In my 20s – young, similar age to students who are in their early-mid 20s, studying abroad White, middle class, but not wealthy[a] Early in career Working for a private language school (low stakes, low authority, low responsibility) English language instructor/ teacher Using a textbook and supplementing	Foreigner 'English native speaker' – Minority, immigrant (ex-pat?), not fluent in Japanese In my 30s – quite young but 16+ years older than students (around twice their age), who are 18–20, many still living at home Non-Japanese (White), established middle class Established in career (Full-time, tenure-track member of faculty) Working for well-respected university (high-stakes, high authority, high responsibility) English language and literature teacher/professor Responsible entirely for the content of the course
Transportable Identities	Husband (recently married) Northerner (Yorkshire) Music lover, film lover embedded in local culture Has lived abroad Sometimes studies Japanese Doing a masters' degree	Father and husband (to a Japanese wife and mixed-race boy) British (Northern) Dog owner, house owner, not familiar with local or popular culture Quite new to Japan Fellow language learner (of Japanese)

Note: [a] When I worked in London, the high cost of studying abroad in London meant that many of the students were from affluent families. Otherwise, they could not afford to come.

Understanding more about how identities are socially created and presented has led me to a deeper understanding of the way I strive to create a culture of authenticity in my classroom. Table 2.1 compares and contrasts my early and developing teaching persona before and after my move to Japan, using situated and transportable identities to categorise the way I see myself and the way I present myself to my learners.

This is important contextual and temporal information in framing the narrative of this study, as all of these identities have a role to play in the way I present myself as a teacher and the way I may invoke different transportable identities during personal interactions with the students as I attempt to socially authenticate the learning by embarking on a 'personal process of engagement' (van Lier, 1996, p. 128). It is also worth noting that the students in my classes, especially those in their first year in the spring semester (as with CLERAC) are likewise undergoing a large transition in identity as they move from high-school student to university student, along with the implications of adulthood and preparing to join society. Two further aspects of identity which we all bring with us to the classroom are schemata and habitus.

2.2.1.1 Schema and habitus

In language teaching, the idea of schematic knowledge is quite well established (see for example Hedge, 2000). Teachers often talk about 'activating schema' in staffrooms, training sessions and discussions of their practice. Schema is primarily a theory of cognition which involves frames of knowing that exist in an individual's mind, and the theory is often used to refer to cultural background. Widdowson (1990) points out that there are two types of schema; 'ideational', which refers to background knowledge, and 'interpersonal', which incorporates knowledge about modes of communication (p. 104). In fact, to language teachers, schema very often carries with it specific cultural connotations. Mishan (2005) discusses schema as one of the most important psycholinguistic theories for providing support for authentic instruction, because the 'emphasis it places on acquiring knowledge of the target language culture is one of the strongest arguments for the use of authentic texts which incorporate this cultural information' (p. 79). She later expands on this to advocate problem-based learning (2011).

However, schema's dependence on a cognitive view of knowing puts it somewhat at odds with sociocultural approaches to learning, with emphasis being placed either on the individual or, more troublingly, on essentialising the concept of schema and applying it to an entire culture. Furthermore, schema theory in language learning is most commonly associated with receptive skills, and so again its place is perhaps rather limited within the context of this inquiry, which focuses much more on language and identity than on the acquisition of linguistic competence.

A related concept to schema is the work on intertextuality, which looks at the shifting patterns of meaning between texts in wider context (see for example Lemke, 1992). This places a clear emphasis on the historical connections of prior texts, and is mainly a term from literature and translation, with its main application in the field of language study being with critical discourse analysis (most notably Fairclough, 2015).

For this reason, Bourdieu's notion of habitus from sociology might be more appropriate. Habitus is a rather ambiguous concept, although it can basically be seen as an embodied type of cultural capital (Longhofer & Winchester, 2016, p. 128). Broadly, habitus relates to the embodiment and internalisation of certain patterns of behaviour and networks of belief, which are socially constructed and often unconscious.

There is, around the notion of habitus, an implication that reflexivity is a desirable social humanistic trait (Adams, 2006), and Bourdieu originally discussed habitus with the intention of critiquing power stratifications and challenging them, thus making it relevant for critical schools of thought which attempt to uncover the subtle authoritative discourses that seek to understand and resist hegemonic constraints (Blommaert, 2005; see also Blommaert, 2010; Blommaert & Varis, 2011; Scheuer, 2003). In this sense, habitus may be a step too far in terms of practitioner research (although this will depend on the teacher's philosophy of practice), and yet schema seems unsatisfactory to describe the phenomena I am attempting to understand in relation to myself as a British man, living and working in Japan and attempting to create authentic links with my students based on social and cultural shared values and interpretations. Therefore, in this inquiry I refer to habitus as an extended sociological version of schematic knowledge which also incorporates assumptions and dispositions that may often be so deeply internalised as to be unconscious, and therefore implying the need for reflexivity.

More importantly, habitus incorporates a 'way of being' or manner, or even a sense of place (Hillier & Rooksby, 2005). Although 'thoroughly individualized, the habitus in fact reflects a shared cultural context' (Adams, 2006, p. 514). This describes well what I am trying to establish when I create the small culture of my classes by emphasising authentic interactions.

2.3 Instructional authenticity and educational philosophy

Authenticity is something that occupies the working lives of not only applied linguists and language teachers but also philosophers, tour companies, banks, museums and restaurants. From Swiss watches to Japanese toilets (see Campbell, 2014 for more on Japanese toilets), the issue of authenticity revolves around many aspects of our existence. Authenticity is a paradoxical construct (Cobb, 2014; Lindholm, 2008; Straub, 2012), and one which is often defined through negatives rather than positives (Golomb, 1995, p. 7). In other words, we can define easily what is not authentic, but it is much harder to identify what is really authentic. As such, authenticity is nebulous, not concrete or definable but shifting and subjective, a performance or a process rather than a trait or property (Waskul, 2009).

In the field of education, authenticity is seen as an important component of learning and knowledge acquisition. However, as Petraglia (1998, p. 14) notes, classical treatises dealing with education never seem to question the relationship between education and the everyday activities of the world beyond the classroom. The notion of authenticity in Western education seems to be a twentieth-century phenomenon, largely due to developments in educational philosophy and attributable in no small measure to the work of the American pragmatists, in particular American philosopher and educational reformist John Dewey (1897), who highlighted the importance of *experience* in learning, and who was greatly interested in authenticating the learning process so that it prepares learners for the 'real world' outside the classroom, claiming in one of his early writings that 'school must represent life' (p. 78), making numerous reference to social and community life. Later, Dewey (1938) expanded on this theme to suggest the famous metaphor that education was 'growth' (p. 36), which implies the type of personal and meaningful validation at the heart of the definition of authenticity used in this inquiry. However, Dewey was criticised from a number of sides, and the term 'authenticity' was used often to highlight problems with a particular view of education. For example, the notion of authenticity differed depending on whether the goal of education was to help society, to foster the individual, to prepare individuals as adaptive and flexible for a range of multifaceted possibilities in their lives or to prepare individuals for certain specific vocations. Thus 'authenticity's rhetorical potency is preserved by its ambiguity' (Petraglia, 1998, p. 30) as essentially the definition of authenticity depends on a person's definition of the *purpose* of education. As such, educators must reflect on their own beliefs in order to understand what they mean when they are constructing authenticity, something advocated by Glatthorn (1999), who asks the reader to reflect on their beliefs at the start of his book on authentic learning. This type of authenticity is best known as authentic instruction, and is something that I will return to repeatedly throughout this inquiry. I found links between this fundamental belief in what we were doing in class to be very influential in motivational synergies in the classroom. In other words, both my and the students' motivation was positively synergised at times when our belief in the validity of what we were doing was convergent. In this way, we all worked together to create the 'socially constructed authentication' (van Lier, 1996, p. 128) discussed in the introduction. From here on I will refer to this as *social authentication*, which I argue will be a defining aspect of teacher-student motivational synergy. It is not just the teacher's job to be concerned with authentic instruction. I will later argue that motivational synergy and social authentication rely on quality feedback between teacher and students, and that part of this process is involving the learners to help improve the 'quality of classroom life' (Allwright, 2003, 2005, 2006a; Gieve & Miller, 2006). I will highlight such instances in the narrative of this inquiry (Chapters 4 and 5) and further expand on the implications for teaching practice in Chapter 6.

Authentic instruction is a familiar term in the field of education. In an important and well-known paper, Newmann and Wehlage (1993) put forward five standards of authentic instruction. These are shown in Figure 2.1.

This was later developed into an authentic pedagogy (Newmann & Wehlage, 1995), which focused on providing a set of standards to evaluate the intellectual quality of teaching, again with a focus on achievement and measurable results, particularly writing. For Newmann and Wehlage (1993), authenticity was about

1. Higher-Order Thinking

2. Depth of Knowledge

3. Connectedness to the World Beyond the Classroom

4. Substantive Conversation

5. Social Support for Student Achievement

Figure 2.1 Five standards of authentic instruction

having 'worthwhile educational ends' (p. 8), and they used the term 'authentic' to discuss educational achievement, which is actually meaningful to all the major stakeholders in the learning (starting, of course, with the students). In many ways, this definition of authenticity is also well accounted for in the fields of applied linguistics and SLA as it relates to language assessment. However, teaching languages merely for assessment purposes is generally seen as undesirable, because even within the work of language assessment, the fallibility of basically any form of assessment is regularly acknowledged (Bachman & Palmer, 1996; Fulcher, 2013). A language test can never be perfect, and thus teaching solely around a single assessment should generally be avoided. Interestingly, and with particular relevance to this inquiry, it is the washback effect of Japanese university entrance exams which is very often held accountable for the perceived failures of Japanese foreign language education (Apple, Da Silva, & Fellner, 2013; Matsuda, 2011; McVeigh, 2002; Sasayama, 2013; Seargeant, 2011; Torikai, 2011; Watanabe, 1997; Yano, 2011; Yoshida, 2001, 2003, 2008, 2009, 2013). This excessively long list of references to support the point represents only a fraction of the discussions on this issue, with more and more added year on year. I will revisit this issue in Section 2.4.4 when I discuss Japan's motivational landscape. In my own experience as a language teaching practitioner in Japan, I can corroborate this with personal experience as well, with both students and teachers often laying the blame on the unchanging monolithic gatekeeping practices of universities, despite university academics being in a position to act as the most powerful voices *against* such practices (Hawley Nagatomo, 2012). Again, reiterating the previous paragraph, the notion of instructional authenticity is hinged upon one's belief about the purpose of education.

2.3.1 Authenticity in language teaching and the 'classic' definition

It has been argued that much of the literature on authenticity within language teaching tends to focus on the authenticity of materials at the expense of examining the *experience* of learning (Henry, 2013; Henry & Cliffordson, 2015). Within language learning and teaching, authenticity has a rather distinct meaning closely resembling *artefact authenticity*, akin to the definition that would be the primary concern of a museum exhibit curator or art dealer. According to this view, something either is authentic or it is not (i.e. It is a fake). This binary view of authenticity pervades much of the practical literature on language teaching, although it has been contested and debated for decades (Gilmore, 2007a; Mishan, 2005; Pinner, 2016b). On the whole, the 'authenticity debate' can be usefully divided into two major strands. The first is a continuation of authenticity as it relates to identity and self, much in the tradition of existential thought. Primarily, such distinctions focus on the process of 'authentication', whereby learners (and teachers) create authenticity themselves through personal and social interactions (Henry & Cliffordson, 2015; Külekçi, 2015; Mishan, 2005; Pinner, 2016b; van Lier, 1996; Widdowson, 1978, 1994). The second strand discusses authenticity generally as a trait or property of the text. This strand is usually dominant in discussions about authentic materials, and hence it is the one most familiar to practitioners. Widdowson (1978) made these two strands clear when he famously put forward the distinction between *authentic* and *genuine* materials: genuineness is an absolute property of the material, referring to its original purpose not being for language teaching, whereas authenticity is relative to the learner's relationship to and the way in which they engage with the text. In fact, it is difficult to say anything new about authenticity following Widdowson's work, especially given that he sometimes 'throw[s] water on the flames he himself had helped to kindle' (Mishan, 2005, p. 17) in suggesting that 'inauthentic language-using behaviour might well be effective language-learning behaviour' (Widdowson, 1990, pp. 46–47 following Breen, 1985; see also Widdowson, 1979). This was the exact dilemma that surfaced very early on in my narrative and became part of my philosophy of practice. I will discuss this more in Sections 4.7 and 6.6.2 as the teach/learn dichotomy, in which I talk about the nature of experience in language teaching as a component of authenticity, and the balance between making the experience of learning intrinsically rewarding or choosing instead to focus on learning gains and language development. The idea of making the learning process itself rewarding also links with the concept of motivational flow and eudaimonia, which is discussed in Section 2.4.

Echoing this fundamental and widespread dilemma, within materials there is an excellent definition put forward by Tomlinson and Masuhara (2010), which states that authentic materials are 'designed not to transmit declarative knowledge about the target language but rather to provide an experience of the language in use' (p. 400). Clearly, this has much in common with Dewey's philosophy of education, which I discussed in the previous section. A further useful definition from the materials literature is Mishan's 3Cs framework, which I draw on later in the narrative and analysis sections. Mishan (2005) argues that SLA research can be 'encapsulated' by a pedagogic rationale based around the 3Cs of authenticity: Culture, Currency (as in time) and Challenge (pp. 44–64). These two valuable contributions mark a clear attempt to combine the two stands of the 'authenticity debate' into one useful and workable approach.

However, within language teaching the construct of authenticity has a tendency to be reduced and oversimplified, especially in relation to materials. For example, even the newest fourth edition of the Longman *Dictionary of Language Teaching and Applied Linguistics*, defines 'authentic materials' as something 'not originally developed for pedagogical purposes' (Richards & Schmidt, 2013, p. 43). This definition completely excludes every textbook, adapted or purpose-made material which is used in the classroom from being authentic, unless it is something like a newspaper from the target language-speaking community which has been 'untampered' with. Basically, under this definition, almost none of the materials actually used for language learning are authentic. This definition is echoed repeatedly throughout the literature on authenticity:

> Authentic material is language where no concessions are made to foreign speakers. It is normal, natural language used by native or competent speakers of a language. This is what our students encounter (or will encounter) in real

life if they come into contact with target-language speakers, and, precisely because it is authentic, it is unlikely to be simplified or spoken slowly.

(Harmer, 2008, p. 273)

I have come to label this definition of authenticity the 'classic' definition; classic in the sense of a classic car which is still widely respected and admired but is no longer economical and in constant danger of breaking down. This 'classic' definition is fundamentally the very widespread assumption that Widdowson (1990, p. 44) labelled the *means/ends equation*, where authenticity is defined in terms of learning aims and outcomes. Authentic language material is a means to an end because the authentic 'real world' is the ultimate destination of the learner. However, this view of authenticity is simply too reductionist to be of any use to language learning, and it also undermines the 'reality' of the classroom, not to mention placing an undue emphasis on the native-speaker model and tending to gravitate towards culturism and native-speakerism (Copland, Garton, & Mann, 2016; Holliday, 2005; Lowe & Pinner, 2016; Pinner, 2014a, 2015, 2016b; Swann, Aboshiha, & Holliday, 2015). This reaction against definitions which unduly venerate the 'native speaker' model was my main impetus for conceiving of authenticity as a continuum.

2.3.2 Authenticity as a continuum

I have been promoting the idea of authenticity as a continuum since I first wrote about it in 2012. The continuum looked much simpler then, and it had slightly different labels on its axes. As it has developed, this continuum has become part of my academic identity, but underlying it is also a much more personal reflection of my professional beliefs and my 'philosophy of teaching' (Crookes, 2009).

There are two major axes to the continuum which are presented as linear due to the limits of the two-dimensional diagram, but they are not meant to be polar extremes. Rather, they are supposed to represent a landscape where both ends of the continuum can mutually exist. The horizontal axis is the social representation, with the individual learner at one point and community represented at the other. Of course, individuals interact with society and often position themselves as speakers dependent on their social position, which changes from context to context (Goffman, 1959). So, these two aspects are in constant interaction as learners and teachers authenticate language-using activities and materials in relation to themselves and also in relation to the perceived society with which they imagine themselves communicating, or with which they find themselves actually communicating. In this way, the continuum draws heavily on Anderson (2006) for the notion of imagined communities, which strongly connects the notion of authenticity to current considerations of motivation which focus on the Self as a complex, dynamic, multifaceted and socially constructed aspect of an individual's identity (Benson & Cooker, 2013; Dörnyei, MacIntyre, & Henry, 2015b; Dörnyei & Ushioda, 2009; Mercer & Williams, 2014; Ryan & Irie, 2014; Ushioda, 2011b). So, along this axis, language is authenticated according to how it relates to an individual's sense of self (which is multiple and complex), and it can also relate to how the communities actually use language and how the community is conceptualised in the mind of the individual. For example, a learner might enjoy reading children's books in their L2, and for them this might be a personally motivating and authentic language using activity, but if the learner mainly uses L2 for business transactions, they may also be aware that they are not likely to interact with children and they may not be planning to communicate with children in the L2. In this case, the learner might feel that an article from the *Financial Times* would be more authentic in terms of the community with whom they intend to interact, but yet this would be less individually authentic as the motivation for reading such articles is less connected to the learner's sense of individuality. Of course, this is an oversimplification because quite probably the articles from the *Financial Times* also have a degree of individual authenticity, just as the children's books have a degree of community authenticity. This would be a dynamic interaction dependent on context, and as such it needs a real example and much more space to explore fully, as I will present in the narrative later.

There are only two general contexts represented on the vertical axis of the continuum. These are the learning context (which may in all likelihood be a classroom, although it could be a crowded train and a person using an educational app on their smartphone or a person in a library) and the use domain, which is basically any context where language use is prioritised over learning. Note again that learning and use do not necessarily exist in isolation, and in my own experience as a language learner I feel that some of the best learning contexts have been actual use domains for me. In other words, I have learned things best when I use them for a 'real' purpose. Learning is not simply switched on and off like the lights in a classroom, of course, and hence the two-dimensional nature of the continuum is merely a graphical representation of a much more complex and dynamic set of interacting contextual and social factors, as shown in Figure 2.2.

Basically, the authenticity continuum may only be useful to describe in retrospect, and after deep self-reflection, particular moments or heavily contextually situated tasks as they relate to real people. The continuum is intended to encompass almost any type of material or task or situation that might occur as language users interact to produce meaning. Its main strength (flexibility) is also its greatest weakness (vagueness). The continuum is my best attempt to present in a simple and easy-to-disseminate format the complexities of authenticity, specifically as it relates to motivation, self, identity, autonomy and other complex phenomena that manifest themselves in language classrooms as students and teachers interact with one another.

2.3.3 Authenticity, global English and native-speakerism

One of my main motives for promoting the concept of authenticity as a continuum was born from my desire to resist the hegemony of the 'native speaker'

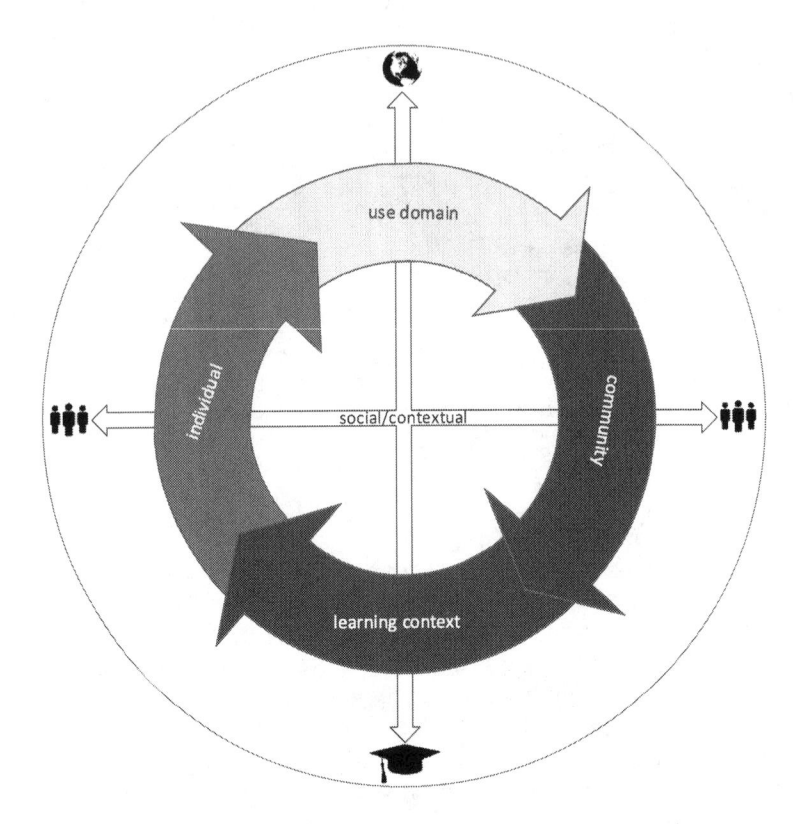

Figure 2.2 The authenticity continuum

of English as the authentic model speaker. Despite the widespread criticism of any definition of authenticity which is grounded on (or uses the word) 'native speaker', I found that the 'native speaker' was still either explicitly or implicitly present within many of the other definitions used to explain authentic language materials (Pinner, 2014a, 2014b, 2015, 2016b). If the authenticity continuum is a crowbar to dislodge this unfair and pervasive native-speakerism, then the concept of global English was the crack into which I first tried to give it leverage. To put it more simply, I always felt that the position of English as the world's only 'hyper-centralised language' (de Swaan, 2001) was the best argument *against* defining authenticity according to 'native speakers'. There exists a strong chorus of voices arguing for greater equality and recognition of the prejudicial practices that are widespread in the English Language Teaching industry (Braine, 2010; Kiczkowiak, 2015; Kumaravadivelu, 2016; Mahboob & Golden, 2013; Swann et al., 2015). Research in this area has uncovered employment discrimination (Clark & Paran, 2007; H.-K. Kim, 2011; Mahboob & Golden, 2013; Mahboob, Uhrig, Newman, & Hartford, 2004; Selvi, 2010), student preferences for

Western models of English (Matsuda, 2003; Saito, 2012; Sasayama, 2013), 'non-native speaker' teachers having negative self-images (Bernat, 2008; Brutt-Griffler & Samimy, 1999; H.-K. Kim, 2011) and students having a positive orientation towards 'native speaker' over 'non-native speaker' teachers (Alseweed, 2012; Lasagabaster & Sierra, 2002; K.-h. Wu & Ke, 2009). Indeed, with an estimated 80 per cent of ELT teachers being identifiable as 'non-native' (Canagarajah, 2005), Silvana Richardson noted in her 2016 International Association of Teachers of English as a Foreign Language plenary that ELT is the only industry which prejudices against the majority. The issue of authenticity has been a feature of several discussions around native-speakerism, especially in terms of authentic model speakers (Edge, 1988; Goto Butler, 2007; Seargeant, 2005), the marginal presence of international speakers in textbooks (Canagarajah, 1993; Matsuda, 2002; Siegel, 2014), the ownership of English (Matsuda, 2003; Widdowson, 1994), and wider sociological issues relating to identity and legitimacy (Creese, Blackledge, & Takhi, 2014; Kramsch, 2012; Myhill, 2003; Widdowson, 1996). These issues make the 'classic' definition of authenticity extremely contentious, often directly linking it with prejudicial practices (see Lowe & Pinner, 2016 for an in-depth review). Clearly, any definition of authenticity which potentially excludes L2 speakers of English from being recognised as 'authentic' could have a very demotivating, depersonalising and disenfranchising effect for both teachers and learners of English.

In *Language and Symbolic Power*, Pierre Bourdieu (1991) borrows the concept of different forms of *capital* from economics and applies them to sociology. Cultural Capital is the most often referred to form of capital with relation to the learning of other languages, because this is seen as a form of social currency which entitles speakers to certain other resources (Kanno & Norton, 2003; Norton, 2013; Norton Peirce, 1995). Cultural Capital is either consciously or subliminally ascribed to speakers with particular accents (Block, 2014) and who match certain visual/racial stereotypes (Amin, 1999; Braine, 1999; Kubota & Lin, 2009b). This is a deeply embedded cultural phenomenon which has plagued human history, and yet the acquisition of social or cultural forms of capital is often regarded as a major component in the motivation (and pressure) to learn English (Dörnyei & Ushioda, 2009; Irie & Brewster, 2014; Maehr & Braskamp, 1986; Noels, Pelletier, Clément, & Vallerand, 2003; Norton Peirce, 1995). Motivational orientations towards English also heavily implicate the idea of *imagined communities*, as proposed by Benedict Anderson (2006), because the target-language community is not a physical reality but rather a social extension of the individual's vision of a group in social context, although it is based on a real group of people or an actual discourse community. This is especially complicated by the process of globalisation and the position of English as a global language (Matsuda, 2011; Pinner, 2016b; Ryan, 2006; Seargeant, 2009; Ushioda, 2013b). This is a theme I revisit in this inquiry, with particular emphasis on the students' perceptions of me as a teacher (a white, middle-class British male), and their attitude to the status of English as a global language and widely established lingua franca.

2.3.4 Empirical studies in ELT on authenticity and motivation

The belief that authentic materials are more motivating is generally held by the language teaching community, is widespread throughout the literature on authenticity, and is a common selling point for textbook producers (Gilmore, 2007a, p. 106). Although there are studies which have attempted to test empirically the connection between authenticity and motivation in language teaching, as I will demonstrate shortly, these studies are generally flawed, but more disconcertingly as a whole the field is marred by a 'dearth of empirical studies' (Pinner, 2016b, pp. 83–97). The below chart shows how journals in our field refer to authenticity in published research, from the first issue of the journal through to March 2015. For example, in its 69-year history since 1946, the *ELT Journal* mentions authenticity roughly 2.43 times per issue, and yet the ratio of articles which deal specifically with authenticity (based on the title) drops significantly to a ratio of 0.04 mentions per issue (see Table 2.2).

Perhaps the best-known and most-cited study looking at the relationship between authenticity and motivation in language teaching was conducted by Peacock (1997). This study reports data collected for Peacock's doctoral thesis (1996) and was also used in at least one other article (1998). Working with low-level learners in South Korea, Peacock tried to empirically prove the widely held belief that authentic materials are more motivating for learners than contrived ones. This was a thorough and important study which has become the bedrock to support the widespread claim. However, as Peacock himself agrees, the study was inconclusive and uncovered seemingly contradictory observations.

Interpreting Ushioda's (1993) paper, Peacock erroneously attributes to her a 'practitioner validated' view of motivation, which he defines as 'learner enthusiasm, attention, action, and enjoyment' (1997, p. 145). The practitioner-validated idea of motivation is in fact attributable to Crookes and Schmidt (1991). Ushioda was advocating a *learner validated* concept of motivation, in which learners are directly asked to explain their own motivation for studying French, later developed more fully in her doctoral work and subsequent publications of that time. However, Peacock interprets these as teacher-observable indicators of motivation in order to quantify the construct so as to be

Table 2.2 Journals surveyed for mention of authenticity (from Pinner 2016b)

Journal	Whole text Hits	Title Hits	Whole text Ratio	Title Only Ratio
Modern Language Journal	1090	0	1.70	0.00
ELTJ	692	10	2.43	0.04
Language Learning	175	3	0.77	0.01
Applied Linguistics	198	2	1.53	0.02
Language Teaching Research	110	0	1.86	0.00

able to draw comparisons between authentic and inauthentic materials. Despite reporting that students experienced authentic materials as more motivating, he also reports that learners found the authentic materials to be *less interesting*. This seems to be something of an oxymoron. Gilmore (2007a, pp. 106–108) also points out this flaw in Peacock's study, and yet concludes after his state-of-the-art review that it is to date the most convincing empirical study examining the connection between authenticity and motivation. Interestingly, Gilmore ranks Peacock's study as the most convincing out of only three that he is aware of – the other two (González, 1990; Kienbaum, Russell, & Welty, 1986) were also cited in Peacock's paper, which suggests that nothing had been done on the subject in the ten years between Peacock's study and Gilmore's review. Furthermore, the study by González (1990) is an unpublished doctoral dissertation in Education from West Virginia University, unavailable digitally and thus rather obscure. This paucity of empirical studies is quite troubling, especially given the widespread nature of the claim.

A final key criticism I have of Peacock's study is that he fails to actually define what he means by the term 'authentic' materials. However, to me it is clear that he is using the 'classic' definition which I criticised earlier for denying the 'reality' of the classroom and implicitly gravitating towards the 'native speaker'. Gilmore's (2007b, 2011, 2016) own important contributions have shown some indirect evidence for authentic materials being more motivating whilst mainly providing support for their beneficial effect on actual language acquisition. However, these studies also draw on a definition of authenticity which heavily implies the 'native speaker' and often use these as norm-providing models.

These limitations in the previous literature have made the present study very difficult, and yet I would argue all the more essential. I hypothesise that the reason for this lack of research into authenticity stems from the unsatisfactory emphasis given to authenticity as a trait belonging to materials. Under the definition used in this study, it would be just as unenlightening to talk about autonomous materials as it would be to talk about authentic ones. By this I mean that authenticity as I am envisioning it, is not something that can be ascribed to a text but something that must be socially constructed by mutually validating the learning enacted in the class. Therefore, this inquiry is markedly different in both the methodological approach and how the key concepts are theorised. However, the more traditional studies which rely on the 'classic' definition of authenticity are no more meaningful and no less abstract than the core concept at the heart of this inquiry. Studies like Peacock's and Gilmore's that attempt to compare one type of material with another do not shed any light on the processes going on in the classroom. At present this is rather unexplored territory, although please see Külekçi (2015) for a step in this direction.

2.4 Motivation

For some, motivation is the single most important factor in determining the success of a learner in achieving their linguistic goals (Dörnyei, 1994; Dörnyei

& Ushioda, 2011; Gao & Lamb, 2011). The importance of motivation is rarely understated, so it is little wonder that the research on motivation in both educational psychology and SLA enjoys a rich and complex history. And yet, despite its frequent occurrence in language teaching and research, motivation is a difficult term to define.

In this section I will briefly touch on some of the development and evolution of motivational theories in SLA, paying special attention to the 'fluidity of today's learning contexts' (Ushioda, 2013b, p. 5) and the nature of theoretical motivational models based on different research paradigms, that is, the move from positivist to ontological approaches (Ushioda, 2009) and the tension between reductionist and comprehensive theories (Dörnyei & Ushioda, 2011, p. 8). Because I wish to trace a strong conceptual link between authenticity and motivation, and the basis of this link is the content, materials and tasks being selected by the teacher in order to facilitate language interaction with the students, I will also examine teacher motivation. Teacher motivation has an important relationship with student motivation, and this is a vital link in the chain between authenticity and motivation. I will then outline the link between authenticity and motivation as two concepts essential to successful classroom learning and with deeply entwined theoretical roots. Authenticity and motivation are common collocates in the literature on language teaching and learning, and perhaps even more common in staffrooms around the world. However, very few studies have tested this connection empirically. In trying to recognise the complexity of this relationship I hope to explain it more clearly and recognise it as part of a complex dynamic system with interconnected components.

2.4.1 Motivational theories: a brief overview

Recently there has been a flood of interest in motivational studies, described as an 'extraordinary surge' and an accompanying 'landscape shift' in the number of studies, the research methods employed and the way motivation is conceptualised (Boo, Dörnyei, & Ryan, 2015, p. 145; see also Dörnyei & Ryan, 2015).

The literature about second-language motivation largely developed separately from the general motivational literature of psychology (Ushioda, 1998) and is still described as 'a rich and largely independent field' (Dörnyei & Ushioda, 2011, p. 39). These two strands do often converge, especially within educational psychology; see current work on motivational dynamics such as Dörnyei et al. (2015b), Muir and Dörnyei (2013) and Ushioda (2013c), for example. However, on the whole L2 motivational theories can still be regarded as distinct from other theories about motivation. This is because learning a second language is often perceived as having a very different and individual position due to the size of the task of learning another language and the long time periods involved. It could perhaps be argued that language learning is a much more sustained and cognitively demanding task than almost any other type of learning.

Dörnyei (2001b, p. 13) refers to this as 'parallel multiplicity', highlighting the very different nature of L2 motivation to that discussed in the mainstream psychological literature. Examining the motivation to learn to drive a car, for example, and that to learn another language will necessitate a very different concept of motivation.

Dörnyei and his proposal of a 'self' framework (2005) is one of the most significant contributions to recent understandings of L2 motivation. He later developed this framework into the *L2 Motivational Self System* (Dörnyei, 2009), best summarised by its distinction between the learner's L2 *ideal self* and *ought to self*. Within this system the *ideal self* is predominantly defined as a 'desire to reduce the discrepancy between our actual and ideal selves' (Dörnyei, 2009, p. 29) and as such incorporates both integrative and internalised instrumental components of motivation. In contrast, the *ought to self* has a focus on avoiding negative outcomes, such as failure or embarrassment or being unable to meet with social expectations. Dörnyei (2009) states that this theory 'represents a major reformation' (p. 9) of previous L2 motivational theory because it incorporates theories of the self from mainstream psychological literature whilst maintaining the roots of previous L2 approaches.

Dörnyei (2009) argues that 'the self approach allows us to think BIG' (p. 39), and as such it has the flexibility to relate to a multicultural and globalised view of L2 motivation which is necessary when considering the cross-cultural implications of English education around the world, now perceived 'as a basic educational skill alongside literacy, numeracy and information and communication technology (ICT) skills' (Ushioda, 2013b, p. 2, following Graddol, 2006). The requirement of English as a basic skill is further intensified by the powerful educational reforms which are being undertaken as a result of the burgeoning array of bilingual methodologies such as English as a Medium of Instruction (EMI) and Content-Based Instruction (CBI) and especially Content and Language Integrated Learning (CLIL).

Elsewhere I have argued that language education which puts content at the top of its learning aims alongside language proficiency will inevitably achieve a higher level of authenticity (Pinner, 2013a, 2013b), or what Coyle, Hood and Marsh (2010) refer to as 'authenticity of purpose'. This is because students need to use language as a tool to understand the content. Thus, following Vygotsky (1964), language acts as a tool through which other aims and objectives are achieved, with knowledge being socially constructed. This also means that CLIL and CBI are deeply situated in a sociocultural framework of learning.

At the institution where this inquiry is based, CLIL has been an important principle in the large-scale restructuring of foreign language education programs (Ikeda, 2013; Izumi, Watanabe, & Ikeda, 2012; Watanabe, Ikeda, & Izumi, 2011), and as such this is an important part of the background to this study. Nevertheless, although content is seen as important in connecting authenticity and motivation, it is still secondary to the need to personalise the learning experience.

2.4.2 Learners speak as themselves ...

One of the most interesting developments in recent concepts of motivation has been the clear need to incorporate contextual variables and with them the social dimensions of learning on the one hand, while on the other recognising the need to incorporate the individual more as a vital factor (Dörnyei & Ushioda, 2011, pp. 30–33). Thus, motivation is seen as a set of various dynamic systems which will inevitably need to take account of a huge myriad of factors. In terms of authenticity and motivation, one particularly insightful view of motivation is what Ushioda (2009) advocates in her *person-in-context relational* view of motivation, which is 'emergent from relations between real persons, with particular social identities, and the unfolding cultural context of activity' (p. 215). In other words, motivation is not fixed, and any attempt to examine motivation must make allowances for various fluctuations as motivation moves along a temporal axis. Ushioda stresses that to study such complex phenomena requires ontological approaches which do not compartmentalise learners according to individual differences but look directly at the *person* who is a learner. For Ushioda, the individual identity of the learner is essential in their motivation to learn the target language, stressing the importance of allowing learners the autonomy required to speak as themselves. The importance of autonomy in motivation has also been established for many years, most notably in Deci and Ryan's (1985) self-determination theory, which posits that autonomy, competence and relatedness are essential factors in motivation.

In this theory, both autonomy and relatedness are conceptually very close to the broadened view of authenticity which I have attempted to put forward so far in this study. In the following statement, van Lier (1996) demonstrates how closely the concepts of authenticity and autonomy can interact:

> An action is authentic when it realises a free choice and is an expression of what a person genuinely feels and believes. An authentic action is intrinsically motivated.
>
> (p. 6)

As the above remarks show, authenticity is about free choice, what an individual feels and believes. Autonomy is about the ability to act on this authentic belief; it is about having a 'capacity to take control' (Benson, 2013b, p. 61). In this way, authenticity is knowing what you want, feel and believe, and autonomy is about being able to act on this. For van Lier, authenticity and motivation go hand in hand, and his definition of authenticity echoes Ushioda's *person-in-context relational* approach to motivation (see also Allwright & Hanks, 2009, pp. 2–3). A triadic relationship is observable from these three components, which I call the Language Impetus Triad.

2.4.3 The Language Impetus Triad

In this section, I will propose that authenticity forms a triad with autonomy and motivation, which I name the Language Impetus Triad, following Martin

Heidegger's work on modes of Being, in which he argues that by living inauthentically (without what he terms *Dasein*, or being-there), we are basically propelled through life without any reflection or development of the self. The reason authenticity, autonomy and motivation form a triad is partly because of the 'synergistic' relationship between student and teacher motivation (Deci et al., 1997; Dörnyei & Ushioda, 2011). It is my belief that teachers will be more motivated if they are working with content and tasks in the language classroom which they feel are authentic, and validate as such. The teacher's validation of the learning materials becomes *social authentication* when it is conveyed to the students and validated by them in turn, thus creating a series of dynamic feedback loops, or a 'reciprocal and recursive pattern of causality' (Dörnyei & Ushioda, 2011, p. 191). The process of authenticating the learning might not actually start with the teacher, but the teacher's investment in the process is essential, since the teacher has been shown as one of the main factors contributing to student motivation (Chambers, 1999; Dörnyei & Csizér, 1998; Montalvo, Mansfield, & Miller, 2007). Finally, autonomy is essential, both as an ingredient of motivation and as part of the students' self-image and place in the imagined community of the language being learned. In this way, autonomy and authenticity are very closely entwined as concepts, because authentication is a process of 'personal engagement' (van Lier, 1996), and autonomy is a necessary ingredient of authenticity as it entails a personal choice.

As these concepts are interdependent and closely related, one aspect of the triad cannot be understood without knowing its relation to the others, which necessitates a complex dynamic systems perspective to examining these relationships. I also propose that not understanding this connection previously may account for the low number of empirical studies investigating authenticity and motivation. The Language Impetus Triad (Figure 2.3) shows the interdependent relationship between authenticity, autonomy and motivation. It is my strong belief that one of the reasons for the dearth in empirical studies on the relationship between authenticity and motivation is because this triadic relationship has until now been avoided for fear of adding another term ('autonomy') into an already unwieldy mix of abstract concepts. However, I think rather than overcomplicating the issue, this relationship allows for a clearer picture of what these concepts are and how they depend on each other. Many well-established theories are grounded in the overlap of these concepts. For example, self-determination theory suggests that motivation is dependent on autonomy, and for van Lier (1996), authenticity and motivation are strongly connected. Furthermore, even down to the basic etymological root authenticity and autonomy are very closely related. Authenticity is knowing what you want, feel and believe, and autonomy is about being able to act on this.

To recap, very basically *authenticity* is being true to the self and a belief in what one is doing. This belief is embedded in the individual, but it also relies on social factors in order to be validated. Next, *autonomy* is the capacity the individual has to realise or act on their authentic beliefs. Authenticity is *what* we do when we have the autonomy *to do* it. Autonomy is influenced not simply by an authority

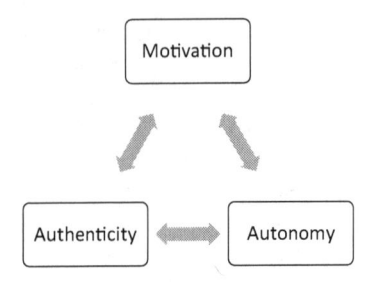

Figure 2.3 The Language Impetus Triad

figure such as a teacher or a department chair but by a myriad of internal and external factors such as time, ability and so on. The final component of the triad, *motivation*, describes the psychological state of the individual as it relates to the authentic action and the physical reality of undertaking it. Again, this is influenced by potentially innumerable internal and external forces, requiring that motivation be conceptualised as a dynamic system.

When looking at the relationship between authenticity and motivation it is my view that autonomy is necessary to understand the connections because the three are essential components in a triadic co-dependent dynamic. As a result of this rather complicated set of factors, empirical studies that look at the relationship between authenticity and motivation will need to put both learners and teachers at the centre of any inquiry and view them as people, each with very different needs and values. I believe that learners achieve their best when they are viewed in this way and allowed to achieve their educational goals in a scaffolded learning environment; an environment which allows them to authenticate the learning taking place by engaging all three elements of the triad with their own personal identities.

2.4.4 *The importance of context: Japan's motivational landscape*

This research will focus on Japan, specifically at the university level, because the Japanese context presents a very interesting motivational dilemma (Ryan, 2009) or even what Berwick and Ross (1989) refer to as a 'wasteland' of motivation. In the Japanese university setting there are two distinct types of learners: English majors and those for whom English is a compulsory subject or module, perhaps bearing little or no relevance to their chosen degree.

In Japan, the need to speak English is held in very high esteem, often sold on trains and advertising boards as a key to success, a key to the world and an integral part of a new self-identity (Seargeant, 2009). Japanese society is very open to foreign cultures; many loan[1] words have been incorporated into the lexicon from English and other European languages, and in fact there is a special writing system called katakana in which loan words are generally written. Examples range from words such as dance, silhouette, get, present, apartment, after-service and ice cream from English, *arbeit* (part-time work) from German and *avant-guerre* (pre-war) from French (Kamiya, 1995). Despite the elevated status of English in particular, Japanese Test of English as a Foreign Language (TOEFL) scores are amongst the lowest in Asia (Yoshida, 2003), and there are complaints of a lack of coherence between government proficiency targets and syllabus design and implementation (Ikeda, Pinner, Mehisto, & Marsh, 2013). This seeming contradiction actually provides a reasonable lens from which to view English language learning in Japan, and makes any attempt to study motivation rather problematic and yet highly essential. Any attempt to examine motivation would do well to include Japanese students' attitudes towards foreign or global culture, paying particular attention to the modern context which includes rapidly globalising perspectives and advancing communicative technologies. Educational reforms, changing societal perspectives and heightened professional expectations regarding foreign languages make the Japanese context a fertile ground for motivational studies.

For a more emic perspective, I would like to share part of an essay written by a student in my English Linguistics Seminar class from spring 2016. Emi Uchida, the author of the following remarks, is about to finish a teaching certificate course which is offered as a pathway through Sophia's English Literature Department where I work. As part of this, she took three weeks of practical teaching experience by visiting a junior high school and working as a trainee teacher. In her essay for my seminar, she made the following first-hand observations:

> Almost all the lessons were taught mainly in Japanese and consisted of reading, listening, and pattern practice of speaking. First, teachers make students do some pattern greeting or easy question-and-answer as a whole class. Second, they check the meaning in Japanese and practice pronunciation of new words in textbook. Third, they do some listening and pattern practice of speaking in textbook. At last, they practice pronunciation and check translations of the texts in textbook. There are few opportunities to make sentences by themselves. [...] The second-year students could make a short speech which is about five sentences. Its topic was about familiar topic such as memories of Golden Week. However, some students could not distinguish between verbs and adjectives like the first-year students. For example, they wrote 'It was enjoy' or 'I was enjoy'. In addition, almost all students did not take their eyes off the manuscript which they wrote before presentation during their speech and read it aloud with flat accent and an expressionless face. These examples are only a part of the present situation in many schools, but they reflect the reality more faithfully because public schools are influenced more strongly by policies of the government.
>
> The [...] problem is the lack of motivation for communication. The reason students did not speak emotionally in speech is because they did not have motivation to make themselves understood by other people and communicate with them.
>
> (Emi Uchida, July 2016)

From Emi Uchida's description, the learning of English seems very mechanical, as well as appearing to be quite unsuccessful in either creating communicative students or even students who know how to speak English correctly, making the use of the target language 'ritualistic' rather than personal (Rampton, 1999, 2002). Such practices have been linked to student demotivation in Japan (Kikuchi, 2013, 2015), particularly because the students are well aware of the 'gap' between the communicative practices advocated by the Ministry of Education (MEXT) and the exam-focused grammar translation methods actually applied in most classes (Kikuchi & Browne, 2009). As stated in Section 2.3.1, the emphasis on exams is widely recognised to be a major failing in terms of English education, and yet the situation persists indefinitely because many private universities in Japan rely on entrance exams for a large portion of their income. Multiple choice tests are the most economical to create and administer, so they provide the highest revenue margins. However, there is no rule that teachers must prepare learners for entrance exams to the next tier of education. Although university is not compulsory, over 50 per cent of high-school graduates enrolled in higher education at either a university or junior college, and this figure increases to 70 per cent if colleges of technology and other vocational higher education institutions are included (MEXT, 2012). However, this still means that in every high-school class being prepared for university entrance exams, at least 30 per cent of the students have no intention of taking such exams. This means that in a class of 40 students, 12 will have no reason for undertaking such instruction. A large group like this will certainly be able to exercise an effect on the motivational dynamics of the class, even if we assume that the other 28 students are all highly motivated to practise grammar and rote learning.

These problems contribute to the 'hyperbole' and 'permanent sense of crisis' that surrounds Japan's L2 motivational literature (Ushioda, 2013a). In the introduction to his book, Kikuchi (2015) relates his own experience of learning English in Japan, blaming the teacher (Mr K) as the primary 'demotivator'.

In their extensive review of the landscape of psychological factors relevant to language learning, Dörnyei and Ryan (2015) chose to omit several 'other motivational themes' from their revisited work because 'the study of the particular topics in question had not produced sufficiently stimulating new results over the past decade [since 2005] relative to other, more fruitful areas' (p. 99). One of these omissions was demotivation, because 'the underlying theoretical basis of the issue has hardly changed since Dörnyei's (2001a, p. 100) first summary'. Dörnyei and Ryan criticise the lack of emphasis on dynamics in this field, essentially sidelining it from mainstream motivational research. Another omission from Dörnyei and Ryan's revised volume is teacher motivation; however, this time they justify the omission not on a lack of theoretical development but on the '*indirect* link of the concept to student achievement' (p. 101; emphasis in original) and the necessity of teacher motivational research to make connections with student motivation and, ultimately, student performance. Clearly, this view is somewhat at odds with that of Exploratory Practice, which seeks only to gain a deeper understanding without placing undue pressure on teachers and learners to increase their performance (Allwright, 2003, 2005, 2006a; Allwright & Hanks, 2009). One study that does address the issue raised by Dörnyei and Ryan was conducted by Sampson (2016), who details his own attempts to connect students' identities with their English learning from a complexity perspective (see also Sampson, 2012, 2015). In the present inquiry, I attempt to establish a link between my students' motivation and my own. In the following section I will examine the dynamic interplay between authenticity and motivation, especially focusing on how this can create a bridge between student and teacher motivation.

2.5 Authenticity and motivation

Authenticity is a very common collocate with the term 'motivation' in language teaching and learning, usually with reference to materials (although see Dörnyei, Henry, & Muir, 2016 for an alternative perspective). By association, authenticity is thus central to language teaching because motivation can be seen as perhaps the most important contributor as to whether or not learners are successful in acquiring a second language.

2.5.1 Teacher motivation and the relationship to student motivation

> The rationale for combining the topics of teacher and student motivation in one book is actually quite simple: the two are inextricably linked because the former is needed for the latter to bloom.
>
> (Dörnyei & Kubanyiova, 2014, p. 3)

Good teachers are motivated intrinsically by a desire to teach, to impart learning, to facilitate the growth of education and the attainment of academic goals in their students. This is proved in quite a number of studies (Dinham & Scott, 2000; Richardson & Watt, 2006) and also covered in some detail by Dörnyei and Ushioda (2011). The relationship between student and teacher motivation can be 'either positively or negatively synergistic' (Deci et al., 1997, p. 68), and so it follows that teachers who are motivated by what they teach will be more motivating for their students in the way they teach. Why is this important in understanding the connection between authenticity and motivation? The main reason is that, like learners, teachers are subject to the same general principles of motivational dynamics. Teachers need to be able to self-actualise (Deci et al., 1997; Deci & Ryan, 1985; Niemiec & Ryan, 2009) and that means they need

- to feel competent in what they are doing (a sense of efficacy in their ability to teach and in what they are teaching about),
- to have the autonomy to make decisions about what they do in their own classroom (often the choice of materials will make up a large part of this

as classroom content is essentially the bedrock of the day-to-day classroom experience of a teacher), and

● to see the relevance of what they are doing and feel it meets their teaching and learning goals.

The concept of 'relevance' in Deci and Ryan's (1985) self-determination theory shares a great deal of conceptual overlap with authenticity. Some of the prerequisites of Csikszentmihalyi's Flow theory (1990, 1997b, 2013) also overlap with self-determination theory (such as *control* with *competence* and *skill/ challenge balance*). Feedback is also an essential component of self-determination theory and Flow, and this was something I also came to recognise as vital during the narrative of this inquiry. Flow is

> characterized, above all, by a deep, spontaneous involvement with the task at hand. In flow, one is so carried away by what one is doing and feels so immersed in the activity that the distinction between "I" and "it" becomes irrelevant.
>
> (Csikszentmihalyi, 1997b, p. 82)

The following seven factors are identified as prerequisites for the experience of Flow:

1. There must be clear goals.
2. There must be immediate feedback.
3. Challenges and skills must be in balance.
4. Concentration is essential.
5. Control must be made possible.
6. Growth and self-transcendence must be enhanced.
7. The autotelic nature of true learning must be highlighted.

Flow has been investigated in language teaching in terms of teacher motivation (Tardy & Snyder, 2004) and more generally in terms of its significance in SLA (Egbert, 2003). Task conditions under which Flow is most likely to occur in language learning can be organised according to four dimensions: Concentration, Control, Skill/Challenge Balance and Authenticity. Here, authenticity is taken to mean that 'the participants find the task intrinsically interesting or authentic' (Dörnyei & Ushioda, 2011, p. 95). Csikszentmihalyi (1997b) also notes that during the flow experience, 'the ego that surveys and evaluates our actions disappears in the flow of experience. One is freed of the confines of the social self and may feel an exhilarating sense of transcendence, of belonging to a larger whole' (p. 82). This is a very important aspect and part of the nature of authentic synergy, as the individual merges with a 'larger whole', in this case the class. The importance of this feeling of Flow is that it creates a sense of belonging to the class, of belonging to the activity (of learning), and by extension a sense of belonging to the language of instruction and hence the wider community of that language. Making the learning itself an intrinsically rewarding part of the class is something which has long been argued to be important to language learning.

> Motivation which is principally founded on immediate intrinsic rewards arising directly from involvement in L2 learning activity, and which is bolstered by experience of such affective rewards and perceptions of ability gained from prior L2 history, seems a rather more solid sustaining basis for continued engagement in L2 learning.
>
> (Ushioda, 1993, p. 10)

Although at the time Ushioda did not connect this idea with Flow, the observation was built on Csikszentmihalyi's earlier research. I later connect this idea to my philosophy of teaching, when I realise that I am prioritising the experience of learning over actual gains in language proficiency (Section 4.7).

Building somewhat on Csikszentmihalyi's Flow theory, Dörnyei et al. (2016) have linked the feeling of eudaimonia (a sense of well-being and connectedness with one's inner-self) with authenticity in their discussion of Directed Motivational Currents (DMCs), which are long-term periods of highly motivated activity that emanate from a sense of congruence from working towards future-self goals. These concepts are also relevant to language teaching as an activity requiring a great balance of skill, prolonged concentration and being a very central aspect of one's identity.

2.5.2 Factors affecting the motivation to teach

The feeling teachers attain when learners are engaged has been shown to be one of the main contributors to teaching satisfaction, making the work intrinsically rewarding and potentially leading to a sense of Flow when teaching which, as one participant in a study by Tardy and Snyder (2004) expressed, is 'why I do it' (p. 123). Looking at the longer-term aspect of teacher motivation, it may be more useful to think of this feeling in terms of DMCs rather than Flow, because the former relates to more sustained periods of activity (Dörnyei et al., 2016, p. 4). Thus, in certain cases, the feeling of congruence in one's teaching approach may potentially lead to a sense of eudaimonia, which helps maintain the hard work of the endeavour by connecting a feeling of self-congruence with the activity of teaching (Bullough, 2009; Bullough & Pinnegar, 2009). Because teaching is often intrinsically motivated, it is therefore a deeply personal calling, and as an academic vocation, teaching well and liking it requires 'extremely high energy, focus, and *total* commitment' (Bess, 1997, p. xi; emphasis in original). This is dependent on the development of one's own 'philosophy of teaching', which must then be aligned with the actual practices of the classroom if the teacher is to feel truly authentic in him or herself (Kreber, 2013). Although these factors influence teaching at any level, as this study focuses on the tertiary context it is also important to note that 'it is less clear just how salient the activity of teaching is in the professor's job description and self-concept' (Deci et al., 1997, p. 58), because university teaching involves a range of other activities besides teaching, such as conducting and publishing research.

Teacher motivation is highly dependent on contextual factors such as faculty support, student ability and engagement, autonomy within the curricula and other personal factors such as health and mental well-being. It also fluctuates according to a temporal axis (Carbonneau, Vallerand, Fernet, & Guay, 2008), as does student motivation to learn (de Bot, 2015; Ushioda, 1998, 2015). Moreover, teacher motivation is fragile. Teaching is identified as a high-risk profession in terms of burnout, despite being less well remunerated than other high-burnout positions like being a lawyer or a stockbroker (Dörnyei & Ushioda, 2011). Avoidance of burnout is one of the justifications behind Exploratory Practice as a research approach, which forms a link between this Exploratory Practice and teacher motivation (Allwright, 2003, 2005; Allwright & Hanks, 2009).

Despite the fact that many teachers are intrinsically motivated by their work, teachers are certainly not perfect Disney-esque agents who teach purely for love and the realisation of a lifelong dream. I am a teacher and I love teaching. I never think about how much I am earning whilst teaching, although I did do this when working as a bartender. However, if I were given the choice between teaching and being a full-time novelist who could live on a self-sufficient island and tend to my own vineyard, I think my teaching days would soon be over. Also, there are, I am sure, any number of teachers who are in their profession simply from habit or from complacency, not to mention a great many teachers who have become disenfranchised with the endeavour due to a myriad of personal and contextual variables. Therefore, a large aspect of this study has been the creation of my own philosophy of teaching and an attempt to gain a better understanding of my own motivations to teach. Understanding my own motivation is essential if I am to investigate the synergy with the motivation of my students.

2.6 Motivational synergy

I have already touched on the idea that teacher and student motivation can be synergistic (Deci et al., 1997), that there is an interactive, bidirectional relationship (Dörnyei & Ushioda, 2011, pp. 190–191) which creates reciprocal feedback loops. This idea has become the main focus of this book, as it is where the interplay between authenticity and motivation seems to be most apparent. This is not what I set out to find in this inquiry, but this theme emerged as the most salient whilst other concepts aligned themselves to the research design. Therefore, it is worth tracing the roots of this relationship in some detail, especially given the paucity of language teaching specific studies related to authenticity and motivation.

In their discussion of self-determined teaching, Deci et al. (1997) overview a number of studies that show how teachers' behaviour is influenced by their perceptions of the students and vice versa. For example, they cite an unpublished study by Jelsma (1982) which found that teachers enjoyed their work when the students were cooperative and interested, and when students were unruly the teachers exhibited more controlling behaviour. This type of authoritarian controlling behaviour has been linked to lower levels of satisfaction and performance in both teachers and students, and is very much an aspect of teacher and learner autonomy (Pelletier, Séguin-Lévesque, & Legault, 2002; Pelletier & Sharp, 2009; Reeve, 2009; Roth, Assor, Kanat-Maymon, & Kaplan, 2007). Other factors also affect classroom dynamics, for example, the students' perceptions of the same class based on whether or not they believed the teacher was being paid, which was intended as a simple way of invoking the concept of intrinsic or extrinsic motivation (Wild, Enzle, & Hawkins, 1992).

A study by Montalvo et al. (2007) found that simply *liking* the teacher led to better student achievement and motivation. The study also looked at what the students liked about teachers, finding that

> liked teachers create a classroom environment that emphasises learning, promotes mastery and supports students by providing confidence-building feedback [...] promotes student interest and cooperation, encourages them to adopt learning goals, see the value of school to attaining personally valued future goals and to persist when tasks become difficult.
>
> (Montalvo et al., 2007, p. 154)

Although only indirectly linked with student motivation, Carbonneau et al. (2008) found that 'harmonious' passion (as opposed to the more destructive form of 'obsessive' passion) was an important part of teachers' long-term sustainability, avoidance of burnout and contributed greatly to teachers' sense of well-being, something that could be linked to a sense of authenticity as discussed in the previous sections.

Crucially, Martin (2006) found that teachers enjoy their work more when they perceive that their learners are more motivated. Although thorough, this quantitative study was based on the teachers' perception of their students' motivation utilising a parallel version of Martin's 40-item Student Motivation and Engagement Scale, which was adapted for administration to the 1,019 participating teachers. One reported finding was that male teachers tended to report higher student motivation than female teachers, which for me highlights the lack of detail in favour of quantifiable generalisations that, as Ushioda (2011b) has argued, 'focuses not on differences between individuals, but on averages and aggregates that lump together people who share certain characteristics' (p. 12). So, although this is an important study, it comes from a methodological background that focuses on quantifiable results, presumably because these tend to be more widely accepted by academic journal editors (Hyland, 2015), and thus the research is less about teachers and their practices than researchers and their publications. This has led to a call for teachers themselves to conduct research that 'focuses the lens more sharply on how motivational and metacognitive processes develop through dialogic interactions around particular cognitive or linguistic problems in the L2 learning process' (Ushioda, 2014, p. 46). I will revisit this criticism in the justification for my research design in the next chapter, but it is also worth noting here that Exploratory Practice seems especially well suited to exploring these types of links. For example, speaking specifically about authenticity, Akyazı (2016) explains in the rationale for her study that

> I often question what students feel about being made to talk about topics that they may not have an interest in or familiarity with, and talking for no other reason than to please the teacher; I strive to make language learning a more authentic, meaningful and enjoyable experience.
>
> (p. 191)

Returning to the concept of motivational synergy, in the same volume as Deci et al. (1997), Csikszentmihalyi (1997b) postulates that students will certainly be able to recognise whether their teacher enjoys his or her work.

> If a teacher does not believe in his [or her] job, does not enjoy the learning he [or she] is trying to transmit, the student will sense this and derive the entirely rational conclusion that the particular subject matter is not worth mastering for its own sake.
>
> (p. 77)

He goes on to state that teachers (specifically university professors) who do not enjoy the work of teaching serve only to 'spread cynicism down another generation' (pp. 77–78). However, the onus must not lie exclusively in the teacher as this denies the agency of our learners. Dörnyei and Ushioda (2011) observe that teacher motivation is neither an antecedent nor a consequence of student motivation, but a bilateral and interdependent process of exchange that 'may best be captured within a complex dynamic systems framework' (p. 191). Therefore, convergent or divergent might be useful ways of describing this phenomenon.

2.6.1 Convergence and divergence

From a complex systems perspective, it would be reductive to talk about an entire class being 'synergised' with the teacher intrinsically, as the reality is that learners will always experience the class differently, and some will be highly motivated at one point whilst others experience positive motivational charges to a much lesser extent as a social phenomenon. It may be more helpful to talk about teacher-student motivational synergy from the point of being either *convergent* or *divergent*, borrowing concepts from accommodation theory (Gallois & Giles, 2015; Giles, Coupland, & Coupland, 1991). In other words, when the participants all work together towards the same educational goals in the class, this could be described as mutually accommodating, or *convergent*. More realistically, the class may be predominantly convergent, meaning not all of the participants but certainly the majority are working together and share the teacher's fundamental aims. At other times, the class may be partially *divergent*, meaning that there are some students who share the teacher's aims and are synergised with his/her motivational orientation; however, there are many other directions in the class. It may also be possible that this orientation could develop a rebellious orientation, in which students align their energies *against* the teacher or the content. This then becomes a power struggle, something that many teachers around the world, especially those working in state education, may recognise as a constant force in their teaching contexts. The final scenario is then fully divergent, when nobody is working towards the teacher's aims and perhaps everybody in the class has their own orientations, or alternatively there are no discernible orientations which could also lead to divergence of this kind, as there are no discernible aims to gravitate towards. These scenarios could be represented in the following way, as shown in Figures 2.4 to 2.7.

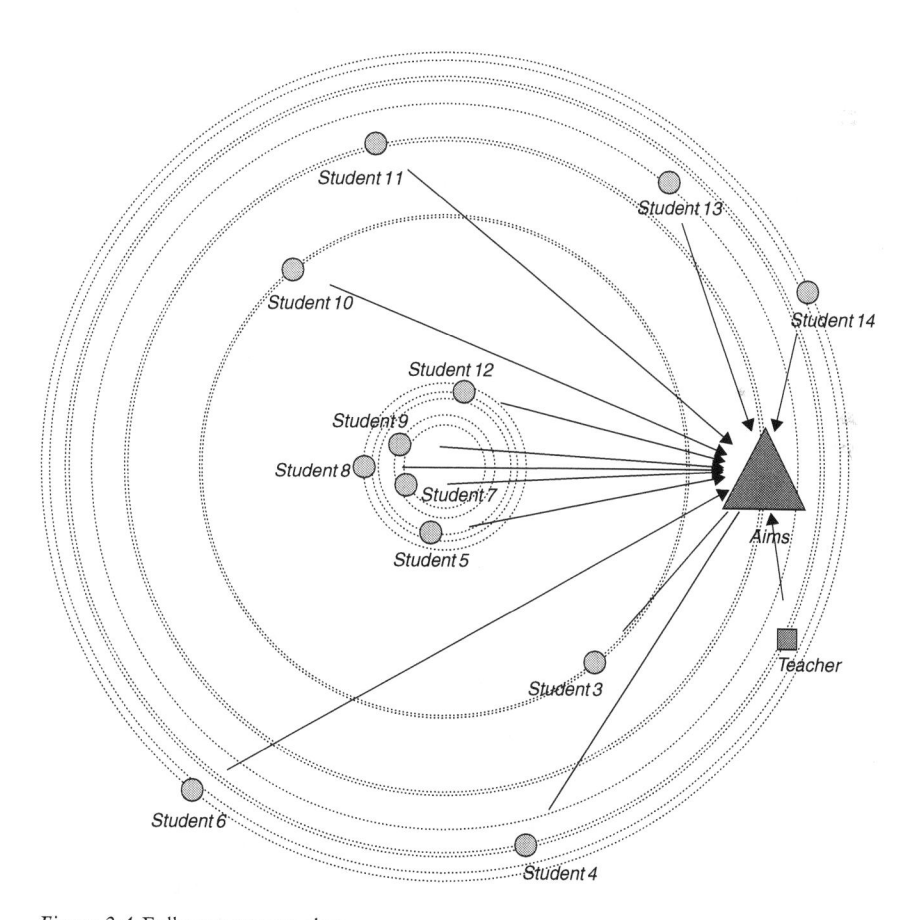

Figure 2.4 Fully convergent class

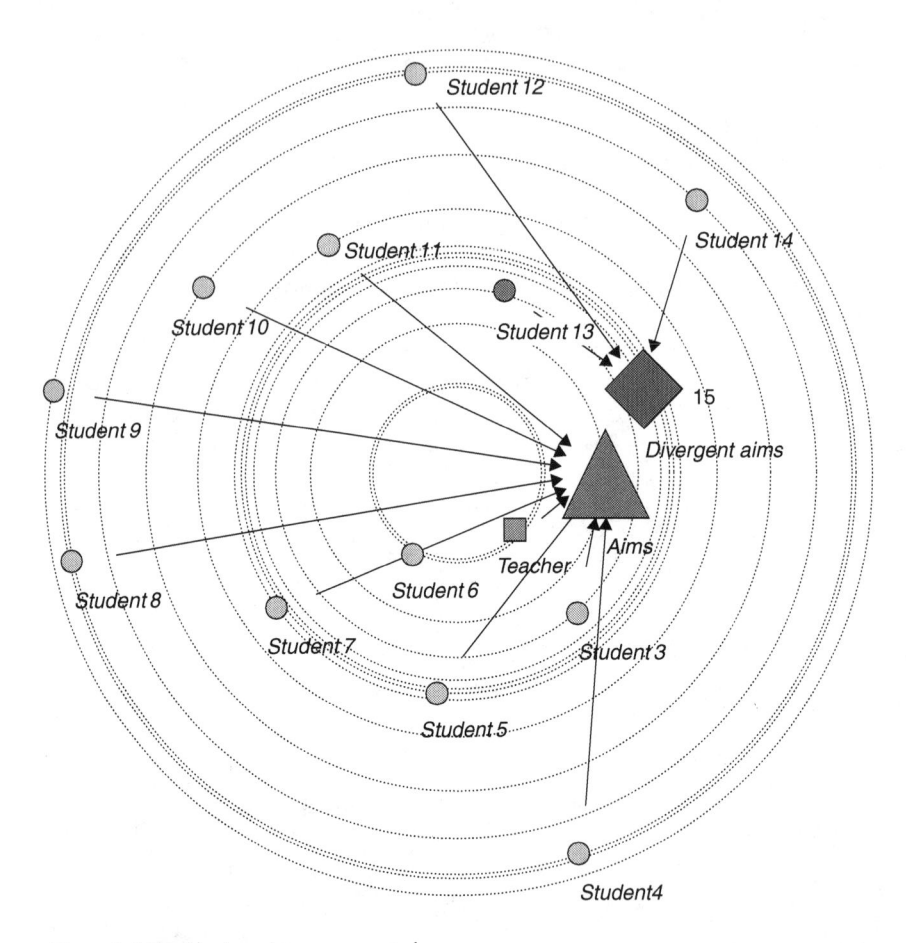

Figure 2.5 Predominantly convergent class

Of course, these diagrams are oversimplified, and it should be noted that 'divergent aims' do not represent a set of shared aims that the students are all moving towards. Rather, divergent aims represent either a lack of clear aims, or simply a lack of convergence towards the aims of the teacher and the class. A further complication would arise if the teacher were unsure of his or her aims for the class. This is why it is essential to have at least a strong sense of one's philosophy of teaching in order to underlie each lesson, as this can provide a focus for class synergy, if properly conveyed to learners.

2.6.2 Synaptic crossings

This inquiry focuses mainly on times when the students and teacher were able to work together in harmony; a state of positive motivational synergy that resides as

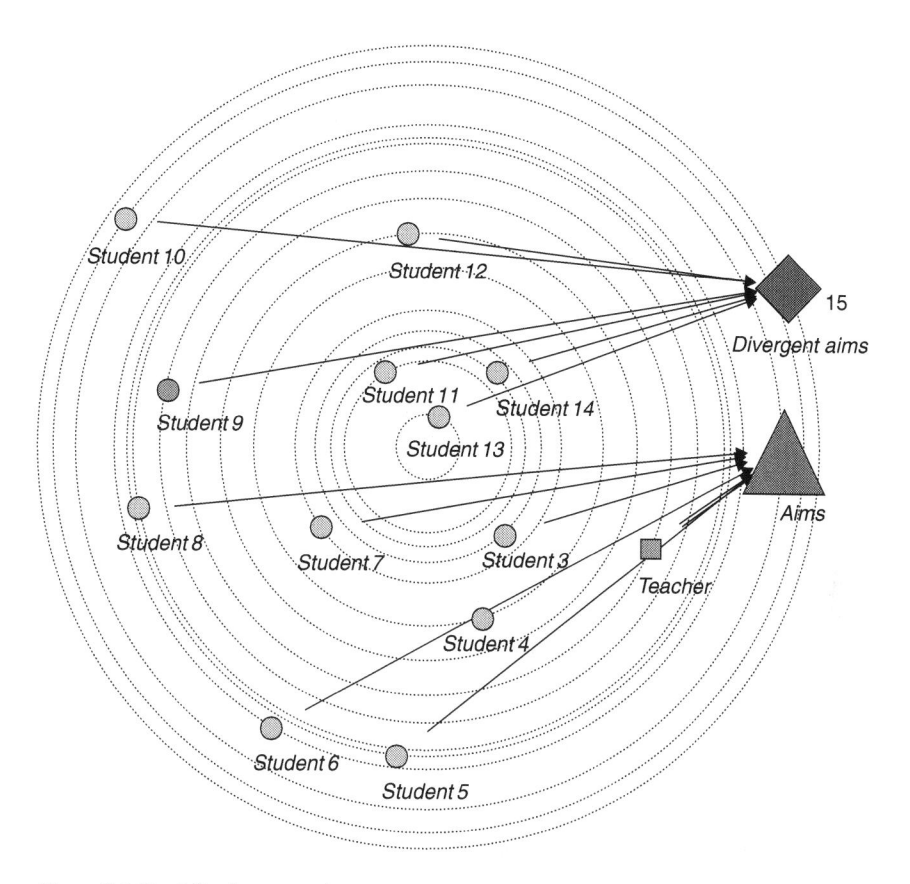

Figure 2.6 Partially divergent class

the final overall impression of the class and has possible long-lasting effects on the students' mid- to long-term motivational dynamics. In the narrative, this will be referred to as *motivational synergy*, defined in this inquiry as basically a period of lesson time in which the teacher and students appear to unite their motivational energies in a social act of mutual validation, or *social authentication* (following van Lier, 1996). At such times, although there may be one or two students who invest at a lower level in this process of synergising, overall the class as a whole is 'on the same level' as it were and working with each other for the same basic educational outcomes. The creation of these synergies is dependent on what I will label *synaptic crossings*, usually in the form of bidirectional feedback that facilitates positive charges of emotion and encourages positive motivational behaviour towards the class. Hattie (2012) suggests that feedback should be thought of as something *received* rather than *given* (p. 122). Furthermore, his large-scale meta-analyses of empirical studies in education have revealed that the students are the main beneficiaries of feedback received by the teachers, especially if this feedback

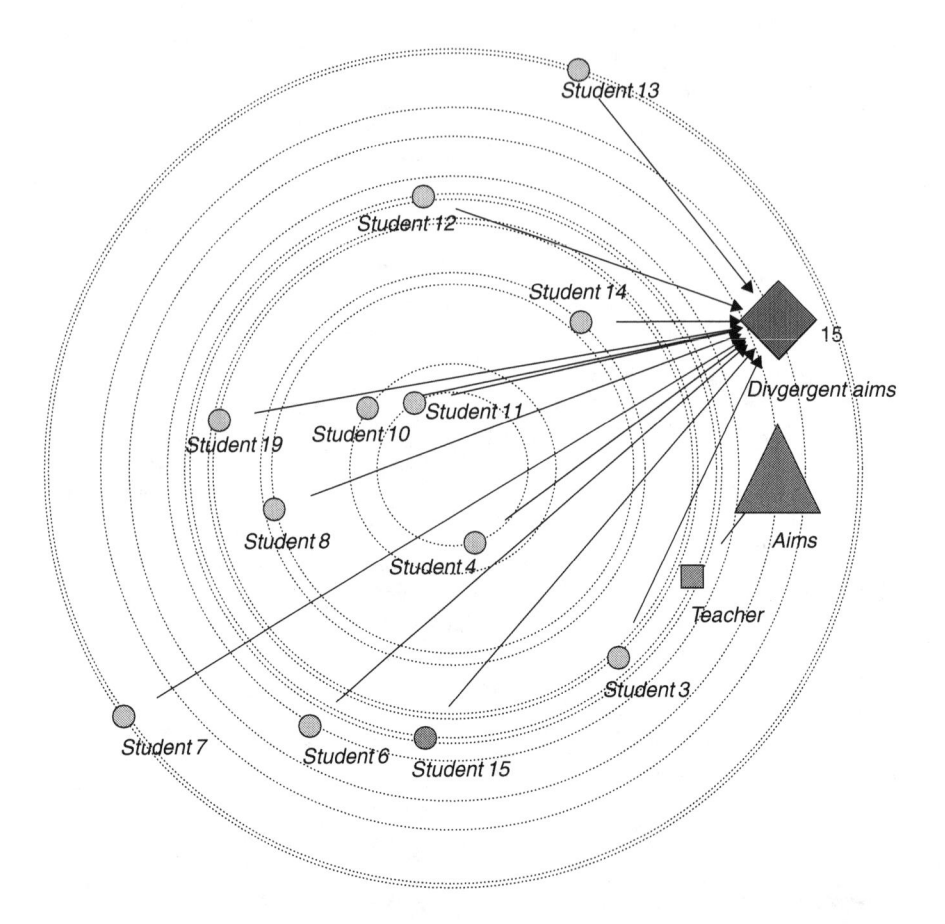

Figure 2.7 Divergent class

tells teachers something about their impact on the students' learning (2008, pp. 181; see Hattie, 2012 for further expansion). This is particularly important in light of events from the spring narrative which I discuss in Section 4.11, involving the institutional evaluation.

A second essential aspect to synaptic crossings is the exchange of *energy*, specifically energy return on investment (EROI). This is a term taken from physics and ecology, often used to explain the efficiency of fuels. For example, oil and gas have high EROI, which has led to great economic prosperity since the Industrial Revolution. However, as the fuels diminish, the amount of energy required to extract them goes up, which reduces their EROI and could lead to serious economic problems (Heinberg, 2005). Energy is fundamentally defined as the ability to do work, and EROI is very basically the payback received (Costanza, 2013). If the EROI of a fuel is 1.0, this means that for every kilowatt of energy I put in, I get back exactly the same amount in terms of work.

In terms of teaching, I apply EROI to refer to the amount of energy a teacher invests in the class, and how much energy (work) is returned by the students. I hypothesise this to be the way that social authentication is forged. If there is a high congruence between teacher and learners, this creates a close synergy with reciprocal and mutually beneficial energy flow. At other times, unresponsive learners mean that a teacher will naturally reduce the amount of energy they expend on a class, which in turn has a knock-on effect for motivation. In this way, EROI has very close links with the concept of teacher immunity as a coping strategy (Hiver, 2015b, 2017; Hiver & Dörnyei, 2017). The same is true for students. If the student works hard but does not feel their investment is reciprocated by the teacher (or other members of class), they will naturally reduce the amount of energy they expend as a reaction grounded in self-conservation. In other words, positive synergy means a high EROI, with students and teacher perceiving energy returns that are congruent with the energy they invest. In this way, synaptic crossings feature feedback and the transfer of energy into work. For simplicity, we could imagine work as the final product of motivation.

Following this description, the most pressing question would seem to be 'how does a teacher know if his or her class is synergised?' This brings me to the question of indicators of synergy, around which the narrative at the centre of this inquiry is structured.

2.6.3.1 Indicators of synergy

Authenticity comes from the Greek word *authenteo*, which means 'to have full power' (Dörnyei et al., 2016, p. 110). The word is made of two parts: *auto-* means 'self' and *hentes* refers to the doer or being, and thus has etymological roots with autonomy (self and *nomos* as in law, self-governing). As I have already shown the necessity of autonomy for motivation, it should be clear how authenticity is also implied as a prerequisite for motivation. As such, one of the main links between authenticity and motivational synergy comes not from any data but from how the interactions are conceptualised. Thus, collecting evidence for synergies is not the primary aim of this study (see Chapter 3 for an expansion on the justification for this inquiry). However, it is unsatisfactory and unscientific to simply say that a practitioner 'just knows' when his or her class is synergised, and to base the inquiry on subjective observations alone. Researchers, particularly those with a preference for positivistic methods which seek to find conclusive findings that represent an objective 'truth', based on empirically tested and generalisable evidence, may well question the notion of motivational synergy as a socially constructed sense of shared positive energy in the classroom, especially in the light of how I am conceptualising the central constructs. If simply defining the constructs is elusive, surely finding evidence for them would be fraught with difficulties. However, there are well-documented precedents for this form of socially constructed authentication. Although the nature and design of this inquiry naturally resists the positivist notions of 'truth' and 'proof', I do draw my observations from what I label *indicators*, which I argue are a form of observable evidence that, when combined together, allow me to make critical observations regarding the dynamics of authenticity and motivational synergy.

These types of indicators themselves have an established position in educational philosophy and SLA research. Sociocultural theory, for example, draws on the theory that learning is a collective process, and does not happen according to a simple pattern of development. Such a theory is inherently difficult to observe in action, which is why Vygotsky (writing shortly before his death in 1934) said that uncovering 'the internal relations of the intellectual processes' was 'analogous to the use of x-rays' (1978, p. 91). Vygotsky felt it was of primary importance to uncover these processes, which on the same page he referred to as complex and dynamic. Despite the difficulty of finding so-called 'hard evidence' for sociocultural theory, it has become an established part of educational philosophy and is also very strongly interwoven into theories about second-language learning (Lantolf, 2000b). As Kramsch (2000) puts it, many scholars

> rejected the binary oppositions of mind and body, individual and society, text and context, Self and Other. For them, the great question was: 'What is it in language that binds individuals into groups and at the same time enables individuals to exist as selves?'
>
> (p. 139)

Recently, the sociocognitive aspect of language learning was explored in an edited volume by Batstone (2010), which develops a synthesis between more traditional cognitive approaches to SLA with perspectives that prioritise social processes of interaction.

In this inquiry, I used the following observable patterns of behaviour and data sources as indicators of synergy in order to add veracity to my observations.

1. Group dynamics and intragroup behaviour – drawing on sociocultural theory and social identity theory, the idea that groups are likely to attempt to converge in terms of their wider social aims is deeply rooted in our evolutionary history. In other words, working together is not just a simple choice, but something that could be hardwired into our genetic makeup because the 'proliferation of group-beneficial behaviours [had substantial effects] that were quite costly to the individual altruist' (Bowles, 2009, p. 1293). Thus, whilst there will always be those outliers who do not concord with the main group, in general group-wide behaviour is easily observable within the classroom (Dörnyei, 1997; Dörnyei & Murphey, 2003; Murphey, Falout, Fukada, & Fukuda, 2012; Tudor, 2001).

2. Student's on-task engagement – this is something a teacher becomes very attuned to as he or she walks around the classroom. It is easy to tell whether the students are talking in English or Japanese, especially with intermediate students, who are less adept at switching from one language to the other quickly. It is also possible for me to tell whether the students are working

on the task even when they are communicating in Japanese, as although my Japanese is far from advanced, I do at least have a working proficiency in the language. In the CALL room, where over 50 per cent of the lessons took place, the teacher's screen shows a thumbnail view of whatever the student is looking at, along with the icon for the program they are using. Thus, it is easy for a teacher to see if a student is on YouTube or a social networking site when they ought to be working on PowerPoint or editing a video. Broadly, the idea of on-task engagement may also be linked to the concept of practitioner-validated motivation, discussed briefly in Section 2.3.4. Teachers also become very attuned to the way a student may glance in their direction, monitoring them to see if they are coming closer. This is actually a very primitive level of awareness that dates back to our earliest evolution. We can often sense when another organism is being vigilant of our presence or not, as this is an essential skill for hunting (New, Cosmides, & Tooby, 2007). In other words, we have evolved to know or sense how others respond to us. This connects also with the concept of empathy.

3. Empathy and mirror neurons – recently, studies into empathy have been able to benefit greatly from insights into how the mind works, learned from neuroscience. This has developed alongside the discovery of *mirror neurons*, which are neurons in the brain that fire when an action is performed and also fire in the same way when the action is simply observed. The most famous example comes from neurophysiologists working in the University of Parma, who observed that rhesus monkeys fired the same neurons when they observed another grasping or eating. In effect, the monkeys saw another eat and their mind reacted as if they had also eaten (Iacoboni, 2009). This has become largely one of the scientific bases for understanding human empathy. In this inquiry, empathy is very relevant as it concerns how individuals react to others and synergise their feelings together in the furtherance of a collective goal. From the teacher's perspective, empathy is one of the cornerstones of facilitating and being a good leader (Rogers, 1961), and its importance is well recognised for language learning (Gkonou & Mercer, 2017; Mercer, 2016; Mercer & Gkonou, 2017). Using mirror neurons as a key piece of evidence for social cognition, Atkinson (2010) claims that '[m]irror neurons may further provide a neural basis for imitative learning and behavioural synchronisation' (p. 26). Empathy also connects strongly with group dynamics, and there is evidence for 'emotional contagion', which is the phenomenon where feelings are copied by individuals and spread through groups (Hatfield, Cacioppo, & Rapson, 1993). Empathy and its relationship to group dynamics and social authentication will be examined in more detail throughout the inquiry.

4. Intuition – contrary to popular belief, it is not unscientific to speak of intuitively knowing something (Hodgkinson, Langan-Fox, & Sadler-Smith, 2008; Lieberman, 2000; Lieberman, Jarcho, & Satpute, 2004), especially from a practitioners' perspective (T. Atkinson & Claxton, 2000). As I will discuss later, intuition became something that I experimented with as I attempted to make my lessons more learner-centric. The feeling of intuitively knowing

something is based largely on experience, and develops over time to become more reliable. Intuition itself is constructed upon subtle yet observable indicators that arise from contextual social interactions. However, the danger of intuition is in not knowing its limitations, or in using it to allow the fossilisation of untested assumptions.

5. Performance indicators – based on the pedagogical data collected from students, I have been able to make certain observations which can be used to infer broadly about the participant's motivation and investment in a given task or topic. Naturally, it is not possible to make specific claims from these, but by looking at the quality of work and the amount produced, I have been able at times to further triangulate observations regarding the students' individual and collective levels of motivation towards the class. A further benefit of this type of data is that I am able to analyse the data in other ways, in order to look at the learners' development in language and communicative skills. In this way, performance indicators are an important part of this inquiry.

6. Feedback – perhaps the most important and conclusive indicator for synergy is the feedback I received from students, and also institutional feedback. Sadly, the idea of meaningful feedback is further fraught with complications (as I will discuss Chapters 4, 5, and 6). However, feedback comes not just in the shape of formal assessments and comments on work but also as socially interpreted reactions during informal discussion with both students and colleagues. As Denise, a participant in Allwright and Hanks' (2009) research, exclaims, '[discussing] with other people who are involved in the same process that we are help[s] us to see our own pedagogic practice from a different perspective' (p. 228). One form of feedback that I relied on heavily was reflection, in other words self-generated feedback. I utilised reflection myself as the main source of data in the study, but I also heavily incorporated reflection into the students' workloads and even conducted self-assessment for class participation. This is something strongly advocated for Exploratory Practice research (Allwright & Hanks, 2009, p. 26), and also aligns with Ushioda's (2014) recommendation for conducting classroom research that examines 'how processes of motivation may interact with the metacognitive dimension of language learning' (p. 31).

Figure 2.8 is a visual representation of these six indicators. When making claims about the motivational orientation of my learners in the narrative, and indeed throughout this inquiry, I am generally drawing on not just one of these indicators but also the general notion of indicators as an array of dynamic interacting processes that contribute to my understanding of the classroom ecology.

These indicators of synergy are likely to be apparent only in retrospect, in keeping with complexity approaches to observation (Larsen-Freeman, 2015; Larsen-Freeman & Cameron, 2008b). Also, although I label these as retrospective indicators of synergy, they are simultaneously thought to represent prerequisites for the creation of *synaptic crossings* of positive motivational synergy. In other

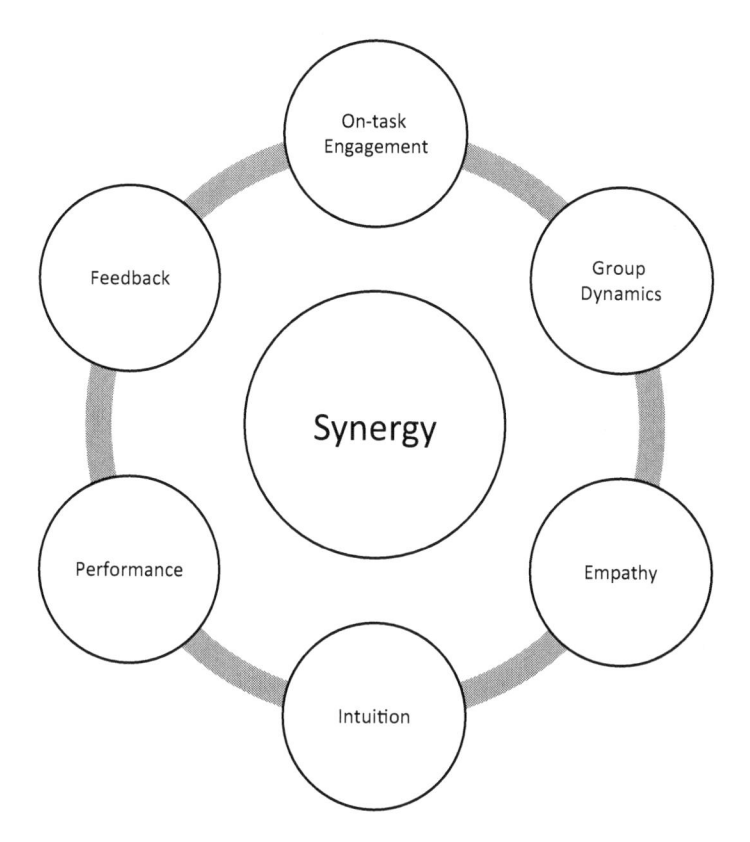

Figure 2.8 Visual summary of indicators of synergy

words, these are the channels through which motivational synergy is created and also the way it can be retrospectively observed. Synaptic crossings are the dynamic and multifaceted processes in which social authentication is achieved.

In terms of teaching, during the course of a normal class the teacher may engage with the students at different points throughout the lesson. At some of these points, the students receive feedback and there is a sense of energy investment in the task of learning. When teachers see students working hard on tasks, or get feedback from the students (for example, students looking alert, listening when the teacher talks, asking questions), they intuitively recognise this as a return on their investment (EROI). These moments, when feedback is exchanged and energy is invested in the learning, are synaptic crossings. Synaptic crossings are the individual moments of connection between people in the classroom ecology, and as such they happen repeatedly in short sequences throughout the class. Furthermore, such synaptic crossings are not limited to exchanges between students and teachers. Students working in groups also create synaptic crossings by displaying their investment in the learning process to their peers. Each synaptic crossing contributes to the overall process of social authentication.

I argue that teachers often intuitively recognise such moments in the classroom, and this is how we know if a class is generally motivated or not. We can tell what the attractor state of a class is from these intuition-based observations. By using indicators of synergy, I have attempted to retrace this complex constellation of classroom events and to reflect on its nature in order to gain a deeper understanding of the connection between social authentication and motivational synergy.

These initial indicators for synergy will be the basis for many of the reflections that I make as I discuss the interaction between my motivation and my students'. However, clearly there will be a limit to the type of conclusion I can draw from such observations, and therefore I must be careful when making generalisations, especially when I discuss how the observations can be used to achieve a kind of praxis between the theoretical framework presented in this chapter and the final practical suggestions presented in Chapter 6.

2.7 Summary

In summary, I have attempted to establish that definitions of authenticity need to reflect the modern context of international language use around the globe. In overviewing some of the definitions and important concepts that contribute to authenticity, I found that for many decades, scholarly definitions of authenticity had attempted to acknowledge that a simple 'native speaker' definition was in no way tenable. However, I also argued that current definitions were not overtly inclusive enough of international varieties, and therefore I presented an authenticity continuum and adopted a much more philosophical concept of authenticity, something that relates to how a person 'genuinely feels and believes' (van Lier, 1996, p. 6). Instead of authenticity relating purely to the origin and function of a piece of material or a learning task, I proposed that authenticity be considered as something which incorporates contextual, social and individual aspects. I then briefly looked at how motivational theories have evolved to include more dynamic variables and based my understanding of motivation around the need for ontological studies.

In faithfully following Ushioda's work I have come to regard motivation as something that needs to be understood qualitatively at a personal and individual level, yet also incorporating wider social and contextual elements. Therefore, I have conceptualised the motivational aspect of this research through the lens of complexity theory and employed what Ushioda (2016) terms a 'small lens' approach. However, my personal starting point or *puzzle* developed around my own shifting identity as I tried to make sense of the issue of authenticity as a teacher adjusting to a changing ecology and steadily evolving professional landscape. In this way, authenticity will provide the belief about *what* my inquiry is looking for, and motivation provides the belief about *how* to look for it. In the next chapter, I will present the evolution of my research design and explain the narrative of how the present inquiry unfolded around itself in an organic fashion. I argue that this natural evolution of the research design was a necessary component of the originally inductive approach I took to this inquiry.

Note

1 Known as *Gairaigo* (外来語) in Japanese – lit. 'foreign came words'.

3 Research methods
The evolution of my design

Most ESOL teachers are natural researchers. We're used to working out
the needs of our students, evaluating the effects of particular approaches,
spotting things that work or don't work and adjusting our teaching
accordingly. Very few teachers approach their work mechanically and nearly
all of us reflect on what we do in the classroom.

K. Richards (2003, p. 232)

3.1 Introduction and overview

This inquiry is a hybrid combination of Exploratory Practice, Evidence-based
Reflection and autoethnography, which are employed to create a narrative based
on my professional development. This narrative is intended to shed light on the
evolution of my philosophy of teaching as my professional identity alters based
on several contextual changes in both my personal and working life. At the heart
of my philosophy of teaching is the belief that motivation is one of the central
components of successful language learning, and that social authentication is an
essential aspect of creating a culture of motivation and mutual investment in
the classroom. Exploratory Practice was chosen mainly because of its focus on
improving the 'quality of classroom life' (Allwright, 2003, 2005). It was also
selected because of the emphasis on what Allwright and Hanks (2009) refer to as
'pedagogic data', or data arising naturally as a result of the teaching and learning
which comes from students' work done in class.

In this chapter I will present the rationale for my approach, a detailed description of the original design and a narrative of how this design changed and
emerged as I responded to the unfurling research context and insights that the
inquiry offered. I will present a detailed description of the context of the inquiry
in time and space, as well as the participants (myself and the 25 learners). Finally,
I will detail the collection and analysis techniques used to harvest and process the
large data set. As one of the most important contributions to knowledge that this
inquiry is seen as making relates to the method itself, this chapter attempts to
map out the many stages in the design in some detail.

3.1.1 *Where are we and how did we get here?*

As I discussed in Chapter 1, the starting place for the puzzle at the heart of this inquiry was the 'authentic high point' in my teaching career. After choosing to examine why I felt the Discussion on Contemporary Topics (DCT) class in 2012 had been so successful, I identified 'authenticity' and 'motivation' as the main reasons for its success. I had already begun to explore the concept of authenticity in my own research, and I decided to launch a further inquiry on a class I was going to teach in 2014.

In the DCT class I was able to encourage my students to produce work which went 'beyond the walls of the classroom' and had a direct interaction with what I called the 'real world'. For me, this was part of the spectrum that made the class authentic, but there were other factors at play also. One of my lasting memories of DCT was the students' level of engagement and responsiveness to the ideas we discussed. The extremely high quality of the final video projects seemed to me to be an indication that the students were very motivated and had worked hard in the class. Looking back at my experience of actually teaching this class, I seemed to have been experiencing a state of Flow (Csikszentmihalyi, 1997a), and I felt that this was, on the whole, mutually experienced by the learners and was therefore socially constructed. I have now come to view this phenomenon as *social authentication* (following van Lier, 1996).

In retrospectively analysing a successful class I identified a possible connection between authenticity and motivation which stemmed from the relationship between the students' and teacher's experience of the learning environment, content and materials. From this position I tried to gain a deeper understanding of what authenticity is, specifically from the context of English as an international language, and to examine how it could relate to motivation as a complex dynamic system.

3.1.2 *Evolution of the design*

David Silverman uses the term 'natural history' to describe a modified research methods chapter in which the story of the research is presented as a natural process and reported in an engaging way. Although I use Silverman's idea, I have changed the name for my section. This is mainly because the words 'natural history' have an unshakeable connection with dinosaur skeletons for me (in a good way!) from visits to the natural history museum in London as a boy, and Silverman (2013) is using the term to get away from metaphorical dinosaurs (in a bad way), or as he sees it the 'dull to read and write [...]desperately boring methodology chapter' (pp. 305–306). Partly as a reference to the natural history museum, I am calling this chapter the evolution of my design. It is basically a natural history of the research design and implementation, the story of my best-laid plans and my responses to the inevitable 'difficulties and dead ends that we all experience' (Silverman, 2013, p. 306). I use the word 'evolution' to suggest an organic and natural process of adapting to the ever-changing environment in which the research took place, and I use the term 'design' both in reference to the research design and also to suggest that there was an intended process and outcome. The words evolution and design do not tend to sit well together in theological discussions, and that tension was also present in my mind when I chose the name for this chapter.

The choice of approach to collecting research was one which caused me quite a considerable amount of consternation when I began working on the proposal for this project in February 2013. I had initially wanted to do a case study, envisaging myself as a *researcher*, because I did not want to be too much part of the phenomenon I was observing so that I could avoid any kind of 'observer's paradox' and I felt I should avoid subjectivity. I was specifically worried about my own strongly formed ideas about authenticity bleeding into my research and about collecting data not based on the actual beliefs of the participants but on what the subjects believed *I* wanted to hear. This issue had also informed my research design in other studies, and admittedly I was never truly comfortable with that type of research as it did all it could to avoid the role that I primarily identified with: that of teacher. Instead I had to be a researcher, which I did not want to see as being mutually exclusive. Although case studies do not necessarily require the researcher to be an outsider or to leave completely their persona as a teacher, for me it was a thin line, perhaps because of my teaching style or because of my growing interest in classroom research. It was only later that I realised the so called observer's paradox could in fact be viewed differently and reimagined as something positive, if thought of in terms of the teacher/researcher's role. The term 'reflexivity' was better suited to describing the process. Julian Edge (2011) explains that, as he sees it, reflexive teaching has 'cast the mould for our vision of what it means to be a teacher' (p. 14), and this is mirrored by Keith Richard's comments which I used to start this chapter. Teachers are researchers, because as a teacher one must constantly question one's own rationale and try new things out. As I was undergoing a very dramatic change in my professional identity, I was also about to find my own 'philosophy of teaching' (Crookes, 2009). It might be a cliché, but it is certainly very true that 'to teach is to learn'. This is what makes the act of teaching very reflexive and very exploratory. Creating a link between our beliefs and our actions is how we achieve praxis (Crookes, 2013). It was always my intention that my research should help me improve my own practice, and so this is a central part of the justification of this inquiry. Although improvement is not the main aim of Exploratory Practice, if development occurs as a result of gaining a deeper understanding, this is generally seen as positive (Allwright, 2005, p. 361).

As such, I quickly rejected the detailed plan for the case study which I had initially developed in favour of practitioner-based inquiry. I began learning more about Exploratory Practice and reflexive teaching because they advocate self-reflection and do not require any particular catalyst or change in the order of the classroom. As such they are quite 'safe' in that students are not being compared and their educational experience is not being used as a control group for that of another. Contrary to how it sounds, students who are part of an exploratory study

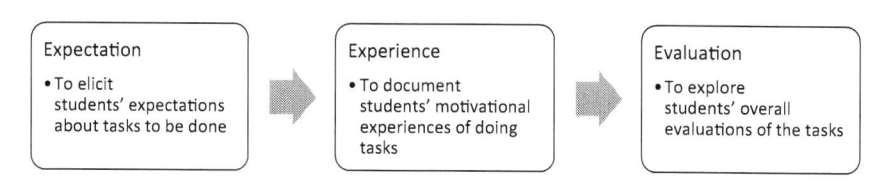

Figure 3.1 Li's (2007) 3Es framework for *balanced research*

are not guinea pigs. Specifically, it seemed unethical to me to assign a group of students to an 'inauthentic' control group or to purposefully use materials which I felt were not authentic. I was not trying to problematise my own teaching or make specific improvements; rather, I wanted to understand the mechanics and underlying values from both my and the students' perspectives.

When I was reading Li (2006), I became much more aware of the fact that I would not be required to leave one persona at the door when I entered the class-room. Her article was fascinating to me for two main reasons. First, she makes a connection between Exploratory Practice and the developments in motivational research from a social-psychological approach to one which centres more on the educational setting, with a focus on examining 'classroom reality, and identifying and analysing classroom-specific motives' (Dörnyei, 1998, p. 125). This is an interesting connection, since the reason for my adopting a practitioner research inquiry was due to my beliefs about how research into motivation should be conducted. Secondly, Li's article takes van Lier's call for *balanced teaching*, by which he means that lessons are made up of 'both planned and improvised elem-ents' (van Lier, 1996, p. 200) and develops this into a plea for *balanced research*. Li suggests that researching, like teaching, is also a creative and dynamic pro-cess which requires the teacher/researcher to make intuitive decisions as things unfold. It is not always possible to stick to the plan, and indeed it would actually be detrimental to the research if the teacher/researcher were not able to adapt to contextual and situational occurrences that could not have been foreseen. She also developed this idea further into the 3E Framework (see Figure 3.1 and Li, 2007).

It was in reading about Li's experiences with Exploratory Practice and in discussions with colleagues, as well as in conducting wider reading, that I became interested in this approach for my own research inquiry. However, I still had some reservations. In the next section I will address my concerns about adopting the Exploratory Practice approach and explain in more detail why I decided to choose it for my inquiry.

3.1.3 The observer's paradox

> To obtain the data most important for linguistic theory, we have to observe how people speak when they are not being observed.
>
> (Labov, 1972, p. 113)

One reason behind my aforementioned consternation was the so-called observer's paradox. This paradox goes beyond linguistic research and permeates through nearly all scientific fields, including quantum physics. For example, in Young's double-slit experiment light was found to alter the way it behaved (either as a wave or a particle) after particle detectors were employed. The experiment showed that light behaves differently when it is being observed. Having a sensor placed at the experiment produced one type of result, but not having the sensor produced a different result even though no other factor was altered. To date it is not yet fully understood why light behaves differently depending on whether it is being observed, but it has led scientists to theorise about the possibility of alternative dimensions, sometimes known as the multiverse (Greene, 2011). I provide this example simply to illustrate that even the so-called 'hard' sciences come up against this paradox, and not understanding it well led me originally to conceive of my research as a project in which I would leave my teaching persona at the door and become a researcher.

I was very happy when I learned that the paradox can be turned on its head through the lens of Exploratory Practice because in this type of research the teacher/researcher acknowledges both personas and tries simply to understand more about what is happening in the classroom. It was this that led me to my current line of inquiry. Since my research is based on my own teaching, the basic starting point was to look at something I have done or am doing in the classroom and frame it as a puzzle, then working from that point try to deduce what I need to know and what data I need to gather in order to gain a better insight into the nature of the puzzle. Rather than trying to 'solve' the puzzle, the aim of this inquiry is to inform my own practice through a much deeper understanding of the situation and the perspectives of the main stakeholders (myself as the teacher and of course the students as the learners). Therefore, I am also part of the puzzle, and I would like to be able to observe what my impact on the learners is, with a view to continuing my own growth as a teacher. In learning this, I hope not only to develop my own practice but also to contribute valuable insights into best practice in general and lend further credibility to the observable benefits of reflexivity in language teacher education.

3.2 Rationale

The original intent behind this inquiry in terms of its contribution to research was to empirically establish the links between authenticity and motivation in language teaching. As my understanding of the constructs under investigation deepened, and as I embarked upon my own 'quest for authenticity', I came to realise that the two were already so tightly interwoven conceptually as to make my initial attempt at *proving* this connection neither practical nor desirable. Authenticity is structurally a part of motivation just as motivation is an inevitable consequence of authenticity (Dörnyei et al., 2016; Kreber, 2013; Vannini & Burgess, 2009). Weigert (2009) even goes so far as to claim that authenticity is a 'master motive' for social interactions. If such is the case, then what forms the basis of this inquiry?

The main purpose of conducting this inquiry was to make sense of my own development; to try to understand why the DCT course was so successful; to examine if I could ever recreate those conditions; and if so to what extent they could be turned into practical lessons for teacher education and techniques to empower students in their own learning. This rationale is later expanded on in this inquiry, when I discuss the main findings of this study and its wider implications (see Chapter 6, particularly 6.7). Another potential contribution from this study is the method itself, which was developed as a response to the call for more emic insights into teacher development as a classroom-based process (Kumaravadivelu, 2012; Ushioda, 2016; van Lier, 1988; 2007). I have also been able to apply a similar version of this methodology in order to retrospectively examine the DCT class itself, which could almost be seen as a pilot study for the current inquiry (Pinner, 2018b).

In examining two very important yet complex phenomena such as authenticity and motivation, one of my biggest problems was being able to maintain a grasp on the gestalt nature of the phenomena at the heart of my inquiry. In order to maintain this, I often found that every aspect of my life, both personal and professional, seemed to take on meaning and become highly relevant. This is rather inevitable, due to the way I am conceptualising authenticity and motivation as complex dynamic factors which are the sum of many parts, and due to my choice of adopting complexity theory as an underpinning framework for the investigation. However, such a view poses many troubling logistical and ethical problems in terms of keeping the study on track, useful and manageable. To put it simply, one of the major difficulties I faced was the balance of quantity and quality. I had to collect so much data in order to draw from all the relevant sources, and even then, those I was able to draw from were not able to fully capture the complexity of the phenomena I was attempting to investigate. At the same time, I needed to find areas to focus the inquiry in order to do justice to the qualitative approach and keep the narrative coherent. This is something I was painfully aware of right at the beginning of the collection phase, as the following comment from my research journal shows:

> I feel a great sense of panic that my data could end up as a meaningless avalanche of dusty sheets of paper.
>
> (TRJournal 15/04/2014)

In this extract I was reflecting on the large data set of mainly pedagogic materials I had amassed from previous classes and what a shame it was that I had rarely been able to turn these into formal studies or write-ups. However, I knew that simply because of the length of time that would pass between conducting the class/collecting data and writing up, any data I collected for this inquiry would no doubt lose some of its meaning and saliency. As the dust collects, I teach other classes and my interest and passion shift to something else. Also, as time passes, the data becomes harder to interpret, the rationale for its use or collection lost in the memory or buried in some scribbled note which no longer makes a great deal of sense. In some way there is an aspect of deixis to the logs and field notes of the classroom researcher; an element of context which loses clarity as time moves away from the actual event. This is somewhat ironic due to the emphasis on context required for complexity theory approaches (King, 2016a; Larsen-Freeman, 2011; Ushioda, 2015). Based on this, I decided to collect new data from a new class and be more methodical about collection. I would ana-lyse the data while it was still 'hot' and while it still made sense. This is also an important part in the management of autoethnographic data (Chang, 2008). Of course, analysis-as-data was an inevitable part of the research design, because in constructing my narrative I was engaged in *narrative knowledging* (Barkhuizen, 2011, 2013b), and the collection and analysis therefore were often one and the same thing. However, this was only the first part of the process. The second stage was a more detailed analysis, and in this stage I also wanted to be more inclusive of my students and *their* experiences. This is when I went 'wading' back into the 'sea of data' collected from pedagogical materials and other sources, and this pro-cess became something like an archaeological excavation. Finally, the writing-up processes also became a stage of analysis, as I began to consider what commu-nicable findings I could present and how to situate them in context for a reader coming from outside.

3.2.1 *Motivation paradigm*

In the popular book *Freakonomics*, Dubner and Levitt (2005) explain that until recently, the common view of economics had been that people were motivated by incentives, perhaps best exemplified by the apocryphal idea that the more money a person earns, the harder they will work. This is actually not the case, and in fact experiments which have been replicated several times and in several coun-tries have found that larger monetary incentives actually have a negative effect on performance in tasks requiring even a small amount of cognitive processing (Ariely, Gneezy, Loewenstein, & Mazar, 2005). Such findings showed that larger incentives have the effect of limiting focus and are thus demotivating to some extent. The main requirements for motivating people and increasing their per-formance, according to the experiments cited in Dubner and Levitt (2005) and also the bestselling book by Daniel Pink (2009) are autonomy, mastery and pur-pose. I show this example to highlight the danger of oversimplifying complex dynamic systems such as motivation, and to demonstrate that basic assumptions which may seem at face value to make sense (more money = work harder) rarely carry water.

Economics tends to take a quantitative approach through the necessity of its particular branch of science. But what about language motivation research? Mostly it is also characterised by the same type of positivist research. Whilst this has led to some fascinating insights and large-scale research projects (see for example Dörnyei & Csizér, 1998, 2006) it is not always conducive to getting a clear picture of what exactly is going on in L2 motivation at the ground level and in some way 'depersonalises learners' (Ushioda, 2009, p. 216). In fact, the very idea that we might ever be able to fully understand this complex and dynamic system is probably rather optimistic. However, Ushioda and others (Bandura, 2001; Larsen-Freeman & Cameron, 2008a) advocate a more qualitative approach, and certainly current trends in L2 motivational research are moving towards an understanding based more on complex dynamic systems (Dörnyei et al., 2015b; Muir & Dörnyei, 2013; Ushioda, 2013b) which require an understanding of people as individuals within complex social settings. It is partly as a response to this call for more research which takes into account the individual and their social contexts that led to the design of the current inquiry. The relationship between motivation and authenticity is the main focus of the research questions, but whereas my beliefs about authenticity shape my teaching and the materials I use to facilitate learning with my students, my interest in motivation is the driving force behind my research inquiry and thus my beliefs as a researcher about motivation have led to the current design.

3.2.2 Puzzling (research questions)

Richards (2003, p. 235) recommends a descriptive approach rather than an interventionist one, and thus I have been constantly revisiting my own questions as I conducted this research. In the first month of starting this inquiry, when I was planning the new design, I came across a very enlightening example in Richards, Ross, and Seedhouse (2012, p. 5) which helped me to realise that I was embarking on a very complex quest. In a section about how to narrow down the research questions, the authors provided some bad example dissertation titles which were much too broad. Of course, one of them was dealing with authenticity and motivation – the two topics at the heart of this inquiry.

In order to ensure my questions were a little more manageable and also that I was following the right procedure with my general research design, I utilised a technique suggested by Richards (2003) to create a *focusing circle*, in which the researcher writes the main question in a circle and draws a larger circle around that. The larger circle is then divided further and in each section a key concept is written. This limits the amount that one can put in their diagram, so rather than being a free brainstorm activity, it is designed to generate a focus. Figures 3.2 and 3.3 show two such diagrams I made in my field journal in the first months of starting the project.

A clear advantage, especially from the perspective of autoethnography, about doing such an activity is that not only is it useful in achieving its aim of developing focus, but also it creates a piece of data which can itself be analysed. For example, roughly a year later I produced the following focusing circle, shown in Figure 3.4.

There are marked differences between my original concept of authenticity in February 2013, which seemed to gravitate around linguistic elements and classroom-based issues, and the circle I produced a year later which more overtly incorporates concepts related to motivation and broader psychological states. I was actually surprised when I compared these two circles because until doing so I was unaware just how much my 'focus' had changed. Thus, these circles were also useful reflective tools as well.

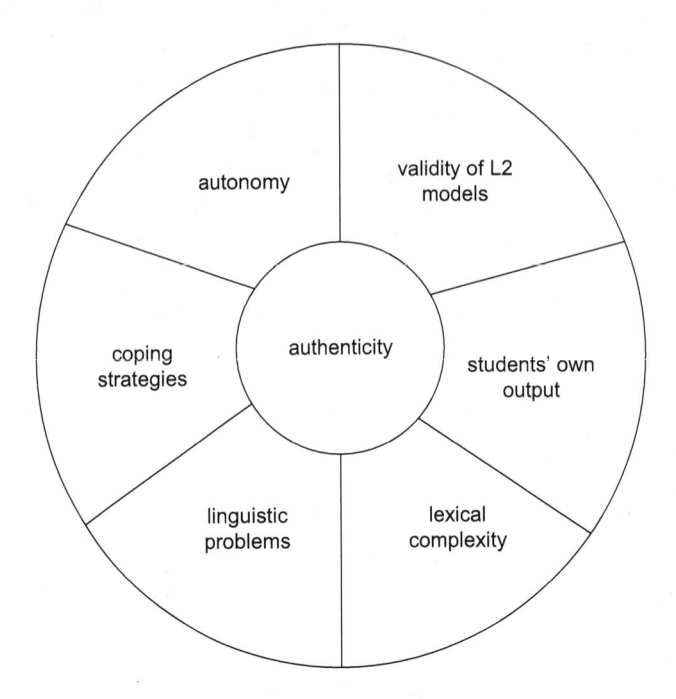

Figure 3.2 Focusing Circle Feb 2013 A

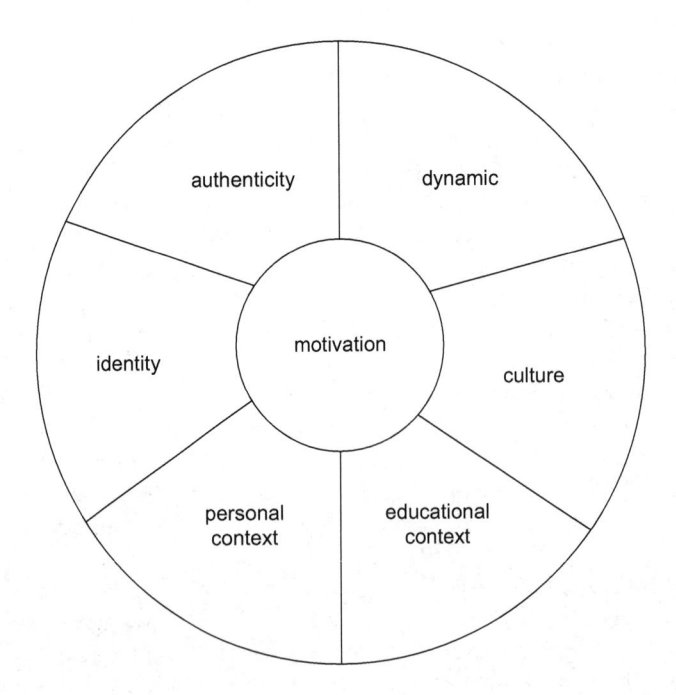

Figure 3.3 Focusing Circle Feb 2013 B

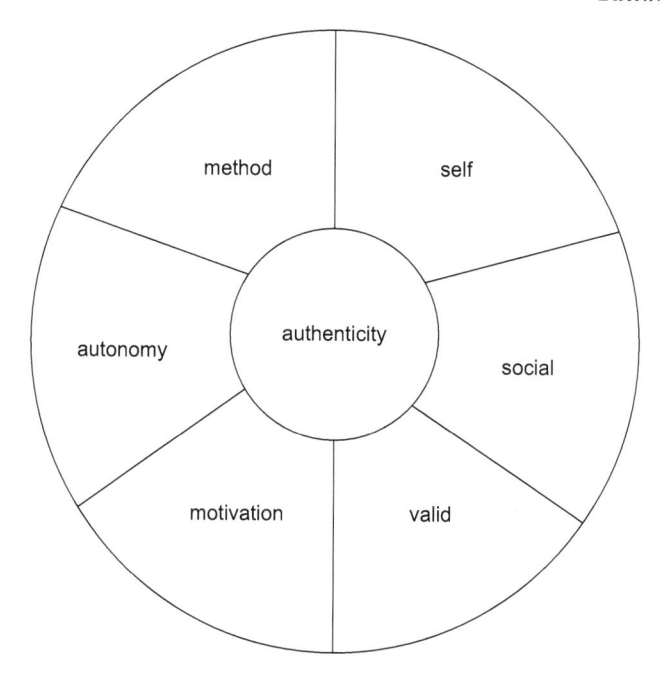

Figure 3.4 Focusing Circle Feb 2014

Another useful model which helped me develop the current inquiry's design was the research design flow chart, as suggested by Richards et al. (2012, p. 4). Although the research design did not always follow its plan and emerged as part of an interaction with the context, I was very conscious that my design needed to be robust and justifiable. Therefore, although many aspects of the study were in a constant state of flux, the purpose behind the study was always one of practical self-improvement. Finally, the modular model of teacher education proposed by Kumaravadivelu (2012) has also been influential for me. Kumaravadivelu's (2012) knowing, analysing, recognising, doing and seeing (KARDS) framework seems to apply very well to the design of this study in that it 'constitutes a network of mutually reinforcing sub-systems that are engaged in a dialectical interplay resulting in a holistic learning environment' (p. 17).

In Chapter 1, I provided a list of the initial questions that I developed by reflecting on DCT as the authentic high point of my career. In order to identify the two broader puzzles presented earlier (authenticity as 'bridge' and authenticity as 'gap'), I undertook a careful puzzling process, as described in Allwright and Hanks (2009). As I began collecting data and reflecting on my teaching, I found that, rather than focusing, the constructs I was examining actually began to expand.

The entire course of teaching and reflecting could be called a puzzling process, and the broader puzzles emerged retrospectively as 'hidden' puzzles that I found myself answering during the write-up and analysis, but that were not necessarily overtly present at the start of the inquiry. These puzzles were only brought to consciousness through the process of narrative knowledging, a natural by-product of the autoethnographic design. The main puzzle that surfaced in this way was the concept of authenticity as a 'gap' and authenticity as a 'bridge'. This conceptualisation of authenticity as possibly something that distances me from my students arose as I deepened my understanding of my own developing teacher identity, and my role as a foreigner in Japan who represents an 'other' culture and hence brings an 'outsider' perspective. The idea that authenticity could be a 'bridge' was the response to this, which became the main key to my understanding of motivational synergy.

Although I could have chosen many other avenues to focus this inquiry, I decided to pursue the concept of teacher-student motivational synergy as a natural by-product of social authentication because this theme emerged as the most salient, the most manageable in terms of research questions, and seemed to provide the most tangible link between authenticity and motivation. In this way, although I had specific ideas in mind when I started the study, it can still be said that the themes were emergent from the data, and that this started as an inductive inquiry and developed into something that was data driven and theory led.

Fundamentally, the research questions being addressed in this inquiry have often shifted or taken on new meanings as the inquiry evolved, and this section is intended to detail part of this process. The final research questions were the following:

- What is the relationship between the concept of authenticity and motivation in language learning and teaching?
  - o   Why do I feel the need to engage in social authentication (mutually validating the learning process and personally investing in the content together)?
  - o   What practical lessons can I learn to facilitate social authentication?
- How is the teacher's motivation linked with the students'?
  - o   Why is positive motivational synergy hard to achieve?
  - o   What features of teacher-student motivational synergy are controllable by the teacher in a practical sense?

These questions have closely followed the puzzling process of Exploratory Practice, as detailed by Allwright and Hanks (2009), and also expanded on by Hanks (2017). Generally, puzzling questions in Exploratory Practice take the format of 'why' questions, as this encourages reflection and avoids framing the puzzle in terms of problems that seek solutions. Echoing Allwright's (2003 see section 3.3.3) concerns about falling into a technicist trap with Exploratory Practice, Hanks (2017) describes the effect of framing puzzles as 'how' questions because, she claims, they seek out 'an answer' and reduce the puzzle to mere problem-solving. Chapter 12 of Hanks' book, which deals exclusively with this issue, lists examples of puzzling questions which all start with 'why'. Despite this, my questions are not able to take only a 'why' format, because although these questions were arrived at though an inductive process, they have developed to become theory led through the effects of other aspects of the design and methodology. Therefore, I have provided two main questions which each contain a central 'why' puzzle.

3.3 Design

This inquiry uses aspects of Exploratory Practice alongside autoethnography and evidence-based reflection. As such, this study is something of a hybrid of classroom-based practitioner research. In the following section I will explain the main component of each design and which parts are utilised in this inquiry.

3.3.1 Narrative Inquiry

> The universe is made of stories,
> not atoms,

> Muriel Rukeyser (1968 IX)

Arguably, the main research method underpinning this study is Narrative Inquiry, which has recently regained attention as a line of qualitative inquiry that seems to fit very well to the needs of applied linguistics research (Barkhuizen, Benson, & Chik, 2014). Barkhuizen (2013b) describes the last 15 years as an explosion of narrative studies, but the ideas of Narrative Inquiry have roots that date as far back as Dewey. Clandinin and Connelly (2000) succinctly explain that Dewey's ideas about *experience* have greatly impacted on the work of Narrative Inquiry because experience is 'both personal and social' (p. 2). People need to be understood as individuals, but they cannot be fully understood merely as individuals; they also need to be seen in the social context. *Experience* is also something continuous, and one experience will lead to another all the time, in a continuous sequence of identity creation and evolution.

> The self is not something ready-made, but something in continuous formation through choice of action.

> (Dewey, 1916, p. 408)

For this reason, narratives are important tools for research into complex psychological phenomena because they offer a rich source of data which simultaneously deals with the self and identity from a personal perspective, whilst situating that within a wider social context. Jonathan Gottschall (2012), who specialises in literature and evolution, claims that stories are not just important to humans in creating their view of the world. He argues that stories *are* how we view the world. Even if we take a mild view of the importance of storytelling, Narrative Inquiry has a lot to offer in terms of insights into personal and shared social phenomena. In this way it ties in well with my definition of authenticity as a social and individual component of identity, and with Ushioda's *person-in-context relational view* of motivation.

Narratives are basically
- Spoken or written texts
- Produced by people who have something to tell
- Situated in time and space
- Involve development over time
- Have structures that correspond to the developments they describe
- Encapsulate a point that the narrator wants to get across
- Have purpose and meaning within the context of their telling

(Barkhuizen et al., 2014, p. 7)

One of the ways I make sense of my own research (and indeed my existence in general) is to write things down in journals or compose stories. Stories are how I, and many people, make sense of the world around us.

Narrative research generally relies on a small number of participants (however, see Barkhuizen and Wette (2008), which contains narrative data from over 200 participants). Narrative inquiries may be seen as limited by researchers who are looking for generalisable findings which address an issue in a way that provides definite answers, applicable to multiple contexts. Such positivistic conclusions are seen as reductionist within Narrative Inquiry (Clandinin & Connelly, 2000, p. 142). Narrative Inquiry is a method of research which actively resists calls for generalisability (Barkhuizen et al., 2014), and in doing so it retains the focus on individuals and steadfastly holds ground as an ontological method for seeking a deeper understanding of complex phenomena. However, the findings of narrative inquiries are not irrelevant or meaningless except to themselves. On the contrary, a lot can be learned from such studies. It is through the act of storytelling or 'narrative knowledging' (Barkhuizen, 2011) that people create and understand their self-image, and in the process 'individuals and groups make sense of themselves; they tell what they are or what they wish to be' (Cortazzi, 2001, p. 388). Because people often make sense of their experiences through the stories they tell, reflecting on their experiences through narratives is a way of gaining an insight into 'the richness of human experience' (Johnson & Golombek, 2002, p. 4). Stories, when told, connect the individual to society because the story is told in order that it might be interpreted by another person. In the act of telling the story, the narrator re-examines the experience at the centre of the story, and in externalising what were probably, until the act of telling, internalised or personal reflections the narrator gains a deeper understanding of themselves in a socially constructed learning context.

There are different types of story, broadly categorised as *small stories* and *big stories* (Phoenix & Sparkes, 2009), where big stories tend to be biographical and deal with past experiences, often life-shaping ones, and these stories are often elicited in formal research settings. Small stories occur in natural conversation and are more likely to centre around the everyday features of life. These types of stories mainly refer to the ones told in formal narrative data elicitation, but both of them are essential tools for us to make sense of our experiences and reimagine our self and identity, which is especially important when dealing with the complex issue of identity in SLA (Ryan & Irie, 2014).

Johnson and Golombek (2002) note that narratives have become central to teacher education 'as both a method in and an object of inquiry' (p. 4), not surprisingly because of the sociocultural context of narratives, which allow for insights into teaching that are simultaneously individual and social. I would argue that narratives are especially valuable in the field of applied linguistics and SLA. The way we speak and communicate is an essential part of who we are and how we construct social relationships.

Another pertinent feature of this inquiry is the idea of context. Contextual information is central to Narrative Inquiry because stories 'don't fall from the sky (or emerge from the innermost "self"); they are composed and received in contexts – interactional, historical, institutional and discursive – to name a few' (Riessman, 2008, p. 105). The importance of context is key to Narrative Inquiry, because analysis needs to take account of the context in order to bring the level of sensitivity and understanding which is particularly prevalent in narrative research. Indeed, it seems that context is the main tenet of this type of research, and yet much narrative research is marred by reportage which seems to take place in a 'social vacuum' (Barkhuizen, 2013a, p. 6).

In terms of relevance, one essential feature of narratives is that, although they may focus on one context and a select few individuals, narratives often say more than what is explicitly stated in the text (Barkhuizen et al., 2014, p. 7). Thus, presenting a narrative which revolves around my own practice can still have relevance to a wider audience. Another aspect of this inquiry is autoethnography, which is a form of research based in Narrative Inquiry but using ethnographic data collection tools.

3.3.2 Autoethnography

Autoethnographic research provides a framework in which the researcher becomes the research subject. There are many contrasting opinions about such research, not least within descriptions of the methodology itself (Denzin, 2006, 2014), and criticisms of the approach are generally aimed at the idea that it is 'nonanalytic, self-indulgent, irreverent, sentimental, and romantic' (Denzin, 2014, p. 69). However, autoethnographic research seems to make a lot of sense for classroom research, particularly as a way of expanding Exploratory Practice and self-reflection.

Autoethnography is defined as research in which the author/researcher attempts to 'systematically analyse [...] personal experience' (Ellis, Adams, & Bochner, 2011, p. 273). In this inquiry the story becomes the reality in some sense, or rather it is a representation of one of a multitude of realities (Polkinghorne, 1988). Benson (2013a, p. 247) explains that the 'veracity' of the narrative is not in itself the main purpose of narrative data, in terms of it describing 'real-world' events. The value of the narrative comes not from its representation of the unrecoverable 'truth' but rather from the alternative perspective that it provides. In this way, this inquiry is not concerned with reliability, as with more positivist methods of research; instead, narrative research is evaluated in terms of validity (Polkinghorne, 2007). Plummer (2001) explains that this validity comes from the reader being able to 'enter the subjective world of the teller – to see the world from her or his point of view, even if this world does not "match reality"' (p. 401).

In a crucial chapter in his seminal work on teacher education, Kumaravadivelu (2012) examines the importance of *interrogating the teaching self*, for which he proposes critical autoethnography as a key to recognising teacher values, beliefs and identities. Canagarajah (2012) has also utilised autoethnography as a tool for deepening his understanding of his different and developing teaching identities, particularly as he began to embrace more global perspectives of teaching. The process led Canagarajah to question the centre/periphery dichotomy that had propelled him towards Western educational values, and allowed him to reflect on the way his teaching career had been loosely structured around the acqui-sition of cultural capital in the form of 'centre' qualifications and experiences. There is a growing body of work in teacher education and TESOL/TEFL (Teaching English to Speakers of Other Languages/Teaching English as a Foreign Language) teacher education that utilises autoethnography, and yet the method still often struggles to be taken seriously due to the highly personal and inevit-ably subjective nature of this form of inquiry. Such criticism misses the point of autoethnography, because it was developed entirely as a way of accommodating 'subjectivity, emotionality, and the researcher's influence on research, rather than hiding from these matters or assuming they don't exist' (Ellis et al., 2011, p. 274). Furthermore, autoethnography may place the researcher/practitioner at the centre of the narrative, but they are not the sole agent of the unfurling narrative (Chang, 2008). Autoethnographies place central emphasis on context, making them ideal for in-depth qualitative reviews in institutional, local and social settings. They are not merely about one person in this respect, but draw on the interactions of the community in order to make observations, just as ethnography does.

> It is a common misunderstanding that ethnography is an analysis of 'small things', local, one-time occurrences only. It is, and always has been, an approach in which the analysis of small phenomena, is set against an analysis of big phenomena, and in which both levels can only be understood in terms of one another.
>
> (Blommaert, 2005, p. 16)

Similarly, like ethnography, autoethnography is often used as a way of empowering people whose voices might otherwise not be heard (Boylorn & Orbe, 2014). In utilising this approach, I hope to further repudiate the perceived dichotomy between theory and practice, between teachers and researchers, and between students and teachers by presenting in this inquiry a narrative of how these viewpoints all converge into one.

I have further utilised the autoethnographic method in another study in which I returned to the experience of teaching the DCT class in order to gain a deeper, more methodical reflection of the experience (Pinner, 2018b). This experience overall has led me to be a much more critical observer of my own actions and to develop simultaneously as a teacher and a researcher. However, this study developed into an autoethnography during the process of data collection as a result of my own reflections on teaching, which were originally intended to be part of the Exploratory Practice design.

3.3.3 Exploratory Practice

The principle of 'thinking globally, acting locally', advocated by Allwright (2003) in the introduction to the special issue of *Language Teaching Research* that focused on Exploratory Practice, ties in closely with Narrative Inquiry's distinction between 'small stories' and 'big stories'. Allwright and Hanks (2009) actively encourage the 'harnessing' of Narrative Inquiry as a way to encourage reflection, particularly when refining puzzles for inquiry. In addition, the ideas from ethnography concerning the interrelated dynamics of local/global perspectives connect closely with this view. Furthermore, the multilevel analytical approach of autoethnography and its focus on empowerment creates a clear link between ethnographic approaches and the central principles that give structure to Exploratory Practice, an approach that was originally a reaction to the 'received wisdom' that had informed much of practitioner research. These reactions are often phrased as principles, which are the following:

1. a concern for the improvement of '*quality of life* in the language class-room' over 'instructional efficiency'
2. a view to developing understandings rather than improving our teaching;
3. the belief that teaching and researching should be social and therefore benefit learners and teachers as well as those who are interested in research. In other words it should 'involve everybody', as opposed to research which is generally concerned with 'cause and effect relationships'.

   (Adapted from Allwright, 2003, p. 114; emphasis in original)

Although many of the *academic* origins for Exploratory Practice were put forward in the final seven pages of Allwright and Bailey (1991), the *practical* origins arose from Allwright's work in Rio de Janeiro in the early nineties, which Allwright (2003) notes, made his initial aims at making teaching more *efficient* seem like 'an embarrassment' (p. 117). Allwright notes a dissatisfaction with what he labels a 'technicist' description of Exploratory Practice, itself ironic given that Exploratory Practice was developed initially as a set of ethical guidelines against such technicist approaches to practitioner research (Allwright, 2005). As a reaction to the initial eight steps of Exploratory Practice (Allwright, 1993), a reformulated list of 'global principles' was developed, and this attempted to shed the technicist agenda that made Exploratory Practice into a method and rather help it maintain its position as a set of ethical principles that inform practitioner research and make it practical, as something that integrates with the actual practices of teaching in a sustainable way. Thus, Exploratory Practice is about practitioners working towards understanding and professional development rather than change.

Exploratory Practice was developed collaboratively through academic writing and practical experience. Although fundamentally it is also an ongoing work in progress and personal experimentation is always encouraged, Allwright (2003) formulated a 'principled description' of Exploratory Practice which features seven points as follows:

1. put 'quality of life' first
2. work primarily to understand language classroom life
3. involve everybody
4. work to bring people together
5. work also for mutual development
6. integrate the work for understanding into classroom practice
7. make the work a continuous enterprise

(pp. 128–131)

Later, additional emphasis was also given to the learners themselves as agents in the process of Exploratory Practice. Allwright and Hanks developed five propositions about learners, that they are (1) unique individuals and (2) social beings who are (3) capable of taking learning seriously and (4) of independent decision-making, (5) and capable of developing as practitioners of learning. However, the lists which try to pin Exploratory Practice down serve merely as markers, in that they show where the ideas have come from and where they are headed, but fail to ultimately provide a description of Exploratory Practice as a method. Indeed, such a description would not be in keeping with the philosophy of practice around which Exploratory Practice was collaboratively built. In my own personal experience, the only way to really understand Exploratory Practice is to try to have a go at doing it.

In any case, my own reading of Exploratory Practice has led me firmly to the conclusion that this is perhaps one of the most promising avenues for teachers to explore in terms of understanding complex dynamic processes in their classrooms such as motivation. This is further supported by a recent paper by Ushioda (2016), which presents a research agenda not at all unlike the one I have used throughout this inquiry. This is, of course, not a coincidence but merely further evidence of the collaborative nature of this inquiry. In addition, although the discussion of motivation is short, it is framed as a centrally important aspect of Exploratory Practice and directly linked with proposition two: that learners are social beings. Furthermore, Exploratory Practice more broadly connects motivation with the 'quality of classroom life' (Allwright & Hanks, 2009, pp. 88–89). Such ethical considerations are echoed in Kumaravadivelu's (2012) comments on motivation, which he later connects strongly with the concept of authenticity, in the development of his modular approach to language teacher education. Furthermore, all of these approaches support Ushioda's persons-in-context relational view of motivation (Ushioda, 2009, 2011b), which has always been the starting place for my conceptualisation of motivation and part of my philosophy of practice.

Exploratory Practice as a framework for research is, in many ways, a development which takes action research as its point of departure. However, action research is still classed by Allwright and Hanks (2009) as *third-party research*, and they see it as still being unsatisfactory in terms of how well it is able to integrate itself as a form of research within the practice of actual teaching. Ellis (2012) explains the differences between the two methods:

> One is the starting point – a 'problem' or, perhaps, a 'task' in the case of action research and a 'puzzle' in the case of exploratory research.[1] Another difference lies in the methodology of the two approaches. Action research employs similar methods of data collection to those found in formal research and involves going beyond the materials used for teaching; exploratory research embeds data collection into the actual practice of teaching. What they have in common is an emphasis on the continuous nature of the inquiry. Action research is 'cyclical' (although to what extent this is actually achieved by many teachers is doubtful); exploratory research is a long-term enterprise and, because it is part of teaching is potentially more sustainable.
>
> (p. 31)

This inquiry was originally envisaged as Exploratory Practice because this way I did not have to view the relationship of the teacher/researcher as a problem or get tangled up with the 'observer's paradox' by having to employ formal data collection tools other than those used for teaching. From this research tradition I am able to make it clear that I *do* intend my participants to have a full understanding of my role as teacher/researcher and to know that I am trying to observe the effect of my interaction with them and gain a better understanding of the consequences of my actions in the classroom situation.

Another pertinent reason for basing this inquiry within the framework of Exploratory Practice is the fact that data should come from pedagogic sources, and that the data should serve a pedagogic purpose in its own right (Allwright, 2003, 2006a; Allwright & Hanks, 2009). This is done by recognising potentially exploitable pedagogic activities (PEPAs), which usually requires a more reflective and analytical approach to the ordinary work produced in class (Allwright & Hanks, 2009; Hanks, 2015b). Whereas action research neglects 'the agency of *learners* as potential researchers' (Allwright & Hanks, 2009, p. 108; original emphasis), Exploratory Practice is also seen 'a less daunting proposition than [action] research' (Mann, 2005, p. 108) because it is based more on the activities which take place in the classroom without intervention. This way the research sits alongside the actual teaching, and as a result the two aims (teaching and researching) are more closely entwined under the broader concept of learning. This appealed to me because this method of data collection would seem to be very authentic in itself. With authenticity being at the centre of this research, such an approach seemed a perfect and familiar fit, even though I had never embarked on a research project of this kind before.

One possible shortfall of this inquiry in terms of its being Exploratory Practice was, however, the way I saw the learners as potential researchers. This is a consequence of the hybrid nature of the study as it utilises autoethnography and Reflective Practice in order to gain a deeper understanding of my developing professional identity. As I found the reflective data and journals taking prominence in the study, I consciously or unconsciously chose not to invite the participants to make their own puzzles, and thus I retained the monopoly as the researcher. I did often invite the learners to reflect and to look at issues such as their understanding of authenticity, as well as their own fluctuating motivation, but I did not encourage them to look beyond the central themes that I was examining. The main way I explored the learners' own agency as researchers was in the forms of self-assessment and reflective essays, both of which are strongly advocated as tools for developing 'practitioners of learning' (Allwright & Hanks, 2009). As such, I do believe that this study was successful in 'involving all the participants' and improving the 'quality of classroom life' (Allwright, 2003, 2005; Allwright & Hanks, 2009) in the true sense of Exploratory Practice. However, it is important to admit that I feel I did not fully explore the learners' agency as researchers in terms of them selecting their own areas to focus on or encouraging them to develop their own puzzles. Exploratory Practice is resistant to prescriptive and dogmatic instructions of method, and is self-referentially called a 'work in progress'.

> EP is still and must always remain in the process of development, as we learn from the different circumstances in which the framework is invoked.
>
> (Allwright, 2003, p. 137)

I feel my having neglected my 'learners' agency as researchers' is an important admission and part of my own development as a teacher. Since completing this inquiry I have made an effort to attempt Exploratory Practice as it was originally envisioned and ask learners to create their own puzzles, present research in areas that they choose to learn about themselves and to take more agency in their own learning. However, the student/participants in this study did benefit from many techniques in my teaching that aimed at increasing their own agency, such as the self-assessments for class participation (see section 4.6), the many reaction papers and reflexive exercises we conducted together, and overall they were made very much aware of my ongoing research and often expressed an interest in my research. So, perhaps it is not accurate to say that I neglected their agency as potential researchers, but rather I kept the focus for this research on the theme of authenticity and motivation, and often asked the students to reflect on their own motivation rather than looking at other areas of learning that they might have been interested in.

Although it does not strictly conform to all of the principles of Exploratory Practice, much of the central justification and data collection tools are based in this type of research, and there are several other studies which have been published as Exploratory Practice that do not invite participants to engage in the act of making their own puzzles. For example, Zhang (2004) used Exploratory Practice to restructure an intensive reading class in China which worked towards improving the quality of classroom life and attempted to involve everybody, although 'not trying to solve problems directly' (p. 335). Later, students were invited to engage in discussing their own puzzles, but these were in no way formalised in the reported study as they were in, for example, Hanks (2015a). Similarly, Wu (2006) conducted a fascinating study which applied ethnography to a 'teacher-initiated research project' (p. 331) that presented a narrative of teacher education and discussed the issue of philosophy and teacher research. This study focuses on the lives of teachers themselves, and several links are made with Exploratory Practice and the concept of authenticity, drawing particularly on existential thought and blending this with Eastern thought such as Taoism. In applying their philosophies and sharing stories, the teachers in Wu's report were able to make a connection between their 'understanding in being' and their work as language teachers.

> The language renames the students from the inside into a category of life instead of standards, and opens their heart of learning which was once covered by the technical criteria of educational values.
>
> (Wu, 2006, p. 347)

This seems to connect the idea of 'teacher as person' (Glatthorn, 1975) with the learner as a person-in-context (Ushioda, 2009, 2011b), which are essentially guiding principles that informed the design of this inquiry.

3.3.4 Evidence-based Reflective Practice and a hybrid methodology

Walsh and Mann (2015) discuss the need for data-driven/evidence-based Reflective Practice. Their paper argues that Reflective Practice is often marred by activities which are insufficiently data led, having a tendency to be overly egocentric and lack collaborative elements; being dominated by teaching journals that are predominantly written methods of engaging in reflection; and tending to lack detail about the nature and purposes of reflective tools. The tools they recommend for overcoming these issues involve Ad-Hoc self-observations which provide snapshots for more systematic reflection and also utilising stimulated recall. More generally, they advocate applying a data-driven approach and opening up reflections to make them dialogic or collegial.

When I read this article, I felt a surge of confidence in the design of my study, because I was already doing many of the things they advocate and even using some of the same vocabulary. I had already collected 'snapshots' and 'Ad-Hoc' data before this article was published. Although I talk about Ad-Hoc interviews and this article promotes 'Ad-Hoc reflections', the justification for research collection being localised and contextualised for specific critical incidents is basically the same. In addition, many of these techniques are advocated by Ushioda (2016) in her research agenda for motivation. Also, that both papers advocate collaborative analysis was encouraging, as I have made a conscious effort not to be doing my research 'in a vacuum', but to collaborate with others or at least talk about it in formal and informal professional settings.

Together, in blending autoethnography, Narrative Inquiry, Exploratory Practice and evidence-based reflection, I have created a hybrid of research methodologies. However, each of these methodologies seems to feed easily into the other and they complement one another in many ways. For example, the literature on Exploratory Practice frequently references Reflective Practice and tends to view it as a step in the right direction in terms of practitioner research and as a form of good, ethical and sustainable practice. However, the criticism is that Reflective Practice tends not to include the agency of learners as potential researchers, and it also points out the tendency to be individualistic (Allwright & Hanks, 2009; Hanks, 2017). Such criticisms are also unfairly levelled at autoethnography, but in fact autoethnography is a type of ethnography, and thus the role of others, the social ecology and context should be highlighted in such research, and indeed a foundation of the method is the idea that the self is created through interaction with others (Boylorn & Orbe, 2014, p. 29). Indeed, autoethnography is fundamentally a research method for understanding the self in relation to culture and society, and of contributing to society by sharing stories and narratives that aim to develop understanding (Chang, 2008, p. 13).

Allwright asserts that Exploratory Practice is not so much a research method as a framework for teachers and learners to develop their own understandings (2006b, p. 15). Similarly, Reflective Practice is not in and of itself a research method but a set of tools for developing practice that closely resembles research which is designed to benefit other practitioners and our learners. Whilst this is a positive thing, I felt in conducting an empirical inquiry I needed a clear process which was a research method in itself. Whilst autoethnography was the main backbone of this design, I added elements from Exploratory Practice and Reflective Practice in order to highlight the classroom context and to attempt to involve my learners and colleagues more directly in the process, adding an education-specific context to the design. This was my main reason for deciding to combine these elements in an attempt to create a robust hybrid methodology which I saw as an appropriate methodology for this particular inquiry.

Farrell (2015) explains the value of teachers creating narratives that reflect back on critical incidents in their teaching, because such events can offer significant insights into what has shaped our teaching practice and how these are affected by lived experience. This is one of the main reasons why I chose to make this study an autoethnography built around the narrative of my professional development, as my teaching identity changes (in part facilitated by the research itself). As such, this inquiry is a hybrid of several interrelated methods. This brings me to an important question, what is the purpose of undertaking such an inquiry?

3.3.5 Purpose

In one way, this study is useful to others because it details methods and techniques which I used and developed as a way of becoming a more reflective practitioner. As such, it is part of an ever-growing body of research which offers evidence that increasing a professional's capacity for reflexivity is a good way of increasing that person's competence and skills as a practitioner (Edge, 2011; Farrell, 2011; Kumaravadivelu, 2012; Mann, 2005; Schön, 1983, 1987; Ushioda, Smith, Mann, & Brown, 2011; Walsh & Mann, 2015). It is also useful from the perspective of research methodology, since studies such as this often differ in their approach. Narrative Inquiry and autoethnography are extremely complex methods of research in many ways, and no two studies are exactly alike in terms of research focus or method (Barkhuizen et al., 2014; Denzin, 2006, 2014; Johnson & Golombek, 2002). In this way, those interested in conducting such research will find it necessary to read other people's work in order to see how the principles of the research are put into practice.

A further justification is in the insights gleaned from conducting this research. By utilising retrospective methods of analytical inquiry and combining them with practitioner research, I was able to see how my previous experiences are connected to my current execution of practice, and to trace my own professional development. This may therefore be useful for language teacher education and research, as it sheds light on teaching beliefs. Also, in reading a study like this, I hope that other practitioners will project their own similar experiences onto the narrative, and therefore by engaging with my study they will be able to learn something about their own experiences. Finally, this study sheds light on a previously underresearched area of motivation, namely the connections between teacher and student motivation. A greater number of studies on language teacher motivation are needed because of a general scarcity of this type of research (Dörnyei & Ryan, 2015; Dörnyei & Ushioda, 2011), but also this particular area of motivational research has long been identified as important, and yet remained hitherto underexplored (Dörnyei & Ryan, 2015; Dörnyei & Ushioda, 2011; Ushioda, 2014, 2016).

Finally, following the main purpose of Exploratory Practice, which aims at improving the 'quality of classroom life' (Allwright, 2003, 2005), this study aims to benefit most those who were directly involved. The students who participated in this research, I believe, did benefit from our time together, and my own practice has developed as a result, meaning that future generations of my students will also experience these benefits as well.

3.3.6 Ethics

As previously stated, I felt it would be unethical to use a control group that did not receive 'authentic' input, however it manifested itself. I felt it would be extremely demotivating to purposefully deny authenticity from a class for the purposes of research, and as such my decision to adopt and adapt Exploratory Practice and reflection were driven by ethical considerations. I have been very considerate of ethics throughout the study. Sadly, it seems that ethics are often treated as a hoop or a tick box, but I have tried to integrate ethics into the centre of my study. As I mentioned in Chapter 2, one of the indicators of synergy is empathy, which of course relates closely to ethical considerations.

The students were all given consent forms to sign which explained the nature of the study in both English and Japanese, and they had been verbally informed of my intention to conduct this inquiry and use the class for my research several times since the first day. I also gave each student a personalised letter which explained my research and that I would be giving them consent forms to sign in the lesson before which I handed out the consent forms (Lesson 107A on Wednesday 28/05/2014). I felt it was better to formally tell the students about the research by letter, and then give them time to decide whether or not to sign the forms; therefore, I administered the consent forms in lesson 107B Friday 30/05/2014.

To my great relief, the students all agreed to the audio recording and other data types I was asking permission to use. Only two students, Mr Nintendo and Mr Dawn, opted out of the use of pedagogical sources. I was actually pleased about this, however, as it showed that I had conducted the procedure in a way which did not too strongly coerce the students into giving consent, and they obviously felt willing to participate and to express doubts or withdraw consent when they felt unsure. After the study was over, students were kept updated about the research via my ePortfolio. At the time I was also planning to collect data from my Writing Skills class, and in this class one person opted out of the audio data. As soon as I received that form I unplugged my microphone, and then deleted all the class audio recordings from that course. This happened after teaching this class, but it made me all the more grateful to the CLERAC students for giving me their consent. I believe this episode shows that I acted ethically and did not place undue pressure on the students to participate in the study.

I strongly believe that I am becoming more ethical by increasing my reflective capacity and by challenging my own assumptions. I also purposefully avoided delving too much into students' lives, and this is why there are several unfortunate 'holes' in my data (such as simple biographical details like age or how long Mr Po has lived in Japan), because I only used the information my students gave me naturally or that was part of my normal teaching. Ethics is actually a very important aspect of my teaching beliefs and is a guiding principle in the choice of content for each lesson as part of my philosophy of teaching.

All participants in this study were adults, and none were identified as vulnerable. The participants' anonymity was carefully maintained throughout the study, and data has been stored on password-protected computers. Participants were given the choice of opting in or out of the research even after data had been collected. Participants were informed that they could access transcripts and data analysis before publication or submission, and I used my online portfolio as a place to communicate findings with the participants, although very few of them remained in contact after the course had finished, which meant there was almost no respondent validation.

3.4 Context

The main focus of the inquiry comes from a course taught through the Centre for Language Education and Research (CLER) at Sophia University in Tokyo entitled

Academic Communication (CLERAC). This is a year-long (two semester) course with non-English majors of various departments, who meet for two 90-minute lessons a week as part of compulsory second-language (English) proficiency classes which make up part of the required credits for the Japanese bachelor of arts degree awarded by the university. CLER was founded in 2014 (the year I taught CLERAC), replacing the general foreign language courses. This institutional restructuring is part of an even longer narrative which I have been involved with since 2011 when I first came to Japan and first started working for Sophia University (Pinner, 2012b). My only experience of teaching for the general foreign language courses was a class called Intermediate (INT), which in many ways represents the old version of CLERAC before the restructuring in 2014, which I shall return to shortly in the overview of the narrative (see section 3.4.1).

CLER is not a full department and does not belong to a faculty, but it provides both compulsory and elective university-wide language education. All students, regardless of their major, have to take a second language class, and in the case of language majors they have to take a third language course. CLER provides an amazing diversity of language options for students, including Italian, French, German, Chinese and Korean as well as Arabic and even Swahili. Classes are taught by full-time lecturers who belong to CLER and also part-time teachers. Due to the large-scale needs for every student to have language courses, some classes are farmed out to language departments such as mine, and as a language teaching specialist and member of the steering committee for CLER, I was chosen to teach our department's CLER quota. So, these classes are compulsory for students even though not directly related to their major, and they are also compulsory for me to teach even though not part of my department's usual contact hours for teaching.

My initial experience of teaching for the general language programs in 2013 was a class called INT (see 3.4.1). I must admit I found teaching INT rather draining, and I did not always relish going into the class. There were 40 students in INT, and I chose to use a textbook called *Global* (Macmillan) which claimed to have 'authentic' speakers of international English. I will return to this point in the analysis section of this book, but I wanted to draw attention to the fact that my experience of teaching CLERAC was markedly different from INT – suggesting, I hope, an achievement in authenticity and motivation.

The CLERAC class I was assigned was made up mainly of students from the Faculty of Science and Technology, with two coming from Economics. There were 25 students in the spring semester, which fell to 24 in the autumn semester as one participant failed on account of low attendance. The aim of the first semester was to help students develop their English skills and academic literacy, and the second semester was supposed to be content focused (or CLIL). Qualitative data was collected in the form of teaching journals and students' pedagogical materials (such as assignments and classwork) as well as classroom audio recordings and Ad-Hoc interviews conducted with students whilst I monitored classes.

We met on Wednesdays in a normal classroom and on Fridays in a computer-aided language learning (CALL) room. Both classes were first period in the morning at 9:15, an unpopular slot with students, especially first-years. CLERAC is an interesting course because, although unique in many ways, as a compulsory English class with non-English majors I feel it is quite representative of the university English language learning and teaching experience in Japan. The fact that many such courses are compulsory and not directly related to students' majors has been cited as a demotivating factor in several previous studies (Kikuchi, 2013).

3.4.1 Overview of the narrative

Because this inquiry represents a very complicated narrative of my own developing professional identity and emergent dynamic elements such as authenticity and motivation, I wanted to explain clearly the overview of the entire narrative. Figure 3.5 shows an attempt at doing so as a simple visual. This diagram was composed in my field journal in January 2016 as an attempt to help myself understand the main elements of the narrative as I prepared the write-up. The complexity of the narrative is due to the shifting analytical lens (narrowing and broadening) which is necessary to adopt when examining context to include 'the wider ecology of external social and environmental conditions' (Ushioda, 2015, p. 51).

In the diagram, circles each represent classes which have the main relevance to the study. Although there were other classes which I was teaching simultaneously, these are not included here for simplicity. The dark circle, labelled CLERAC, is the focus of this inquiry. The first circle, DCT, is the Discussions on Contemporary Topics classes, overviewed in the Introduction and the virtual 'starting point' of my interest in authenticity and thus the first piece of the 'puzzle' at the heart of this inquiry. The second circle, labelled INT, is the class I taught in between DCT and CLERAC, which was part of the general foreign language courses that preceded the formation of CLER in 2014. The circles labelled CONT represent my continued teaching, but the classes are undefined in order to limit the narrative scope. However, I wanted to stress that my teaching and professional

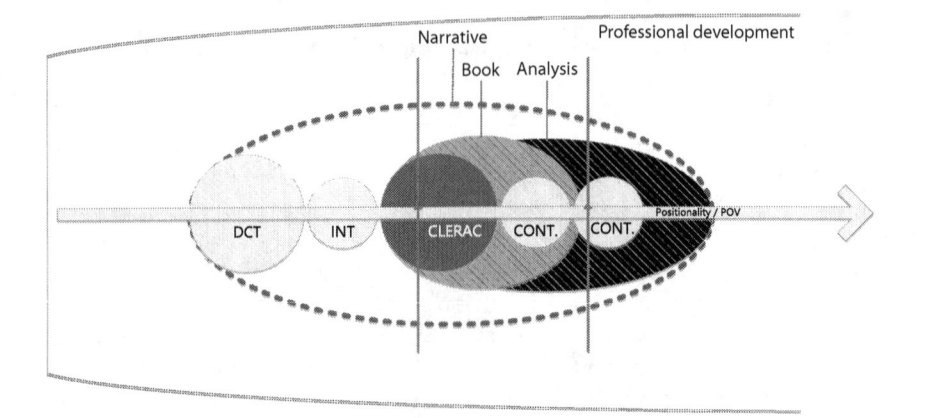

Figure 3.5 Diagram of the narrative

development are still ongoing. This narrative is merely a cross section of the class-room based on what the data provides a window on. Another important point is that my teaching practices were and have been especially influenced *as a result* of this inquiry, as I will discuss in Chapter 6.

The arrow through the middle shows my teacher/researcher positionality and point of view (POV). This is continuous, although I am also able to view things retrospectively. I will argue that in conducting this study, as part of my analysis, I have occupied a dual observational role. First, when I was the teacher and was still working with the class, I had an emic (insider) view of the course and my own teaching. Then, as I returned to the data for the analysis stage, I took on a slightly more (although, obviously not completely) etic (outsider) perspective. However, my POV is most strongly emic in that I am an insider reflecting on my own practice. The circles are shaded to represent that within each circle is another POV for each of the students/participants in those courses, and of course it is a POV which I can appreciate and attempt to examine from the limited data I have, but that ultimately remains elusive to me. In Chapter 6 I will develop this idea to explain this in more detail and claim that time and lived experience act as a force multiplier in the classroom; that in one 90-minute class with 25 students, there is actually 25(+1) X 90 minutes of experience. This is because each student experiences the 90 minutes completely differently, and so does the teacher, thus for each 90-minute class there are actually 2,340 minutes of class-time experienced (see section 6.3.2). This relates to what Holliday (1994, 1999) discussed in his treatment of classrooms as 'small cultures'.

The light grey oval shows the time in which I was writing a monograph about authenticity (Pinner, 2016b), which is significant as it shows when I was most engaged in developing my understanding of the concept of authenticity (detailed in Chapter 2, the theoretical framework). The darker oval represents my conducting analysis for the main research project described in this book.

Finally, the grey lines show the panel meetings I have had as part of this inquiry, as I move towards its completion. These lines represent important opportunities when this very personal and inward-looking quest has received direction and input from outside perspectives, and then the collaboration arising from these interactions has been taken into account. It is also worth pointing out that the entire chron-ology of the narrative is peppered with other such collaborations in smaller or less formal contexts, such as tutorials, conferences or even discussions with colleagues.

The entire narrative is framed by a dotted oval line, indicating that my pro-fessional development and understanding of the key issues at the heart of my 'puzzle' are continuous in nature. Although the inquiry is an autoethnography and thus the central figure is myself, arguably the next most important agent in the narrative are the student-participants from CLERAC.

3.4.2 Participants

There were 25 participants in CLERAC (see Table 3.1). As I moved further with the analysis, I decided to create Focal Participants, students whom I selected

Table 3.1 Participants

	Pseudonym	Department
1	Ms Pine	Economics
2	Mr Montville	Economics
3	Ms Sound	Materials and Life Sciences
4	Mr Swamp	Materials and Life Sciences
5	Ms Redslope	Materials and Life Sciences
6	Ms Widetree	Materials and Life Sciences
7	Ms Smallville	Materials and Life Sciences
8	Mr Cloud	Materials and Life Sciences
9	Ms Downtree	Materials and Life Sciences
10	Ms Saltfield	Materials and Life Sciences
11	Mr Cleyera	Materials and Life Sciences
12	Ms Oldriver	Materials and Life Sciences
13	Mr Po	Materials and Life Sciences
14	Mr Fly	Engineering and Applied Sciences
15	Mr Charge	Engineering and Applied Sciences
16	Mr Wind	Engineering and Applied Sciences
17	Mr Dawn	Engineering and Applied Sciences
18	Ms Forest	Engineering and Applied Sciences
19	Mr Nintendo	Information and Communication Sciences
20	Mr Mouth	Information and Communication Sciences
21	Ms Chennai	Information and Communication Sciences
22	Mr Auxiliary	Information and Communication Sciences
23	Ms Lovehouse	Information and Communication Sciences
24	Ms Hemp	Information and Communication Sciences
25	Mr House	Information and Communication Sciences

because they were interesting or particularly unique (or particularly representative as the case may be). I tried to gain a deeper understanding of these individuals in order to look at the interactions between myself and my students, and avoid generalisations about 'the class' but rather to focus on the individual learners as 'persons in context' (Ushioda, 2009, 2015).

3.4.2.1 Participant list

The creation of the pseudonyms might warrant some explanation here. Names are very important, and knowing students' names shows them that the teacher recognises them as people (Shi, 2002). I made a special effort to learn all the students' names and keep them in memory so that I would remember them as individuals during the analysis. However, I found that when writing the analysis, I was not satisfied with my students' pseudonyms because they were non-descript and did not match their personalities. I created a system where I would adopt one or two kanji characters from the students' names and render them into English. The kanji I chose did not always have meaning for me, but it gave the student pseudonyms a little more personality. Also, certain of the students' pseudonyms were rather apt, such as Mr Charge and Mr Auxiliary. Although these names sound quite unnatural, because they stand out I felt they were good for the Focal Participants and also go some way to describing their student personas. The only exception to this system was Mr Nintendo, who is named after a conversation I had with him on the first day of class. Mr Nintendo did not pass the autumn semester, and so I wanted his name to differentiate him. The other participant with a different name is Mr Po, who is Chinese and so his real name differentiated him in class already. I wanted to retain this aspect of Mr Po's Chinese identity in the pseudonyms, as it was an important aspect of his identity in the class.

3.4.2.2 Focal participants

Because of the large number of participants in the study, I needed to be selective and reduce the focus, in order to prioritise the quality of the analysis. I decided to select just four students as Focal Participants.

The process I adopted in choosing the individual students whom I would give focus to was not simple. I actually began selecting students while the class was still in progress, and this was useful in helping me archive certain interactions or take notes. Whilst the classes were still ongoing and I still had a good personal knowledge of the students, I began to select those who I felt allowed for a diverse cross section of the students in the class. I wanted to choose students who were high achievers and highly motivated, and then students who were in the middle, and finally students who I felt were 'at the bottom of the class' in terms of their own personal involvement. I also tried to strike a balance between gender when making this selection, as I wanted the selection to be representative. It should be pointed out here that this judgement was mainly *intuitive* in that I was not looking at test scores or other indicators of class performance, and these were more personal judgements that I made whilst I was still working closely with the students.

The second step in the selection was based on quality of data, selected after the final class had been taught and when I took stock of the types of data I had at my disposal for analysis. Some of the students I wanted to focus on, for example, had not actually revealed much in their assignments or in their class-room interactions. Of course, this in itself could be revealing in some ways, but I used this stocktaking phase as another way to help focus and refine the sample I would use.

Finally, I compiled learner profiles of the participants I had identified as the main students I wished to focus on for the inquiry. During this phase, I further eliminated several participants simply due to constraints of manageability. Out of 24 participants, my list numbered as many as 12 at one point for detailed focus, which then went down to seven, but finally reduced to four as I felt any larger number than this would compromise the quality of the focus. Of course, I should stress here that the other participants will still be part of the study, but I will not draw on their data as much. In addition, I began listing the most critical reflections on which to focus the narrative. Rather than listing the reflections here out of context, they are presented chronologically in the narrative under designated headings.

Together this shortlist of participants and reflections is hoped to provide the central points around which the main themes for analysis gravitate.

The list of Focal Participants is as follows (16 per cent of participants):

1. Mr Auxiliary
2. Mr Charge
3. Ms Downtree
4. Mr Po

3.4.3 Space (institutional context)

Japan's motivational landscape has already been briefly mapped in the previous chapter. However, I feel it is important to focus the analytical lens on the institutional context as well.

Sophia University is particularly renowned for its international exchange programmes, its integrative and progressive attitudes towards foreign (non-Japanese) culture and for its English language courses. Sophia University advocates a content- and language integrated learning (CLIL)-based methodology and this fact in particular makes it an especially interesting institution for the proposed study because of the focus on content. CLIL methodology strongly advocates authenticity (Coyle, Hood & Marsh, 2010, p. 5). Sophia University takes pride in its reputation as a centre of mixing cultures and international cooperation, as the following message from the president of Sophia attests:

> [W]e develop abilities to address the global society. Intensive language education, overseas study programs, academic exchanges and a campus with a diverse community shared by international students from all over the world help to deepen the understanding of other cultures and to develop qualities that will allow students to play an active role in an evolving global society.
>
> (Takizawa, 2010)

As the world moves towards a greater understanding of culture and greater international cooperation, it is hoped that Sophia will be seen as a representative example of an institution with an emphasis on internationalism and the global society.[2]

3.4.3.1 Environmental conditions and the classroom

To aid the narrative I include photographs of the inside of the classrooms and seating plans, to help the reader place the narrative in a visual space. I always create a 'map' or seating plan of the students in class to help learn their names, but I came to realise this was also useful data in terms of contextualising the narrative (see Table 3.2 and Figures 3.6 and 3.7). I converted this basic sketch of

Table 3.2 Seating plan legend

Department	No. Students (N)	Colour
Economics	2	
Life Sciences	11	
Engineering & Applied Sciences	5	
Information & Communication Sciences	7	

Figure 3.6 Wednesday classroom

the classroom into a diagram, and also used the data to help create the network sociograms shown in Chapter 6.

It is quite noticeable that in the classroom lessons (held on Wednesdays), the first two rows were almost always empty, with a higher concentration of students choosing to sit near the back. It is also quite interesting to note that students who were very active in the class (such as Mr Charge and Ms Downtree) sat towards the front, whereas less communicative students, such as Mr Auxiliary, all sat as far back as possible. On Fridays in the CALL room, although the seating and environment were very different, similar patterns emerged in terms of the physical distance that students choose to sit at from me and in relation to each other. I never allocated seats during the lessons, and students only moved during mingling activities or when doing group work; therefore, these seating plans show the students' own default choices of where to sit. On reflection, it may have aided the classroom dynamics to mix seats more frequently and ensure the students knew each other better (Dörnyei & Murphey, 2003). In the seating plans, students' departments are colour coded.

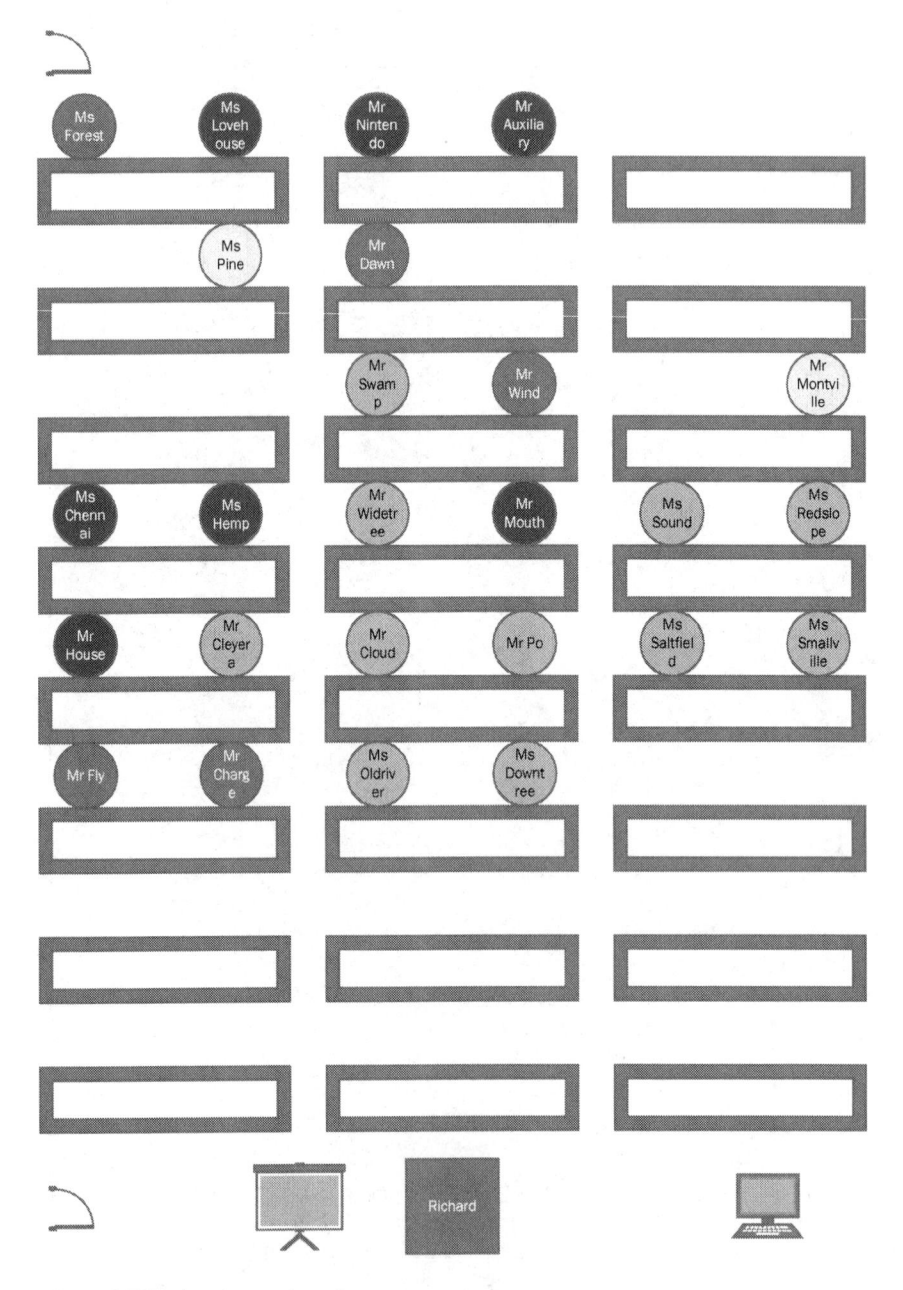

Figure 3.7 Wednesday seating plan

Figure 3.8 Friday CALL room

In addition to the empty tables at the front of the class and a general tendency of students to cluster near the middle, these seating plans also show the relative preference for same-sex seating partners. This is possibly indicative of the students' level of sexual maturity (Degenne & Forsé, 1999, p. 24), termed 'sexual cleavage' by Moreno (1934). This is fairly typical of my seating maps for other classes, and I have even observed several classes where all the girls sit on one side of the room and all the boys sit on the other. Many of the students, particularly the freshmen, are perhaps relatively unfamiliar with members of the opposite sex, especially if they came from single-sex high schools, which are quite common in Japan. Also worth noting is that many students remain living with their parents whilst attending university in Japan. This is quite normal in Japanese culture but somewhat different from my own university experience in which I lived independently for the first time.

As the photograph of the Friday CALL room shows (Figures 3.8 and 3.9), each student actually had two monitors in front of them. One is their own monitor, which I could take control of and project onto the screen at any time, and also see a thumbnail view of what they are looking at on the teacher's control panel; the other was a display monitor which I usually set to show the left-hand monitor of my PC, which is the same as that being projected on the screen. The room was fully networked, had high-speed Internet (although many of the students still had cause to complain about the speeds) and teachers, if they know how, are able to fully control every aspect of the students' PCs, including sending links and opening programs en masse and in sync. Naturally, teaching in such a room created a very different type of classroom atmosphere, which is what gave the Wednesday and Friday classes a very distinct and tangibly different feel, not

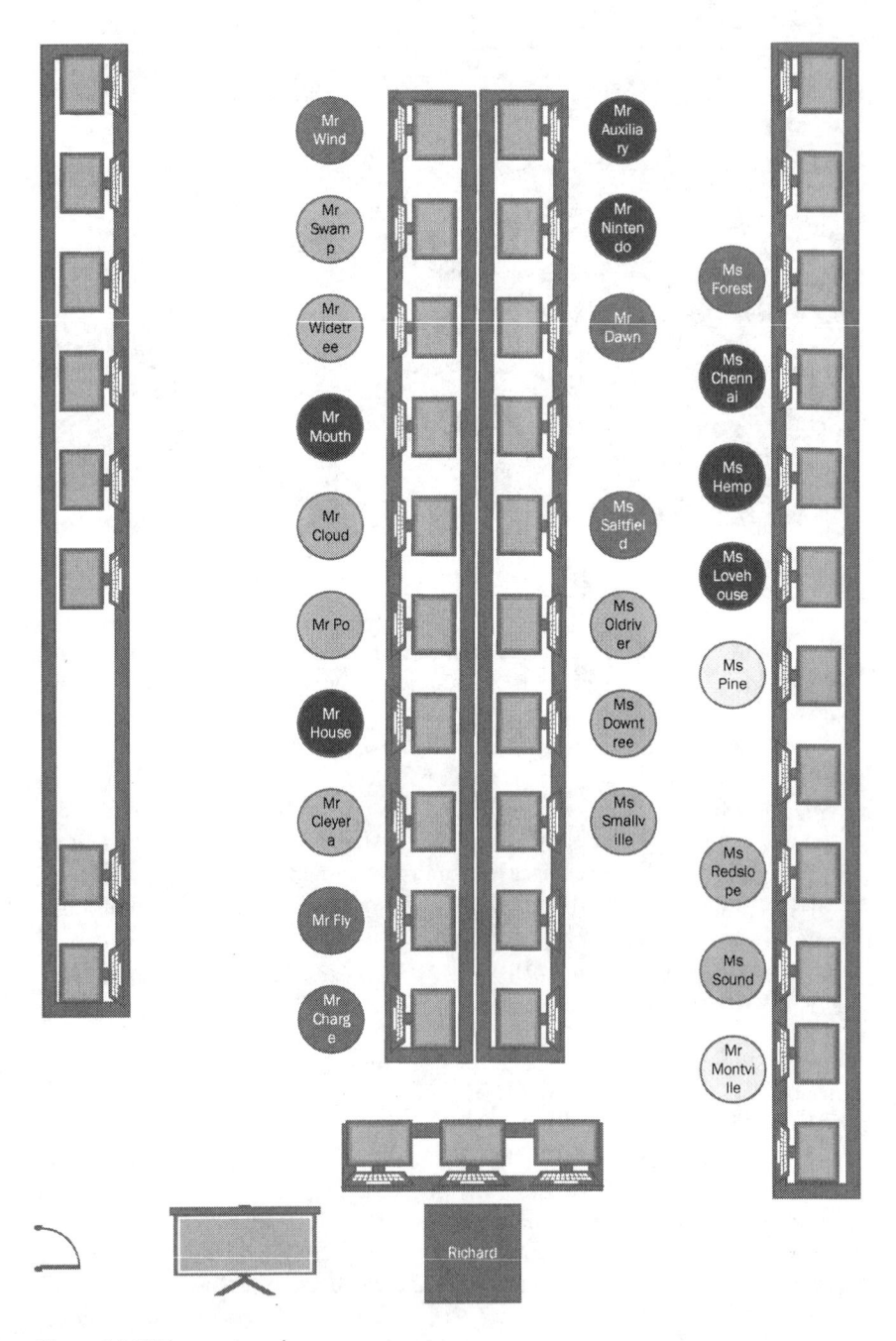

Figure 3.9 Friday seating plan

to mention requiring a rather different teaching approach and set of tasks. As the narrative will discuss, I did not fully become attuned to these environmental differences until the autumn semester, after having attended one INSET workshop and having asked a technician for specific instruction. It is likely that this delay was due to my own stubbornness in the belief that I was already an expert CALL user. This high opinion of my own computer proficiency was most likely a product of several things, such as my MA dissertation having focused on teachers' attitudes to CALL; in 2008 I became the eLearning coordinator for a private language school in London in which I was responsible for a Moodle used by over 20 other schools; and I set up my own eLearning consultancy and presented about setting up virtual learning environments at IATEFL in 2010, as well as actually teaching an information technology (IT) course to pre-master's degree students on university placement programs. I also built my own computer and know how install an SQL database onto a server in order to create websites using content management systems such as WordPress. In short, it came as a surprise to me to realise that I actually needed help with the CALL room, and that I was far from being fully proficient in the employment of computers for my teaching. Sadly, this late realisation is linked to a lower quality of lessons in the spring semester, which has relevance in terms of motivational synergy, as I will explain in the following chapters.

3.4.4 Time

In the previous chapter I gave a detailed description of my identity and the changes that I was perceiving, which were initially important in alerting me to the issue of authenticity in the language classroom, particularly the idea of an authenticity gap between myself and the learners. Although there is no need to reiterate this, I wanted to draw attention to these issues again as they form part of the context of the study.

Furthermore, it is important to note that this was the first year that CLERAC had run, and thus the first (and only) time I taught the course.

3.5 Data collection and analysis

3.5.1 Data types

Before I embarked upon the data collection I made a carefully constructed list of steps which I intended to take in order to gain the insights I felt would best lead me to a better understanding of the central puzzle around which I was framing this inquiry. This was a list of 'snapshots' that I intended to collect by eliciting reflective data from myself and the students on given topics as they appeared in the syllabus. However, the research developed rather organically and independently of my intentions as the students became part of the research, following Li's (2006) call for 'balanced research' and the principles of Exploratory Practice that promote learner-centeredness and flexibility.

What happened when I actually came to collect the first snapshots (related to global English) was that I found the data I collected to be 'blurry', rather like a photograph taken from a moving vehicle – not only was the panorama reduced to something which can only capture a small part of the subject matter from a single perspective, but also the picture that developed was out of focus and unclear. I soon abandoned the map of snapshots. Throughout the course the teaching and research were symbiotic, until the end of the semester when assessments became the main focus of the class and I was unable to even record detailed reflections in my journal.

At first I was undecided which classes I would select for my research, so I initially started by attempting to record every lesson I was teaching and keep journals on all of them. However, within a few days the size of this task led me to quickly narrow down my options and select just two (Writing Skills and CLERAC), which was further reduced to one near the end of the first semester. The reasons behind this choice will be the subject of another article in the future.

Due to my large teaching bank, the work I was doing on my monograph and other constraints on my time, I soon found it very hard to keep detailed notes and make in-depth written journal entries. This was especially true on Thursday, where I teach three classes in the day. Writing Skills is the third class I teach that day, and usually when it came time to write my journal entry, I was so tired that I was literally drifting off to sleep as I typed. I decided to narrate my journal entries instead, which became a reflexive self-interview and contributed a large component to both data and analysis. In this way the teaching journal became an audio journal and I found that my ability to be reflexive on my teaching actually deepened as well. The quality of the journal entries was much increased, but of course the actual amount of work in processing all that data had also increased.

Another important development was in the way I structured journal entries. At first I had only a very basic structure focusing on moment-by-moment reflections as I felt this would be best as part of the inductive approach. However, as I looked back over entries, they already began to make less sense to me, even after a period of a few weeks since the class. Therefore, I decided to structure entries around a format in which I would first explain the steps and procedure of the entire class and use this as a kind of stimulated recall for classroom observations and reflections. This system became even more developed in the autumn semester, when I began making chronologically structured field notes during lessons which I would 'unpack' later into the audio journal. This was specifically a response to my own perceived overreliance on technology, particularly audio files, which created a 'needles in a haystack' issue for me in terms of locating pieces of data such as Ad-Hoc interviews and reflections that got lost in hours and hours of recordings. There were further issues when I came to listen back to certain classes in order to identify Ad-Hoc interviews only to find that the students' responses were virtually inaudible amongst the background of other students' activity. For this reason, I later began employing CALL room headset chats which recorded the students' group conversations with great clarity.

The data centres around myself as the teacher and my students as fellow participants in the act of socially authenticating the learning and creating positive

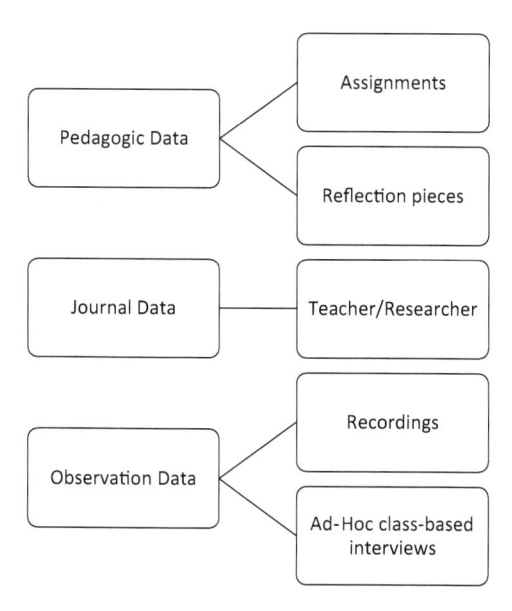

Figure 3.10 Three types of classroom data

motivational synergy. I am trying to triangulate the data by looking at different types of classroom data (see Figure 3.10) pedagogic data from the students, journal data from myself and observational data which is produced when I interact with the students.

Each type of data has strengths and limitations, but all of them are natural products of the teaching and therefore nothing is intervening with the progress of the class. On the contrary, data collection should actually enhance the class experience and allow a better understanding between us, which it is hoped will lead to improvement in the quality of classroom life. During the narratives I will refer mainly to the final written journal, which also incorporated the audio journal after summary transcription, as the TRJournal. Entries are provided along with the date for reference unless this is already clear from context. Other data sources are made clear in the context and provided with a date for reference. Each lesson is also coded to show the semester, week number and lesson (e.g. 101A, 208B).

3.5.2 Analytical approach

Using Ushioda's metaphor of an analytical lens (2015, 2016), I have conducted cycles of analysis, trying to focus in on the critical incidents and most salient moments relating to motivational synergy. The collection of data is also part of the analytical model as well, and I utilised a form of 'narrative knowledging' to make sense of emergent issues and identify the key themes. I also relied heavily on NVivo 11 to organise the data and look for holistic themes by using analytical queries such as word frequencies and sociograms, which will be presented in Chapter 6.

In conducting this inquiry, I recorded twenty-eight 90-minute lessons in the spring semester, and then twenty-seven in the autumn semester. On top of this I have collected hours of recordings from the students themselves, in the form of videos and audio recordings which they produced as coursework, and also recordings from on-task interactions that took place during lessons in the CALL rooms. Furthermore, I have included the students' essays and reaction papers, as well as other samples of their work ranging from test scores to personal emails, as well as trace data (Rodriguez & Ryave, 2002) harvested from the interactions which they participated in on Moodle (the class VLE). I have also recorded my own audio-teaching journals (which serve simultaneously as both data and analysis), as well as my own written journal and field logs and other notes. In addition to all this there are numerous photographs I took of the board work for the lessons, as well as the teaching materials used throughout the course. Although Table 3.3 does not account for all the data sources, it provides the most comprehensive list of the sources and data types which were used in the compilation of this narrative.

All told, I have composed over half a million words on word-processed documents, and recorded 13,609 minutes (227 hours, or 9.4 days) of audio data for this study. My field journal alone runs to over 80,000 words, with students' essays adding up to a total of about 50,000 words. Of course, not all of this is relevant to the focus of this inquiry, and yet in order to do the study justice, I have had to carefully manage how I approach this unwieldy amount of data. One of the strategies I employed was selective sampling, both in terms of participants and events. By this I mean that I had to focus on certain key moments (defined as either snapshots or critical incidents) and pay particular attention to these moments whilst allowing the events which lead up to them to fall away into the background. Snapshots are basically moments when I collected data in the class in order to try to ascertain my students' reaction to the lessons, whereas critical incidents are moments which have emerged through reflection as being of significance to my professional development (Farrell, 2008; Finch, 2010; Tripp, 1993). These two contextual signifiers have thus provided me with a way to clear a path through the data which leads directly through the most important events in the collection phase towards the central themes of the study. Another aspect of the selective sampling technique was to focus on interactions with particular individuals, those whom I identified as being key persons (Focal Participants) within the class who contributed to its dynamics.

In order to manage the data I have also used a combination of structured/strategic and random sampling. In other words, I have gone back over data sources which I had indicated as important in my reflections and I have also selected other areas at random, looking for things which might surface as important. Often this stimulates me to look at other sources and I sometimes 'find a trail' in the data which I follow up based on a random sample. Finally, once the key themes were established (motivational synergy), I listened back to all of the audio reflections

Table 3.3 Summary of data types

Chronology	Data Type	Data Description
Data collected during the CLERAC course (April 2014–January 2015)	Pedagogic data	Work done by students as part of the CLERAC course, also includes my own teaching materials
	Field notes (as opposed to journal entries)	Logs, observations and notes made during the CLERAC course
	Trace data	Includes emails and online interactions as part of the course VLE.
	Audio/Audio-visual data	Recordings of every CLERAC class
		Audio Teacher/Researcher journal
		Recordings made by students as part of coursework
		Recordings of students on-task
		Ad-Hoc interviews conducted whilst monitoring the students
	Institutional end of course (EOC) evaluation questionnaire	End of course evaluation done by the students anonymously when the teacher/researcher was not present and conducted by the institution
Data collected after the CLERAC course (August 2012–June 2015)	Academic writing	My own published or in-progress academic writing that mentions the CLERAC course
	Journal reflections and narrative (as opposed to field notes)	Notes and observations made subsequently and transcribed as teacher/researcher journal entries, many of which use stimulated recall
	Student follow-up emails/meetings	Includes both coincidental and solicited reflections from students after the course. Meetings were only conducted with one participant (Mr Charge)

and wrote a summary transcript which I added to the written journal in order to make it searchable and run queries from NVivo.

Mainly, I prioritised certain data types over others as well. For example, I decided not to listen back to all of the class audio, just the recordings which seemed particularly important.

Another way I have analysed the data is by talking to people about it. For example, despite not being a teacher herself, my wife has been an important person in helping me 'talk things into understanding' (Mann, 2002 p. 195). In particular, I made a special effort to have more social contact with colleagues and other teachers, in which we nearly always 'talk shop'. I would often note down things from these informal social gatherings. I have also made more formal attempts to collaboratively reflect on my practice by joining a research group at my university. Also, my own academic writing (although mainly authored individually) always goes through a process of review, and on occasion I have written collaboratively. This also counts (although often indirectly) towards the analysis of the work I am doing on the current inquiry. Presenting at conferences is similarly collaborative in this respect. This is also something recently advocated in the data-driven approach to Reflective Practice by Walsh and Mann (2015).

3.5.3 *The excavation process*

As I was preparing this chapter I returned constantly to the data I had collected and the notes I had made throughout this process. I often felt lost in the data, and I experienced a 'terrible sinking feeling' when I realised I had just too much data.

> As data accumulate, their magnitude and fragmentary randomness can overwhelm you. Although data collection still continues, it is high time to organize your ever-growing data and move forward with steps of turning data into autoethnography.
>
> (Chang, 2008, p. 113)

At times this process was more like an archaeological excavation than anything else. This is because I did not always know what I would find, or even where to look. Looking back in 2016 on data collected in 2014, the sense of time having passed began to feel very important. It was extremely difficult at times to retrieve all the data.

For the purposes of illustrating the excavation process, I would like to share one particular sequence in the retrieval of pedagogical data. Many of the reaction papers and reflections on class were submitted to the virtual learning environment, Moodle. I had left these documents on the Moodle because this seemed preferable as they were organised, time-stamped, searchable and easily accessible. However, on one day in January 2016 when I came to search back through them, I found that only 14 people had actually done the end-of-semester diagnostic exam, which was worth 10 per cent of the grade for the semester, contingent on them having completed it. At first, I found this odd, but fortunately I had only just finished listening to the last day of the spring semester's class audio, in which I was carefully going around the class, speaking to each student in turn with a clipboard and spreadsheet containing ticks next to their names and detailing which of the numerous assignments were missing. Cross-referencing with this, I soon discovered that the missing assignments had in fact been submitted, but they had been deleted from the system because the students' enrolments had expired from the VLE. After a complicated process of sifting through the system settings, I was finally able to recover the lost data by manually re-enrolling the students and ticking a small check-box to attempt to recover previous grades.

I recount this story because it shows just one instance of the way the data and I interacted. During these interactions I not only learned about the systems I was using (be they computer based or a form of physical note keeping), but I also learned more about the *process* of autoethnography, of Reflective Practice and of data collection. These are valuable lessons, and I felt documenting them was as important as finding the original data. However, again this makes it very hard as a researcher to draw the line as to when the data collection stops and the analysis begins.

3.6 Summary

This section's purpose is to firmly state and justify my research design. I wanted to make sure that the research methods chapter was not just another literature review focusing on research paradigms, and as such I have tried not to go into unnecessary detail about the different approaches which I might have chosen. An important element in both the inquiry's data collection techniques and write-up are informed by work on Narrative Inquiry, and therefore the story of how my research evolved into its current shape is an integral part of the overall research design.

The time frame of this section's narrative is much longer than the main narrative which follows in the next two chapters. However, what follows is the crux of this study and the main source of both data and analysis.

Notes

1 Ellis is using the term 'exploratory research' to refer to Exploratory Practice here. The terms can be confusing, which is why in this book I use the term 'Exploratory Practice' to avoid ambiguity and differentiate between exploratory research, which could refer to unfinished research or research which is exploratory in nature.

2 Please note these comments were made before the BREXIT referendum and the 2016 US elections.

4   Spring semester

4.1 Overview and syllabus

The first CLERAC class in the spring semester was conducted on 16/04/2014 (09.15–10.45), and the last (the 28th class) on 18/07/2014. The total amount of teaching time was 42 hours (28 × 90 mins). The number of students was 25, and all the students passed the semester and continued to study with me in autumn.

The focus of this semester is to prepare the students for the more content-focused classes which start in autumn. In order to do this, the spring semester has a language-based focus and aims to teach academic skills (writing a short research paper with citations, listening to lectures and taking notes), but also with a strong communicative element.

Teachers are required to design their own syllabus around the clear guidelines set by CLER. I opted to structure my classes around interrelated content-topic areas, which would change roughly every two weeks and involve students doing their own research that could then be used as a focus for final projects. CLER stipulates that students must write a 400-word report and give a five-minute presentation, but because my class would spend half the semester (every Friday) in a CALL room, I decided to make more use of the computers by replacing the presentation with a group video project. This had a lot in common with the DCT course mentioned in the introduction as the initial impetus for my inquiry. Since that class, I have done many video projects with students, so I felt confident that, with the time in the CALL room and my experience, I could encourage the students to produce a high-quality video project. As outlined in the participants section (3.4.2), all but two of the students in my CLERAC class were from the Faculty of Science and Technology, and thus I felt that, like English, using computers would be a particularly important life skill for them.

The syllabus was constructed around the following topics:

1. World English: Explanation of English as an international language, introduction to the World Englishes debate, discussion of English as a lingua franca.
2. Online Security: Examination of online security issues and identity, especially focusing on *digital shadow* and communication change through technology exposure.

3. Real or Fake?: Students try to determine the difference between real and fake photographs, then create their own real or fake stories.
4. Fallacies in a logical argument: Discussion of critical thinking skills, debating skills.
5. Final Video Projects: Students choose their own topics and create a video around the theme in groups. This is assessed as a final project. The 400-word research essay is also based on the same topic.

The original syllabus (see Appendix 1) contained several additional topics not covered in the final course, and not all of them had an equal amount of class time. This was because of the flexible, student-centred and emergent nature of the course as I began to focus on personalising the content in order to highlight authenticity and develop mutually motivating content. Topics for the Final Video Project became very diverse. Most students worked in groups, although there were three students who chose to work on their own (lone).

Towards the end of semester, assessments inevitably became foregrounded, and there were many different types of assessment, requiring careful record keeping and grading to ensure each student met the requirements. Assessments were somewhat further complicated by my choice to include a number of alternative assessment approaches, one of which was the self-assessments used to calculate class participation, which was generally complemented by reaction papers which the students composed on the class Moodle. One important justification for these assessments, which came to my attention later, is Ushioda's (2014) call for classwork that highlights metacognition (in terms of thinking about the aims of class) in order to help learners sustain higher levels of motivation. Self-assessment is also advocated as part of an Exploratory Practice framework (Allwright & Hanks, 2009). Another form of alternative assessments were the diagnostic exams, required for the students to earn 10 per cent of their grade, but only awarded for taking the test independently of the students' actual score. These types of assessment were consciously developed in order to foster the students' autonomy as language learners. Another aspect of how I tried to maintain motivation and create an environment of authenticity was based around the concept of the Language Impetus Triad detailed in Chapter 2. These assessment types will be covered in more detail later in this section as they both form the nucleus of important critical incidents and serve as indicators to motivational synergy, especially as a form of feedback between teacher and student.

What follows is the chronological narrative of the spring semester, with certain critical incidents and snapshots given a more detailed focus so as to highlight the most salient parts of the inquiry as they relate to authenticity and teacher-student motivational synergy. In this way, the narrative is presented from the perspective of an 'analytical lens' (Ushioda, 2015, p. 51) which moves in and out of focus, closing in and on the events that would seem most to indicate the synergistic relationship between teacher and student motivation at the heart of this study.

4.2 Initial conditions: the first class

The first day of class is very important in terms of establishing group dynamics, behavioural norms and the learners' attitudes towards the class (Dörnyei & Murphey, 2003; Murphey et al., 2012). In dynamic approaches, initial conditions are defined by Verspoor (2015) as 'the moment one starts measuring', yet she points out that there is a huge amount of inherent variability amongst our learners at this initial state. This snapshot then represents my attempt to understand something of the initial conditions and various attitudes of my learners towards English. I personally find that I will often use the first class as a kind of barometer, and indeed many of our initial impressions and first assumptions, whether accurate or not, will be laid down in the first lesson – both for the students and the teachers. I will return to these issues as I attempt to identify what the attractor states for my CLERAC learners were in terms of their motivation to learn English and their attitude towards the class.

On day one of the class, I was very excited. The lesson plan was to introduce myself (get the students to like me), go over the syllabus (so they had a good idea of what was expected of them, alleviating uncertainty and fear) and then collect some pedagogical data, or a task I had identified as a PEPA. My idea was to have the students draw their Relationship to English as a Diagram (RED) and then explain in English to their partners what they had drawn.

As I taught the class, I used a collar microphone and a digital voice recorder to create an audio file of the entire lesson. From the audio recording of the first class, it is clear that I handed out the syllabus even before the bell went, and chatted to the students, saying, 'It's hot' and 'Could you open the window?'. Just after the bell chimes to start the class, I say 'phew' and the window can be heard opening. My first words to the class go as follows:

4.2.1 Classroom extract 101A

(Please see Appendix 3 for transcription conventions.)
Transcript 4:1

1.	RICHARD:	Okay. Good morning everybody
2.	CLASS:	Good morning.
3.	RICHARD:	And welcome to Academic Communication. So, every morning, FIRST period
4.	CLASS:	@
5.	RICHARD:	On a Wednesday AND a Friday
6.	CLASS:	@
7.	RICHARD:	You and me will spend 90 minutes ... ALL semester, both Spring AND Autumn Semester. So we're going to get to know each other very well, we will spend a lot of time er together in this class...

Noticeably my speech is very clear, very few 'ers' or pauses, but actually the speech is very carefully enunciated and there are very minor pauses between most words. It does not sound (to my ear) particularly slowed down, although certainly this is a moderated way of speaking which I have adopted for classes in order to make my speech easier to follow. Also, it is noticeable that there is laughter coming from the students within the first seconds of the class. This was achieved through my emphasis on the first period. Perhaps I had been able to hit on an aspect of the class which the students and I shared our attitudes toward. As outlined in Chapter 2, empathy is an indicator and prerequisite for synergy. I make many jokes in the introduction, and explain why they are lucky to be in this class. This is a standard introduction I have for nearly all my new first-year classes, in which I explain that Sophia is a good university for learning English because it is high in the Japanese league tables. This is important to create a sense of cohesion by activating 'group pride' (Dörnyei, 1997; Levi, 2017), and I usually make a joke about how Sophia is much better than X University, which became a joke that I returned to often throughout the course. I also state that another reason they are lucky is because they have *me* as their teacher, and I joke that I am very handsome, whilst showing Figure 4.1 my slides (in which I do not look handsome).

This show of arrogance actually opens me up as a person, although very carefully. In saying 'I am handsome', I am actually drawing attention rather to the fact that I am below the average age of other university teachers at my institution, and even now I am still the youngest faculty member in our department. Also, this claim to be handsome shows me as fallible, something I feel is important so that the students feel able to question me and relate to me as an actual person (Glatthorn, 1975).

Later, I asked the students:

> Who speaks good Japanese? *Nihongo pera pera* [are you fluent in Japanese]? Raise your hand. [show of hands]
>
> You speak Japanese, why speak English to each other? It's strange. Although it's strange, try to speak English to your partner, it's the best way to practise. Some Japanese is okay. 20 per cent Japanese, 80 per cent English.

Figure 4.1 'I am handsome' joke

I then set up the task where students have to introduce themselves to their partner in English. After the introduction, I ask for a show of hands for 'who spoke 80 per cent English', and then 'who spoke 80 per cent Japanese?', and from the laughter, it seems more hands went up for the latter. After this I said 'Ah well, it's the first class', as if in consolation. Again, this shows how I tried to create from the very first class an environment of honesty and trust, with mutual empathy. During the class I also made several references to myself as a learner of Japanese, even saying occasional phrases in Japanese (as in the above extract when I say *Nihongo pera pera?*). Just after this, I say:

> Hands up if you have a good partner. Ha, your hand was the last up! [class laughter] I'm sure he's a good partner.

Here is an example of my teasing the students or using that type of humour which is often found in British stand-up comedy. Although I did not realise it at the time, this might be my own attempt to orient the class to my own sense of humour, a key aspect in rapport building (Haugh, 2010; McCulloch, 2012; Medgyes, 2002). Perhaps more broadly, this is also an attempt to establish my own cultural identity. Medhurst (2007) argues that the distinctly British sense of humour is an essential part of cultural identity, and comedy has always been a central part of my own identity; often being a talking point between friends and family and deeply embedded in my own social development. The humour I exhibit in the above extract is very gentle teasing and not particularly face-threatening, although it does draw on a potentially awkward scenario where a person may not really like their partner. In drawing attention to this possibility, I think I was actually trying to diffuse such a situation by making a joke about it. Just before this, I had gone around the room and monitored the students as they introduced themselves to each other. For many of them, they did not know each other and so they were meeting for the first time. Others already knew each other (perhaps from being in the same department, they would know each other only slightly from orientation camp), but few if any of them would know their other classmates well. This is important to acknowledge when teaching a class of mixed-major first-year university students. However, the seating arrangements and pairings rarely changed from this initial class, as I discussed in Chapter 3.

After this introduction task, I found myself explaining to the class about how the CLERAC course was brand new, and very different from the previous year. I told them that last year, my class had 40 students, and now this was reduced to 25 (some of the students could be heard making surprised exclamations in the background). I explained this new course was very exciting, reiterating that they were lucky to be in the class. Again, this could have contributed to the creation of group coherence by highlighting unique features in the context.

Shortly after this, I ask, 'What does compulsory mean?' I ask a student (Ms Oldriver?) to explain, and she says the word in Japanese (although, she said *Hisshu*, which means required). I then elaborate:

So it means you *have* to come to this class. So, you have to come to this class, so I want to make it fun.

Then I explain about the rule that below 85 per cent attendance results in an F, making a joke that even if they give me 10,000 yen, I still have to say no. I explain that the attendance rule is 'not my rule' but CLER's rule, although I have to be 'strict' about it. This way I distance myself from the rules that I represent, showing that 'I am just doing my job, I'm not a bad guy', again showing how I attempt to build rapport with them by downplaying my situated identity and role as the teacher.

I explain about the pair-work approach which I use in class, although by now they have already experienced it. Constantly throughout the class I ask questions and then say 'ask your partner', which is the students' cue to begin a discussion about the question I just modelled. Most of the communication is done between learners and their partner. I say it is their job to find people they like, who 'work hard' and that they want to communicate with.

After going over the class rules, I ask students to create their own class rules, one for themselves and one for the teacher, which I then go around and monitor. Students had trouble making 'rules for the teacher', but when I pushed, asking individual pairs, 'What do you think makes a good teacher?', one pair said, 'kindness' and another said 'enjoy'. When one pair (Ms Lovehouse?) said, 'remember the names [of students]', I became very excited and explained that I also think this is important. Shi (2002) presents a narrative of her experience as a language teacher, talking specifically about her approach to names. She states that remembering a person's name is essential in building a bond with that person, which I agree with completely. However, I work with over 100 different students each semester, mostly for a period of just 14 weeks, after which I may not work with them again. Thus, I have a system for remembering students' names which involves creating a map of where they are sitting. After four to six weeks, I usually know most of the students' names, but if I meet them out of context I can rarely recall their names. I did not explain all this, but I did take the opportunity to explain that it would take me some time to learn all the names, but that I would certainly try. I would probably have also made a mental note to remember that student's name, which is why I seem to recall it was Ms Lovehouse, although sadly I cannot be fully sure as the audio recording is quite distorted by the background noise of the class.

After going around a few pairs and giving a few minutes for this task, I go back to the front and sum up the rules, especially the ones for the teacher. I explain about the rule for enjoying class, saying, 'It's my job to make the class enjoyable, I'll try that'. I then tell the students about remembering names. I say to them, 'You should also try to remember my name', at which point I realise that I have not yet even told the students *my name*! By now, this is 30 minutes into the class. I also have not yet taken the attendance register (although I have explained the 85 per cent attendance rule). This seems to fluster me a moment, and I announce that I will take the register shortly (saying, 'don't let me forget' as if some of the onus is also on the students, which of course it really is not).

Before taking attendance, I finish off my explanation of the style of the class and the rules. I also briefly discuss the issue of sleeping in class. I warn them I will take a photo and upload it to Facebook if they sleep, which elicits laughter and a few 'e::::::h' noises, although it is, of course, a bluff.

I take attendance 30 minutes into the class. Going over the attendance list seems to suddenly remind the class I am a teacher and highlight my institutional power over them and my role as a marker, a grader and a kind of gatekeeper. The attendance register invokes and foregrounds my situational identity as the teacher (Zimmerman, 1998). This is why I consciously avoided doing that until I had built a rapport with them and spoken to them one-to-one before this. However, it is rather naive of me to assume that this was a latent identity until now, when of course the entire class has been led and controlled by me, and to some extent by the institution I work for. Of course, there are other political factors involved which may or may not be in the students' minds during this, such as the position of English as an international language and the educational requirements set out by the Japanese Ministry of Education (MEXT), which is tied to university funding and subsidies (even for private universities like Sophia). These issues will resurface in Chapter 6.

After taking attendance, I go over the assessment weighting by saying, 'the most important thing, how to pass this course'. I explain about the mid-semester and final exams, modifying this by telling them that I have done the Japanese Language Proficiency Test (JLPT) so I know how they feel. This attempt at solidarity is unfortunately ingenuous (or inauthentic?) not only because there really is very little at stake for me when taking the JLPT, and because I chose to take it to test my own proficiency as a diagnostic exam, but also because it contradicts what I say to them in lesson 108A when we discuss the mid-semester exam.

With the overview of the syllabus complete, I move into the next task, which is the Relationship to English Diagram (RED). This was a task designed to get the students talking about how they see English in relation to themselves, but rather than explaining this in words, I wanted them to draw a diagram which would not only transcend some of the linguistic limitations of expressing themselves but also provide a multi-modal data type for analysis later. Without my realising it at the time, this task was also a good way of developing the students' view of English and the 'imagined community' in which it is spoken (Anderson, 2006; Kanno & Norton, 2003; Norton, 2001).

4.2.2 Discussing the REDs

In setting up the task I provide a handout with clear instructions to each student. I also explain the task verbally, giving examples of 'crazy' things they could draw. I do not, at this point, tell them that they will have to explain what they have drawn. I do not want them to know that at this point, as it might limit what they decide to draw. I give five minutes for the activity, which is done in silence. To ease the silence and relax them, I play Bach's cello concertos in the background. The atmosphere is calm and pleasant. I think this downtime helps the students recharge their communicative batteries. Then, after the five minutes, I say, 'Turn to your partner and say, "Hey, check out this. I drew this because…"'

Within a few seconds, the class is very noisy again (perhaps noisier than ever) with many outbreaks of laughter as students show their drawings. I begin to monitor these discussions, which I present alongside the drawing.

4.2.2.1 *Mr Charge*

The first Ad-Hoc interview I have chosen to present in this narrative was with Mr Charge, one of the main Focal Participants from the group. We are discussing his RED (see Figure 4.2).

Ad-Hoc 4.1 101A

1.	RICHARD:	What's your relationship to English like.
2.	MR.CHRG:	Ah. English is the tool that I can connect with foreign people
3.	RICHARD:	A:::::h okay. Yeah that's interesting that you use the word tool. Yea:h I think, I think that's a good explanation. So do you like English?
4.	MR.CHRG:	Yes Very
5.	RICHARD:	Oh good good. Yeah @ that's good. Why do you- Why do you like English?
6.	MR.CHRG:	By using English, I can, I can connect many people
7.	RICHARD:	Aha. Yeah. Oh, that's good. Yeah, maybe on the Friday classes we will try to use English to talk to different people in the world,
		um, using the Internet for example[e
8.	MR.CHRG:	]that's goo[d
9.	RICHARD:	]yeah

Mr Charge mainly wrote his reaction as a paragraph, which he uses to help him when he communicates with me face-to-face. Whether this was intentional or just a result of having already composed the sentence is unclear, but either way Mr Charge is able to convey not only his relatively high ability with English but also his enthusiasm for English and his understanding of English as a tool. When I say, 'that's interesting that you use the word "tool"', I am referring to my understanding of the word 'tool' in the Vygotskian (1964) sense. I instantly liked Mr Charge, and he seemed particularly alert throughout the class. He seemed constantly aware of me, and when I asked him to work with others he would do so, often taking on a kind of leadership role. However, he also remained distant from other members of the class as a whole, as I will examine in later extracts, and only really worked with one other student, his friend Mr Fly. Looking at his RED, Mr Charge has clearly picked up on my joke about being handsome. This emphasis on the teacher is interesting, because I think Mr Charge saw me and liked me instantly as well (just as I took a liking to him). He perhaps saw me as a kind of model, and his engagement with the class could have been due in a large part to his engagement with me.

I am not sure if Mr Charge liked me because he already had a disposition which gave him positive feelings towards English, or if it was more personal than this.

Draw a diagram that shows how you see your relationship to English. Use words and pictures to explain it.

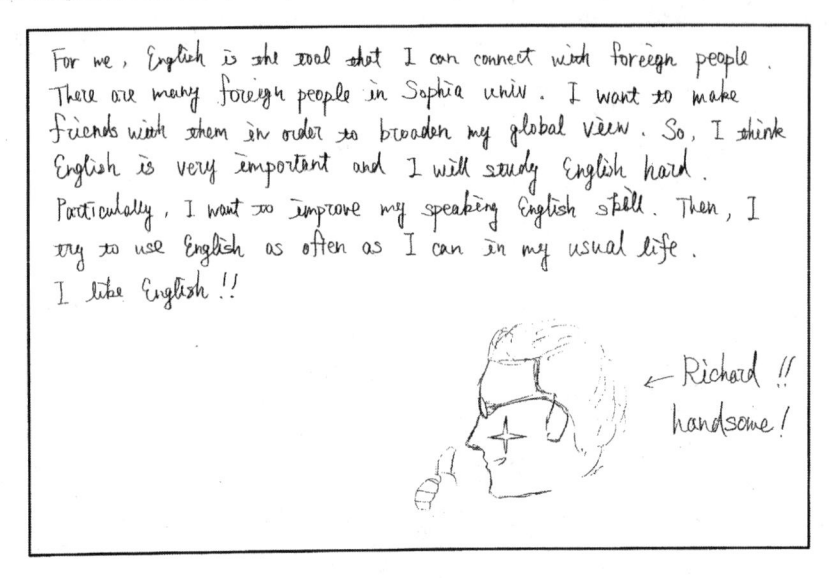

For me, English is the tool that I can connect with foreign people. There are many foreign people in Sophia univ. I want to make friends with them in order to broaden my global view. So, I think English is very important and I will study English hard. Particularly, I want to improve my speaking English skill. Then, I try to use English as often as I can in my usual life. I like English !!

← Richard !!
handsome !

Figure 4.2 Mr Charge's RED

I recorded in my teaching journal that Mr Charge told me later in the year, as we were walking through campus on 10/12/2014, that he is not such a good student in his other classes. Mr Fly also corroborated the fact that Mr Charge does not work so hard in his other classes, and in fact told me that he only works hard in English (lesson 109B). I will discuss this in more detail later, but at least we can observe that right from the start, for Mr Charge, English was not merely an abstract subject, and he seemed (at least to me and from my analysis of his work) to have a good sense of his identity as a speaker of English. One notable feature of our discussion are the parts which slightly overlap each other's utterances in turns seven to nine, indications that the discourse is happening quite quickly and naturally. His ability to express himself probably feeds back into his motivation to study, and from this high position he continued to make progress and maintained his high motivation until the end of the course. Then he went to study abroad in the United States. I also met Mr Charge three times in 2016 when we had an informal chat over coffee, and I was able to learn more about his studies and how his English had progressed, which I will discuss later in the narrative. In his learner biography, Mr Charge states:

> The world is becoming more global. In fact, there are many foreign people in Sophia univ. So I am studying English in order to make friends with them and understand the way they think or their culture.
>
> (Thursday, 17/04/2014, 10:07 PM)

Mr Charge seemed to maintain his high level of motivation throughout the course (generally). However, as this was noticeable from the very outset, it might be explained in relation to factors which have nothing to do with my class:

> A learner who has been highly motivated to learn a language over the course of a few years is not likely to change much, even if he has a negative experience with that language during the course of the study. On the other hand, a learner who is highly motivated to study an L2, but is still at the early stages of his study, may be completely discouraged after one strong negative event.
>
> (Verspoor, 2015, p. 45)

Verspoor is discussing attractor states and initial conditions in dynamic approaches, and thus, in order to truly know more about Mr Charge's motivation, I would need to know more about his learner history in detail. Much later, on 02/10/2014, Mr Charge wrote in the Coffee Room that 'I learned grammar, idioms and reading skills before entering university, but now that I think these are not useful at all in the communication with foreigners. It is the English communication skills that I eager to get.' In our informal discussions, Mr Charge told me that he did not like his previous English classes and he also made English education in Japan the topic for his essay and final video project, in which he again voiced a certain degree of dissatisfaction. This perhaps suggests that, at least with Mr Charge and other highly motivated students, CLERAC was successful in achieving synergy because our aims for learning were largely convergent from the beginning.

4.2.2.2 Ms Downtree

I then began to speak with another Focal Participant, Ms Downtree. Again, Ms Downtree was highly motivated, as was her friend Ms Oldriver, and both sat near the front of the classroom. Early on, I learned that both have the opportunity to use English in their part-time jobs at McDonald's and Starbucks respectively, which they also signal in their respective REDs (Figures 4.3 and 4.4).

Ad-Hoc 4.2 101A

1.	RICHARD:	Hi, what about you guys, what's your relationship to English like
2.	MS.DWN/OLD?:	En... Uh....Like. Like dakedo ((however)) (?although)...(undistinguishable)
3.	RICHARD:	G- good?
4.	MS.DWN:	I like English
5.	RICHARD:	Oh, good good good. Why why do you like English?
6.	MS.DWN/OLD?:	It's so fun [giggling]
7.	RICHARD:	@ Good good @

8.	MS.DWN:	I speak English when I work in Star[bucks
9.	RICHARD:	]oh righ[t
10.	MS.DWN:	]arubaito
		((part time)) @
		hahaha[ha
11.	RICHARD:	]
		ahhh of course yeah
12.	?:	(indistinguishable) [laughing and giggling] @
13.	MS OLDR:	(?I too). Me too. I work in McDonald
14.	RICHARD:	Oh really. Okay so you get a lot of foreigners where you work. OK. So that's good. So, you try to speak English when you have foreigners in the class… ah… in in your shops.
15.	MS.DWN/OLD?:	Shops?
16.	RICHARD:	Oh that's good that's fantasti[c
17.	MS.DWN/OLD?:	]goo:d goo:d
18.	RICHARD:	So you have a real connection to English then.
19.	MS.DWN/OLD?:	Thank you

Noticeable here is the amount of laughing and giggling that goes on. The two girls speak together, unlike the conversation with Mr Charge where his friend Mr Fly remains silent and just listens. The two girls have their part-time jobs in common, and I actually make a mention of this incident in my teaching journal entry after the class, remarking:

Draw a diagram that shows how you see your relationship to English. Use words and pictures to explain it.

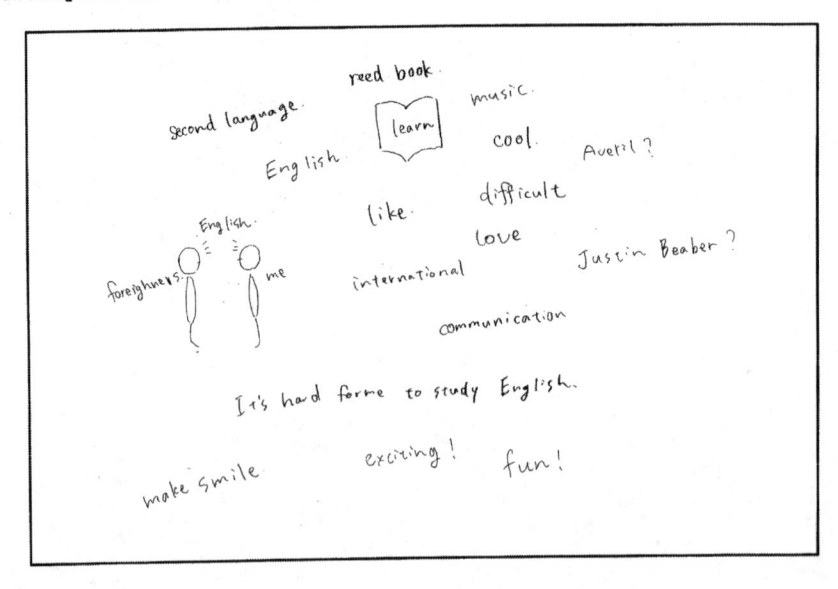

Figure 4.3 Ms Downtree's RED

Draw a diagram that shows how you see your relationship to English. Use words and pictures to explain it.

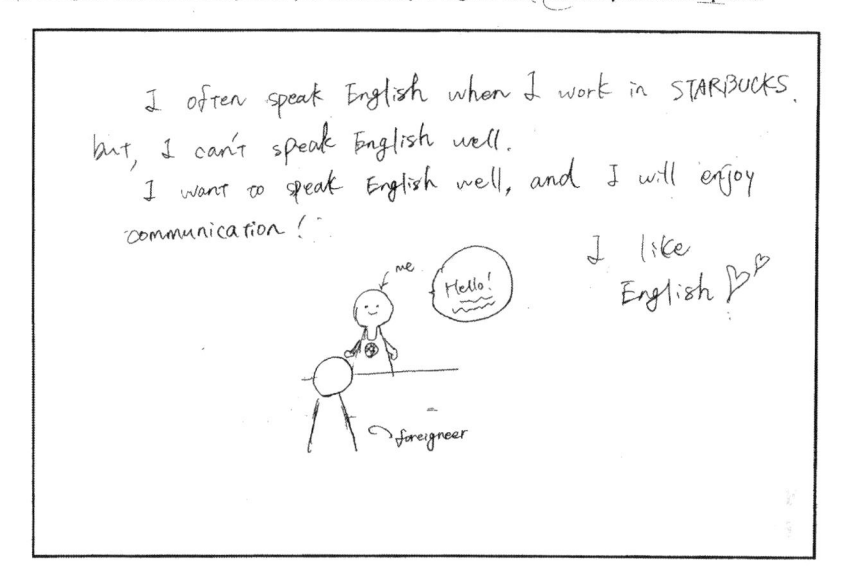

Figure 4.4 Ms Oldriver's RED

Two girls sat in the middle use English in their jobs at Starbucks and McDonald's. Mental note: they seem to like their jobs and it gives them contact with foreigners so try not [to be too negative about] the big corporations too much! Especially McDonald's!

(TRJournal 16/04/2014)

This is because I am often quite outspoken in my anti-consumerist views and I have a particular disdain for McDonald's, both as a food and a business. I later would teach lessons which touched on this subject in the autumn semester.

Although less clear from the transcript, there is something quite flirtatious about the girls' manner, especially Ms Oldriver. Although I was only able to reproduce it slightly, if listening carefully to the recording, it is possible to make out that one of the speakers (or both) are parroting my phrases a little, such as in turn 17. This was happening a little throughout the discussion, and suggests a kind of light teasing which definitely has a flirtatious undertone. I really know very little about Ms Downtree's life outside the class, but in another Ad-Hoc interview on 28/10/2014, whilst discussing a Halloween party, I called Ms Downtree a 'party animal' and Ms Oldriver replied that she was a 'party fox' (creatively altering the expression and referring to her costume). At this point, Ms Downtree was showing me photos on her phone of her fancy dress outfit. Of course, my manner was always kept very professional and I never met the girls outside of the class. And yet, the flirting taking place in the class seems to be very relevant, and certainly draws parallels with the research of Bailey (2006, 2007), Kelsky (2001) and Takahashi (2013), who have examined the concept of *akogare* (admiration/desire) in Japanese women towards foreign culture and men in particular. Although the interaction was very innocent, there was certainly an underlying sense of *akogare* here, and I know that Ms Downtree was a member of the Foreign Circle, which meant she attended many parties with international students, where she would certainly come into contact with foreign men. This shows her independent resourcefulness in finding opportunities not just to use English but also to actually form friendships and possibly romantic relationships with people in English.

4.2.2.3 Mr Auxiliary

Overall, as I walk around the class during this task, there is a real sense of fun and engagement. As I talk to different pairs, the rapport building and joking are quite evenly distributed. There is a lot of background noise and outbursts of laughter. I then move towards the back of the class, where the third of my Focal Participants is sitting, Mr Auxiliary. A quick glance at his RED (Figure 4.5), which depicts English as a snake and himself as prey, shows clearly his trepidation about being in the class.

Ad-Hoc 4.3 101A

1.	RICHARD:	And I have to ask you guys about yours [huh]. You've drawn a… is this a snake?
2.	MR.AUX:	Snake
3.	RICHARD:	So, why did you draw a snake…. Ah, why did you draw a snake
4.	MR.AUX:	English attack me
5.	RICHARD:	Really. And you're a frog? A:w…. Why do you feel English attacks you ((…..5))
6.	RICHARD:	Why does English attack you
7.	MR.AUX:	I can't understand English
8.	RICHARD:	A:h, right. Yeah. Eng-…So English is scary?
9.	MR.AUX:	Scary? (?Scared), yes.
10.	RICHARD:	A:h, now I see. That's a really interesting drawing. [Turning to Mr Auxiliary's partner, Mr Dawn] And you've drawn a stairs… staircase… Wha- What's your relationship to English? ((………………19)) [they speak Japanese quietly]
11.	RICHARD:	Stairs
12.		((………9))
13.	RICHARD:	Ah:, oh:::, I see. And the stairs keep going up. No no no, I like that.

Mr Auxiliary was one of the least communicative students in the class, and he represents a classic stereotype of the uncommunicative Japanese English learner (Apple et al., 2013; Kikuchi, 2013, 2015; Sampson, 2016; Susser, 1998). Despite the fact that Mr Auxiliary was basically always on time, if not one of the first

Draw a diagram that shows how you see your relationship to English. Use words and pictures to explain it.

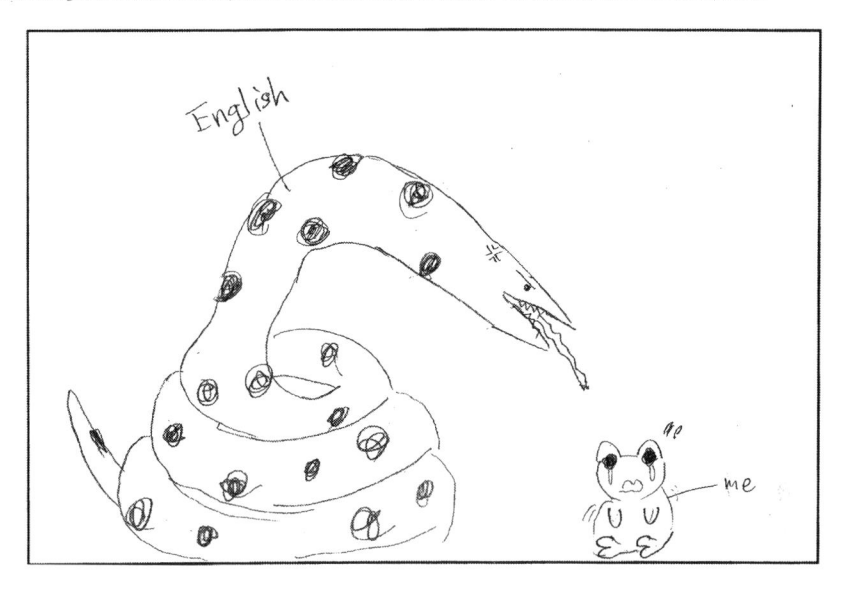

Figure 4.5 Mr Auxiliary's RED

people in the class (he was absent only once), I had to fight against my initial red-flagging of him as a classic 'non communicative' student who just wanted to get a grade at the end, and thought that to do so he just needed to show up and try to stay awake and hand things in on time. In fact, in this way he was a very motivated student and clearly wanted to do well. However, to me he also fit the profile of an 'English Hater' (Erikawa, 2009 cited in Sato, 2015 p.15). He worked hard but seemed very introverted, and whenever I tried to speak to him the dialogue was filled with very long, awkward silences. In contrast to the studies of silence in Japanese university English teaching, such as those by King (2013a, 2013b, 2016b), it was generally unusual for students not to respond in CLERAC. Despite his lack of communication, in every other way Mr Auxiliary was, however, a truly good student, and I am interested in him because he is quite representative of certain stereotypes of the Japanese university English learner, and despite the negative image of this stereotype, I want to highlight the many positive aspects he brought to the class.

Mr Auxiliary's RED is certainly my favourite one from the entire group. It shows a genuine sense of the discomfort that many students must feel when they encounter English. After all, being in the classroom (especially the foreign language classroom) is a *face-threatening* act (van Dam, 2002). Mr Auxiliary was not only uncommunicative in English, but listening back to his recordings while he was on-task in the CALL room, and having observed him in class talking to other students, he rarely spoke in either English or Japanese (see Section 5.8.1). He seemed to be quite introverted and shy as a person, and I can imagine he felt very left out and dreaded the English classes. It is quite likely he sat at the back of each class wishing that he could be more communicative, but that just was not part of who he is and for whatever myriad of reasons he could not do it. However, he did manage to 'survive' the class, and because of this inquiry and my heightened state of reflexivity (a theme I will discuss in Chapter 6), I made allowances for him and did not try to push him too hard. He managed to get an 'A' for the class because he followed instructions and because he did all the work to the best of his (admittedly limited) ability. In his learner biography after the first class, he wrote:

> I have studied English for 6 years.
> I want to go to England and watch Arsenal's football game someday.
> I hope to learn the way of talking with English people.
> I want to enjoy class.
>
> (Thursday, 17 April 2014, 9:25 PM)

Interestingly, the final statement about wanting to 'enjoy class' corresponds with my philosophy of teaching and the teach/learn dichotomy (see Section 6.6.2). Mr Auxiliary actually reveals a strong future self-image here in terms of his motivation, although in order to achieve this he would not actually require particularly high proficiency. This has some connection with a study by Matsuda (2011), in which one of her teacher/participants explained that not all students need to become fully proficient in English, and that 'not everyone can be a star' (p. 45). Mr Auxiliary's perceived reticence and 'unwillingness to communicate', rather than being a lack of motivation, is much more complex than this and probably dependent on personal differences. I do not believe he was simply a demotivated student, as is commonly argued with learners matching his profile (Apple et al., 2013), as I will examine later.

4.2.3 The reality of classroom data

During these Ad-Hoc interviews, it became very hard to hear the students in the recordings due to there being a great deal of background noise. Students were loudly talking in both English and Japanese, but towards the end Japanese seems to dominate. However, overall the class appears to have gone very well, and I collected enough data in one class to almost conduct an entire independent study.

The sheer size of this section illustrates very clearly other logistical issues which came to light during the analysis, namely, the issue of word limits and too much data. This section omits many of the important Ad-Hocs (for example Focal Participant Mr Po) and could easily go into more detail about each learner. However, this was just one of 55 classes.

4.3 Global English, authenticity and native-speakerism

In the second lesson of the course (the first lesson in the CALL room, 101B, Friday 18/04/2014), I introduced the topic of global English, featuring an adapted version of Kachru's circles of English (1988), in which students have to match the countries to their respective circles (inner, outer and expanding). I then show the following statement:

> The future status of English will be determined less by the number and economic power of its native speakers than by the trends in the use of English as a second language.
>
> (Graddol, 2003, p. 157)

We discuss the meaning of these words, and I emphasise the students' importance and ownership of the English language. Throughout the lesson, and after each task, students have a chance to discuss their reaction with their partner. This is very much a lesson in which I attempt to *condition* the students to be more accepting of international varieties of English, in which I attempt to empower them as L2 speakers of English and in which I attempt to open up the reality of English as a lingua franca and a global international language. This is really one of my most developed lessons, one I have taught to other classes many times. However, I felt I underused the CALL room facilities and thus the environment was not as good as it had been on Wednesday.

In the lesson after this (102A), I play a TED.com video lecture of Jay Walker talking about English Mania. This is a continuation of the theme of empowerment and an attempt to purge the embedded native-speakerism which is so deeply entangled with English instruction in Japan and also in other countries as well (Houghton & Rivers, 2013; Kim, 2011; Lowe & Pinner, 2016).

One important point from my journal is that in lesson 102A, during an Ad-Hoc interview with Ms Downtree and her friend Ms Oldriver, I realised how little impact my efforts in these two classes had really made. As I learned in lesson 101A, Ms Downtree works at McDonald's and Ms Oldriver at Starbucks. Both girls like their job because it gives them opportunities to use English. Ms Oldriver told me during her class about a recent exchange with an American customer who she said 'forgave' her for her 'incorrect English'. I found this rather sad, as she said it towards the end of the class and after I had exerted so much energy in trying to explain that there is no such thing as *correct English* (although this is an oversimplification I use to empower the students). In my journal I recounted another story I learned:

> [Ms Downtree] said she went to a party [as part of the international circle which she recently joined] which was made up of around 50% foreigners [non-Japanese]. She was very motivated and had joined an international circle based on the World English lesson and she was super-motivated. Then, at the end of the class I asked her how to improve listening and despite all said about World English she replied 'listen to Native Speakers, listen to Richard's class.' Native speakers still dominated her idea of English.
>
> (TRJournal 23/04/2014)

The theme of embedded native-speakerism became one of the major causes of divergence in motivational synergy, as this was an area which tied in strongly with my philosophy of teaching and was at the heart of my teaching persona, yet it seemed that the students could not all shake the monocentric view of English and the self-discriminatory preference for 'standard' varieties.

4.4 Authenticity of the speaker-ranking activity

The prominence of globalisation in the discourse surrounding language teaching and motivation means that students' reasons for learning English, both now in the late 2010s and in the foreseeable future, will necessarily be quite different from learners of the past. Advances in technology, the increase in travel opportunities and the need for English in order to compete for jobs in the workplace and the global market all have made a significant contribution to the reshaping of the language learner's motivational landscape (Ushioda, 2013b, 2013c). I therefore felt it was important not only to learn how the CLERAC class saw themselves in relation to English but also to explain to them what I felt were the realities of English, which did not always match the way in which English is actually taught (Holliday, 1994, 2005; Pinner, 2016b). This has important implications for motivational synergy as I am exposing the students to my core beliefs about teaching and attempting to align them to it, or more succinctly, this was a very important attempt at convergence and at achieving congruence with the class in terms of my philosophy of teaching. Such a sense of congruence is vital to achieving a sense of authenticity (Dörnyei et al., 2016; Kreber, 2013).

As I explained in the previous section, we had just spent three entire classes talking about the global status of English in which I specifically de-emphasised so-called 'native speaker' varieties. On 25/04/2014, in class 102B I created a task specifically for the CALL room featuring video content and online interaction, designed to expose the students to different varieties of spoken English, which they would then rate according to the simple criteria of 'authenticity'. At this point I also told the students that I was researching authenticity, but I purposefully left the word undefined and very open. I chose eight videos, trying to represent a diverse set of speakers within a limited (and therefore practical) task design. As I will discuss in the next sections, the students tended to favour videos featuring speakers who use the more standard varieties of English, such as that of the Queen of England or Barack Obama.

4.4.1 Authenticity of the speaker-ranking activity

On 25 April, in class 102B (the fourth class) of the spring semester, I wanted to gain another 'snapshot' of the students' attitudes to English as a global language, particularly how this influences their conception of authenticity. I created a task specifically for the CALL room which would feature video content and online interaction but would also expose the students to different varieties of spoken English, which they would then rate according to the simple criteria of 'authenticity', which I purposefully left undefined and very open. I chose eight speakers, trying to create a fairly diverse set of speakers within a limited (and therefore practical) task design. The speakers I chose are listed in Table 4.1, along with the

Table 4.1 Authenticity of the speaker-rating activity

	Speaker	Nationality	EL1/EL2	Average /10	Mode /10	Overall /250
1	Ban Ki-moon	Korean	EL2	5.12	4	133
2	Shinzo Abe	Japanese	EL2	5.54	8	144
3	Arnold Schwarzenegger	Austrian	EL2	5.77	6	150
4	Barack Obama	North American	EL1	6.58	8	171
5	Dynamo	British (Northern)	EL1	7.88	8	205
6	Queen Elizabeth II	British (RP)	EL1	8.58	8	223
7	14th Dalai Lama	China (Tibet)	EL2	8.58	10	223
8	Naomi Watts	British/Australian	EL1	9.00	10	234

average score (out of 10) and their overall score (out of a maximum of 250). The table also indicates whether the speaker can be considered as a speaker of English as their first (EL1) or second (EL2) language, along with their nationality.

The chart below shows the nationality and average rating in visual form, from which it is clear that EL2 speakers were generally rated lower for 'authenticity' than EL1 speakers. The most notable exception is Arnold Schwarzenegger, who many of the students seemed to believe was a 'native speaker' of English, which I will discuss shortly. It should also be pointed out that Steven Frayne (aka Dynamo) is a Northern English magician who was born in Bradford, in the same city and the same year as I was. Dynamo has never publicly discussed his ethnicity, but he has dark skin and that might mean that he does not fit the racial model of a native speaker of English because of the 'tendency to equate the native speaker with white' (Kubota & Lin, 2009a, p. 8), although he is every bit as much a 'native speaker' as I am, in fact more since he still lives in the United Kingdom and probably does not speak the code-switching blend of English and Japanese which I tend to use in my daily life. His inclusion in the task, like all the speakers here, was motivated by a specific intention on my part to test certain working hypotheses about the race and social class of the idea of so-called 'native speakers'. As such, I felt it was notable that Steven Frayne's average was rather low compared to other EL1 speakers (see Figure 4.6).

4.4.1.1 Ban Ki Moon

After each rating, students had to explain their reasons for awarding the speaker that score. The speaker with the lowest average was Korean national and current Secretary-General of the United Nations Ban Ki Moon. This speaker was selected because he most likely would be familiar to the students in CLERAC from news broadcasts. I have seen him on the television in my own home and so I felt he would be known to the students. Also, Korea is often compared with Japan in Japanese media and educational discourse, with the perception being that Koreans have a better system for studying English, which is often traced to superior or

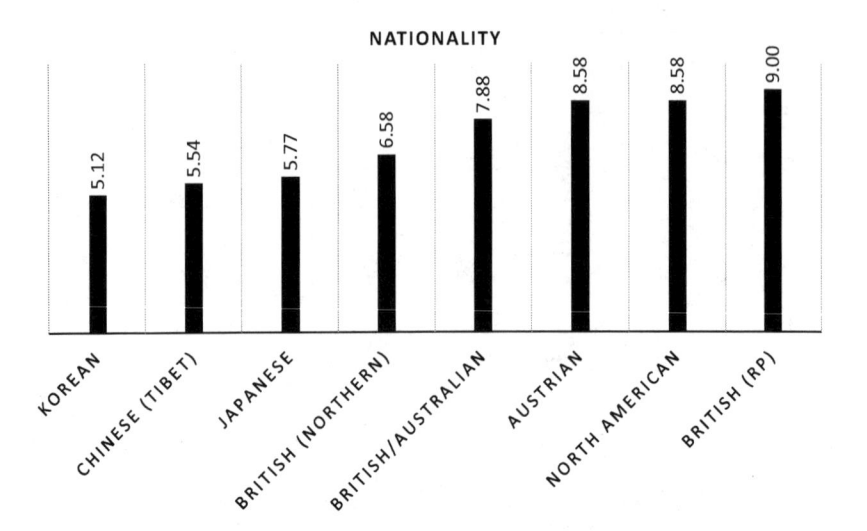

Figure 4.6 Authenticity of the Speaker Rating activity (averages)

more communicative textbooks (Takeda, Choi, Mochizuki, & Watanabe, 2006; Yuasa, 2010). This has been a popular topic for the undergraduate thesis students I supervise in the English Literature Department. Despite this, there are also many similarities with the Japanese and Korean English teaching contexts, and similarities between the Japanese and Korean languages, making it a useful comparison. I will discuss Japan/Korean relations in more detail shortly.

Mr Po rated Ban Ki Moon a 4/10, and when asked to explain the reasons for giving that score, he simply wrote, 'He is Korean.' This shows clearly a form of discrimination against nationalities where English is not an official spoken language.

Ms Smallville had very different perception of Ban Ki Moon's English, awarding him an 8/10 because 'His English is formal and like native speakers!' It is noticeable that Ban Ki Moon's high score is attributed to his sounding 'like native speakers', when Ms Pine awarded him a much harsher 2/10 score for exactly the opposite reason, stating that 'He is not good at speaking English natively.'

Mr Widetree awarded Ban Ki Moon the maximum score of 10/10 because 'He is top of United Nations', clearly showing that he had factored in Ban Ki Moon's status and position in his estimation of his authenticity. Ms Lovehouse awarded the speaker an 8/10 for a similar reason, stating that 'He is in a high position.' Somewhat confusingly, Mr Auxiliary also awarded 10/10, but his reason simply stated, 'He reads paper.' This could either mean that Ban Ki Moon was reading from a script (surely, not a good thing?) or that Mr Auxiliary had read about him in the paper, although I feel that Mr Auxiliary would have been able to express that if it truly was what he meant to say. Either way, the score was confusing, until

I noticed that Mr Auxiliary had awarded almost every single speaker a maximum score of 10/10. The only speaker he did not give 10/10 for was the magician Steven Frayne (Dynamo), whom I will discuss shortly.

Another interesting feature of the comments was that the speech patterns or English ability were not the sole criteria the students used to judge levels of 'authenticity'. For example, Ms Forest awarded Ban Ki Moon 4/10, noting that 'He speaks English fluently. But he doesn't make eye contact with people. Because his speech isn't persuasive.' Clearly, authenticity is more closely connected in Ms Forest's mind to the concept of 'sincerity', something Lionel Trilling (1972) has discussed at length but that is worth mentioning here briefly, as this is something I will return to in the Second Stage analysis in Chapter 4. This type of authenticity, which I will refer to for now as non-linguistic authenticity, was quite common, with six out of 25 responses relying on sincerity/authenticity judgements, although the others relied on the linguistic (and therefore native-speakerist) analysis. Mr Charge, who noted from the first class in his RED that he took a very global and practical orientation towards English, did not have very much to say about this speaker. He awarded Ban Ki Moon a 3/10, saying simply, 'His pronunciation of English is not very good.'

Similar to the non-linguistic conception of authenticity, but at the same time potentially very much linked to discriminatory concepts, was Ms Hemp's comment below:

(5) 'I don't think he is poor at speaking English. However, he is a Korean.'

In Japan, there are many issues surrounding the Japanese perception of Koreans and other East Asians, particularly those who immigrate to Japan (Castro-Vázquez, 2013; Schreiber, 2013; Sugimoto, 2010; Tamaki, 2004). In Japan, hatred specific to Korea is called *Ken-Kan* (featuring the kanji characters for hate and Korea respectively). According to Schreiber (2013), writing in *The Japan Times*, anti-Korean sentiments are spreading in particular amongst young Japanese. This could also explain Mr Po's earlier comment of simply 'He's Korean.' Perhaps Mr Po (as a Chinese immigrant in Japan) is trying to express solidarity with his Japanese host country by taking an ironically xenophobic stance, positioning himself as anti-Korean in an attempt to foreground his Japaneseness. However, this is quite frankly a rather small piece of evidence to make such a bold claim on my part, but it would certainly be something that never would have occurred to me if I had not collected this data and conducted a detailed analysis of it. In order to justify any of these observations I would need to do respondent validation. Despite her harsh comment, Ms Hemp, it should be noted, awarded Ban Ki Moon a 5/10, which is not ungenerous and reflects the average score, and is one higher than the mode of responses. In the autumn semester we did look at issues of prejudice, so I will revisit this theme later in the narrative, but I should note here that I doubt any of these students were harbouring strong racist sentiments, although Mr Swamp also said, 'He is a foreign politician' in justifying his low score of 3/10. At the very least, these comments demonstrate that these students lack sensitivity to their words being construed as racist, which might be more related to their English proficiency than their actual beliefs (although see Kubota & Lin, 2006; Kubota & Lin, 2009b; Liggett, 2009; Pinner, 2018a).

4.4.1.2 The Dalai Lama

Mr Po, himself a Chinese national, self-discriminated when he rated the Dalai Lama's extract; the reason for his low score of 3/10 was only one word, 'Chinglish'. Self-discrimination is a term used by Reves and Medgyes (1994), and is a feature that occurs often in the literature on 'non-native speakers'. This is not just speakers being harsh on themselves but also other 'non-native speakers' being particularly challenging towards 'non-native speaker teachers'. It has been pointed out that when so-called 'native speaker' teachers of English make language usage errors or cannot answer a question about grammar, it rarely impacts on their self-image. Conversely, when a 'non-native' English teacher makes a mistake or reveals that they 'do not know everything about the English language, their teaching abilities are often immediately questioned' (Moussu & Llurda, 2008, p. 323). Mr Widetree also seemed to self-discriminate when he stated that 'I feel his English is not good. His English is similar to mine.' However, Mr Widetree awarded the speaker 7/10, which is rather high, and above the average for this speaker (5.54). This is also higher than I would probably award Mr Widetree for his speaking as well, as he was very firmly a middling student in terms of his performance in class (or at least my perception of his performance and the grades I gave him – he took 83 per cent overall for the spring semester, the class average was 91 per cent).

Ms Forest gave the Dalai Lama a score of 1/10, explaining that 'I don't like him. I think he isn't a gentleman.' Mr Mouth also graded the Dalai Lama lowly, giving only a 3/10 because 'He is a suspicious-looking person.' Again, this comment demonstrates the Trillingian concept of sincerity which I have called non-linguistic authenticity. Somewhat similar but taken as a polar opposite, Mr Auxiliary (awarding his usual 10/10) said, 'He looks noble person.' Several other students also judged the Dalai Lama positively in this way. Ms Redslope for example gave him a 7/10 and said, 'I don't know him well. But I think he is a great person.' Mr Charge was unimpressed, however, awarding a 1/10, again judging him purely on his English and stating rather humorously, 'I cannot understand his English. Does he speak English really?' Mr Charge only gave one other minimum score, which was for Shinzo Abe. [omitted from this data due to writing up constraints]

4.4.1.3 Steven Frayne (aka the Magician Dynamo)

As I have already touched upon, Steven Frayne is a British magician, born in Bradford in 1982. I was also born in Bradford in 1982, and although Frayne's accent is perhaps thicker than mine (as I have acculturated mine to my international English teaching context), we have very similar ways of speaking. Frayne was chosen specifically because we speak the same dialect of English and are the same age. It is therefore very interesting to me that Frayne received overall the lowest score of any EL1 speaker. I wondered to what extent this was due to Frayne's ethnicity, which although he is British, he is mixed-race and has slightly dusky skin. In this way, he does not match the predominantly 'white' view of a native speaker (Amin, 1999; Kubota & Lin, 2006; Liggett, 2009; see also Kubota and Lin, 2009a, for edited volume). I also wondered if this might also have somewhat influenced Barack Obama's lower rating than Queen Elizabeth (Obama was given the same rating as Arnold Schwarzenegger [Obama is also omitted due to writing-up constraints]).

Interestingly, when looking over the comments on Frayne's rating, only 3/25 contain a reference to his speech or style of language, and two comments make specific reference to his being a native speaker of English. Those three linguistic authenticity ratings were made by Mr Widetree (9/10), who said, 'It is easy to hear'; Ms Pine (4/10), who said, 'Because he used slang'; and Mr Montville (5/10), who said, 'He doesn't open his mouth so that it's hard to understand what he is speaking.' Although there were two students who mentioned Frayne being a 'native speaker' (Ms Saltfield, 10/10 and Ms Hemp, 7/10), there was a third (Mr Dawn) who gave Frayne 10/10 and said, 'I think all first speaker is "authentic"', which seems to be based on the fact that Frayne is perceived as a 'native speaker'. From this, it seems that Frayne's relatively low authenticity rating was not specifically due to his way of speaking or dialect. The non-linguistic ratings were mainly based on Frayne's ability with magic, which was either rated positively or negatively. Examples of positive ratings were:

'So cool.' (Mr Cloud, 8/10)
'He is very interesting.' (Mr Mouth, 10/10)
'His magic is amazing.' (Mr Cleyera, 10/10)
'His magic is fantastic!' (Mr House, 8/10)
'His magic is nice.' (Mr Charge, 6/10)

From this it is clear that the students enjoyed the video but did not have much to say aside from expressing their enjoyment.

The more negative comments were characterised by the following types of statements:

'He may deceive me.' (Mr Swamp, 1/10)
'He is a magician. He is good at deceiving.' (Ms Oldriver, 5/10)
'He is a magician.' (Mr Wind, 3/10)
'I think he isn't a regular person. He is always full of fun.' (Ms Forest, 3/10)
'He doesn't look sincere.' (Mr Auxiliary, 6/10)

From these comments, we can see that not only do the scores alter greatly even if the students were giving what can be construed as either a negative or positive rating, but also the comments do not offer much insight into the students' perception of this particular speaker. However, Frayne was still awarded a small amount of preferential treatment on account of his perceived 'native speaker' status. The same was also true of Arnold Schwarzenegger.

4.4.1.4 Arnold Schwarzenegger

Schwarzenegger's speech was chosen for several reasons. First he represents an incredibly successful model of a person who has learned English as a second language, and secondly this speech in particular is an extract from the famous motivational speech which he gave as part of his University of Southern California commencement address in 2009. I'm a little embarrassed to say that Schwarzenegger is a personal hero of mine, in fact, and I even have a picture of him on my fridge. This could have influenced the students' in their ratings, as I was going around the class saying 'Arnie... *Schwar-chan*!' (which is the Japanese name for him, -chan being a suffix indicating a close friend). Schwarzenegger got the same average score as President Barack Obama, which is quite a notable achievement, although perhaps not so surprising. However, this high rating can be partly attributed to at least four of the students not knowing that Schwarzenegger has learned his variety of English, as the following comments attest:

> 'I love Arnold Schwarzenegger and He is native English speaker.' (Mr Widetree, 10/10)
> 'He is native and it is easy to hear.' (Ms Smallville, 9/10)
> 'He is a native speaker.' (Mr Dawn, 10/10)
> 'Native speaker, he is stoic, his timing is good.' (Ms Saltfield, 10/10)

This shows that the students were not able to detect the speaker's Austrian/German accent. This not only shows the students' own proficiency in English being inadequate to discern a foreign accent, but it also shows a gap in shared cultural schemata. This is closely linked to my previous discussions of the authenticity gap, when I spoke of *Star Wars* and *Jurassic Park*, which will arise later in the narrative and analysis. In addition, Schwarzenegger received 9/25 (36 per cent) comments relating to his way of speaking or use of language, all of which had positive valence. His other comments were generally positive. The lowest score he got was 6/10 from Ms Lovehouse, who said, 'He use English always.' Many of the positive comments may have mirrored comments I was making as I went around the class:

> 'He is very masculine!' (Mr Charge, 8/10)
> 'He is very nice guy' (Mr Nintendo, 9/10)
> 'I like Arnold Schwarzenegger.:-)' (Mr House, 10/10)
> 'Because I think so' (Mr Swamp, 10/10)

Again, the above comments do not reveal much other than that students may not always base their authenticity rating on linguistic features of a speaker. One of the most interesting comments was made by Ms Chennai, who seemed genuinely moved by the content of the speech:

> I don't know him ever. But after this speech, I know he is very great. I can't have my confidence in myself. But he made me thought I may have my confidence in myself. (9/10)

Although Schwarzenegger received exactly the same average score as Obama (making him joint second place), his mode of responses was slightly lower at 8/10, whereas Obama's was 9/10. The only person whose mode was 10/10 was, of course, the queen.

4.4.1.5 *Queen Elizabeth II*

The queen came out with the highest score, which I must admit felt like I had lost my battle and seemed to be evidence of my failure to convince the students to 'unlearn' the embedded native-speakerism that seemed to dominate much of their attitude to English. Although I doubt very much that the Queen's English is actually what any of my students aspire to sound like, or are likely to encounter in their English-speaking careers, it seems that she still represents the most 'authentic' speaker model to them. Reasons for the queen's high score are exemplified by the following comments, with the score they assigned in brackets and the student's pseudonym:

> 'I want like Queen Elizabeth II. I want to go to England someday.'
> (Ms Chennai, 8/10)
> 'Hers is royal.' (Mr Wind, 10/10)
> 'Se [sic] is more 'authentic' because she must speak collect [sic] English.'
> (Mr Dawn, 10/10)
> 'She is queen' (Mr Auxiliary, 10/10)
> 'She is the queen' (Mr Po, 10/10)
> 'She's a Queen' (Ms Lovehouse, 10/10)
> 'Queen is cute!!!!!!!!! Forever!!!!!!!!!!!!!' (Mr Fly, 10/10)
> 'Her native language is English, and her end of a word is not clear'
> (Ms Hemp, 9/10)

This selection of quotes shows that the students enjoyed seeing a video of the queen. As the reader will notice, the results only raise more questions than they are able to answer. However, a clear preference for unrealistic native models is evident here amongst my students, few of whom had lived abroad, although the student quoted above who gave our beloved yet dispassionate queen a 5/10 had been to Australia for a two-week homestay. The two students in the class who had lived abroad for a longer period of time (Ms Lovehouse and Mr Montville), having attended schools overseas, both assigned the queen a score of 10/10.

4.4.1.6 Language correctness

One reason which may explain the students' preference for the highly standardised (RP) model of the queen is the 'Language Correctness Act', which is in place in Japanese education. This is an official policy by the central government to teach 'standard Japanese' at schools, which actually explicitly disparages regional varieties (Heinrich, 2012; Sugimoto, 2010). Not only this, but as most television shows, news broadcasts and newspapers are edited in Tokyo, 'the Japanese public is constantly fed views of the world and of the nation that are constructed, interpreted, and edited in Tokyo' (Sugimoto, 2010, p. 72). This act gives a great deal of influence to the way class and language are perceived in Japan, which no doubt would have an influence on class perception in English. In another study (Pinner, 2013a) I found that students' ideas about authenticity in English were often tied to the notion of 'correctness' and even 'dictionaries'. At the time I did not realise it, but both these findings may be linked to the issue of Japan's overall suppression of regional dialects and the highly political enforcement of the idea that there is, in fact, a single 'correct' way of speaking. This ties in with Bourdieu's notion of 'cultural capital' (1991), which has been linked to language motivation by a number of scholars (Block, 2014; Lowe & Pinner, 2016; Norton, 2013; Norton Peirce, 1995).

4.4.1.7 Overview

I added up the average scores for EL1 and EL2 speakers, and the results are shown in Figure 4.7.

I would again like to highlight that this experiment was conducted directly after several lessons in which I explained about the importance of global English and in which I attempted to empower my learners as speakers of an international

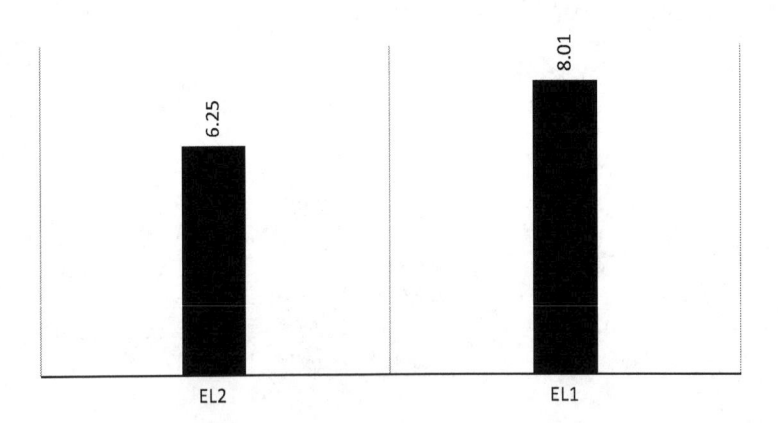

Figure 4.7 Averages for EL2 and EL2

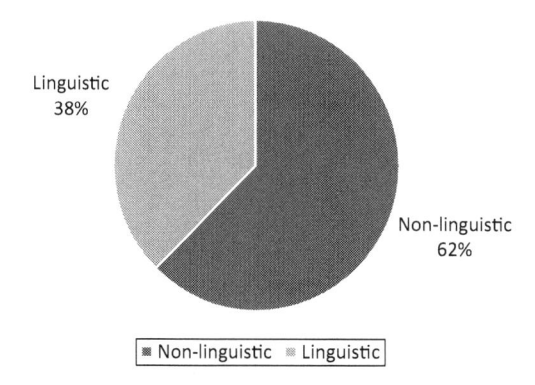

Figure 4.8 Authenticity judgements

variety of English. I think that this shows the deep level of ingrained preference towards 'native speaker' varieties. As I have already stated, this task was designed as a snapshot, but I am (and was even directly after the lesson) none the wiser as to what it means. I also counted up how many of the authenticity ratings were based on linguistic considerations and how many based on 'sincerity' or non-linguistic aspects (see Figure 4.8).

Interestingly, despite the ingrained native-speakerism present in many of the comments, the overall summary of the comments seems to indicate that authenticity is primarily a non-linguistic construct for the students, with many 'authenticity' ratings being based on a personal response to the speaker and the content of their speech.

The task was basically much too simple and the instrument much too blunt to ever really hope to gain any specific insights into the nature of authenticity and the orientation of my students towards English. In many ways, the task was mainly a reflective tool for me in order to show areas for deeper focus.

In addition to the videos, I adapted the eight interrelated definitions of authenticity identified by Gilmore (2007a) into a questionnaire with Likert items for the students to express agreement or disagreement to these established definitions identified from a state-of-the-art review the literature (see Table 4.2 and Figure 4.9).

I have used a similar questionnaire in another study which I conducted with both teachers and students (Pinner, 2016a), but I wanted to just briefly draw attention to this additional perspective on authenticity which I tried to collect as part of the snapshot. As can be seen from the graph, the students generally agree with each of the definitions equally, except for the 'native' definition which received the lowest average. Initially, when looking at the authenticity of the speaker rating task, with I queen receiving the highest score, I felt I had 'failed' to shift the centre of gravity of authenticity away from 'native speakers', but looking

Table 4.2 The eight definitions adapted into questions

Question (adapted from Gilmore, 2007a)	Short Q.
Authenticity means the language produced by native speakers for native speakers.	Native
Authenticity means the language produced by a real speaker/writer for a real audience, conveying a real message.	Real
If I think something is authentic, that makes it authentic. Each person decides how authentic they think something is.	Self
The interaction between students and teachers is authentic.	Classroom
Authenticity is the types of task chosen. It is not the texts we use in class but the way we use them in class.	Task
The social situation of the classroom affects how authentic things are.	Social
Things are authentic if they help me prepare for my assessments.	Assessments
Culture is authentic, and the ability to behave or think like a target language group in order to be recognised and validated by them.	Culture

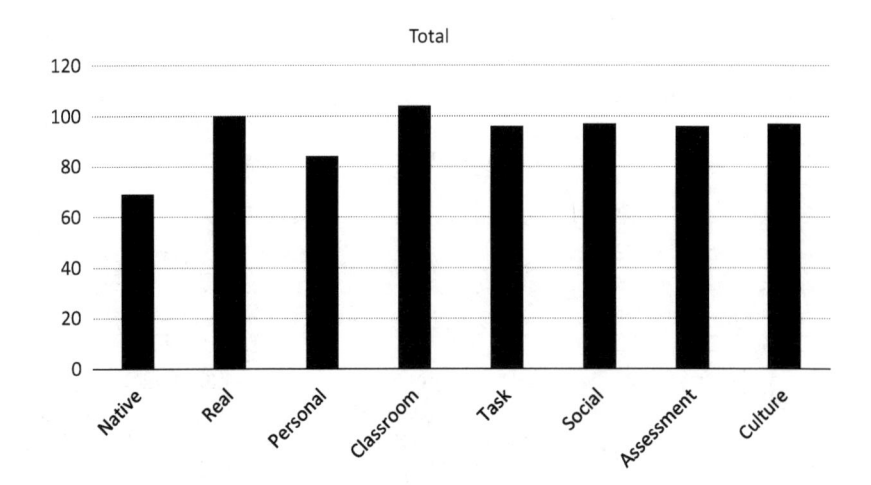

Figure 4.9 Agreement with definitions of authenticity

also at the ratio of linguistic to non-linguistic authenticity judgements, it seems that actually the students have a much more complex view of authenticity than I had originally given them credit for.

I did further triangulate this data with two written tasks which were set as homework on the class Moodle. The first task asked students to state their reactions to the global English lessons (before the speaker rating activity), and the second one asked them to further explain their ideas about 'authenticity' in English (directly after the rating task). I have tried to factor this additional data into my analysis, but I have chosen not to present it at this stage because the data provides a very unclear picture as each student clearly has a different definition of authenticity. Furthermore, all this data was collected very early on in the course of the inquiry, and therefore I would rather focus on critical incidents that arose later as the course progressed.

My 'philosophy of teaching', when compared with the admittedly rough findings from the Authenticity of the Speaker snapshot, reveals a possible divide in the teacher's perception of what English *is* and the views and orientations held by the students. This could manifest itself as a barrier to positive motivational synergies in future lessons if left unchallenged. It is for this reason that methodologies such as Exploratory Practice, which highlight the students' agency and encourage critical reflection, are powerful tools in reaching an alignment, or at least an understanding, of beliefs between teacher and student, and thus fostering greater levels of synergy.

Although the task was overly simplistic, it was mainly a reflective tool for me in order to show areas for deeper focus, and a way of engaging the students with the otherwise rather abstract notion of English as a global language. Although I initially felt the results showed my failure to alter the students' view of English in a way which I felt would lead to self-empowerment, as a pedagogical tool I feel the Authenticity of the Speaker task was successful in raising the students' awareness of varieties of English, and provided a useful form of feedback for me as to the students' orientations towards English.

4.5 Online security and the living textbook

As I will discuss more in Chapter 5, one aspect of the way authenticity facilitated teacher-student motivational synergies was the way I negotiated and adapted the learning content to specifically suit the CLERAC class. In discussing this process of tailoring content and constantly revising my own materials later on 21/05/2014, a colleague of mine dubbed this *the living textbook*. What he meant by this was that my materials were alive because they were constantly being updated, adapted and altered for each class, to fit the individuals that made up the class as a whole.

One of the earliest incidents of this process was when the course moved away from global English and on to the next topic, online security. I noted in my journal that:

> I felt a sort of reluctance to be moving to a new topic and saying farewell to the topic of Global English and authenticity, which had related so directly to my research. This is because the snapshot is now over and yet I feel it is incomplete. However, I think that this might actually be where the *real* authenticity comes in, as I chose a topic of genuine relevance to the students.
> (TRJournal 30/04/2014 [adapted for clarity])

This observation seems quite prophetic upon retrospect, as it was around this time that I felt I really began to work *with* and *for* the students in the class, despite the aforementioned lack of convergence over our beliefs about global English. The main aim for my global English lessons was always to empower students as speakers of the language, to create a more realistic picture of how English is used in the world, and to tackle discriminatory preference against 'non-native speakers'. However, we worked better together as we moved away from this topic and on to areas for which I had less of an agenda in terms of my own research.

The topic of online security spanned two lessons, (103A and 103B), which then transitioned into the real or fake lessons (104A and 104B), which then eventually led to a workshop on fallacies and critical thinking in preparation for essay writing. In this way online security was more directly tied in with the learning aims and assessments than the global English topic.

In many ways, this topic area was a negotiation between my own interest, areas I felt confident teaching, and my perception of the students' needs and areas of interest. All but two of the students are from the Faculty of Science and Technology, so overall I was definitely tailoring the content towards the students, albeit in a very generic way based solely on their department and choice of major.

Lesson 103A featured a TED video lecture by online security expert Mikko Hyponnen. I noted that 'it's probably not a coincidence that the speaker [...] is an L2 speaker of English. I made sure to point this out before we watched the video' (TRJournal 30/04/2014). This was my attempt to link the current topic to the previous one of global English. I also make a note of the fact that the online security lesson gave rise to issues of authenticity in another sense, namely in the Trillingian sense of sincerity and in the fact that there might be scam emails, fakes and phonies, which was then expanded more fully in the real or fake lessons.

In my journal entry, I seem annoyed at myself for not having properly planned the lesson, and for not having allowed myself time to design the handout and 'jazz it up' a little by adding logos or images in order to improve its *face validity*. This is a testing term which I have adopted from Bachman and Palmer (1996, p. 42), which is used to refer to the basic appearance of a test and how it 'appeals to test takers and test users', and which is a 'function of authenticity and interactiveness' in their definition. However, Bachman (1990, pp. 285–289) discusses the fact that this term is very problematic and often used to refer to different aspects of a test's validity. I use the term in its simplest sense to refer to the initial and purely superficial judgement about the way a piece of material looks to a student, in particular whether or not they feel it might be interesting to learn from.

This must have influenced the way I prepared for the next lesson (103B 02/05/2014), which was in the CALL room. I had the students Google one another in order to trace their *digital shadow*. In the class audio recording, several students can be heard laughing and making surprised exclamations during this lesson, even saying '*kowai* [scary]' and '*usso* [it's a lie]' when I showed them how I could trace Ms Forest's IP address and find her Internet service provider, where she was in Tokyo when she logged on to do her homework and what time it was, as well as longitude and latitude.

I first taught some necessary vocabulary (VPN, digital shadow, cookies, encryption etc.) and had students learn them via a WebQuest format in which they Google the word and then teach their words to their partners. I then put students into random pairs (assigned by the CALL room student management software CaLabo) and told them to trace each other's digital shadow. They have ten minutes to create a profile and then make a 'stalker style' presentation about their partner.

However, this lesson was also rather unsuccessful because it required the students to find each other on Facebook, which quickly became problematic when I found that 'just under half the class did not have a Facebook account'. Also, listening back to the audio I can hear that seven minutes into the Digital Shadow Tracing task one unidentified student did not know his/her target. There is also a moment where a huge amount of laughter breaks out between students, and when I say, 'what what what, what did you find?', they reply, 'nothing' and I am not brought in on the joke. Many students were unable to uncover much about their targets, especially those with no social networking accounts.

I also had to begin disciplining some of the students, and in particular I noted that the lesson had been 'dossy' (i.e. the students did not stay on task and messed around) and I had to use 'The Stare'. Listening back to the classroom audio recording, I also noted that in this lesson the students used Japanese a great deal whilst on task, although there was a lot of banter and teasing going on as I moved around the room. I also made note of some troublesome students.

> There were two boys in particular [Mr Widetree and Mr Mouth] who I iden-tified as trouble. I even wrote 'bad?' next to their names on the register (they were the two talking mostly as I read the attendance register and I felt a bit of a yellow flag there). As I wrote that next to their names, I hoped that I wouldn't get into a Pygmalion [Golem] cycle by highlighting them, and I wanted to be careful about that.
>
> (TRJournal 02/05/2014)

When I checked back through my materials, it still said 'bad?' next to those two students' names on the attendance register. I have to question to what extent these observations were intuitively right and to what extent I challenged my own snap assumptions about these students. Again, this will be discussed in Chapter 5, along with an examination of the Pygmalion/Golem effect (Dörnyei & Ushioda, 2011; Rosenthal & Jacobson, 1992).

For Mr House, one enjoyable aspect of this class was being able to interact with other students from the class, as he indicates in Figure 4.10.

Ms Smallville was also quite impressed with this lesson (Figure 4.11).

Ms Smallville indicated that she would actually make a lifestyle change based on what she learned in the class, although this was not my intention. Likewise, Ms Downtree also seemed to reconsider her current Internet usage in a very personal response (Figure 4.12).

I felt a great deal of professional pride when reading these responses, because it showed that I was teaching the students more than just English but also other life skills such as digital literacy and facilitating critical thinking skills. Most importantly, the students were coming to their own conclusions based on the task, which meant that the learning was more authentic in that it was based on the

Re: Online Security Your
Reaction
by Mr House Sunday, 4 May 2014, 3:25 PM
Hi, Richard.
Class of this time was instructive because I have learned information technology.
In paticular, I was interested in Hackers.
I was surprised by their technical capabilities.
The two movies also was very interesting.
In addition, class of this time was nice to interact with people other than the usual
    partner.
I am looking forward to the next lesson.
See you next time.

Figure 4.10 Mr House's reaction to online security

Re: Online Security Your
Reaction
by Ms Smallville Monday, 5 May 2014, 5:57 PM
Hi! Rechard!
I learned the terror of Internet by this class.
I was surprised by the technology of Huckers, and interested in IP adress.
Because IP adress tells me where pc is!
I think I don't use net shopping by cash cards.
If I use cash card, I use it carefully.
Thanks!!

Figure 4.11 Ms Smallville's reaction to online security

Re: Online Security Your
Reaction
by Ms Downtree Tuesday, 6 May 2014, 12:40 AM
I have Face book acount and twitter account.
And they are found in the class.
I surprised and frightend at SNS.
I've never cared about my information:(
So I thiught I want to be carefully.

Figure 4.12 Ms Downtree's reaction to online security

students' personalised responses to the classroom content (Dörnyei et al., 2016; Henry, 2013; Henry & Cliffordson, 2015).

Basically, this series of lessons marked the beginning of a more organic approach to the teaching and learning content, which led to me experimenting with planning, often adopting a kind of *Dogme* approach to the lessons. *Dogme* is a term borrowed from the Danish film directors Lars von Trier and Thomas

Vinterberg's Dogme 95 manifesto and applied to English teaching at the start of the millennium, most notably in a book entitled *Teaching Unplugged* (Meddings & Thornbury, 2009). *Dogme ELT* attempts to focus on the interactions between students and teachers and to de-emphasise the role of published textbooks and especially the role of technology (McGrath, 2013). Ushioda (2011a) has already connected this approach to motivation, and I believe it also works well as a connector between authenticity and motivation in a very practical sense, because such an approach encourages the organic flow of learning and the bespoke creation of personally meaningful social interactions between teachers and students, again a kind of *living textbook*. This type of attention would naturally lead to greater synergy.

Later in the course, I began experimenting even more with this idea by purposefully refraining from planning the lessons beyond a very general list of ideas. Although initially this went against my ordinary teaching style, and did occasionally lead to dissatisfying lessons, as I became more confident and got to know the students better I found that these lessons were the most rewarding ones. I also discussed this issue with my colleagues in quite some detail (hence the term 'living textbook'). Ironically, it emerged through this type of experimentation and discussion that having made my own materials, I had actually just created yet another static textbook which I found myself as dissatisfied with as I would an impersonal mainstream one from 'off the shelf'. I had been striving to reach a point in my teaching where I no longer needed to plan, and thus I felt my life would be less stressful and busy, and my lessons would be more consistent and higher quality. It was upon realising through this Exploratory Practice inquiry that such a view was actually unattainable, undesirable and based on untested assumptions that I was able to take a less sentimental view of my self-authored materials and come to terms with the fact that I will always need to plan, adapt and update my teaching. From this point on, I made an effort to attempt to synergise what I wanted to teach with what I felt the students would respond well to. This was not always successful, however, which I will return to when I discuss the Output Sessions in the next chapter.

Mr Po also showed not only a good understanding of the main content but also went on to write a deeper reflection in the Coffee Room (Figure 4.13).

Notice also Mr Po's very eloquent and appropriate use of the 'double edged sword' idiom, which I commended him on in my reply.

Ms Hemp, who was always very quiet and tended to work in a small group with Ms Lovehouse and Ms Pine, is in the department of Information and Communication Sciences, which explains her reference to ninjas because I said that anybody in this department must be good at computers and therefore a 'digital ninja' (Figure 4.14).

Ms Hemp invoked Mishan's concept of Currency in her description of why she felt the class was very 'near' to her. Currency is one of Mishan's 3Cs of authenticity (2005, see Section 2.3.1), and here Ms Hemp is referring to the fact that there was a worldwide news story and official university warning about a known security flaw with Microsoft's Internet Explorer, which I capitalised on at the introduction to the lesson. I also explained that today's lesson was about

---

Re: Online Security Your
Reaction
by MR PO Wednesday, 7 May 2014, 12:07 AM
Online security is Important for our computers.
We can't live without Internet but it's a doubleedged
sword.
It's convenient that we can share something interesting on Internet.
It's also dangerous that we are being seen by all people.
If we upload the picture on SNS,our location will be known.
If we open the private information to the public on SNS,our private information will be
    known.
So we should be careful on Internet and don't write our private information on
    Internet.

Figure 4.13 Mr Po's reaction to online security

Re: Online Security Your
Reaction
by Ms Hemp Sunday, 4 May 2014, 8:04 PM
I felt this class near me because the news about internet explorer was reported recently.
I like watching YouTube. I usually watch the animations from the foreign countries.
However, I think it serious. So, I want to be careful about the dangerous sites.
I have used Facebook since I was high school student.
However, I was not able to know the degree of risk of my Facebook by the last class.
I may be ninja!!
Therefore ,I was interested in degree of risk of my Facebook.

Figure 4.14 Ms Hemp's reaction to online security

learning how to 'protect your identity online' (Class Recording 103B), which seems to make it less about English and more of a lesson which will be useful to the students and keep them safe. As with global English, this is part of a much deeper underlying belief which has developed in my philosophy of teaching, which is that teaching language as a subject is inherently inauthentic. In other words, I see myself as an educator who teaches language whilst raising awareness of other issues. Language is both medium and content, but I draw the core content from my own personal beliefs about what is important and what should be central to education. I will return to this issue in Chapter 5, but it also leads on to the next section in which I tried to foster greater autonomy, motivation and a sense of agency in learning by expanding the students' locus of control to include a degree of control in how they grade themselves for classroom participation.

4.6 Self-assessment 101

As alluded to briefly at the end of Section 4.4, Exploratory Practice would seem to be a powerful approach to teaching and research in terms of fostering positive motivational synergy because it enables a deeper understanding to be forged between teacher and learners in terms of their orientations towards learning. This is because Exploratory Practice encourages teachers and learners to 'explore their practice(s) together, in order to develop their own understanding(s), for mutual development, by using normal pedagogic practices as investigative tools' (Hanks, 2016, p. 22). The relevance of this approach to motivational synergy is therefore key. One way that I have persistently tried to engage the learners in the process of learning and to take greater control of their learning is by encouraging reflection and increasing their 'locus of control' (Benson, 2013b). Allwright and Hanks (2009, p. 26 following Oscarson, 1989) also specifically advocate the use of self-assessment.

In lesson 104B on Friday 09/05/2015, I introduced students to the idea of reflecting on their learning by asking them to post in the Coffee Room forum a simple response using a + (strengths), - (weaknesses), = (target or solution) template. During this lesson I had an interesting discussion with Mr Auxiliary, whom I tried to motivate into being more positive about his performance in class by focusing on his strengths.

Ad-Hoc 4.4 104.B.1

1.	RICHARD:	How're you guys doing? Ar... y you guys you guys okay? ((....3.2)) Okay?
2.	MR.AUX:	Ah oka[y.
3.	RICHARD:	[Do you need any any uh:: help or yu uh did you upload the file okay?
4.	MR.AUX:	[nodding]
5.	RICHARD:	OK. Good good good
6.	RICHARD:	So what do you think is your strong point in the class/ ((.........9.5)) I think you're good at computers aren't you? Your- you're good with computers? ... You have high IT Skills ((......3.2))
7.	MR.AUX:	I don't have IT skill
8.	RICHARD:	Oh really? Oh/ ... MM:: What do you think is you:::r... (?wha) y- your strong/ point\ ((.......6.9)) You're usually ... you're always on time, right... you're not late usually. So that's a strong point I think. That's a good point. Many many people chose... If you/... let's have a look at this. [I lean over to his workstation computer and begin looking for something] (?wrong bit) if you have a look at this one. Huh? Oh. Nobody posted. ((.....4.1)). Ah no postings yet. Oh ok. N:: never mind [slight laughter]. But many people said being on time or being active in the class, so I think that's a that's a good/ strength\

As the Ad-Hoc transcript shows, it was extremely difficult to have anything like a natural conversation with Mr Auxiliary. It was almost excruciating every time I went over to where Mr Auxiliary, Mr Dawn and Mr Nintendo were sitting, which was always as far away from me as physically possible. Ordinarily, I have found having even one uncommunicative student in my class can act as a kind 'fly in the soup' that pollutes the entire class. For the CLERAC course, though, I managed to avoid this feeling of contamination by trying to learn more about these 'uncommunicative' students and maintaining very good rapport with the other students. In contrast, here is an Ad-Hoc interview from the same class with Mr Fly and Mr Charge:

Ad-Hoc 4.5 104B.2

1.	RICHARD:	How about you guys, what's your strong point?
2.	MR.CHRG:	I have a so hi-high motivation
3.	RICHARD:	You DO. I, I can see your motivation. I already know you are highly motivated?
4.	MR.CHRG:	I use TED usually to study English and in other, in other this class I usually talk with foreign peop[le.
5.	RICHARD:	]yes
6.	MR.CHRG:	I speak English and do everything in English
7.	RICHARD:	Yeah, so you are working really ha[rd
8.	MR.CHRG:	[yeah yeah y[eah
9.	RICHARD:	]Yeah I can tell. Ah, every... You always sit at the front of the class and I always hear you speaking English in the class, so I know. But why are you so motivated
10.	MR.CHRG:	The, the world become more and more global, so in the future, if I could... If I could not use English can't, ah... [uh
11.	RICHARD:	]Yeah, you're right, your right. I have a lot of respect for you. You [huh] that's great. I, I live in Japan and I, I, I want to speak Japanese better but I find it hard to make myself study, you know, but you found a good way 'cause you enjoy watching TED videos. I need to do this, I need to be more like you
12.	MR.CHRG:	Thank you.
13.	RICHARD:	[to Mr Fly] Do you think he's highly motivated?
14.	MR.FLY:	Crazy boy
15.	ALL:	@
16.	RICHARD:	You think he's just crazy
17.	ALL:	@

Ordinarily, it would appear that Mr Charge is motivated and successful, and Mr Auxiliary is not motivated and (therefore) less successful at communicating in English. However, the picture was not as simple as this, as I will draw attention to as the narrative progresses and in the praxis section.

In lesson 105A on Wednesday 14/05/2014, we negotiated the self-assessment criteria for class participation. Self-assessment is something which I have been using as a motivational maintenance tool since 2011, and which has developed as a separate aspect of my overall practice (see Pinner, 2016c; 2016d for an in-depth justification and description of the development). I recorded in my field journal that:

Today was an excellent class, conducted with no handout whatsoever and all the content was generated by the students based on tasks which I put on PowerPoint slides. I planned the lesson a few days ago but made the slides just this morning before class. The idea was that today we would create the self-assessment (participation) marking criteria. I asked students to work in groups and brainstorm/list 5 things which meant good participation. The list was then written down (by me) as a speaker from each group presented them, and then I explained that I would use the list to create a marking criteria questionnaire which they will then use to give themselves the 30% participation score. I also explained other assessments and the students brainstormed ideas that they would like to work on as projects.

(TRJournal 14/05/2014)

The significance of the self-assessments almost warrants a separate study. I have found that the motivational effect of the self-assessments is highest when the students have multiple chances to reflect on their participation, rather than just once at the end of the class. I have also found that students seem to take more ownership of the self-assessment when we negotiate the criteria together as a class. I employed both these strategies with CLERAC, and we actually renegotiated the criteria in the autumn semester as well. I will return to the self-assessments later in the narrative and praxis sections.

As part of the class I also gave the students a very basic overview of L2 motivation by explaining the difference between intrinsic and extrinsic motivation to make my research accessible and relevant to the students in order to 'confess' about my research. It was in this class that I announced my intention to use CLERAC as the focus for a research inquiry, and I informed the students that I would give them a letter explaining about my research, and ask them to sign consent forms in the next class (105B).

In lesson 105B on Friday 16/05/2014, we conducted the first self-assessment for class participation based on the criteria of what makes a good participator elicited in the previous lesson.

The grid I designed for CLERAC at the time appears in Figure 4.15.

This creates in the students an opportunity to reflect on their goals and progress in the class, and provides a feedback loop between us. They are able to write down their goals and assess their own participation (or perhaps investment, another form of motivation). In grading themselves, the students' own sense of agency is reinforced, and I feel these classes to be very good at reinstating the high levels of motivation that we experienced in the first lesson. More evidence of this will be provided later.

Mr Auxiliary wrote in his strengths column, 'I have high motivation.' This would be a recurring theme in all his self-assessments (Figure 4.16).

In contrast to Mr Auxiliary's reflection, Mr Charge did not specifically mention motivation as an abstract concept; instead, his reflection is slightly more fine-grained and shows that, although he and Mr Auxiliary share similar aims, Mr Charge has a more developed version of his future self in that his goals are more specific and focused (Figure 4.17).

Negotiated Self-Assessment Criteria

30% of your grade comes from Class Participation. This grade will be entirely based on self-assessment.

Last lesson you worked in groups of 4-5 and created a list of criteria which make good participation.

The list below is a combined list of all these factors:

1. Speak English as much as we can
2. Communicate and cooperate with partner and group
3. Enjoy myself in class
4. Conduct further research
5. Keep deadlines

Class Participation (10% of grade x3)

This score is derived from Self-Assessment. We will complete this 3 times for a total of 30%

To what extent do you agree with these statements? 1 = strongly disagree, 5 = strongly agree.

	1	2	3	4	5
1) I try to engage with the tasks and work hard in class					
2) I speak English as much as possible in class (about 80%)					
3) I try hard to do homework and research outside of class					
4) I communicate and cooperate with my classmates					
5) Overall, I feel I am doing the best I can					

Use the chart below to add comments about your performance in class

+	
-	
=	

Figure 4.15 Self-assessment grid

To what extent do you agree with these statements? 1 = strongly disagree, 5 = strongly agree.

	1	2	3	4	5
1) I try to engage with the tasks and work hard in class					✓
2) I speak English as much as possible in class (about 80%)				✓	
3) I try hard to do homework and research outside of class				✓	
4) I communicate and cooperate with my classmates					✓
5) Overall, I feel I am doing the best I can				✓	

Use the chart below to add comments about your performance in class

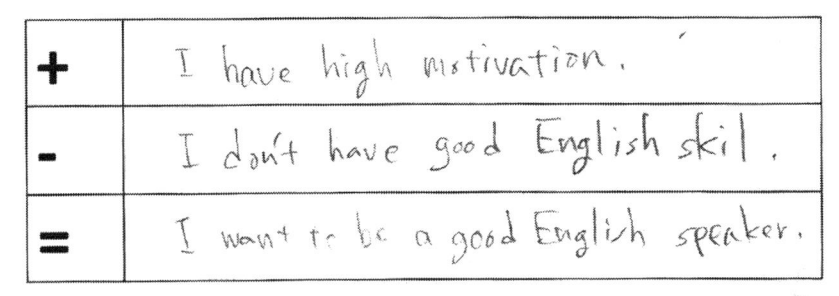

+	I have high motivation.
-	I don't have good English skil.
=	I want to be a good English speaker.

Figure 4.16 Mr Auxiliary's self-assessment goals

Class Participation (10% of grade x3)

This score is derived from Self-Assessment. We will complete this 3 times for a total of 30%

To what extent do you agree with these statements? 1 = strongly disagree, 5 = strongly agree.

	1	2	3	4	5
1) I try to engage with the tasks and work hard in class					O
2) I speak English as much as possible in class (about 80%)					O
3) I try hard to do homework and research outside of class				O	
4) I communicate and cooperate with my classmates					O
5) Overall, I feel I am doing the best I can					O

Use the chart below to add comments about your performance in class

+	I eager to improve my communication ability, and I always try hard.
-	I still often can't transfar what I want to say into English well.
=	I want to communicate with foreign people in fluent English.

Figure 4.17 Mr Charge's self-assessment goals

Unlike Mr Auxiliary, who said, 'I want to be a good English speaker', which is rather unfocused, Mr Charge can clearly imagine himself 'communicat[ing] with foreign people in fluent English'.

The self-assessments took up roughly 30 minutes of class time, and then with the remaining time I asked the students to complete an online Myers-Brigg personality test. Several of the students (most notably Mr Charge, Mr Fly, Mr Po, Ms Downtree, Mr Montville and Mr Wind) found this activity fascinating, and they seemed to agree with their evaluations and also learn something about themselves. The fact that they had to answer complicated questions about hypothetical situations meant that they certainly had to demonstrate quite high-level English comprehension skills, and the fact that they agreed with their final Myers-Brigg personality types demonstrates that they had been successful in the task. In essence, the reward for this task was finding themselves, which may have helped them to link their English identity to their L1 identity. Merging their L1 and L2 identities would also seem to be a way of encouraging motivational synergy, as identity plays a key role in motivation (Dörnyei & Ushioda, 2009; Norton, 2013; Ushioda, 2011a, 2011b; Ushioda & Dörnyei, 2009).

One other important observation from this class was that, even though I told the students I would give them the explanation letter about my research and consent forms to sign as participants in this research, in actual fact I was not quite happy with my letter at that time. I wanted to use mail merge and personalise each letter, adding a few lines of individual feedback for each student in order to give them a pedagogic rationale. However, although some students were easy to write something for (such as Mr Charge, Mr Wind, Ms Downtree and Ms Oldriver), many of them were (and a few remained until the end of the course) rather 'grey' in my mind. I could think of nothing particularly personal in a positive way for certain students (such as Mr Widetree and Mr House), and I could only really think of negative things for some students (such as Mr Auxiliary and Mr Nintendo). Therefore, I delayed giving the letters. In my own words from the audio journal, 'I forgot and I failed [because] the perfectionist in me kicked in.' However, I felt a strange mixture of happiness and guilt when Ms Oldriver and Ms Downtree came to ask me at the end of the class where the letter I had promised was. This, for me, communicated that 'they had obviously been, you know, looking forward to reading [the letter and learning about my research]. So that's obviously my bad. I get the feeling that this group are actually excited and keen to be part of this research' (TRJournal 23/05/2014).

4.7 Philosophy of practice – Learning aims versus experience

On the way home from a long day on Friday 23/05/2014 I picked up my Dictaphone as I cycled back from the train station to my house and began talking into the machine to make an audio note. At this point, I had not yet fully decided that I would keep an audio journal and so really this was just meant to be something I would type up later. However, the nature of the reflection was quite different than if it had been put into writing.

Er... I'm kind of... too... too focused on authenticity, and... the search for authenticity, and the search for [a] sort of personal connection. And as a result I am kind of neglecting the ... er, the learning aims, the outcomes, of the class. The purpose of the classes. [sigh] no I'm not neglecting that. That's a secondary thing. Language- measurable language acquisition, er... you know, provable, statistical, quantifiable gains in fluency, accuracy, these things don't interest me. Really. To be honest. Er, their [the students'] ability isn't' – I'm not looking to quantifiably measure changes in their ability because for me, th- the whole thing is about giving them an experience of the language, giving them a redefined er... redefined concept of the language. I don't want them to think of English as a school subject, you know, where they learn grammar and stuff like they often, invariably have at high school. I want them to redefine language as English classrooms and the English language itself not as a school subject but as a living breathing thing which they have some ownership of. So, measurable gains and measurable language progress and all these kind of things, these are secondary aims for me. Which I have known all along, but I have only just put that into words. [...] I am not there to.... [ah] I'm still there to teach them something, but what I am trying to teach isn't something that you would quantify in the standard way, it's not something that you can really express or measure or, or clearly define. And I think that's what authenticity is in a way. I am trying to teach them a ... er... new way of engaging and a new way of conceptualising the [English language].

(Audio TRJournal 23/05/2014)

This is a prime example of narrative knowledging taking place as I verbalise the words and bring to consciousness my own beliefs about *why* I am teaching and *what* I am trying to teach. This might not necessarily be the first time I had ever articulated this belief, but it certainly became a formative reflection in the study and laid down a seam of justification for my inquiry as well. This also became the crux of the view I tried to express in my monograph (Pinner, 2016b), which I was just at this time beginning to write and work on. This is an important realisation that I have referred to as the teach/learn dichotomy, and will reflect upon further, especially in Section 6.6.2.

4.8 Research statement letter and *The Economist* debate

In lesson 107A on Wednesday 28/05/2014, I gave the students the letter I had written which explained my research. Each letter also contained about two lines of personalised feedback for each student. For example, in Mr Auxiliary's letter, I wrote 'you are a little quiet in the class sometimes but work well in groups and take the class seriously. You do the homework tasks and are attentive during lessons.' The rationale behind including feedback in this letter stating my research intentions was to use the chance to demonstrate that this research could be beneficial to the students as well, and to make the administrative aspect of gaining ethical approval still a pedagogical material, to fit the Exploratory

Practice framework. I told the students that they should read the letter carefully at home, and that I would ask them to sign (or not sign) the actual consent forms in class on Friday.

As mentioned earlier, the online security lessons (103A and 103B) segued into the real or fake lessons (104A to 104B) in which students had to choose between real photos and Photoshopped hoaxes, as well as discerning between genuine and spam emails. This then naturally moved into the discussion of fallacies in a logical argument, spanning four lessons (106A to 107B). The students had their first debate in English in this lesson, based around an advertising campaign that was on billboards when I lived in London. There were three different adverts, each presenting two sides of an argument. I felt these were great primers to get the students talking about difficult, emotive (although, crucially not too taboo or sensitive) topics.

Students could choose their debate topic and also which side they were on, although I had to move a few students into opposing teams to balance the numbers. While I did this, I also tried to balance out the proficiency levels of the groups as well, to ensure a more even-sided debate.

Before the debates, and during them as well, I observed that the students helped 'scaffold' each other by discussing, checking understanding and using L1 to clarify concepts. I also monitored each group before we launched the debates.

I reflected that the lesson went well, although of course the students spent a lot longer planning the debate than they did actually holding it. In the instructions on the handout it says that each group should elect a speaker, but in reality anybody was encouraged to participate in the debate, and they composed their arguments as a team. It was an impressive class and listening back to the lesson recording, I was not surprised to see that it was the highly motivated or more proficient speakers (those who possessed a certain degree of self-confidence) who became the main spokespersons for each group. Mr Charge, Mr Wind, Mr Montville, Ms Saltfield and Ms Downtree were particularly vocal during the debates. Around one hour and 19 minutes into the lesson, Mr Montville expressed his exasperation that although he explained as simply as he could, his opponents did not understand his argument. This is perhaps because Mr Montville was one of two students who had lived abroad and as a result he was one of the most proficient speakers in the class. I explained that he could use Japanese in this case, although I am not sure how well I handled the situation, because I tried to stay out of the debates and leave the students to 'fend for themselves', which they managed admirably for the most part.

It was not until later that I realised that Mr Montville's frustration during the task was not entirely aimed at his interlocutor (sadly whom I can no longer identify, although Mr House, Mr Cleyara, Ms Saltfield and Ms Sound were on the opposing team). Figure 4.18 shows what Mr Montville wrote in the Coffee Room.

It is interesting to note that for Mr Montville, like so many students, the task was challenging and pushed their English to the limit, and yet it was done so within a supportive enough environment so as not to be demotivating. In fact, *every* student who wrote in the Coffee Room, except one (Mr Cleyera), mentioned specifically that the task was 'difficult' but highly enjoyable. Mr Wind expressed that having debates 'is the best way to use and learn English for me' (Figure 4.19).

Re: Debate based on *The Economist* Ads
by Mr Montville Thursday, 29 May 2014, 9:41 PM
Hi, Richard.
My topic was selling internal organs.
I was in disagree team and my real opinion was same.
Because I know helping each other is very important thing.
But now our medical skill is getting higher and higher so we can make some persons clone.
If someone had no arms or leg or some other thing we could see, he can make his clone and get what
he lost and transplant it.
This mean is I think everone will lost he or her personality.
Not having arms is personality, not having leg, cannot walk is personality.
And if someone will die due to cancer and there is no way to live by transplanting I think it is destiny.
Our destiny is god only knows.
I had really good time in discussing.
To tell my theory in English is very hard but I thought that will improve my english skill.
So I want to debate more and more.
Thank you

Figure 4.18 Mr Montville's reaction to the debate

Re: Debate based on *The Economist* Ads
by Mr Wind Friday, 30 May 2014, 12:26 AM
My topic was Prisoners voting.
I thought prisoners should be allowed to vote.
The first thing we focused on is prisoners have a fundamental right.
Certainly, prisoners commited a crime, but all prisoners don't have dangerous thinking.
Some prisoners are innocent, other prisoners couldn't help commiting a crime possibly.
So I agree with allowing prisoners to vote.
I enjoyed the deate.
I felt it is very difficult to convey my opinion.
If we have a chance, I want to do more debate.
I think debate is the best way to use and learn English for me.
Thank you for your reading.

Figure 4.19 Mr Wind's reaction to the debate

Mr Charge headed up the discussion for legalising drugs. He was in the same group as his friend Mr Fly, making this team quite strong, despite the fact that very few people actually agreed with this opinion.

Figure 4.20 shows what Mr Charge later wrote in the Coffee Room Forum as a follow-up.

In the Coffee Room forum, when people wrote their 'real' opinions, I was pleased to see that most of them said they had highly enjoyed the task although it was difficult.

For example, Mr Cloud posted the following about prisoners being allowed to vote (Figure 4.21).

In my responses to four of the students in the Coffee Room, I posted links to films or videos which I thought would be good for them as follow-up watching and as a way of practising English outside the class. Sadly, I have no data about how many of the students actually took up any of my suggestions, although Mr Fly wrote back later on 02/06/2014 that he had watched them 'in the train' (Figure 4.22).

Atkinson (1997) argues that culturally, Japan is poorly suited to argumentation because language is used mainly not for self-expression but for expressing group solidarity. This echoes more generally the argument that Japanese education prioritises collectivism, whereas Western education has a more individualistic focus (Holliday, 1994, 2005; Kim, 1995; see also Littlewood, 2000; Palfreyman

---

Re: Debate based on *The Economist* Ads
by Mr Charge Thursday, 29 May 2014, 11:24 PM
My topic was legalising drugs.
In my opinion, drugs had better be legalised. Whether drugs are legalised or not, sensible people do not use them, foolish people use them. Rather, I think that '' banning drugs puts big money in the hand of bad people like Taliban'' is right. Then,there is no reason to ban drugs.
That debate was fun, but I also felt difficulty. I had to use more complex and logical sentences than
usual, so I could not out put my thought easily.
However, it is trying hard things that makes me strong. I wanna do many debates.

Figure 4.20 Mr Charge's reaction to the debate

Re: Debate based on *The Economist* Ads
by Mr Cloud Thursday, 29 May 2014, 8:53 PM
My topic was prisoners voting ,and I agree with this opinion.
It is difficult to distinguish a good man and a bad man, also prisoners.
Prisoners and murder do not always go together.
So, I think voting is good thing.
Debating is difficult, but it's fun.
Listening other opinion is very exciting.

Re: Debate based on *The Economist* Ads
by PINNER, RICHARD Thursday, 29 May 2014, 9:15 PM
Hi Mr Cloud,
Yes, I'm glad you took this view. Prisoners are people in prison, they are not all "bad" in some
ways. The movie Shawshank Redemption is a good example of this. Have you seen this movie?
The Shawshank Redemption - Trailer...
I think it's one of my all time top 3 movies ever. Just brilliant.

Figure 4.21 Mr Cloud's reaction to the debate

Re: Debate based on *The Economist* Ads
by Mr Fly Monday, 2 June 2014, 11:38 PM
Thank you for giving nice videos!
I have watched them in the train:)
I whish my skills were growing!

Figure 4.22 Mr Fly's reply to my post

& Smith, 2003). This is an area of much debate, and even within Japan there are mixed messages about the place of critical thinking within educational policy (Kubota, 1998, 1999; Rear, 2011). From my discussions with colleagues, the general image of debate classes held with Japanese students is that, because of the strong sense of community and avoidance of face-threatening behaviour, debates often fall flat or result in everyone just trying to agree. This was certainly not my experience, however, and perhaps one reason for this is that the students worked together and prepared their debates as groups, and therefore there was no individually face-threatening behaviour. Based on my findings from this inquiry, I might try to hold more debate-style classes like this, and I would certainly challenge the stereotype that Japanese students do not do well in debates.

Rear (2010) has recorded great success in using debate classes with low-level learners in Japan. I was aware of Rear's study before I conducted this lesson (him being a former colleague and close personal friend), and so his findings, that students need adequate time to prepare and should be attended to on an individual basis during the preparation phase and reflection, would have been in my mind at the time I was conducting this lesson. This is evidence of how reading, researching and interacting with colleagues contributes to my professional development and allowed me to create lessons in which motivational synergy seemed highly positive overall.

4.9 Consent forms and your dream in the future

In the next lesson, 107B on Friday 30/05/2014, I gave the students the consent forms for participating in the research (see Appendix for the form). To my great relief, the students all agreed to the audio recording and other data types I was asking permission to use. Only two students, Mr Nintendo and Mr Dawn, opted out of the use of pedagogical sources.

After collecting the consent forms, we concluded the work we had done on fallacies by doing a WebQuest in which I asked students to find real-world examples of arguments with fallacies from newspaper sources and other media. They were encouraged to search for examples in Japanese, but then they had to present their findings in English in the form of a mini-presentation.

Additionally, in an INSET CALL room training course I had attended which was hosted by other CLER teachers, one of my colleagues shared an idea in which each week, a different student or pair of students is responsible for creating a new discussion in the Moodle forum, which every class member must contribute to. I instantly applied this idea to CLERAC, and I nominated Mr Fly and Mr Charge

Your dream in the future.
by Mr Charge Monday, 2 June 2014, 1:42 PM
Hello everyone.
Today, we have a new topic. The topic is about "Your dream in the future".
Please write down your dream and what should you do or learn in Sophia Univ in
   order to achieve it. But, "I have no dream" is not allowed. If it is vague, try to write
   something.
My dream is to be a engineer, and to design airplanes or air fighter for myself because
   I have loved them since I was a child.
Then, I will learn many things, for example, mechanics(力学),thermodynamics(熱力学),
   aerodynamics(空気力学),material science(材料科 学)...etc. These seem very difficult.
   So I am studying fundamental mathematics and physics.
One day, I wanna see the plane which I designed flying in the sky.

Figure 4.23 Mr Charge's Coffee Room dream

to be the Coffee Room Forum Managers for the week. They posted the question
'Your dream in the future' (Figure 4.23).

This is particularly interesting in that it shows that Mr Charge is a person with
a strong vision of his future self, and it also demonstrates the importance he places
on this future vision. In my discussions with Mr Charge in 2016, I learned that he
still maintains this vision, although it is slightly less specifically about planes and
now more connected with designing engine parts. He is currently preparing to
go to graduate school and further his studies with a Master's. Even though he is
not yet in his final year of university, he told me on 28/07/2016 that he studies
for graduate school almost every day. In the Coffee Room, Mr Fly expressed an
interest in becoming a professor of physics at university. I subsequently learned
that he and Mr Charge were studying for graduate school together, but Mr Fly's
grades are apparently a little discouraging and he has decided to just get a job
working for Japan Railways after he graduates.

Ms Oldriver was one of several students who, unlike the motivational dynamo
Mr Charge, had a less clear future self-image (Figure 4.24).

I found this to be a very charming exchange. Ms Oldriver is talking to
Mr Charge, but it is Mr Fly who replies to her with encouragement and
understanding, indicating a sense of empathy. Ms Oldriver's future self-image
seems to hinge upon her going abroad 'for a long time', where the image ceases,
presumably anticipating further identity construction upon reaching this stage
(cf. Takahashi, 2013). It seems very clear from this exchange that the learners are
speaking *as themselves* (Ushioda, 2011b). I think this was achieved by increasing
the locus of control and actually allowing (or forcing?) the students to choose
their own topics to discuss in the Coffee Room.

4.10 Preparing for assessments

In the next lesson, 108A Wednesday 04/06/2014, the students wrote down
three things that they would like to focus on for their final video projects and

Re: Your dream in the future.
by Ms Oldriver Monday, 2 June 2014, 10:56 PM
Hello!Your deame is so wonderful!
I belong to department of matetrials and life science.
But I don't like physics... I want you to teach me physics:)
My dream is my life will be happy!!!!
First,I don't have dream in the future,I don't know I will do in the future.
But I hope I will speak English fluently,and I try to go abroad for long time.
I will study Science English. I will make an effort to study it.
Second,I love dancing!!!!
I will enjoy dancing with my friends.
Last, I will be make a happy home:)!

Re: Your dream in the future.
by Mr Fly Monday, 2 June 2014, 11:47 PM
It's very difficult to expect in the future.
But to think that we do in the future is very very exciting!!!
Because "Our future is shining"!!!
It is hoped a good dream is found.

Figure 4.24 Ms Oldriver and Mr Fly's Coffee Room discussion

then found groups based on their preferences. Some of the groups were a little unexpected; students were given the option of working in groups or 'lone wolf style' by circling the corresponding symbol at the top of the handout I used for this class (Figure 4.25).

This handout is exactly like the one I used in DCT in 2012.

The groups which the students formed are shown in Table 4.3.

It is very interesting that of the three 'silent' students, both Mr Auxiliary and Mr Dawn actually chose to work in groups, and only Mr Nintendo worked alone, suggesting perhaps that they were not necessarily anti-social, but merely uncommunicative. It is also interesting that both these students paired up with members of the opposite sex, something which rarely happened naturally, as indicated from the seating plans (see Section 3.4.3). I was particularly curious to see that Mr Dawn found a group with Ms Oldriver. Mr Dawn actually chose 'soccer' as his preference, and I was surprised that he changed his topic in order to work in a group, despite not being particularly interested in dance – something Ms Oldriver was decidedly passionate about. It also seems strange that Mr Auxiliary did not join with Mr Dawn despite their shared interest in football. I also wondered later in my journal entry that day, 'Why aren't Ms Oldriver and Ms Downtree working together?' I would later reflect that this pairing may have actually impacted on Ms Oldriver, whose attendance began to slip after being placed with Mr Dawn. She had been late a few times, but in lesson 111A she actually missed the class entirely, and again in 112A. On the other hand, the pairing between the quiet and hard-working Ms Chennai and Mr Auxiliary actually seemed to benefit both of them, although they did not form a close friendship, it seems, and only sat together when instructed to work in their

Projects

Circle the symbol to show if you are a groupie or a lone wolf.

What interests you?

Write down a topic that you would like to conduct broader research on. This should be something you are intrinsically motivated to study about, related to your own interests. *Remember, your topic shluld be suitable for academic research – something you can write an essay and give a presentation about.*

_____

Which of the topic areas we looked at in class most interest you?

1) _____

2) _____

3) _____

Do you want to work in groups or individually? If you want to work in groups, move around the room and find people with similar interests. Based on your prefernece, from groups to decide who will collaborate on projects. Keep away from the lone wolves though, they will be working individually.

Standard Assessments

- Presentation 20% (5 minutes)
- Essay 20% (400 words)

For Group presentations, each member should speak for around 5 minutes with time for Q&A at the end. Individual presentations should be between 5 and 10 minutes (no more than 10 minutes) including time for Q&A

Video
Presentations must also include a short multimedia video which is authored by the student or group. This will be worked on together in class.

Figure 4.25 Working on projects

Table 4.3 Video project topics

Name	Topic	Final Video Length (MM:SS)
Mr Wind	Cloning (lone)	02:19
Ms Oldriver	Dance	05:05
Mr Dawn		
Mr Cloud	Deep Sea Creatures	08:53
Mr Cleyera		
Mr Po		
Mr House		
Mr Fly	Education in Japan	05:50
Mr Charge		
Mr Nintendo	Free Online Games (lone)	02:00
Ms Sound	*Koshoku* (eating problems)	01:10
Mr Swamp		
Mr Widetree		
Ms Downtree		
Ms Redslope	Management of Disney	12:24
Ms Smallville		
Ms Saltfield		
Mr Mouth		
Mr Montville	Medical Robots (lone)	05:11
Ms Pine	Projection Mapping	01:43
Ms Forest		
Ms Lovehouse		
Ms Hemp		
Ms Chennai	Steve Jobs	08:01
Mr Auxiliary		

groups. Also worth noting is the fact that Mr Charge and Mr Fly circled 'lone wolf' but chose group only on the condition that they could work together. I found this rejection of the rest of the class rather interesting, and at times I would notice that Mr Charge would often 'prickle up' or become slightly withdrawn when working in groups with other students, especially those who I personally (and presumably he also) felt were not hard workers.

As part of lesson 108A we also discussed the issue of the mid-semester exam, which was set to take place in lesson 108B. In lesson 108A, I asked the class about the usefulness of exams, explaining about my own experience taking Japanese tests in order to demonstrate my status as a language learner and build solidarity. I also asked about their experience of language tests.

Only 3 had done TOEIC, no one had done TOEFL, All have done Eiken (except 1?). Mr Po likes exams. Mr Dawn feels so-so about exams. Most students hate exams. Mr Wind thought exams were 'useless'. Explained that exams can be useful to direct study, will do a diagnostic exam on Friday.

(TRJournal 04/06/2014)

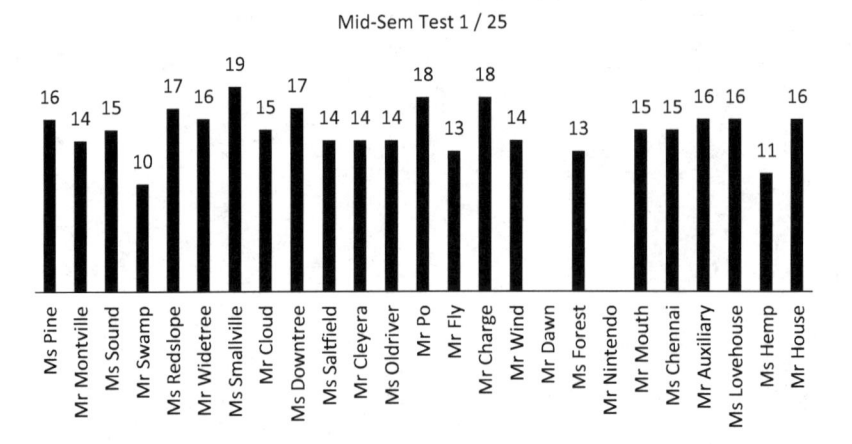

Mid-Sem Test 1 / 25

Figure 4.26 Mid-semester diagnostic test scores

Later that day, I quickly looked online for a test which I could use in the class. In my reflections and also subsequent discussions with students, I have come to realise I was quite defensive about my choice of test, but now in 2016 I feel that in truth I was hasty. For the first mid-semester exam I chose the Cambridge Online Test for Adult Learners.[1] I had wanted to use the DIALANG test, but this required installation and, furthermore, at the time the site was showing up as unsafe due to a security breach. I had also planned to make my own test, but again I found myself limited by practical issues, mainly time constraints.

In lesson 108B, we conducted the mid-semester diagnostic exam, which certainly seemed to have a negative effect on motivation. I had been reluctant to include exams in my syllabus, but doing so was a requirement of the CLER guidelines. Also, I felt it might be a useful opportunity to measure the student's learning (see Figure 4.26).

The class average was 15. (Mr Dawn and Mr Nintendo are excluded as they did not give permission for their pedagogic data to be used in this study).

As the graph shows, Ms Smallville scored the highest with 19/25, with Mr Po and Mr Charge in close second with 18. Mr Montville, who had lived abroad, scored below average with 14. Also interesting is that Mr Auxiliary did well, scoring 16, which is just above average, the same score as Ms Lovehouse, who had also lived abroad. I was surprised to see that Mr Wind, who I felt was one of the most capable students and very able to express complex ideas, only scored 14. Clearly, this test is only a very blunt instrument and is not intended to be as accurate as something like DIALANG, which is exactly the problem with it. It presented a very skewed picture of the students' ability and progress, and in that way, rather than motivating them, I feel this diagnostic exam ended up being demotivating for the class.

I recorded in my journal that I received instant feedback from Mr Charge in the Coffee Room forum. He was unhappy that the diagnostic test had been what he perceived as primarily a grammar test. He seemed demotivated by the whole thing. I had been telling the class that tests can be motivating but can also be demotivating, and my attempt to make the diagnostic exam a motivating experience seemed to have backfired, to the extent that it even managed to unseat Mr Charge from his position as a highly motivated and confident user of English.

I had intended the mid-semester exam to be a form of feedback, which I felt would help motivate them and provide useful information about where to improve, but sadly I feel I actually caused the class quite a bit of damage with this exam.

4.11 Number one

By this point in the semester assessments were taking over. The analytical lens will now focus on one critical incident in which both the students and I reported a 'dip' in motivation and then a rise, followed by another lull. This is something I reported in my journals, but also that the students showed in their own self-reports of motivation, as I will present shortly.

On Wednesday 11/06/2014 lesson 109A, the students conducted an institutional evaluation of the CLERAC course. This questionnaire was conducted for internal quality auditing and is required for each course. The teacher explains to the students about the process, and one student is put in charge of collecting the questionnaires. Then, the teacher leaves the classroom and the students complete the questionnaires anonymously.

In lesson 109B on Friday 13/06/2014, I went over the syllabus again and discussed the assessments in detail. I turned the class aims into 'can do' statements, similar to those in the European Language Portfolio (CEFR, 2016), and in this way I attempted to remotivate the students and make them feel more capable after the mid-semester exam. I explained that they had chosen their own topics for the final assessments (video and essay) and tried to convert their interest in these topics into positive action in terms of English. Class aims state that students should be able to listen to a ten-minute lecture in English.

Ad-Hoc 4.6 109B.1

1.	RICHARD:	You say no Ms Saltfield. Ho- How long can you listen to me speak English. Until you fall asleep or get tired or stop listening
2.	MS.SALT:	Five minutes
3.	RICHARD:	Five minutes! Oh, you're... you're half-way there. And that's okay because this is half way through the class.

Around 41 minutes into the lesson, I start talking about the essay. I ask, 'How long does the essay need to be' and elicit that 400 words is the length of the essay as dictated on the syllabus. Around 44 minutes I ask Ms Redslope if she can write a 400-word essay in English? She replies, 'No', so I ask, 'Can you write a 400-word essay in English about Disney?' To which she replies 'Oh, yes!'

Ad-Hoc 4.7 109B.2

1.	RICHARD:	Who's writing about Disney who's writing about Disney... Aha... Can you write a one-page essay about Disney
2.	?:	(inaudible)
3.	RICHARD:	YEAH! Oh, oh suddenly it's different. Okay. Mr Wind what did you chose for your project
4.	MR.WIND:	(?cloning)
5.	RICHARD:	Cloning. Can you write a 500... a 400-word essay about cloning? Yeah, it's interesting right? Oh, suddenly a one-page essay is not so bad because you can write about something that you chose that you find interesting.

Knowing that they would feel a higher sense of efficacy in writing about topics that they had chosen, I highlighted the autonomous aspects of the class assignments in order to try to motivate the students and give them a sense that the target was actually not only accomplishable but also something they should be looking forward to.

After this, we worked on projects in groups as a class workshop, and I showed the students how to make a video project. Also very crucial is that I showed CLERAC the Wold Hunger video project made by my DCT class. I noted in my audio journal that they were impressed but a lot of them said 'we can't do that' or 'it's difficult'. Mr Wind said that he had never made a video, while Mr Fly and Mr Charge were also worried. Seeing such a high-quality video may actually have, ironically, demotivated the class, as they saw something which they knew they would not be able to do. However, I told them they needed to be working on this and only had five weeks. I learned that Mr Charge had already written his script; however, Mr Fly told me that Mr Charge is focusing so much on his English that he is neglecting his other subjects.

In lesson 110A on Wednesday 18/06/2014, the class was focused on how to write an academic essay, and specifically on how to conduct research and cite it in their 400-word essays which were due at the end of semester. This lesson was given early the morning before teaching from 'hashed together materials that I have used countless times in the Academic English course [the pilot for CLERAC]'.

During the class, I explained the structure of essays such as thesis statements and topic sentences. One tried and tested way I use is to explain that the thesis statement is like the DNA of an essay, after which I use the movie *Jurassic Park* to explain what DNA is and how it is possible to clone something from DNA (just as, theoretically, a good thesis statement should allow someone to know the structure of an essay). Around 30 minutes into the lesson, the following exchange took place:

Ad-Hoc 4.8 110A.1

1.	RICHARD:	Thesis statement is like Jurassic Park okay. In Jurassic Park they make dinosaurs. How do they make the dinosaurs in Jurassic Park? What do they use to create dinosaurs. Yu-... who-... did you say something?
2.	MR.MONT:	(?computer graphic)
3.	?:	[cough]
4.	RICHARD:	COMPUTER GRAPHICS/? No no that's.... Well, ye::s\.
5.	CLASS:	@
6.	RICHARD:	But no...@ in the story. In the story@. Imagine the story is real. How @ you're very clever. How do you... how do they make the, eh... dinosaurs IN THE STORY. Yes, I know it's computer graphics. In the story though. Ms Hemp how do they make... have you seen Jurassic Park. No? Ah. Ms Pine do you know? You forgot. Oh man. @ er. Does anyone know. Ms Downtree do you know. Help, help me somebody help me, how do they make the dinosaurs. Mr Wind do you... you know. You're the best person to ask. Y...have er. have you seen Jurassic Park. Have you seen Jurassic Park, with the dinosaurs. Ahh. Okay. Sorry. It's to do with genetics, your, your topic for your essay. They take dinosaur DNA from mosquitoes

Although this incident was amusing in itself, it hints at a deeper problem, the very problem that initiated this inquiry. It is just a very simple episode, yet it does quite clearly illustrate the authenticity gap which I will discuss in more detail in Chapter 6, and how this lack of cultural schema can potentially lead to problems with the way a teacher might frame ideas and explanations, leading to a misunderstanding of central concepts being learned. We started to lose sight of the aims as the means for communicating them took focus. The divergence occurred here as a result of the authenticity gap. The lesson was not very dynamic, and I noted that I had to tell Ms Lovehouse off for using her phone, and that Mr Auxiliary 'fell asleep almost with his head on the desk and I had to go and wake him up and he seemed confused. But I am not surprised. I did not particularly enjoy teaching that class.'

Lesson 110B on Friday 20/06/2014 was another workshop in groups on the final video project. The students had to give a progress report as a kind of presentation, and the idea for each group's video is discussed as a whole class.

After lesson 110B, I reported in my audio teaching journal that I was feeling:

not so chuffed about today. My heart's not in it as much. Not just the teaching, but even the research. Too many things going on today...

(Audio TRJournal 20/06/2014)

Following this statement, I made a list of other things I had to do and tried to work out how to get through to the end of semester. I reported how I felt very low and demotivated, and I reported negative feelings towards Mr Po and Mr House, who were on their phones during other students' presentations. I reported that the students did not seem to give each other their due respect while presenting in front of the class, something that resurfaced during the output session in autumn. I felt I saw 'a gap between what I expect and what they are doing', which I put down to perhaps 'too much autonomy'. Reflecting in the audio journal, I noted that 'perhaps I shouldn't blame them, perhaps the problem is as much with me as it is with them, in terms of demotivation. Let's see what they do on Wednesday.' I could be heard getting irritated with a colleague (quietly muttering to myself into the recorder) who was rattling his/her keys in the corridor, which indicates my general feeling of stress. Then, tagged onto the bottom of another email about a totally unrelated matter, I received the following comment from a colleague with access to privileged information.

> Oh, and one more thing – your [CLERAC] lesson evaluation was the highest of the 98 courses. Congratulations!
> (Undisclosed source, personal email 20/06/2014: 10:19:17)

Hearing this made me unspeakably happy. As I noted in my journal, it made me feel 'amazing' and helped 'pique my motivation again'. I expanded on this, discussing the feedback which is required for motivation. I was particularly pleased with this because not only will this feedback be logged and recorded (and noticed) by my institution, but it also *comes* from the students. It was evidence that all the hard work I had been putting into this class, all the personalising and the extra effort at 'authenticating' it had obviously paid off. However, officially I should not know this information, as the questionnaires are evaluative and they are purely for feedback purposes. It is certainly not a competition. Normally we would have no idea where we place in terms of the ranking of feedback. And yet, I had been told this information from a very reliable source, and so I could not help but be moved by it. I decided, after some deliberation, to tell my students that our class had the number one feedback out of the 98 other courses, and to use this as a motivational 'booster', because prior to learning this I had reported a serious motivational lull. There had been enough consistently 'low motivation' classes that the class may have been about to shift to an attractor state of lower motivation, and so I felt that it was necessary to 'rescue' the class.

4.11.1 The institutional evaluation

The letter which contains the breakdown of the students' evaluation of the CLERAC course is dated the 16/06/2014, which is before I learned that my class was 'number one'. I am not sure if I had already seen this letter before I heard about how well I had done here, as there is no mention of it in any of my journals until the 20th. It seems likely, however, that I had received it and paid it no attention until its significance was revealed to me.

Table 4.4 Student responses to CLERAC evaluation (%)

		5	4	3	2	1
1	The aim of this course is clear.	29.2	50.0	20.8	0.0	0.0
2	The syllabus of this course is easily understandable.	33.3	37.5	25.0	4.2	0.0
3	The level of this course is appropriate for me.	37.5	37.5	12.5	12.5	0.0
4	The teacher is committed to teaching.	83.3	16.7	0.0	0.0	0.0
5	The teacher's explanations are clear.	62.5	29.2	8.3	0.0	0.0
6	The teachers' feedback is useful.	66.7	25.0	8.3	0.0	0.0
7	I perceive I am learning language knowledge and skills on this course.	16.7	54.2	25.0	4.2	0.0
8	Overall, I am satisfied with this course.	58.3	33.3	8.3	0.0	0.0

Table 4.5 Student responses to CLERAC evaluation (people)

		5	4	3	2	1
1	The aim of this course is clear.	7	12	5	0	0
2	The syllabus of this course is easily understandable.	8	9	6	1	0
3	The level of this course is appropriate for me.	9	9	3	3	0
4	The teacher is committed to teaching.	20	4	0	0	0
5	The teacher's explanations are clear.	15	7	2	0	0
6	The teachers' feedback is useful.	16	6	2	0	0
7	I perceive I am learning language knowledge and skills on this course.	4	13	6	1	0
8	Overall, I am satisfied with this course.	14	8	2	0	0

Table 4.4 shows the table in English, based on the official translation which was circulated with the letter (5 = strongly agree, 4 = agree, 3 = don't know, 2 = disagree and 1 = strongly disagree[2]).

I have reverse-engineered the percentages to show me how many people marked each response. There were 24 students present when we did this survey (Mr Nintendo was absent that day) (Table 4.5).

I would like to pay particular focus to Item 4, which I feel is the most important to this inquiry. Students could all agree that I was committed to teaching, which seems the most important factor to me in terms of authenticity as a bridge and teacher-student motivational synergy, which are at the centre of this inquiry. This will be discussed in more depth shortly and also in Chapter 5.

4.11.2 *Falling off my bike*

On the day of the next class (lesson 111A Wednesday 24/06/2014), I was riding my bike to the nearest train station on my way to work when it started to rain quite heavily. Rather than stopping to open up my umbrella, I foolishly chose to attempt to open it whilst still riding. I, of course, fell off the bike whilst going at quite a speed. Luckily, my work bag (containing laptop and iPad) was able to slightly break my fall, but I landed in a puddle feeling very stupid and unhappy. I got up and continued my way to work, although my back felt bad. Amazingly, nothing else was broken or damaged, just my back. I have been plagued with back problems all my life, ever since I was 16, so I was a little concerned as I stood on the train, feeling the pain in my lower spine. However, I made it to work and arrived on time to teach the CLERAC course.

In the class recording, I can be heard groaning, and at the start of the class I explain that I fell off my bike. I make it into a funny story, and some of the students laugh with me. I explain I will teach most of the class sitting down, although I do actually spend much of the lesson walking around and monitoring. After explaining about my fall, I ask the students, 'Do you think I am having a bad day?' to which the class generally responds, 'yes'. I tell them that I am actually having a good day, and ask them to guess why. I say it is because I am here to teach this class. Then I remind them about the class survey, and I tell them that we have 98 other classes and ask them to guess where we placed. I walk around and a few people give me their answers, most of them somewhere in the top 30 (although Mr Charge guessed it was number one). Then, after drumming up a certain amount of interest in this, I announce that we were 'number one', and a cheer goes through the classroom. I recorded that I felt 'a big well of emotion' as I told them about this, and doing a stimulated recall by listening to the class audio again, I was able to feel that sensation again. It was something like a wave of social energy, a very reciprocal EROI and sense of Flow. It was, with little doubt, one of the best motivational speeches I have ever given to a class. I then go on to explain that from here we have to earn our position and that we should work even harder. As luck would have it, this also happened to be the day that we were to conduct the second of three self-assessments for class participation. This, again, is a very motivational day and one of the built-in mechanisms I used to help students maintain their own motivation and reflect on their performance in the class.

One useful indicator of the dip and rise in our motivational synergy came from a very simple tool in which I had students create a self-report, hand-drawn line graph of their motivation as it progressed through the semester. Although this graph is in no means quantifiable, it is a clear indicator that the students' motivational landscape was very similar to my own, and again lends a great deal of support to the idea that our motivation was synergistic. This lesson seemed to become a large-scale synaptic crossing for motivation, and it was primarily based on the reciprocation of feedback. Having received such good feedback from CLERAC motivated me to do my best for them, which I could then feed back to them through encouraging words and through synergising with them in the class.

Below are three representative examples (see Figures 4.27, 4.28 and 4.29). Eighteen out of 25 (72 per cent) of these graphs depicted some kind of dip, which was then followed by an increase, with the notable exception of Mr Auxiliary

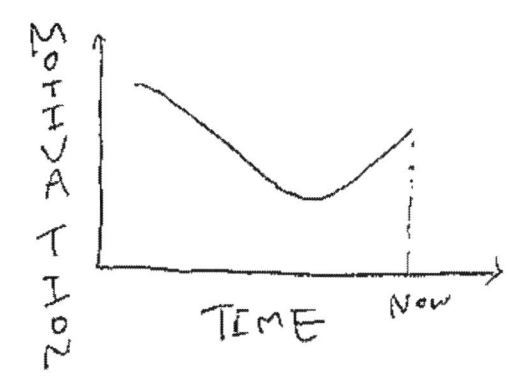

Figure 4.27 Ms Pine's self-report on motivation

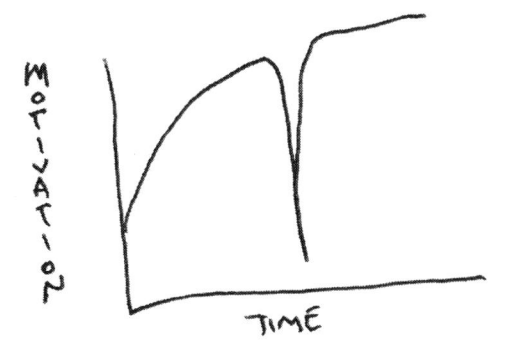

Figure 4.28 Mr Widetree's self-report on motivation

Figure 4.29 Mr Po's self-report on motivation

and Mr Charge, who both reported a constant level indicated by a straight line. The general consensus about how motivated we feel in all our self-reports would strongly suggest that our motivation was synergistic, even when the valence of our orientation was not always positive. However, despite this, this incident became a formative aspect of the group dynamics, becoming a 'class legend' (Dörnyei & Murphey, 2003, p. 67; Hadfield, 1992) and establishing a positive aspect to our overall class reflections.

Much later, near the end of this inquiry, I met with Mr Charge for a friendly coffee on 10/06/2016 after not having seen him for nearly two years. We chatted a little about various topics, but when I brought up the CLERAC class, he instantly said, 'Number One!' with a good deal of pride. Until that moment I never realised that this had been a big achievement not just for me but also for the students together as well.

By the end of the class, I felt I had got everything back on track and really sent a surge of motivation through to all the students, a real transfer of energy. The EROI for this lesson was very high, and I had achieved such a sense of Flow that I hardly noticed the pain in my back. However, my back was steadily getting worse, and almost as soon as the class ended I realised I could barely stand straight. I did not know it at the time, but I was actually suffering from a herniated disc.

Throughout the day, my back only got worse. I sounded in agony when I recorded the audio journal and to make matters worse, Wednesday is the day I teach a very late class, so I did not get back home until almost 10 p.m. and had nowhere to lie down all day. Sitting was very painful. Standing was even more painful. I also had to carry a heavy bag with a laptop in it, and ride a very busy train home through rush-hour Tokyo. When I returned home I went to bed feeling exhausted.

In the morning, I woke up and the thought of riding the busy Tokyo trains to work literally terrified me. I knew I could not do it, and that would only be the first hurdle. On Thursdays I taught three classes in a row for the English Literature Department. I called the Centre for Academic Affairs and cancelled all my classes for that day, and also emailed the department chair, who was very sympathetic. That day, I also received several emails from my students asking if I was okay, expressing concern and sympathy. I felt very loved by my work, but also 'blue' and 'very bummed', as I noted in my journal. I could not work, I could not sit in a good position to write and moving at all was very painful. I was still hopeful I would feel better enough to teach CLERAC on Friday.

4.11.3 Cancelling the class

My back was not better on Friday 27/06/2014. If anything it was worse. I cancelled the CLERAC class, and I also would have been teaching at another university, so I had to cancel two classes there as well. Altogether I had cancelled six classes, which I described as a 'haemorrhage' in my journal.

Figure 4.30 shows the message I wrote to the students through the Moodle News forum.

Cancel Class (27.06.2014) TODAY
by PINNER, RICHARD Friday, 27 June 2014, 6:49 AM
Dear Students,
I am really sorry but I've had to cancel today's class at short notice. As you know, I fell off my bike and hurt my back on Wednesday. Yesterday I could hardly walk and today I am not any better so I am afraid that I can't come in and teach your class today. Please notify the other students who may not have got this message.
I am even more sorry to cancel at such short notice. Please use the time to work on your projects, catch up on reading or chat with your classmates about work (in English as much as you can).
I will arrange a makeup class near the end of the semester and we will hopefully not be too inconvenienced by this cancelled class.
I'm really sorry to have to cancel class and I promise to be more careful in the future whilst riding my bike ;)
Sincerely,
Richard

Figure 4.30 Message to students cancelling class

I went to the doctor on the Friday, when I should have been teaching CLERAC, for back x-rays and medicine. After a very long wait of over three hours, I finally had the results and prescriptions form my doctor. I learned that not only did I have a herniated disc, but I also had an extra lumbar bone in my back. This discovery was quite earth shattering for me. It suddenly explained why all my life I had bad posture, why I was susceptible to back pain. I hated my back and always wondered why it was so weak. Finally, I had a reason. So, in many ways this was a very personal revelation, which had nothing to do with my work. And yet, it did have a lot to do with my work in other ways, because it affected my vision of myself and how my health is very directly linked to my motivation and ability to do the stressful work of teaching. I realised from this point that I had to take better care of myself, and ever since I have done regular back exercises in the morning, which have improved my overall fitness and happiness.

The letters I received from students expressing concern were therefore all the more valuable to me. And yet, I had not received a single letter or email or note of concern from any of the CLERAC students. This did not escape my notice, but it was further exacerbated when I finally arrived back at work ready to teach again on Monday. By Wednesday 02/07/2014 I felt a lot better, although I was still wearing a back brace, taking medication and using a stick to help me walk. In my journal I recorded my disappointment that the CLERAC students did not seem particularly concerned about me (as a person). I was also very disheartened that my perception of their motivation was back into the lull, and now we were a class behind and would need to do a make-up class. Make-up classes had to be held on Saturdays, and the students, rather than being happy that they would not lose a class, seemed understandably annoyed at losing a Saturday. Overall, the entire incident was very eye opening about the nature of motivation and the complex, chaotic (unpredictable) events that make up a person's life and have a profound impact on the few moments we have together in the language class-room. I had attempted to 'cheat' motivation and to create positive synergy by telling the class that we were 'number one', but through events beyond my control the class returned to the lull state and our motivation returned to a negatively valenced orientation.

In my reflective audio journal, I noted that the semester was 'in disarray' and that 'motivation took a big hit because of these missed classes'. I also noted that the lesson was not fun. Also, somehow I felt that the CLERAC students didn't care about my back, which was for me rather life altering. Since my back injury I had decided that I needed to take much better care of my health and to change my lifestyle. However, I felt that, as far as CLERAC was concerned, rather than seeing me more as a human, they saw me more like just another teacher. There were four people late to the class with no explanation. Ms Oldriver did not come at all (as previously mentioned – her first absence). I noted that the class 'doesn't feel like number one anymore. Crimp in motivation. Peak turned into trough.' Further evidence of this perceived lack of concern for my personal welfare is the fact that almost two years to the day later, I asked Mr Charge about the incident during our second informal coffee meeting and he could not recall me falling off my bike or cancelling any classes (28/06/2016).

Also, at this time I observed in the reflection that I did not know what to reflect on, that I was 'too busy to reflect' and that I could not think about the past because I had to focus on the future.

4.12 The last leg of spring

In Japan in July, the weather is extremely hot and humid. This also has an impact on one's motivation and the type of activities a person might want to do. People try to avoid venturing out into the heat during the middle of the day; they sweat and feel easily tired. The Japanese word *natsubate* describes the type of lethargy that overtakes people around this season. In lesson 112A on Friday 04/07/2014, we worked on our essay introductions. The class was supposed to be a peer-review workshop using the Moodle workshop module, but only 15 out of 25 students managed to upload their introductions for peer review. This hints at the possibility that high motivation was actually a strange attractor for the CLERAC class, as I will discuss in Section 6.3.4.1.

I had somehow managed to create all the marking criteria for the assignments, and I was much better prepared for the class, having also made a very strict plan to 'get me through to the end of semester'. It was a survival plan. During the lesson, because very few students had their essays ready, we worked on the video projects. I had a moment of inspiration and told the students that they needed to create a project trailer of 10 or 20 seconds in length, but that it should quickly show the rest of the class what each group's project was all about. I did a demonstration on the screen and made a handout as I went with instructions. I felt this task timely and appropriate because it made the video suddenly very tangible. I was beginning to worry that the students had done very little on their projects, and I was also concerned about their digital literacy, as many things can go wrong when making a video project. The trailer was a chance to iron out any such issues before the actual assessments were due. Like with the introductions, very few members of the class were able to complete the task on time, so these two things became homework. By lesson 112B on Wednesday 09/07/2014 I was very disappointed to note that Mr Nintendo, Mr Dawn and Mr Cleyera had still not finished their introductions, and that only four out of ten groups had managed to create a project trailer.

I began to feel like we were 'drowning' in assessments, and the CLERAC course had become a very different animal to the one it started out as. This is actually very common with university courses. Certainly my colleagues also have very similar complaints, but it is inevitable, and so both teachers and students have to just 'get on with it'. I attempted to avoid this in the autumn by introducing staggered assessments, which led to its own problems. However, due to my eagerness to collect rich pedagogic data, I believe I may have had an excessive number of deadlines, which was made worse by the missed class. Furthermore, the CLERAC students had not yet actually submitted anything for me to assess or give feedback on, so I reflected that they were 'working blind', which was why they might have felt like they had been 'smacked in the face with all these assessments'. It was around this time that I realised that feedback seemed to be vital for creating a culture of authenticity, and especially for establishing positive motivational synergy. The teacher-student motivation was still synergised, but at this point I felt it was in a negative phase of synergy. In other words, the energy I was investing did not have a high return (EROI). The attractor state of the class was one of low motivation, and high motivational orientation seemed to be a strange attractor that we often gravitated towards but never quite reached. In part, I think this was because I was still investing high levels of energy into the class, quite possibly because it was also a research project. Reflecting back, I realise that feedback is an essential component in creating the synaptic crossings to positively charge motivation between teacher and students and facilitate social authentication, and that although I was investing energy in the teaching, I had not done enough by way of feedback.

In lesson 113A on Friday 11/07/2014, the students finished their 400-word essays, which were all on the same topic as their video projects. The lesson was a final workshop and review, and the deadline was set for the end of the day. Ms Lovehouse was the only student who submitted late. I also found some evidence of plagiarism (an entire paragraph copied and pasted) in Mr Po's essay. Both these students were reprimanded and their grades were adjusted accordingly. The next day was a Saturday, but this was the class we had set as a make-up lesson, so lesson 113B was also held in the CALL room. Not all the students could attend, which meant that those who could not work in their groups on their video projects (such as Mr Charge, whose partner, Mr Fly, was absent) were given a 'fun task' of watching an entertaining YouTube video which was an animated history of the universe in three minutes. They were then supposed to write down the sequence, basically creating a summary of their own very fast observations.

Mr Charge and Mr Wind (who had already finished their video projects anyway) both enjoyed the task. I spent the rest of that day marking in my office. My plan was to have the entire semester marked by the last day of class, not just for CLERAC but also the other five courses I taught. There were just two lessons left until the end of semester.

In the last week of spring semester, on Wednesday 16/07/2014 in lesson 114A, we watched the students' final video projects together. We could not watch them all because three out of ten were late. Mr Wind was late, as was Mr Nintendo because they submitted the wrong type of file (a .wlmp project file instead of an.mp4 video file). This is exactly why I had wanted to do the trailer project. I was disappointed in this and gave both of them a late penalty as I had been very clear in my instructions. The dance group, Ms Oldriver and Mr Dawn, were also late, and I recorded that they 'couldn't even explain why'. They were given an even harsher late penalty. In the lesson, we watched only four of the projects because each one took about 15 minutes due to questions and answers, plus a large amount of class was used on administration and submissions, and reprimanding those who were late. I noted that overall I felt 'very disappointed', particularly in terms of the quality of the videos.

In lesson 114B on 18/07/2014, the last lesson of the spring semester, we watched the last of the video projects and I went around the class with a chart, ticking off everybody's name and ensuring I had each of their assignments. Some people had not yet finished mid-semester reaction papers or diagnostic essays for either the mid- or end of the semester, and I ensured everybody knew what I had and what was missing. The class ended well, and I recorded that it had been a really good class. However, overall I was quite disappointed with the low-quality videos. I reflected that even though my expectations were not particularly high, the results were still lower than I had hoped. I felt that, given the large amount of class time dedicated to the projects (ten lessons, 35 per cent of the semester), the final videos were rushed, with some groups seeming to have basically done everything on the Saturday make-up class. In terms of the quality of the work, the DCT class had not (and still has not) ever been duplicated, except in some stand-alone cases for other classes. I was particularly upset that the *Koshoku* and Projection Mapping groups' videos were both under two minutes long, although the class average was 05:16 (see Table 4.3 for summary). This struck me as evidence that they had not worked hard on their projects and had not worked hard during the classes, indicating a much lower level of motivation than I had originally credited many of them with. However, I must bear in mind CLERAC's overall lower language ability than DCT, as I am inevitably comparing these two classes. I discuss this more when I expand upon motivation as a strange attractor (see Section 6.3.4.1).

4.13 Roundup of spring semester

Towards the end of the semester, the atmosphere of the class changed as the assessments inevitably took precedence. Early on in the semester, as I had stated in the TRJournal (23/05/2014), I basically wanted to provide an *experience* of the language in use (following Tomlinson & Masuhara, 2010). However, towards the end I had to help the students understand what my expectations of them were. I had to instruct them in how to write an academic research paper, how to create a video project, how to write a reaction paper, as well as keep them well informed of the deadlines for submitting this myriad of assessments. As the teacher, I also found it hard to keep up with all the work, and the CLERAC class became less about teaching and more about administration, as I frequently noted in my reflective journal entries. This was of course added to by the other classes I was teaching, and further compounded by the fact that I had to return to the United Kingdom for my first PhD panel whilst also working on the monograph related to authenticity and presenting other research at the 2014 BAAL annual conference.

Despite all of these things, I tried to be very careful about ensuring that the students were given fair treatment, plenty of warning about deadlines and ample feedback for their assessments. The main aims of the spring semester were related to language skills and academic literacy. As previously explained, the first semester is designed to prepare students for the more content-focused instruction of the autumn semester, which in turn then prepares students for the second-year CLIL-based elective courses.

Notes

1 Available at www.cambridgeenglish.org/test-your-english/adult-learners/
2 Please note, in the Japanese version, no. 5 (strongly disagree) is worth 1 point and no. 1 (strongly agree) is worth 5 points. I simplified this by reversing it in the English translation.

5 Autumn semester

5.1 Overview and syllabus

The first CLERAC class in the autumn semester was conducted on 01/10/ 2014 (09.15–10.45), and the last (27th) on 21/01/2015. The total amount of teaching time was 40.5 hours (27 × 90 mins). The same rooms and times were used as the spring semester. During this semester the number of students was 25; however, Mr Nintendo dropped out of the class due to absences. He attended just 25 per cent of the classes, meaning he fell below the minimum requirement of 85 per cent set by CLER.

In the autumn semester, there was a large shift in the nature of the class as it became more content focused, in line with the stipulations from CLER. As previously stated, this is part of an innovative restructuring of general foreign language courses offered by the university, which was piloted for three years before being implemented for the first time in 2014. I also taught on the pilot courses from 2011, although they were actually rather different in structure and the content I used was completely different. However, the underlying pedagogical principles are the same; the belief is that students are more likely to learn to use the target language effectively if a CLIL-based methodology is applied, meaning that there have to be 'dual focused aims' (Marsh, 2002, p. 2). Another underlying belief in the content-focused approach is that it affords a greater 'authenticity of purpose' (Coyle et al., 2010, p. 5) because, as I have argued elsewhere, authenticity is a defining aspect of the CLIL approach (Pinner, 2013b). This means that having a real reason to use the language is what defines CLIL and what makes it 'the ultimate dream of Communicative Language Teaching [...] and Task Based Learning [...] rolled into one' (Dalton-Puffer, 2007, p. 3).

One fundamental difference between the two semesters was also in the way they were assessed, and the type of coursework I set. In the spring semester, the main coursework to be done was a video project, which made a lot of sense as we took 50 per cent of lessons in the CALL room and a large number of students came from the IT and technology departments. In the original syllabus for autumn, the plan was again to do a video project. However, as I noted previously, I had been very dissatisfied with the quality of the videos from the spring semester. Rather than working on this to improve the videos, I decided to abandon the video projects and use an assessment I called *output sessions*; interactive presentations in which one group of students leads the class and involves the other students in discussions, sets them quiz questions and presents information in an engaging way. These output sessions work on the premise that I will give an input session, which is a mini-lecture and interactive discussion in the first week, and then in the second week one group will lead the interactive output session. At the time, I was working part-time at Tokyo University of Foreign Studies (TUFS), a national university specialising in foreign language instruction. I taught on the general English programs there (much like the CLER programs at Sophia), and one of my classes was a content-focused course titled Introduction to Language and Communication. As part of this course, I required students to work in groups to create an output session. At TUFS, I had enjoyed a great deal of success with the output session format. My course was structured along a path which alternated between input sessions (teacher led) and output sessions (student led), with time devoted to preparation in the class in addition to online materials and additional support outside of class. I felt it would not be too hard to import this system to the CLERAC course in autumn, and indeed I felt it would be a good way of changing the previous semester's structure and highlighting the new content focus. Although I had already created the autumn syllabus before I even met the class in spring, as the syllabi all had to be uploaded to the course management system of the university by February 2014, I actually altered it to feature the input/output format over the summer break. When I came to start teaching CLERAC in the autumn semester, I did not feel the output session format would be any problem, and indeed I felt I had no reason to worry. In my teaching journal on 17/10/2014, I wrote, 'Output idea was a gut reaction/impulse decision but not intuitive perhaps.' The outputs form an important part of this inquiry, because during the output sessions I took a seat amongst the students as a participant, and therefore I was able to see what happens to the classroom dynamics when our roles were reversed. In terms of motivational synergy, this led to some exciting insights and provides certain indications that the teacher is not necessarily the only agent in the relationship capable of generating largely positive charges of motivation. For example, in her end of semester reaction paper, Ms Smallville noted:

> Honestly, the class was not a pleasure for first. But I made friends with my classmates as we repeated the number of times, and I enjoyed it. I thought that the motivation would go up by the relation with classmates. I think that we were not able to make friends with classmates if we do not have time to talk our partner.
>
> (20/01/2015)

Furthermore, Ms Chennai and Ms Forest, Ms Pine and Mr Montville among others commented that they had particularly enjoyed the chance to communicate with their classmates, allowing them to practise English and also to build a relationship. This hints that motivation was connected to the individual's view in social context, and thus lends weight to the idea of social authentication as a motivating factor.

Apart from this difference, the assessments were very similar to spring, with self-assessment for class participation, final essays, mid- and end of semester diagnostic exams and regular reaction papers being assigned as coursework. As in the spring, we teachers are required to design our own syllabus around CLER's guidelines (see Appendix 2). The content I chose to be the focus of the second semester was Awareness and World Issues, making it very similar to DCT. This shared content focus between CLERAC and DCT was intentional, especially because I wanted to use and develop the materials that I originally used in DCT. This was partly motivated by a desire to use tried and tested materials, thus saving myself a lot of work in developing an entirely new content-focused course, but also as a way of trying to compare the CLERAC course with the puzzle's ancestral roots, the DCT course.

The syllabus was constructed around the following topics:

1. Prejudice:[1] Students watched part of a documentary featuring a facially disfigured man and discussed issues related to prejudice such as race, gender, ethnicity, social position and so on. We talked about social justice and how to be better people.
2. Food: Students researched a range of food activist movements, especially pertaining to the treatment of animals in the production of meat. There was a special lesson about free-range chicken in which we watched a video from River Cottage, the UK food and nature series hosted by Hugh Fearnley-Whittingstall.
3. Consumerism: We discussed a number of consequences of consumerism, such as being overly materialistic, the dissatisfying effect of marketing, the paradox of choice (Schwartz, 2004) and the environmental impact of consumerism. I introduced the class to the documentary *No Impact Man* (2009), which follows Colin Beavan and his family as they try to change their lives in order to be greener and live more sustainably.
4. Economics and Oil: In this section of the course we discuss the phenomenon of peak oil, which is an economic doomsday scenario currently unfurling amongst developed nations due to the global economy's dependency on cheap oil (see Heinberg, 2005 for further information). Note that no students chose this topic for their output sessions.
5. The Environment and Wildlife: This topic looks at how our current way of life impacts the environment and contributes to mass extinction and the endangerment of wildlife. This topic was split into two as a large number of students chose it for their output sessions, which meant that there was an environment output and a wildlife output.

What follows is the chronological narrative of the autumn semester, again using the shifting analytical lens and narrative style employed for the spring.

5.2 Initial conditions 2: lesson 201A

I arrived 15 minutes early to class (as usual) to get set up and say hello to people. However, the projector was broken and I could not get it to work. I thought this was a bad omen at first, but I noted in my audio journal that it 'worked out okay and I managed to muddle through and get my head back on'. I abandoned trying to set up the projector, despite having spent a long time creating slides for the lesson, and had to just rely on the handout. This lesson was very similar to the first lesson of spring in that we went over the syllabus and discussed the assessments. I explained the two main differences between the autumn and spring semesters (content focus and output sessions format). I explained that we would focus on Awareness and World Issues, and that this semester we were going to use English to discuss important social and environmental concerns. When I say 'important', perhaps I should also make it clear that these were topics which I intrinsically feel are important and which I am extremely passionate about. In the handout for the first class (see Figure 5.1), I wrote under the aims and objectives that we were going to try and 'make the world a better place'. This, of course, will have a bearing on my motivation (and thus on the students' motivation) throughout the course.

In the first class, students ranked the topics from the syllabus in order of preference, then found groups based on this preference. These then became the output groups, and at this point I explained to the students in what order the topics would be dealt with and when the output sessions would be. The first output, dealing with the theme of prejudice, would be held on 15/10/2014, just two weeks away. I also noted that many students were late. The first class was otherwise rather uneventful, and I have not chosen to present it with such a high degree of detail as the first class of spring because I already knew the students, although I did note that I accidentally referred to Ms Chennai as Ms Forest, which I felt embarrassed about. Reflecting on the lesson, I also noted that I was out of the habit of recording journals, and that it 'feels weird to be recording'. I observed that there was a 'black hole' in terms of my experiences over summer break. I also noted that my personal and professional life seemed to be 'knitting together' for me now. However, I was also cautious that the quest for authenticity might lead me to be too reflective and to 'go round in circles'. I had read that being too reflective can impair intuition and in extremes of self-consciousness can lead to 'paralysis' and be 'deleterious' (Claxton, 2000, p. 35). This fine line that I had walked in spring became even finer as the year progressed, and my reflections became even more wide ranging, structured and systematic.

I explained to the class that, unlike in the traditional presentation format where students have a strict time limit (usually between five and ten minutes), the output session can last up to the full 90 minutes of class. In my reflective journal I noted that the students 'seemed shocked about output sessions but I am going to make sure they get lots of help'.

Academic Communication: Awareness and World Issues

Richard Pinner (rpinner@sophia.ac.jp) Office: 7-511. Office Hour: Mon Period 2

Introduction and Overview

Nelson Mandela
1918–2013

> 66 *Education is the most powerful weapon which you can use to change the world.*"
> Nelson Mandela, Rights Campaigner and President of South Africa

Aims and Objectives

In this class, we will try to make the world a better place whilst also learning to use our English for authentic purposes. **It will be a real challenge!**

Classes will be arranged as either teacher-led **input sessions** or student-led **output sessions** in which the students lead the discussion and give short, informal presentations.

Presentations

Presentations will be given in class and conducted as **output sessions**. Please refer to the class schedule to see which classes are output sessions. Depending on the number of students, different groups will each be assigned a certain topic which they will research and present as an output session. Each student will conduct between one and two output sessions depending on class sizes.

- What do you think is the benefit of conducting your own research on a topic?
- Why do you have to present in front of class?
- What skills will conducting output sessions help you to develop?

What are some World Issues?

Work in groups and make a list of World Issues. These are usually social problems which affect all of us.

Figure 5.1 Starting the content-focused semester

5.3 Prejudice

In lesson 201B, held on Friday 03/10/2014, we began the first of the content topics, prejudice. The lesson was designed around a WebQuest which I created and a discussion forum task (Figure 5.2).

The class was split into groups and given a question to discuss together, after which they had to post a response in the Prejudice Forum. I noted that Mr Po mentioned his own experience of prejudice as a Chinese person living in Japan; he seemed 'a bit emotional', and he was 'really personal and opened up about his identity', although sadly this was not recorded in his written work for class. I indicated that I felt I had started to increase their awareness of certain issues, but it was still too abstract. For example, in the Prejudice Forum, attempting to answer the question 'are you prejudiced?', Mr Fly discussed his work at a cafe and how people were prejudiced that he spoke good English just because he is a Sophia student. Ms Smallville similarly missed the mark by discussing the lack of bullying at her all-girls high school (Figure 5.3).

In lesson 202A on Wednesday 8/10/2014, we watched part of a documentary series called *Beauty and The Beast: The Ugly Face of Prejudice* (Channel 4, UK, 2011–2012). Simply because it was available on YouTube, the episode I had chosen for class was season 2 episode 2, *Reggie and Gary*. This episode follows Gary, a homosexual man who is 'addicted' to cosmetic surgery in order to improve his (already good) looks. Gary then meets Reggie Bibbs, who has neurofibromatosis, a genetic disease which causes tumours to grow on the body, often leading to disfigurement. It is the same disease that caused John Merrick to become known as the Elephant Man, a story that had fascinated me since I was at high school.

We only watched the first 15 minutes of the video, and afterwards I asked the students 'who is really "ugly"?', clearly expecting the students to answer

Prejudice and Social Justice WebQuest

What is the Halo effect. How could this affect your score on an essay?

Read about Stop and Search Statistics http://www.bbc.com/news/uk-24902389. Why are black and Asian people more likely to be stopped and searched in the UK? What is your opinion about this? What can you find out about this problem in the USA?

What is the gender pay gap? Can you find a graph?

Prejudice Forum

The Face of Another (他人の顔)

Figure 5.2 Moodle screenshot of Prejudice WebQuest

Are you prejudiced?
by PINNER RICHARD Pinner, Richard - Thursday, 2 October 2014, 4:33 PM

**Are *you* prejudiced? If so, what are some recent instances in which you behaved in
a prejudiced way? If not, how do you know that you're not prejudiced?**

Re: Are you prejudiced?
by Mr Fly　- Friday, 3 October 2014, 10:25 AM

I'm workikg in the cafe at shinjuku.

when I taught other people of the cafe staff that I'm sophia univer,student,people said
　　"Oh, you are good at using English,aren't you??? Please attend to the customer!"
I can't denied because they looks like very happy,so I said "...yes,I will do the best..."

I didn't feel good when I hear that.
But I think it is very difficult to break this prejudice...

Re: Are you prejudiced?
by Ms Smallville - Friday, 3 October 2014, 10:30 AM

I said that I went to girl's high shcool,
many people say there is bullying and it seems that girl's high school studesnts are evil
　　minded person.
But in reality, there is not any bullying.

Figure 5.3 Replies in the Prejudice Forum

Gary, because he seemed primarily concerned about what was on the outside,
as opposed to Reggie, who was content with his appearance despite being seriously facially disfigured. In dealing with a topic like this so early on, I was
clearly trying to establish the new, more serious tone of the content-based
class. I noted that the learners were 'kind of transfixed by the video, especially when Reggie Bibbs came on'. However, I reflected that, with the exception of Mr Wind, Mr Charge and Mr Fly, 'they weren't really able to express
their opinions', and I wondered how much they had connected with the video
as it was very different from their own experiences because it presented such
extreme contrasts. I also began wondering if the content was too advanced for
them. Overall, though, I was still very upbeat and the class had gone well. My
written reflection discusses many personal issues such as health and study and a
desire to 'reinvent' myself.

　　By lesson 202B on Friday 10/10/2014, I was feeling quite different. I noted
that my motivation was very low, and that the class was 'slipping at certain points'
because I tried to 'wing it' too much, based on my reading about intuition and
an attempt to respond to the students and build the content of the lesson around
them. I had set some video comprehension questions based on the previous class
(202A), and I was disappointed to learn that 19 of the students had not done the
task. I tried to be positive about the fact that six of them *had* done it. In my audio

journal, I discussed my disappointment and took the lack of uptake as evidence for a lack of engagement:

> When I found that only 6 of them had done the homework it kind of maybe threw me a little bit, it was evidence that they hadn't really connected with the topic. Some of them said that they wanted to watch it but they didn't have time and I believe that, but I think that if they had been really motivated then they would have watched the video.
>
> (TRJournal 10/10/2014)

I felt that perhaps we had only scratched the surface of the topic, so I showed them the final 15 minutes of the video, because I wanted to show the class how it ends. I made the following observation in the audio journal:

> It [the video] just seemed a bit stupid really. I felt it was actually quite shallow and superficial, because the guy [Gary] was changing himself because of the cameras. I didn't really believe in the video myself, but I didn't realise that until I was showing it. It felt like I was squeezing the last bit of juice out of it. Today was a 'vapour trail' of Wednesday's class. Hadn't prepared what to do, thought I could feed back off the students but it wasn't there. Maybe they didn't care much about it. There was nothing to feed back from. My fault for being less prepared, as opposed to Wednesday.
>
> (TRJournal 10/10/2014)

Interestingly, I attempt to blame the students for there being nothing to 'feed back' from, whilst failing to notice that I myself also failed to truly 'authenticate' the video (and perhaps the content as a whole). In this way, our motivation seems to be negatively synergised, perhaps due to there being a lack of clear aims, as represented by the divergent model presented in Chapter 2. This led me to a deeper reflection, about whether or not I was using the video of Reggie Bibbs to teach the students about prejudice, or if I just wanted to shock them into some kind of a reaction.

I started to feel conflicted, comparing myself to Frederic Treeves, the doctor who treated John Merrick. I noted that 'just as he doubts his own ethics, I feel like that as a white male middle-class person shining the spotlight on prejudice'. In retrospect, it seems that I ran out of legitimacy and could no longer discuss the topic of prejudice and feel 'authentic' because of my own conflicted feelings on the subject. This is a deeper cause, which was likely exacerbated by the lack of uptake on the homework task, which I took as negative feedback from the students. Another type of negative feedback I observed was that some students, such as Mr Po, were looking at their smartphones during the class when they were supposed to be working in groups on their output sessions. As this was a CALL room class, it was almost certainly evidence that they were not working on the task, because if they had needed to search for something, they could have used the CALL PCs.

My reflection presents a rather polar view of the class. Despite the class having been relatively successful I also seemed to have found it decidedly unsuccessful.

A bit full of doubt, woke up full of beans, the class was ok but somehow it sapped my confidence. It wasn't so bad really, but it wasn't great. Because I wanted it to be great and it wasn't, I kind of let them and myself down.

(TRJournal 10/10/2014)

In an attempt to reinvigorate the topic after the lesson, I sent an email to Reggie Bibbs through Facebook to tell him that we had watched the documentary in our class here in Japan, to which he replied on 22/10/2014, although I did not inform the students until nearer Christmas. I also posted a link to a trailer for David Lynch's *The Elephant Man* (1989) with a personal story about why I became interested in this topic. Also noteworthy, for the first and only time there was not a single reply to this Coffee Room post. The average number of replies to the 23 Coffee Room posts was 26.6, (see Chapter 6 for further analysis of the Coffee Room forum).

5.4 The first output session

Lesson 203A on Wednesday 15/10/2014 was the first of the student output sessions. In the prejudice group were only three students: Mr Fly, Ms Lovehouse and Mr Nintendo. From my journal entry of the same day, it seems clear that I was expecting the session not to go well. My overall reaction to the first output was one of disappointment, not just at the students but particularly at myself for having failed to really scaffold them in terms of how to conduct an interactive style presentation, although I had dedicated roughly 20–30 minutes at the end of each lesson for groups to work together on their sessions, which I then monitored and talked to in turn. I noted in my reflection that Mr Fly was 'over theatrical', and that his writing on the board was 'virtually illegible' (I do not have a photo of his board work as he erased it before the end of the session). I also felt that Mr Fly's comprehension questions were 'either patronisingly easy or too difficult'. In my feedback to Mr Fly I wrote the following:

> Great start with good gestures, very good voice and gestures but the board was very messy and hard to read. Using PowerPoint would have made this better and easier for you. Nice use of video but your questions about the video were too simple (is he a man or a woman, is he black… etc.) At the end you trailed off without a conclusion, but overall this was a good effort and you have a good authoritative style.
>
> (CLERAC2014B Grades)

Like Mr Fly, Ms Lovehouse did not use PowerPoint and her section was very short. She spoke in a very quiet voice and seemed the most nervous of the three. Although Ms Lovehouse was one of the two students (the other being Mr Montville) who had lived abroad when younger, she often seemed to struggle with shyness and to feel difficulty expressing herself in English. Again, after each important assessment, I asked the students to email me with a self-reflection, using the +,-,= template discussed in the previous chapter. Figure 5.4 shows what Ms Lovehouse wrote.

To Richard
Sorry to be late for this mail.
I just forgot...
This is my reflection.
+ I thnk I could make them think,and could convey my message.
- I couldn't make them discuss so many times.
  And maybe my presentation(?) was boring.
= I want be a person who can make peopple amused by my talk.
  So I'll practice talking at my part-time job.(I work at a restaurant)

Richard,I'm readind an English book now!
It's still a very low level book,but my goal is to be able to read Harry Potter by my
  Birthday.
I love Harry Potter too,and I wanted to be able to read it someday from long time ago.
Incidentally,I'm reading "Beauty and the Beast" now. I'll work hard,so I just wanted
  you to cheer me in your mind;-)

see you Wednesday!

Ms Lovehouse

Figure 5.4 Email from Ms Lovehouse 18/10/2014

It is interesting that in a 144-word email, 55 words pertain to the reflection (the main reason Ms Lovehouse was asked to email me) and 72 refer to
additional information about her current independent efforts to improve her
English and the way these indirectly relate to the course. This communicated
two things to me: first, that Ms Lovehouse wanted to connect on a personal level
with me relating to some of the things we were working on in the course, but
mainly relating to the overall main aim of improving her English; and secondly,
that the reflection was less important than maintaining/repairing this personal
connection. Ms Lovehouse had struggled to do the output session, and I think
she was reaching out to me in this small way as an attempt to replenish rapport,
as no doubt like me she felt personally responsible for her poor performance.
In contrast, Mr Nintendo's reflection was only 39 words, although it is omitted
from this study as he opted out of the use of pedagogical data.

To my great surprise, Mr Nintendo was the best of the three presenters. He
spoke about the theme of 'mudbloods' in *Harry Potter* (hence Ms Lovehouse's
mention in her email), which I felt was very interesting, relevant and showed that
Mr Nintendo actually had a lot of interesting things to talk about. He was clearly
nervous to be doing an output session, yet he carried himself well and I felt that
he should have received an 'A' for his performance if it had been a standard presentation. However, in terms of making the session interactive, Mr Nintendo had
made no attempt to engage the audience or make his talk interactive for them.
It took me several days to finish marking the output sessions and a full week to
return their results, because I was torn between awarding them an 'A', which is
what I felt they wanted and expected, and a 'B', which was what I felt they actually

deserved in terms of their performance. I would still be pondering this decision for several weeks in the journal entries, along with other grading decisions.

In my reflection, I wondered:

> Why did I want them to do output sessions? My justification was to be able to stagger the assessments instead of getting the bottleneck, but it would have worked just as well with a normal presentation. At TUFS they never needed much preparation for output sessions. Comparing TUFS with CLERAC's output session tells me a lot about the kind of instruction that they have had previously. For example, Mr Fly must have had a very aggressive teacher based on the aggressive way he conducted the session, at times calling on other students to offer their opinions by simply pointing and saying 'you'.
>
> (Audio TRJournal 15/10/2014 [edited for clarity])

Overall, this first output session rather 'set the tone' for many of the ones to follow. I would feel I had not given them enough preparation, I would feel that I should have communicated my expectations more by providing a clearer marking scheme, and I would award grades which I felt were right and yet which I struggled to give to the students because they were low and thus demotivating and mutually disappointing.

Although it does not directly suggest that they were demotivated, the fact that Ms Lovehouse and Mr Nintendo were absent and Mr Fly was late to the next class seems to indicate negative motivation. Because both the students and I were feeling this orientation, we are still synergised, albeit negatively. This is best conceptualised as a result of my failure to clearly communicate my aims for the output sessions, which inevitably led to divergence as the aims were unclear.

5.5 Food

In lesson 203B on Friday 17/10/2014, we began the topic of food, which I knew would be successful as food in Japan is a very important cultural issue, and the previous semester several of the students had chosen *koshoku* (societal eating problems) as their video project. My 42-minute audio reflection and subsequent transcript present the polar extremes of my reaction to this class. At one point, discussing how I used the CALL room software to facilitate group discussions, I say:

> it was really exciting and the work went well, not enough time to present so using Coffee Room for homework. Very successful when they were using technology groups went well and improved tech handling on my part the lesson went well.

And yet later on, about 29 minutes into the recording, I state:

> CLERAC class was horrid. I wasn't really prepared. And then output session, two of the outputters were absent in today's class. I wonder why they were absent, perhaps it was related to their feeling about a bad output.

These two reflections seem almost to be about two different classes, but they are of course discussions of the same class, and indeed from the same reflection. This would seem to be an early example of how, as Claxton (2000) notes, too much reflection can actually be detrimental to the intuitive practitioner. It should also be noted that I claim to have stayed up working on preparing the lesson until midnight the day before, and then after waking up around 5 a.m. to have still been working on it right before the lesson started. Again, this would perhaps indicate the complexity of classroom motivation, as a simple thing such as amount of sleep can have a great influence on a person's cognitive functioning and the amount of energy reserves they have not just to accomplish a task but also in their reflections and long-lasting memories of the activity.

On 21/10/2014, I received an email from CLER which stated that the next year I would not be teaching CLERAC. This came as a surprise to me as I had expected to be teaching the course again. I noted in my journal that I was actually very pleased to learn that I would not have to teach CLERAC again, and this information had the paradoxical effect of investing me more in the CLERAC class as individuals but less in terms of materials development. Rather than thinking of the course as something I would teach again and again, I realised this would be a special class which I only taught once, and which, like DCT, would be a formative part of my teaching identity.

In lesson 204A on Wednesday 22/10/2014, I did my 'famous' Chicken Lesson. This is a lesson that I have taught many times, to several different groups of students, and for which I even have a special Christmas version. The lesson handouts are carefully designed with vocabulary items, warm-up tasks and a video from the Channel 4 food and lifestyle programme River Cottage with subtitles and comprehension questions which were written in order to guide understanding. Hugh Fearnley-Whittingstall interviews professor Michael Crawford, director of the Institute of Brain Chemistry and Human Nutrition. The focus of the video is not chicken welfare, but the fact that intensively reared chicken has a much lower omega-3 content to free-range chicken, which Crawford links to an impending mental health epidemic (many foods are now lower in omega-3). According to the video, factory-farmed chicken is also much fattier, containing up to 100 more calories per chicken thigh than in the 1970s. I use this video because when trying to 'make students care' about animals. I have often received the response of *shougannai* ('it can't be helped' in Japanese). Perhaps the general consensus is that cruelty to animals is a necessary consequence of producing enough meat. The United Kingdom has approximately 4 million vegetarians, with some accounts claiming up to 12 per cent of the population, and rising to 20 per cent for 16–24-year-olds (Mintel, 2014). Unlike the United Kingdom, vegetarianism in Japan has a low profile, and it can be difficult for vegetarians to find food which has not been prepared alongside meat dishes. According to a survey of 1,188 participants (Animal Rights Center, 2015), 4.7 per cent of respondents claimed to be vegetarian, although the figure may be even lower nationally. In the CLERAC class, nobody identified themselves as vegetarian. However, by highlighting the health issues connected to factory-farmed meat rather than the animal welfare issues, I sincerely hope to effect change in my learners in their behaviour as consumers. I always get extremely passionate about this issue, and go into detail about my experience of taste-testing the difference between free-range and 'cheap' chicken, even going so far as to offer a 'money back guarantee' if the students cannot taste the difference for themselves. In feedback I received from the DCT course (which was the first time I ever taught this lesson), I learned that at least one of my students had made lifestyle changes based on this lesson and had not only reduced her meat consumption but also completely vetoed intensively reared chicken.

I recorded feeling very happy with the banter that occurred between me and Mr Fly, who had jokingly said, 'I hate you' to me on the stairs when we met on the way to the lesson because he was hungry and I told him today's lesson was going to be about food. The other two members of his output session were again absent from this class.

In both class reflections of 15/10/2014 and 22/10/2014, I had noted my growing frustration with the three uncommunicative students, Mr Auxiliary, Mr Dawn and Mr Nintendo. Mr Nintendo's repeated absences were beginning to cause issues, and in this lesson there was nobody to work in a pair with Mr Auxiliary.

> Mr Dawn and Mr Nintendo away so Mr Auxiliary alone. When Ms Pine arrived late I asked her to sit with Mr Auxiliary but then I saw her eyes dart towards Ms Hemp and I said 'or you could work with Ms Hemp'. And of course she went to work with Ms Hemp. Then I asked Mr Auxiliary if he wanted to move, to work with Mr Montville and I could see Mr Montville put his head down because obviously he didn't want to work with this silent guy [...] nobody wants to work with him.
>
> (Audio TRJournal 22/10/2014)

I was already worried at this point that Mr Nintendo would fail the course on account of too many absences. When I asked Mr Auxiliary and Mr Dawn, they seemed to know nothing about him outside of the class and could not offer any insights as to why he was not attending. I felt that perhaps the output session had 'broken him', despite my feeling that he was the best of the three presenters and had finally talked about something interesting. Much later, when Mr Nintendo had definitely failed the class and ceased coming altogether, I asked Mr Dawn and Mr Auxiliary about him on 26/11/2014 and recorded that 'they had no idea and didn't seem to care'. This hints at a lack of empathy, which I will discuss more in the next chapter.

The following lesson, on Friday 24/10/2014, we conducted Food WebQuests, but I felt they went badly as I was unprepared. Again, I was still experimenting with the idea of responding to students and not being overprepared, skirting rather too close to being unprepared and therefore not being able to support or scaffold the students sufficiently. I recorded a great deal of frustration, noting that I felt their use of Japanese was a 'rebellion' against my lack of planning and lack of authority. I felt I needed more training about how to effectively use the CALL room.

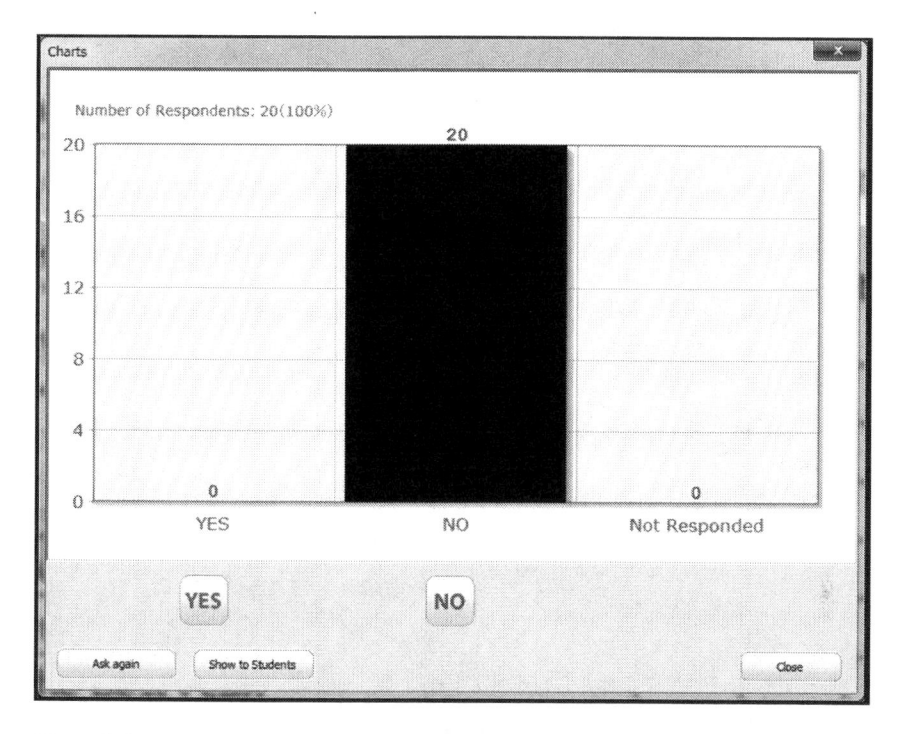

Figure 5.5 Do you speak 80 per cent English in class?

I feel like a cyclops trundling around class, half blind, I don't hear what they say, if I talk to them I interrupt. I tune out and even if I tune in [to what they are saying] they are talking in Japanese anyway.

(TRJournal 24/10/2014)

Tuesday 28/10/2014 was a 'Virtual Friday' which meant we were in the CALL room. I had intended to start the topic of consumerism, but the entire class was taken up with administration. In particular, we renegotiated the self-assessment marking criteria slightly and did self-assessment 201, the first of the autumn semester. During this class we decided to alter the 80 per cent English 20 per cent Japanese to 70/30, as I had noticed that the previous target was not being kept. Using the CaLabo response analyser, I asked the students, 'who used 80 per cent English during the class?', which produced the following result shown in Figure 5.5.

I then asked if we should change our participation criteria on the self-assessment sheet, which returned the answers given in Figure 5.6.

As I am able to see exactly how each student voted, I noted that the two who voted 'no' were Mr Charge and Mr Fly. Finally, I asked them how much they use English outside of the class (Figure 5.7).

A meant 'always', B 'regularly', C 'sometimes' and D 'never'. Mr Charge, Mr Po and Ms Downtree chose B and Mr Auxiliary chose C.

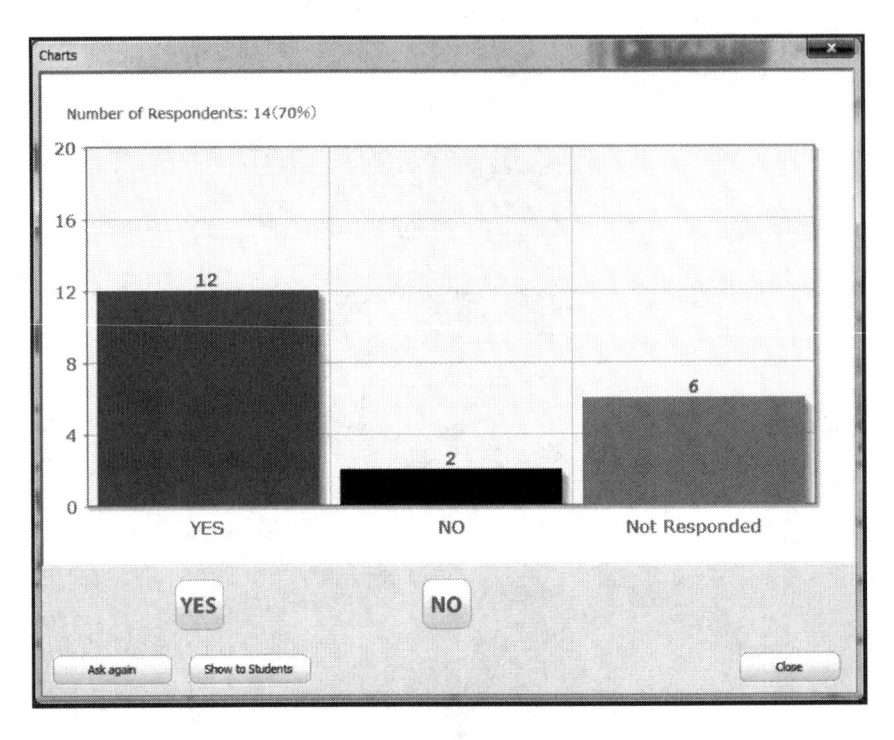

Figure 5.6 Should we change the participation criteria?

After completing the first self-assessment for autumn, we did the 'WAY task' detailed in Williams and Burden (1997), in which students have to make a list of 20 sentences, each starting with the words 'I am'. Initially this is very easy, but as the task progresses the replies become more personalised. My reflection on this lesson shows that I had made a very strong connection with the learners through this highly personalised task. I provided my own version first as an example. In my reflection I noted that nearly all the students started in the same way as mine. Many of them wanted to just copy and paste mine, and then as they worked down they realised they would have to write their own responses. The ones who were using my model got more stuck than those who did their own from the start, and I noticed Mr Po was the last to finish as his initial comments were very closely mapped to my example. I noted that I already knew Ms Saltfield played lacrosse, but today I learned that she played in goal. I learned that Ms Downtree loves teddy bears, and that Mr Charge had taken up boxing in order to protect the people he loves. Mr Fly made fun of him at first, but Mr Charge said, '*Urusei! Demo, honto da yo* [shut up! But, really you know].' I was strongly moved by this task, and I noted that I was really seeing the students as people today, 'not just seeing myself as a teacher but as a "person who teaches" and the same with the students, seeing them really as people'. However, I also reflected that:

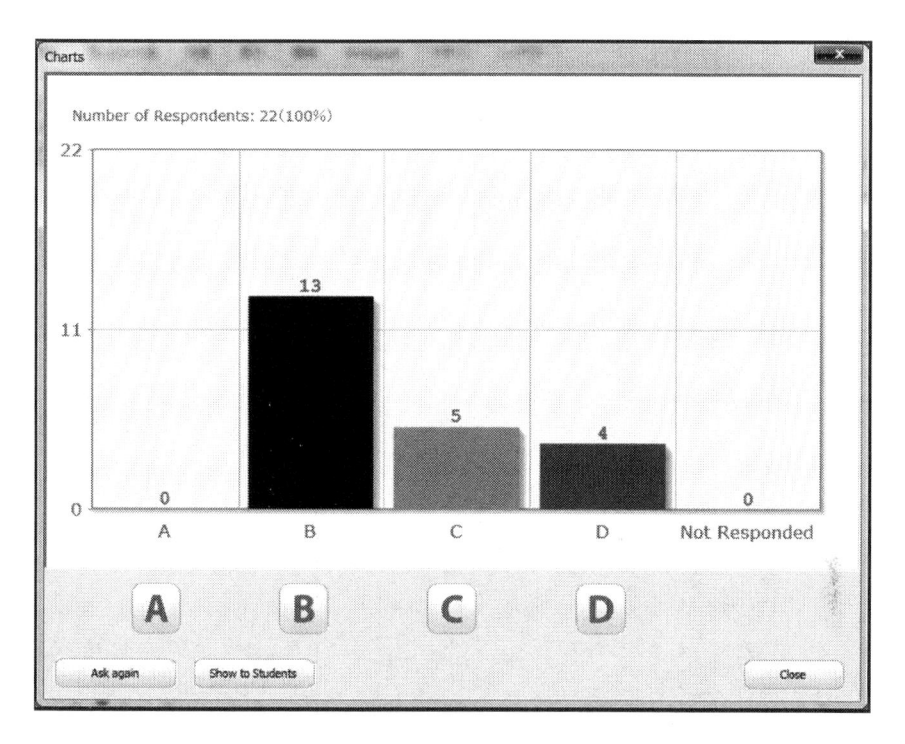

Figure 5.7 How much do you use English outside of class?

Learners as people – it's easy to say the words but to actually remember that and build that into everyday classroom interactions is challenging. As a teacher I see about 200 people a week – people who I am their teacher and that's our only connection. People who are younger than me, who may be very different, people with whom there is a linguistic barrier (especially from their perspective) but also there is a depleted amount of shared cultural capital, and the social capital changes too as I get older, as I identify myself more with the generation above them, see myself as very different to them in terms of my level of experience, of education. But I can still connect with them as people but there might also be negative effects of doing so... like for example getting too close so I can't grade them objectively (is being objective even that good?) and also might put the personal relationship as a higher priority than their learning... sometimes to be a good teacher you have to be strict... there is a fine balance and also that goes for them as well.

(TRJournal 28/10/2014)

I will expand on this reflection in Chapter 6, particularly in Section 6.6.2.1, when I discuss the 'David Brent Effect'.

The very next day, Wednesday 29/10/2014 lesson 205B, was the second output session, focused on food, featuring eight learners in the group. These

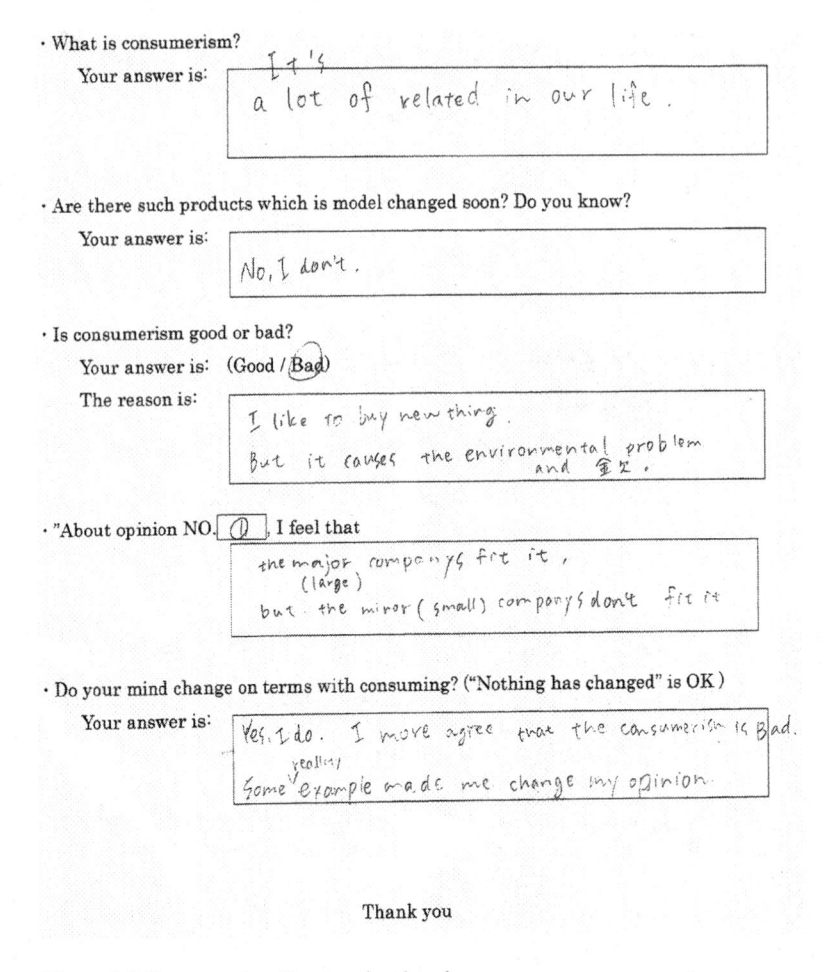

· What is consumerism?

Your answer is:

> It's a lot of related in our life.

· Are there such products which is model changed soon? Do you know?

Your answer is:

> No, I don't.

· Is consumerism good or bad?

Your answer is: (Good / ~~Bad~~)

The reason is:

> I like to buy new thing.
> But it causes the environmental problem and 負担.

· "About opinion NO. ① , I feel that

> the major companys fit it, (large)
> but the miror (small) companys don't fit it

· Do your mind change on terms with consuming? ("Nothing has changed" is OK)

Your answer is:

> Yes, I do. I more agree that the consumerism is Bad.
> Some real example made me change my opinion.

Thank you

Figure 5.8 Consumerism Output class handout

were Ms Sound, Mr Swamp, Ms Redslope, Ms Smallville, Ms Downtree, Ms Saltfield, Ms Oldriver and Mr Dawn. Again, it was not a good session, causing me to further speculate that the output sessions were a bad idea.

> [The output session] is kind of [deep intake of breath] almost like a cancer, eating away at the student's self-esteem. I need to find a way of fixing that.
> (Audio TRJournal 29/10/2014)

The problem I reflected was that, having had two groups give their output sessions, I felt it would not be fair to those who already finished their assessments to now give additional help to the students who were going to present in the future. In this way I felt I was trapped in an inescapable motivational drain. I felt it had been very 'hasty' of me to alter the syllabus to feature output sessions without having properly considered whether the students would be able to do them.

Another problem which I was noticing with the output sessions was that some students who were watching seemed disinterested in their fellow students' sessions, and I felt this was likely to be also having a negative effect on those presenting. This could be due to emotional contagion, a phenomenon closely related to empathy in which feelings spread quickly through individuals and groups of people, such as the spread of panic through crowds or elation through audiences in concerts (Goleman, 2006, pp. 114–117). From my own experience of presenting, it is easy to lose confidence in one's self when it seems that the audience are not paying attention, and I began to worry that it was not just my failure to help those giving the output sessions but also a more deeply rooted form of divergence that I felt possibly spanned from the learners' preference for teacher-fronted lessons. As I will discuss in more detail during the analysis section in Chapter 6, Japan's education system tends to place greater emphasis on the teacher than on the more collaborative, less hierarchical teaching approach employed at universities in the United States and Europe, for example. As a result, the students presenting, *and* particularly the students watching, were not invested in the output sessions, which is what lead to the divergent rift between our motivations and educational ideologies. In this way, although my and the students' negative motivation was synergistic, this was caused by a divergence in our approach and desires about how the class should be conducted.

Noticing this was facilitated by the output sessions themselves, in which I of course took a seat (usually centre-middle) amongst the students. I could only occasionally glance back to gauge the other students' reactions, and doing so obviously altered the students' current state (the observers' paradox), yet as I usually sat very near to Mr Po, I was able to observe him very closely. I made the following observation:

> I don't think they buy into the output session. Several students sleeping during the other students' outputs. Mr Po was basically sleeping right from the start; he was not committed. Someone else was on their phone. Output sessions are a disaster, going to create a lot of damage if I don't repair, but I can't repair because I am already committed. Kind of powerless.
>
> (TRJournal 29/10/2014)

I would follow this up with later observations, and eventually I even confronted Mr Po about his attitudes to the output session, hoping to shed some light on this barrier to class synergy.

5.6 Consumerism

In lesson 206A on Wednesday 05/11/2014, we 'broached' the subject of consumerism. I had been looking forward to this because I had described this topic as the 'first eye opener' of the DCT course in 2012. This is because consumerism is one of the things I find most upsetting about the modern world, so I felt a great personal investment in this topic as I felt that in helping the students to critically examine their own roles as consumers and the impact their choices have on society and the environment, they might actually start to make lifestyle changes. The first thing I did in the lesson was to ask students whether consumerism was a good or bad thing, and many of them impressed me by answering along the lines of 'both'. However, I noted that I was 'off to a bad start' as six or seven people arrived late.

> None of them had printed the handout, so that was kind of annoying. Started to feel a bit disappointed in them all. That started to affect my motivation and I started to feel it sinking and they were also, I felt, not really engaging. They were all very quiet during the discussion. I had to physically work hard to motivate them. To break the ice. They have these lulls and troughs and it was my job to work through them.
>
> (TRJournal 05/11/2014)

The lesson culminated with students working in groups to write discussion questions, which would then be used in Friday's lesson (07/11/2014) where students used the CaLabo software to record a 'podcast' discussion, based on the discussion questions from today. This was a very successful strategy, as the time allowance was generous, and working together the students were able to hold scaffolded discussions on the topics. Despite the 'disaster' of the output sessions, it seemed that I was able, by 'a sheer force of will' (05/11/2014), to manage to motivate the class. I noted that I had to motivate myself in order to motivate them, by having 'banter' with members of the class, by focusing on them as individuals and using our past experiences as a way of creating a good rapport again. Doing this required me to really 'be in the moment' of the class, which invokes elements of motivational flow theory which I will discuss more in the analysis section.

The students needed to work in groups of three or more to write discussion questions, and I noted that I was very proud of Mr Cloud, who volunteered to leave his friend Mr Po's side and work with the 'silent' students, Mr Auxiliary and Mr Dawn, at the back. He seemed to be able to engage them and got them talking, and I was very happy about this dynamic.

I was using several indicators during the class to gauge the student's motivational levels. The main one appeared to be simply the noise levels of the class while the students were doing discussion tasks. As discussed in Chapter 2, it is relatively easy for teachers to accurately gauge students' on-task levels of engagement and to tell whether the class is working hard or not, and this ability is identified as one of the indicators of synergy. At first, the class seemed very quiet, and rather reluctant to speak. I recorded that I needed to turn on more lights (at the expense of being able to see what was on the projector) and open the blinds to let more sunlight in. I did not record what the weather was like that day, but if it was raining this could have also been a factor perhaps.

Around 10–20 mins into the class they were doing the discussion. And I said 'Oh, I know why it's quiet. Because last week you did the self-assessment and you've been trying to speak only in English' and that made them laugh and broke the ice but also made them speak more Japanese. I kind of gradually got them motivated. By the time we did the group work it was good. They had to write six questions and that was a focused task and so they could do it.

(TRJournal 05/11/2014)

Clearly in this context, my concept of motivation really just extends to on-task motivation to accomplish the current activity, and it is mainly measured by my awareness of indicators such as on-task engagement and group dynamics. However, my ability to engage the class came at the expense of being a teacher and doing certain authoritarian duties which I felt needed doing.

Was going to [reprimand] all the late people, but I didn't do it. Didn't want to damage the rapport that I worked so hard to create. Today's class started quite badly but I saved it and it ended up being a good class. But my motivation is down. November, two more months, feels a long way off and yet it will be over soon and then I won't be teaching this class again. Not just the students but also the course. Difficult to invest in it as I know I won't be teaching it again.

Again, this reluctance to invoke my teaching identity as an authoritarian is linked to what I later term the David Brent Effect.

As briefly stated earlier, the task from Wednesday was continued on Friday, which involved students recording a 'podcast' discussion based on the questions they collaborated on previously. Before the class, I had specifically asked for help from one of the technicians, so my own sense of self-efficacy about using the CALL room was higher, which almost certainly led to the higher levels of on-task engagement and the ensuing rise in motivation. Another factor was the increased scaffolding (particularly in terms of preparation time) for the task. Whilst my journal credits my own 'force of will' for 'saving' the lessons from low motivation, it seems that the synergising was greatly facilitated by working within the students' zone of proximal development (ZPD) (Lantolf, 2000a; Vygotsky, 1978) and, to borrow terms from self-actualisation theory, allowing the students to work in areas where they felt competence, relevance and relatedness. During the Friday class, when the students recorded their headset discussions using the CALL room's CaLabo software, I noted that there was something 'a little unnatural, or, dare I say it, inauthentic' about having them talk to one another through voice over internet protocol (VOIP) despite being in the same room, but it seemed to work well as a structured task, and everybody knew what to do and was well rehearsed in how to express themselves. However, I did note that the way the task was set up using a cyclical, turn-taking format seemed very reminiscent of the studies by Dam and Legenhausen (2001) and Legenhausen (1999) which compared the formulaic and unnatural discourse of a German Gymnasium secondary school with that of students from a much more autonomous and naturally free speaking school in Denmark.

With only two lessons on consumerism, the third output session was planned for Wednesday 12/11/2014. The consumerism output group consisted of just four students: Mr Widetree, Mr Mouth, Mr Auxiliary and Mr Charge. Despite my misgivings about the other members, I was quite confident that Mr Charge would not fail to deliver a good session, and his performance in the output session led to what I labelled an 'output session turning point'. Even now, over two years later, I can still feel a great well of emotion as I compose this part of the narrative.

5.6.1 Mr Charge to the rescue

As the narrative has already made clear, the output sessions were a serious problem in the autumn semester, and I came to view them as 'a cancer, eating away at the student's self-esteem' and motivation (TRJournal 29/10/2014). I was certainly attributing the output sessions to the lack of positive motivational synergy and divergence that both the students and I were experiencing around this time in the semester. However, when the consumerism group took charge of the class on 12/11/2014, their session lasted 45 minutes, with an additional 15 minutes for questions and answers, and in that time I felt that they had reversed the negative feelings and doubts I had been experiencing about these sessions. I specifically attributed this to one student in particular, Mr Charge, who I reflected had 'basically carried the whole output session, and carried the whole class, and also single-handedly repaired and turned around the whole output crash, disaster, that was taking place' (TRJournal 12/11/2014).

This group structured their session around the following, rather unpromising looking handout (Figure 5.8); this example also features the answers written by a participating student) which was later followed up with a Coffee Room post.

First, Mr Charge had the students compose their answers in writing before asking them to communicate about the questions. Each box marked a stage in the output session, with the final box being used for the final and concluding part of the session. In this way the session was very tightly structured and also provided each participant with ample opportunity to prepare what they would say during the discussion. Mr Charge was doing *exactly* what an experienced teacher would do; seemingly he already knew about scaffolding. This was particularly interesting, as, despite my almost ten years of teaching experience at that time, due to my working for the relatively high-level literature department I had fallen out of practice with lower groups and was only now working out how to balance difficult content topics from the autumn semester with the slightly lower level of CLERAC. As such, I was less adept at communicating my aims to the class, and it is likely that much of the incidental feedback that occurs between students and teachers during lessons was not always picked up on. Despite the errors in the wording of some of his questions, once explained, it seemed that most students were able to contribute their answers (as the example in the figure shows). When Mr Charge elicited answers from the other

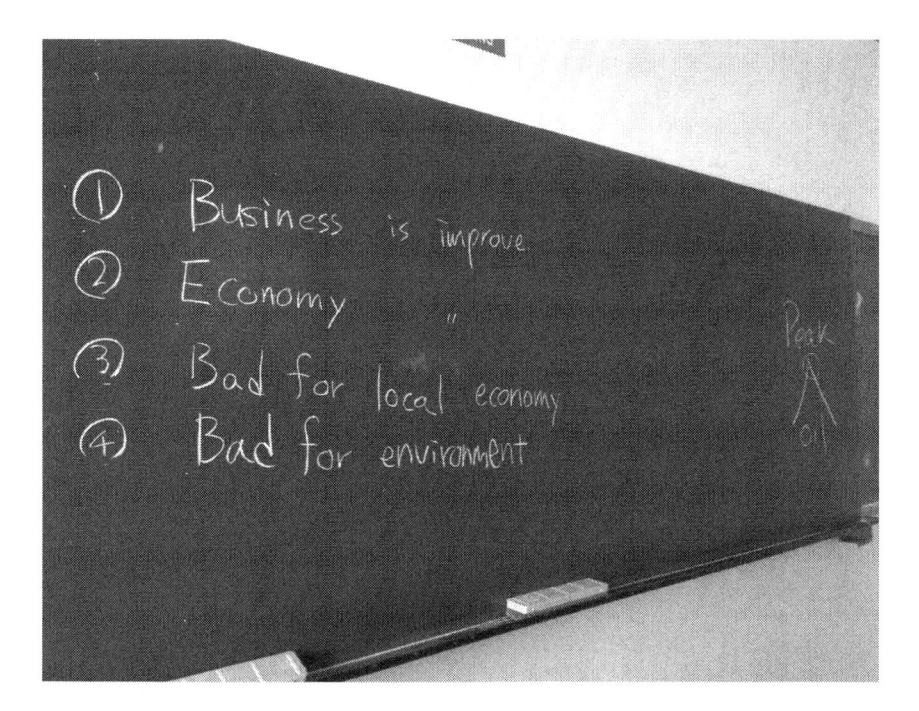

Figure 5.9 Consumerism Output board work

students, he wrote them on the board and used them directly when he moved on to the next topic. In this way he and the class worked together towards a better understanding (Figure 5.10).

Not only was the output session carefully planned and scaffolded, but Mr Charge's manner was also very authoritative yet caring. He called on students by name, thanked them for their answers and created an air of mutual respect whilst retaining his authority. However, it would not be fair to say that Mr Charge was solely responsible for the excellent output session. Beyond any expectation, Mr Widetree, who had been rather ominously late for his own output session and only made it a few seconds before they were to start, was one of the people who contributed to the turning point. I recorded that Mr Widetree actually asked me a question directly, which until now none of the other groups had done. I reflected that this was 'a turning point, shift in power, me as a participant'. I also noted that Mr Charge gave me a thumbs up for my answer, much as I would do to a student, and that he seemed to feel a little awkward about doing so, but it felt good that he did it, although it was just a quick gesture. Even the usually reticent Mr Auxiliary was able to do well in the session.

Mr Widetree was not the only person missing when the class started. There were ten people late in total, with three people absent. This further supports my hypothesis that the students were not invested in the idea of output sessions *as*

Hi Mr Charge,
I was really impressed by your output session today. I was wondering if you could
tell me more about how you planned the session and why you were able to be so
successful with it? Is it from your Juku teaching experience? Were you motivated by
the topic (consumerism)?

I'd appreciate your answers about this!

Thanks again,
Richard

Figure 5.10 My email to Mr Charge

observers, which led to the motivational divergence which I have been able to
describe throughout the narrative of autumn. Further evidence for this comes
from the following excerpt from my journal:

> I noticed Mr Po was not writing anything [for the tasks that involved
> writing]. Didn't even have his pen *on the desk* [it was still in his bag]. Had his
> smartphone on the desk. I identified Mr Po's output session sheet and took
> a shot of it. Has short, basic, non-committal answers on it. He wrote eight
> words in five boxes. Two of them are blank. He really hasn't made an effort
> there. Then I saw him on his phone.
>
> (TRJournal 12/11/2014)

Following on from the incident in which Mr Widetree had caused a 'shift in
power' by asking me a question, I wrote:

> And this is what I think Mr Po doesn't like [the student-teacher role reversal].
> He doesn't invest in the output sessions. He is very motivated and invested
> when it is a teacher fronted class, but he is not invested [in what the other
> students can teach him].

This is a vital snapshot in the narrative of this inquiry, because usually the teacher
is viewed as having a central role in the group dynamics of a class (Dörnyei &
Murphey, 2003). Several wide-scale empirical studies have been able to firmly
establish that perhaps the single most important contributor to classroom motivation is the teacher (Chambers, 1999; Dörnyei & Csizér, 1998; see Dörnyei &
Ushioda, 2011 for further examples). However, this turning point shows that,
given the right dynamics, students can also take on the role as energisers.
Mr Charge was an extremely highly motivated person and an excellent student,
but just as there are less motivated students in every class, there are also more
highly motivated ones too. Mr Charge motivated me in the class and made me
feel much better about myself and the structure of the course. It seems that
he was also able to motivate others, as this comment from Ms Hemp's end of
semester reaction paper submitted in January 2015 shows:

My motivation changed thanks to this class. I didn't like English so much until a high school student because I was not able to understand words which were spoken in English. However, I enjoyed your class. When I saw the person of this class talked in English with a teacher smoothly, I got motivation.

Interestingly, in the mid-semester review activity which I used as a needs analysis opportunity, on 25/11/2014 Mr Auxiliary wrote the following two statements:

- *What have you enjoyed most this semester?*
- It is classmates' output session that I have enjoyed most this semester. I can more relax because they are same age.
- *What have you enjoyed least this semester?*
- I was not able to enjoyed my output session. Because I felt pressure and was not able to afford to enjoy it.

Certainly something I noticed whenever I looked back at Mr Auxiliary during other students' output sessions was that he usually seemed alert, although I had half expected to find him sleeping. I noted that he 'was looking at his fingernails' later on during the Wildlife output on 10/12/2014. Yet, there is something a little strange about this statement as well. As I have recorded, the act of watching most of the students' output sessions was uncomfortable because very few of them were able to do it well. For example, in Ms Saltfield's mid-semester review, she wrote that her least favourite part of the class was the output. She wrote, 'I failed my output, and I had got a tense in a output class' (26/11/2014). Ms Lovehouse also used the mid-semester review to comment on output sessions. When asked which lesson she had enjoyed most, she said, 'I enjoyed the [consumerism] output session. The plan of the class was interesting, and made me fun to think about it.' However, when asked what she had enjoyed least she said, 'My output session:-< I couldn't enjoy at all. Just strained all one and a half hour. And I don't feel my output session was good…' (26/11/2014). The fact that Mr Auxiliary enjoyed watching other people's output sessions, when they themselves confirmed my observation that they were uncomfortable, perhaps might suggest that Mr Auxiliary is not able to recognise the emotions of others to a strong degree, perhaps revealing a general lack of empathic ability. This would explain his reticence in the class to communicate and his poor social status within the group. I will also return to this issue later when I discuss his participation in a recorded CALL room group discussion.

Sadly, my reflection does not mention Mr Auxiliary in great detail, despite having decided to structure my narrative around Focal Participants on 07/11/2014 and no doubt having chosen him to be one of them. My feedback to each of the other members (apart from Mr Charge) mentioned that their part had been rather short. This is what I sent to Mr Auxiliary as his individual feedback:

You did a very nice job of asking your classmates about their answers. You were firm but gentle in asking them for their contribution. You seemed confident and did very well, but your part was quite short overall.

(CLERAC2014B Grades)

It seems from this that even Mr Auxiliary was able to make the session interactive, and to have the confidence to ask his peers to discuss questions in groups. Again, this would seem suggestive of the synergising going on in this lesson, but instead of the students feeding off of my confidence in the social situation, they were feeding of that of another student, Mr Charge. One reason that I suspected Mr Charge was able to do such an amazing job in his output session was that he works part-time at a cram school, known as a *juku* in Japan. I wanted to know if his experience as a *juku* teacher had helped him give such a good output session, and whether he had received any special training.

I also noted that Mr Po had not really engaged in the session as thoroughly as I would have liked. I reflected that, since I was less worried about the output session as it was going well, I was able to relax a lot more and just enjoy it. This meant that I was able to focus more attention on the other students watching the session. As a result of this class, I decided I needed to send two emails, one to Mr Charge and one to Mr Po, in order to learn more about their orientation towards the output session. This could be regarded as an attempt at respondent validation. Although I did not realise it at the time, it seems I was already aware that Mr Charge was convergent with the output sessions, whereas Mr Po seemed to be divergent, and I wanted further evidence to corroborate this.

5.6.2 Mr Charge's email

When I contacted Mr Charge on 12/11/2014, I asked him to offer a little more about his output session (Figure 5.10). He wrote a reflection on 14/11/2014 and then replied to my further email on 15/11/2014 (Figure 5.11), which shows that he perhaps did not notice my email until after writing his reflection.

Another interesting fact from this email is that Mr Charge also seems quite capable of reading what the other students (as a group) are feeling, revealing his ability to empathise with the group as a whole, and he explains that he wanted to communicate his passion and effect change in his fellow students. This would seem to strongly suggest that Mr Charge was seeking to converge with his peers, and that he was synergistically aware of their responses to him. He denies that his *juku* teaching has anything to do with it, although I still feel it must be connected. I should also point out that Mr Charge seems to have no intention of becoming a teacher or working in education, as his ambition has remained to work on engines and to study at graduate level in order to get a good job in the aviation industry.

In his +,-,= reflection on his output session, he further demonstrated his ability for empathy and to understand how he was perceived by the group when he discussed his weakness during the session:

> Bad point; We showed them a video, in which English was fast and difficult for them. I am afraid that they could not understand that video.....We should have prepared the transcript.
>
> (email to me, 14/11/2014)

Hello, Richard.

I was really really surprised that you gave me perfect score for my out put session.
> Surely I made a lot of effort to make my session better, so I am very happy to be able to make you impressed.

But...as you told me, there were some silence in the session. We felt that it is not good while carrying out it. I should also think how I can avoid silence

Next, about how I planed the session.

When I saw previous two group's out put session, I felt that it was only reading the script. It seemed that they did't have the will to tell us something at all....They were not interesting in their topic, just did it because Richard say. To be honest, such a session was tired for the listener.

But. But I am really interested in Consumerism (I always feel that people's behavior of consuming is so bad. Many people don't value things at all. They should change).
> I have a lot which I want to tell everyone.

I want everyone to change.

I think it is all that drove me and let me do successful session. If people have concretely will, they can do themselves best. (Juku teaching experience has nothing to do with it.)

I could enjoy myself in the session very very much. Thank you.

Figure 5.11 Mr Charge's reply

The fact that Mr Charge was able to gauge the students' level of understanding shows that he was keenly attuned to the group dynamics. This seems to be in sharp contrast with Mr Auxiliary, who enjoyed watching other people's output sessions and seemed almost oblivious to their discomfort during their own sessions. However, Mr Charge's enthusiasm was not met by all the students, which brings me to Mr Po's email of a very different nature.

5.6.3 *Mr Po's email*

On the same day that I emailed Mr Charge, I also sent the following email to Mr Po (Figure 5.12).

As the email shows, I tried to avoid scolding Mr Po or from awarding him any blame for his lack of attention. This was a conscious attempt at avoiding a defensive (and thus potentially insincere) reply. The very next day, on 13/11/2014 (Mr Po was always quick with his online posts and correspondence), I received a reply (Figure 5.13).

Despite my efforts, I felt this reply did not really explain the underlying reason for Mr Po's lack of attention. He claimed to be checking words on his smartphone, and made reference to this excuse again in his end of semester reaction paper. However, given Mr Po's relatively high English compared to other learners in the class, I find it very unlikely that the amount of time I observed him checking his phone would be necessary from the lexical density of his peer's speech (see Chapter 6 and the digital appendix (Appendix 5) for performance indicators). This is another reason why I did not pursue the students for respondent validation

Dear Mr Po.

Hi this is Richard, your Academic Communication teacher. I'd like to ask you a little
about the Output sessions we have been having in class.

I noticed that usually in class you are one of the most motivated and attentive students,
and I am very grateful for your attention. However, I also noticed that in the Output
session you seem to be uninterested, and you often just use your smartphone or
don't listen to the presentations. I was wondering if you could tell me how you feel
about the output sessions? Do you think they are a waste of time? Why/why not?
Would you prefer a lesson where the teacher does most of the talking?

I'd appreciate your answers about this, because I have been a little worried in general
about the output sessions. Perhaps they are too difficult?

What do you think?

Thanks a lot,

Richard

Figure 5.12 My email to Mr Po

Thu 13/11/2014, 14:55

I am sorry for it.
I am not knowledge for vocabulary.
So I always check what a word or a idiom means by my smartphone.
And sometime I am really tired and sleepy.
So I can't concentrate.
I am wrong.

I don't think they are a waste of time.
If anything, they are pretty good make me presure.

Figure 5.13 Mr Po's reply

after the course had finished. Although I did have contact with Mr Charge and
Mr Swamp after the course had concluded, for the most part the contact with
students ended when the course ended (see also Section 5.12 regarding the final
class and the second RED, as well as the afterward in Chapter 8).

This snapshot has revealed three broad types of interaction in relation to the
output sessions and with relevance to motivational synergy. First, Mr Charge's
desire to influence his group, his ability to read the group's responses and the
reactions to his session from other students would seem to suggest that Mr Charge
was capable of creating a synergistic link with the class, just as I (the teacher) am
able to do if I invest enough energy. This shows that the students play a very
significant role in motivational synergy, and it would suggest that Mr Charge
was seeking convergence with the group. Secondly, I looked at Mr Auxiliary's
reaction to the output sessions, in which he seemed unhappy with his own performance (despite this having been actually rather good) and to prefer watching
other students give output sessions, even though for a person who can read social

emotions (i.e. someone with high emotional intelligence) this would have been an uncomfortable situation. Nobody else mentioned that they had enjoyed other people's output sessions, except for Ms Lovehouse, who made it clear that she was only talking about the consumerism output. This seems to suggest that Mr Auxiliary was lacking in certain social skills relating to empathy, in stark contrast to Mr Charge, who possessed such skills to a highly advanced degree. Thirdly, I looked at Mr Po's mysterious divergence from his peers' output sessions and I used this to hypothesise that Mr Po preferred teacher-fronted learning and did not recognise his peers as being useful sources of knowledge construction. Sadly, this must remain a hypothesis as Mr Po's response to my questions did not reveal any further insights, but his position as a Chinese student in a class with 24 other Japanese members may have had some unconscious bearing on this orientation, although I can only speculate about this. Overall, these observations seem to lend a very useful insight into the complex nature of group dynamics and motivational synergy taking place in the language classroom of the CLERAC course.

5.7 Oil and the economy

Although this was an important part of the course, because there was no output session for this topic I will give only a very cursory treatment of this part of the semester, in order to give more focus to other sections. In lesson 207B on Friday 14/11/2014, I introduced the topic of peak oil and had the students watch five- to ten-minute sections of a 34-minute video on YouTube called *There's No Tomorrow* (2012), which explains through an easy to understand animation why our current reliance on oil for the global economy is unsustainable. The video is rather bleak, and so students were assigned a section of the video to watch and summarise, which was then turned into an information gap exercise conducted using the CALL room's CaLabo software and recorded. This was again a very structured task that worked well, unlike lesson 208A on Wednesday 19/11/2014, in which we watched another documentary called *The End of Suburbia* (2004). Despite having used this video several times and it having been too difficult for the students, I did the same thing again with CLERAC and recorded that it was an 'inevitable disaster' and a 'lazy lesson' in which I basically had just not done the necessary revising of the material because it would have taken too long. Students openly slept during the class, and I even used my notes to draw a picture of Ms Downtree and Ms Oldriver, with the annotation 'fully asleep didn't even wake up at stop vid' (Figure 5.14)

This is an excellent example of low EROI, and my initial energy investment being low meant that Ms Downtree and Ms Oldriver could not even remain conscious for the lesson. Sleeping in class can be seen as a passive act of resistance (Holliday, 2005, p. 98; Tong, 2002). I offer no explanation during my reflection about why I did not do more to improve upon this lesson, although it seems in retrospect to be due to overexertion on my part. There were several other events taking place in my life at the time. However, this lesson did lead me to the interesting observation that one of the problems with the autumn semester's

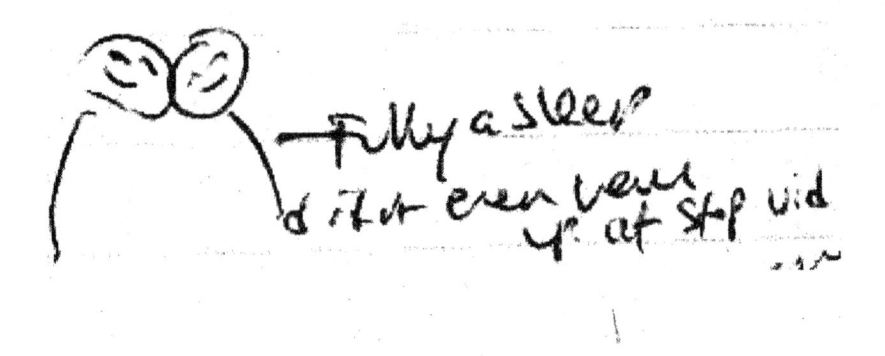

Figure 5.14 My sketch of the sleeping Ms Downtree and Ms Oldriver

content-based approach was that the CLERAC course often did not have the necessary language ability to deal with the content that I was trying to use with them. As touched upon earlier, this could perhaps be due to the fact that most of the content I was using had been geared towards the very advanced DCT course, and that I had failed to properly adapt it for CLERAC. I labelled this problem peak comprehension and noted that I needed to do a lot more in terms of scaffolding in order to overcome this barrier.

5.8 Mid-semester review activity

In lesson 208B (21/11/2014), we held the mid-semester review activity, which was previously the diagnostic exam in spring. In the spring, the diagnostic exams had been one of the divergent experiences which damaged the positive synergy of the class. I did not want the same to happen again in autumn, especially with the difficulties that had surrounded the output sessions, so I had decided to change the exam into a review activity. Until the night before the lesson, I still had no plan as for what to do in the mid-semester review activity. Then I had a sudden inspiration based on something I had read recently, in which I learned that Fridays are very autonomous at Google because workers are allowed to choose whatever projects they wish to work on, leading to several innovations (Gersch, 2013). Based on this idea, I was able to find a way of making the mid-semester exam both a learning and a teaching experience for the students. Rather than setting a standard exam, I explained to the students that they had 40 minutes to research or investigate how to study English in their own way. After 40 minutes, students were asked to present what they did and assess this as a way of studying English on their own, based on the criteria of 1) enjoyability, 2) potential for learning and 3) sustainability. After the initial stage, students used CaLabo software to hold recorded group discussions. They also produced a written report, which provided me with ample data to assess their English progress. I was very happy with this form of alternative assessment, which focused directly on the learners and tried to engage their identities and individual learning styles. I lamented not having had the idea last semester. Watching the students all working on their own ways to practise English for the first 40 minutes of the task brought me an enormous sense of well-being.

I later listened to the discussions that the students had recorded using the CaLabo software. One in particular was very interesting, as it featured Mr Auxiliary and demonstrated once again that he was not necessarily demotivated to study English, but, perhaps more seriously, he seemed to actually have difficulty talking with people in a group, even when he was allowed to use Japanese.

5.8.1 *Student discourse transcript*

Due to the length of the transcript, I provide merely a summary here and the full transcript in the Appendix (4). The conversation involved Mr Auxiliary, Ms Oldriver, Mr House and Mr Widetree. Mr Widetree arrived late to this lesson and also misunderstood the task (despite my having personally explained it to him and the provision of written instructions), so much of his turn is omitted (turn 22) as it was simply a discussion in Japanese about what Mr Widetree should have done, a discussion which Mr Auxiliary did not join and he is the main focus of the analysis of this transcript.

As can be seen, the most active speaker of the group was Ms Oldriver, who had 39 turns out of 124 (31.5 per cent). She also had the longest turns in general. This is in rather stark contrast to findings from Genderlect studies and the normal patterns of male/female discourse. For example, women are reported to generally speak much less when communicating with a group of men, and are interrupted more frequently (Norton & Pavlenko, 2004; Tannen, 1991; Wardhaugh, 2006). This is worth discussing briefly as it would suggest that the usual gendered power imbalances which are prevalent are circumvented by the empowering nature of the English language, especially when the female is the most proficient in terms of communicative ability, as was the case here. This is interesting from the Japanese context particularly, due to the strong genderlect of Japanese and patriarchal social hierarchy. This has been looked at by several other scholars, and links with the idea of *akogare*, which I discussed in the spring narrative (Bailey, 2006; Kelsky, 1999; Takahashi, 2013). When Ms Oldriver elicits speech from Mr Auxiliary in turn 87, it is clear that she holds the power of the conversation and is trying to balance the discourse to include Mr Auxiliary, who until this point had remained silent since finishing his 'institutional' role when he gave the speech he had created for the mid-semester review task (turn 12 is the entire task). Mr Auxiliary has only 13 turns in the entire dialogue. His speech is always elicited, either by other speakers (Ms Oldriver) or by the demands of the task itself. As Mr Auxiliary speaks, he is encouraged by Ms Oldriver but also the other participants through discourse markers (mainly in Japanese), and given scaffolding in the way of concept checking, affirmation and a certain degree of patience. This suggests that there was a degree of empathy towards Mr Auxiliary from the other group members, which is an important part of the positive and convergent dynamics of the classroom synergies.

There are 1,129 words in the transcript (minus translations), although the discussion took almost exactly 21 minutes. It seems quite apparent, from both the number of turns and the total duration of speech, that Mr Auxiliary was severely out of balance in terms of discourse with his peers. Again, this would seem to suggest a deeper social issue rather than merely an aversion (or divergent motivation) towards English on Mr Auxiliary's part. I will return to this issue in more depth in the next chapter.

One other interesting feature of the transcript is that there are two types of classroom discourse contained within. The first is the linear, structured and rather scripted on-task discourse in which students talk about exactly what they have been told to discuss (in this case how to study English), which occurs mainly between turns 9 and 23. In turn 24, Ms Oldriver says *owachatta*, which is the Japanese word for 'to finish', plus an abbreviated form of the verb ending *shimau*, which is often used to express regret (Makino & Tsutsui, 1986, p. 404). Thus I translated this as 'oh no, we finished' as there is clearly a sense of confusion and worry about how to maintain the conversation in English now that each speaker had fulfilled their role in the task. The second type of classroom discourse is the unscripted attempt at continuing the conversation in a 'natural' way. This group was, out of the other five groups, perhaps the one which struggled the most to maintain the second type of discourse. However, the fact that they did try singles them out from the group containing Mr Po and Mr Charge, who made no attempt to continue the conversation once the task was complete and spent the remainder of the time browsing the Internet. The group containing Ms Downtree, Mr Fly and Ms Saltfield was, I noted in my field observations and from listening back to their transcript, three times longer than any other and featured almost no breaks in the discourse. The students discussed singing karaoke in English, which Ms Downtree said she does because 'it's cool'.

The two types of discourse (task-structured and post-task unstructured) are interesting because they seem to combine the two markedly different transcripts presented in Legenhausen (1999, pp. 166–167) into one, although the CLERAC transcript never really goes as far as it could have with a more communicative group like the one featuring Ms Downtree. Rampton (1999, 2002) has also examined the way students used 'ritualised' target language in a German class in London with teenagers, whose 'ragged and reluctant participation' (2002, p. 502) was a result of the teacher's overly ritualistic style of teaching and was 'preserved by a pedagogy that kept the students' own agendas and experience at arm's length' (p. 495). In other words, students were not allowed to personalise their language use because of the ritual nature of the tasks (see Mitchell, Myles, & Marsden, 2013, p. 280 for related discussions).

In my audio journal later after observing another CaLabo activity (09/01/2015), I noted that certain groups did not have much of a discussion because they were 'too structured'. I felt this could be a problem with the inherent 'inauthenticity' of using a headset to communicate over VOIP with someone who is already in the same room (as discussed in Section 5.6). This combines with the other issue of using English to communicate when the students all share a higher proficiency in Japanese, which also makes communication only in English somewhat 'inauthentic'. I will discuss how these issues contribute to the authenticity gap in the next chapter.

5.9 Wildlife and the environment

In lesson 209A (26/11/2014), we began the final of the content topics. Because the number of students who had chosen this as their output topic was very large (N = 10), the group was further divided into a Wildlife group (N = 5) and an Environment group (N = 5) who would conduct their output sessions in concurrent lessons (210B and 211A). In lesson 209A, I introduced the students to the documentary *No Impact Man* (2009), which I briefly explained in the overview of the narrative. The main point of the lesson was to ask the students to list things they had done today which helped the environment, and then to list things which they had done today that damaged the environment. It was very eye-opening for the students to realise that the latter list was much longer. We then used this to create three pledges to become 'a greener you', in which each student stood up and presented to the class what they planned to do next week in order to be a greener, more environmentally friendly person. I also made three pledges, one of which was to no longer use the elevator to get up to my office on the fifth floor (a journey I make around four times a day or more). In the following lesson (209B 28/11/2014), we presented our results. Many of the students had been able to keep their pledges, although many others had only been able to keep one or two. The main thing was the students' honesty and genuine attempt to change, which made me very happy, although I noted that I felt not all the students were honest. For example, Mr Widetree said he had kept all three of his pledges. I asked him, 'really, what did you do?' during the lesson, to which he replied that one of his pledges was 'saving energy'. In my reflection I recorded that this was 'very vague' and I wanted to ask him for more detail. I noted that 'it kind of annoyed me that he has given himself the three but he hadn't really done anything'. I was often suspicious of Mr Widetree, who would appear to be a hard-working person and much more outgoing and communicative than Mr Auxiliary, for example. However, I felt Mr Widetree was 'sly' and wanted to deceive me into thinking he was a hard worker when in fact he rarely invested much effort into the class, as I will discuss more in the next chapter, when I examine the fact that Mr Widetree awarded himself the maximum score and highest in the class for participation on his self-assessment.

Also, during this lesson I was able to find a way of overcoming the earlier problem of peak comprehension by using TED videos, which often feature Japanese subtitles (some TED videos may have as many as 44 language options in the subtitles). In 2013, when I had taught the INT class (the precursor to CLERAC before the course was changed), we had watched all of *An Inconvenient Truth* (2006) which, in my old teaching journal from that time I noted was 'a cop out' (Prior Teaching Journal, 29/05/2013) because neither I nor the students really wanted to do any work. This was actually one of my earliest observations about teacher-student motivational synergy. I rectified that event in the CLERAC course by selecting a TED video presented by Al Gore which was more contemporary, shorter and overcame peak comprehension by using Japanese subtitles in order to help scaffold the students beyond their ZPD and enable them to follow the main content. This shows that I was developing as a teacher, and that the act of reflecting on this development had led it to become much more ingrained in my current teaching practices (a theme I return to in the next chapter).

Between this lesson and the next one, I attended my evening Japanese class which I had been taking since the start of the semester. In the class was a young Frenchman named Nicolas who was working as a research assistant at the Department of Global Studies, having just earned his undergraduate degree there. I liked Nicolas as he was very enthusiastic about Japanese and seemed to be top of our class. After the class we spoke in English and he told me he was interested in environmental economics. I actually have a friend working in China who works for an environmental consultancy, and I wondered if Nicolas would be interested in being in touch with this friend, to which Nicolas responded enthusiastically and seemed very grateful that I had a strong contact working in such a relevant area. Nicolas emailed me later so that I could forward his details to my friend. His being a nice guy, good at English, a recent graduate and now seemingly in my debt somewhat for me putting him in touch with my friend got me thinking that I could perhaps ask Nicolas to come to CLERAC as a guest speaker and give a short lecture on environmental economics. This seemed very authentic to me at the time, and I decided to set it up. I asked Nicolas if he was interested and he responded enthusiastically, especially as this would be an experience he could list on his curriculum vitae. We set up a date and time, although it was hard to find space in the syllabus. I decided that the best time would be right after the final output lesson.

In lesson 210A (Friday 05/12/2014), we began the subject of wildlife, a subject I knew would garner a lot of interest and which I personally had a lot of passion for. We started by watching a video from a charity named Pangea Seed, which aims to raise awareness about the barbaric way sharks are caught for their fins, then thrown back into the sea alive but with their fins cut off so that they sink to the bottom of the sea and drown. I told them that I loved sharks, and that I knew one of the speakers from the Pangia Seed video. I asked if they would like for me to try and arrange for this speaker to come to our class, but 16/24 voted no using the CALABO software, which I was surprised about. Before doing this vote, I had already informed the class that Nicolas, the French research assistant, would be coming to give a short lecture about economics and the environment, so perhaps they felt another speaker would be too much for them. After this, we started the main class, which was structured around a simple WebQuest about endangered animals. Students worked in groups depending on their chosen animals to create an infographic poster using PowerPoint, which one speaker from each group then presented. Again, because the task was very structured, and the students and I were all enthusiastic, I noted this to have been a predominantly successful lesson. I also observed that this lesson worked on 'autopilot' and more or less 'taught itself' because of the clear instructions and the way I had pre-taught much of the vocabulary and done lots to scaffold the task. The overall success of this class meant that we had experienced four consecutively convergent lessons in which we all seemed to be positively synergised for the most part. Sadly, this did not carry over into the output sessions.

Over the weekend I had to come in on Saturday to invigilate an institutional TOEFL test. Mr Charge was one of the students in the group that I was invigilating. I noted in my field journal that I

> felt funny... Like I'd let Mr Charge down by making him think his reality in English would be fun when in fact he also has to experience English in the form of gruelling TOEFL tests with high stakes and dull difficult questions. Also, felt I wish I could have helped him prepare for this reality a bit. Still. It was nice to recognise my students and I tried to be friendly (although serious and professional as chief invigilator).
>
> (TRJournal 06/12/2014)

In lesson 210B (Wednesday 10/12/2014), the environment output session featuring Mr Montville, Mr Cloud, Ms Chennai, Ms Hemp and Mr House was held. The former three students were able to get a low 'A', whereas the latter two received a high 'B'. In my audio journal I recorded an 'obligatory' reflection in which I stated that I was too busy to really reflect on anything. As a result, there is little to report on this output session other than the fact that, although parts of it were good, overall I still felt dissatisfied with the students' performance and felt another negative alignment of motivational synergy.

The same happened in lesson 211A on Wednesday 10/12/2014. In this session there was Ms Pine, Mr Cleyera, Mr Po, Mr Wind and Ms Forest. The group all received an 'A' grade, except for Mr Cleyera and Mr Po, who both took a 'B'. The best presenter was Mr Wind, who found 'the perfect video' for his session, and presented his information in an impassioned way, I felt. Mr Po did something during his session which 'saved him from a C' by asking the other students to discuss a question using the CALL room's chat feature. I reflected in my audio journal that it felt good to have finished the last output session and that

> Mr Charge's session, all the output sessions have been quite good and it wasn't the cancer after all and I actually made a special point of pointing out to them how a presentation is difficult, presentation in English is very difficult, output session is super advanced so well done and I applauded them all.
>
> [5:41]

With all the output sessions finished, the semester itself was also close to completion. After the output session we conducted the second self-assessment, and then I just had time to start preparing the students for Nicolas, our classroom visitor, who would be coming next lesson. I posted a message in the Moodle Coffee Room (see Figure 5.15).

Guest Speaker to our class Nicolas will talk about Sustainable Development
by PINNER, RICHARD Friday, 12 December 2014, 10:37 AM

My friend from my Japanese class, Nicolas, is a student at Sophia's global studies
department. He is French and speaks English, German and Japanese. He is a cool
guy! I have asked him to come to our class to give a short talk to you. Then, after his
talk, you can ask him questions and talk with him.

Please think of at least 2 questions you want to ask him about Economics, The
Environment and Sustainable Development. He will be happy to answer you
questions. Please post your questions here in the coffee room by Monday 14th at
13:00 so I can email him a list of questions so he can prepare (English is his second
language too :)

Thanks a lot!
Richard

Figure 5.15 Preparing for the classroom visitor

Only nine students posted their questions (Mr Po, Ms Redslope, Ms Hemp,
Mr Cloud, Ms Downtree, Mr Fly, Ms Forest, Ms Sound and Ms Chennai).
Interestingly, I noted that there was nothing from Mr Charge, although Mr Fly
did write his questions. Mr Po was the first to post a question, but that is because
he did the homework task during the class, and Ms Redslope wrote straight after
the class with a question about rising food prices based on an observation that
'price for a beef bowl of *Yoshinoya* went up the other day'. A few more questions
came in over the weekend, the most interesting one from Ms Sound, who asked,
'What do you think about that crude oil prices have dropped significantly?',
which I felt may be related to the disastrous peak oil lesson, although clearly this
was an observation about oil prices going down, which is the opposite of what
troubles peak oil economists. In my journal I noted:

> Wanted to email the students their corrected questions, because I was
> worried that their questions wouldn't make sense to Nicolas and I didn't
> want a kind of breakdown like when they ask him their non-grammatical
> questions. Like I got some questions that... that said.... "Do you think that
> how the global environment turns out' by Mr Cloud. And Mr Fly wrote
> a question 'in French (Europe), how does people care about environment
> from economic pollution.
>
> Audio Journal (17/12/2014)

Rather than simply allowing this disaster to happen, as I had done with the peak
oil lesson, I attempted to avert the situation by 'correcting' their questions and
summing them up into a cohesive list. This was done because I was worried they
would ask their questions but Nicolas wouldn't understand, and it would cause a
breakdown of communication and thus a damaging loss of face for all concerned.
The final corrected questions were presented as an anonymous list which the

students could identify their own question from and ask, but basically the whole class was supposed to take ownership of. I also printed out who had asked which questions, so that I could call on them personally if they didn't answer my questions.

Although I did not make any specific mention of this in my journals, I now realise that I would have felt somewhat of a contradiction about 'correcting' the students' work and scripting or 'grooming' them for this encounter. Part of me would have wanted them to use their own words, but I feel that I knew the encounter would be potentially damaging if I did not intervene and scaffold the situation carefully.

5.10 The classroom visitor

In lesson 211B, as planned, Nicolas, the French research assistant from the Department of Global Studies, came to give a guest lecture. Students had written questions for our guest beforehand, which I had edited for comprehensibility, 'corrected' and transformed into a list of 17 questions (see Figure 5.16). After Nicolas' lecture, we used this list to have a structured Q&A session. I had initially asked Nicolas to speak for just 15 minutes, but in the end his lecture lasted around an hour. As with many of my feelings around this episode, I felt torn because I thought it wouldn't really be worth Nicolas' time to come and talk just for 15 minutes, but also his talk was too long, and the 'students got flummoxed' not just by the content but also the delivery and sheer amount of English.

Our Questions for Nicolas
1. What do you think about Abenomics?
2. Do you think that the Japanese government should raise the tax to 10%?
3. What do you think about consumption tax rising?
4. What do you think about a result of this election?
5. Do you think Japan can return to prosperity?
6. Do you think Japan's bubble economy will come again?
7. What causes the recession?
8. How do you think that the recession in Japan is related with the rise in consumption tax?
9. As an economist, do you think the Economy is good?
10. In France (Europe), how much do people care about the environment in terms of economic pollution?
11. The Price for a beef bowl at Yoshinoya restaurant went up the other day. Do you think that price of food will continue to rise from now on in Japan?
12. How do you think the global environment will turn out?
13. What do you think about global warming?
14. What do you think about mass production?
15. What do you think about extravagance/consumerism? Is it a good thing? Is it sustainable?
16. What do you think about the fact that crude oil prices have dropped significantly?
17. What do you think about the fact that the global population continues to grow? Are there any countermeasures?

Figure 5.16 Questions for Nicolas

Overall, the talk went very well, but the speaker spoke very fast and it was not always easy for the students to understand. I collected a large amount of feedback from the students about this lesson, particularly wanting to connect it with the Authenticity of the Speaker activity from spring. The main features were that the speaker was hard to understand for the students, and they felt glad to have been exposed to another speaker but also seemed to lose confidence in their ability to understand people other than myself. Whilst I felt that the speaker had been hard to understand, I had mixed feelings because, although I had initially invited Nicolas because to me he seemed able to represent as a speaker of international English (and was thus a more authentic model speaker than myself), by the end of the talk I felt he had not made enough concessions for the class to be able to understand him well. So, on the one hand I felt it was a good example, and yet paradoxically for the same reasons I felt it was not a good example. The issues that arose from the lesson were certainly likely to crop up in discussions with speakers outside of the classroom setting, but I felt that the learners from CLERAC who do find themselves using English outside of the class were not likely to encounter the type of English that Nicolas used (i.e. somewhat technical economics and environment-related language, spoken quickly in a fairly strong French accent).

5.10.1 *Detailed description of the classroom visitor*

As I noted in my journal, I was extremely relieved that I had invested some time to scaffold the questions and print a list of who had asked which questions. I noted simply that doing so had 'saved us'. Despite having 17 questions, we only had time for three of them because each of Nicolas' answers took about ten minutes, during which time he was using the whiteboard and drawing graphs and other explanatory aids. For me, it was a brilliant talk and I noted that Nicolas is 'a cool guy … but He's French and English is his L2 and I wanted him as an authentic model speaker'. Here I clearly admit my rationale behind inviting Nicolas, having reached the position with my thinking on authenticity that, as an L1 speaker of English and teacher who uses easy-to-understand English, I might not represent an authentic 'reality' of English that my students would encounter in the language use domain.

When students asked questions, I noticed that they all referred to my corrected questions. In my journal I reflected that the corrected list had 'avoided a loss of face because I did not correct any individuals. Saved the last half an hour from death'.

I had, in fact, been a little unsure as to whether Nicolas would show up for his guest lecture, so I had prepared a plan for what I would do if he didn't come, which would have been simply to watch the documentary *No Impact Man*. I was nervous before class, and 'felt it would either be a disaster or brilliant, but I think I was wrong about that because it wasn't a disaster but it wasn't brilliant either'.

One of the main observations I made as I sat amongst the students was that that Mr Po's head was drooping during the initial one-hour lecture, and he was more or less asleep for the whole thing, a very bad sign and also very reminiscent of Mr Po's behaviour during the other students' output sessions. I noted in my journal once again that 'he never sleeps when *I'm* talking!', which further adds evidence to my suspicion that Mr Po respected my authority as a teacher (and as a speaker of English, perhaps) but not others'.

However, Mr Po was not the only person whose attention was lost during Nicolas' lecture.

> Mr House wasn't really listening, he was looking at his fingernails. Mr Mouth sort of had his eyes closed, I think most of them were trying to show their attention and stay awake because they didn't want to be rude to this guy, but you know I think he did do some good stuff, try to engage them, but they were reticent to reply, he had to ask some of them directly but some of them kind of froze... they couldn't reply or he'd asked them a question that was too hard. It's not his fault, he doesn't know what kind of class this is.
>
> (TRJournal 17/12/2014)

I noted that Nicolas' experience was in the Global Studies Department and that he had many friends in the Faculty of Liberal Arts, both of which have very high English proficiency students. Also, this was a cultural issue, as a large proportion of those students are returnees or have experienced education overseas, and so I suspected the classes with Japanese students that Nicolas had taken were more likely to be familiar with a classroom culture in which the student asks a question to the class and expects people to answer (see Vignette 5 by Sal Consoli in Chapter 7). This was one of the most noticeable things I found when teaching DCT to students in the English Studies Department (Pinner, 2018b). Conversely, the students in my CLERAC class were very much from a Japanese educational background, and thus less familiar with this more 'Western style' of education. In further support of this observation, I did note that Mr Montville and Ms Lovehouse (both returnees) did actually speak up more than others, and that they had a bit more to say during the dialogue. However, in terms of asking the students direct questions, I felt Nicolas did really well, and I had taken some pains to tell him about my class and explain their needs to him.

During the Q&A, Nicolas asked Ms Pine and Ms Lovehouse what they specifically do about the environment. After their answers, I suggested that Nicolas should ask Mr Montville the same question about the environment, as this was the topic of his essay. After my having intervened in this way, all the questions somehow fell to me to direct, so I just chose specific people and, as I knew which people had written which questions, I was able to do this quite well. But again, the real issue was what I had previously labelled the peak comprehension problem. Too many of the students were unable to follow easily what Nicolas had said because it was too difficult for them, too far outside their ZPD. I felt that Nicolas may have been given a false sense of the general level of the class, because when Mr Montville, Ms Lovehouse and Mr Fly spoke, they sounded quite fluent and used the questions I had provided and responded with some good follow-up questions. However, when Mr Po spoke, I could see it was difficult for Nicolas to answer, and I felt the only reason he could understand Mr Po's question was because he knew already that the question was about Abenomics,[2] from the list which I had also shared with him.

Nicolas is only just slightly the senior of my CLERAC first-year students, having graduated the year before, and he had no teaching experience. As if to confirm Nicolas' own lack of experience, I noted that

> he got chalk on his jumper and his slides had low resolution pictures. Overall very good although he was mumbly and had a lot of false starts, and he talked too fast and his pronunciation was at times, difficult to grasp. pronunciation was probably the main thing they found difficult to understand.
>
> (TRJournal 17/12/2014)

Following this reflection, I made sure that I should follow up this observation and see if the students really did have trouble with his pronunciation, noting that if I was right, this would be 'proof of synergy and that I know them'. In fact, I noted that even I didn't understand some of Nicolas' answers, especially about Abenomics, which was a question posited by both Mr Po and Ms Forest and which formed one of the longest discussions after the lecture. I noted that I was not sure how much it benefited the students, but I felt that what would make things count would be how I followed up on the experience.

5.10.2 Feedback on the visitor

In lesson 212A on Friday 19/12/2014, we were back in the CALL room and my plan was to collect some feedback about Nicolas' visit, and then as the final lesson before the Christmas holidays, we had a special Christmas lesson planned, in which I wanted to simply watch Raymond Briggs' *The Snowman* with the class and then have a discussion. We also worked together as a class on the final written assignment for around 20 minutes, as the feedback took only 15 minutes and *The Snowman* is under 30 minutes. Most of the students had already finished their first drafts for this assignment by the time we broke up for the Christmas holidays because they were simply planning to work on the scripts from their output sessions.

To collect the data from the students about Nicolas' visit, I had originally wanted to create a questionnaire, but by the time the class started I had not yet completed it. My journal mentions that just as I left my office to go to the classroom, I had a breakthrough based on something I had read in Allwright and Hanks (2009) about talking directly to learners about their feelings and perceptions rather than merely assuming we know what they think. To that end, I decided that instead of a questionnaire, I would simply ask the students directly in a CaLabo chat at the start of the class. I opened the chat and simply asked the students verbally to write what they thought of Nicolas' lecture.

My initial prediction that Nicolas' pronunciation was the main issue turned out to be slightly inaccurate. First of all, as with the Authenticity of the Speaker rating activity, not all the students could recognise the difference between an L1 speaker of English and an L2, as Mr Montville demonstrated in a rather unusually off-the-ball comment in which he said, 'I had difficulty in hearing British English' when referring to his ability to comprehend Nicolas' speech. I felt I had made it clear to the class that Nicolas was French and that for him, like for them, English was a foreign language. Ms Saltfield displayed a slightly better knowledge of Nicolas' English variety when she said, 'I feel that he is a clever man, but it was hard for me to understand what he said, because he speaks so fast and his accent is European English(?).' Prior to this, several students had commented that the contents were interesting, but it was hard for them to understand. Also, Ms Chennai revealed that he had followed some of the more complex features of the lecture when she reflected that 'I felt a little difficult. However, I was surprised to the consumption tax of France.' I should remind the reader that Ms Chennai, like the majority of the students, was not an economics major, and that only two students belonged to this department (Ms Pine and Mr Montville).

After her comments about the European accent, Ms Saltfield began focusing on extra-linguistic features, noting that 'he is handsome' and 'his legs is very long.' As I discussed in the Spring Narrative in Section 4.2.2., this is perhaps a snippet insight into Ms Saltfield's *akogare* towards foreign men (Bailey, 2006, 2007; Takahashi, 2013). She is the only one to voice such comments, as the others focused either on the content or their ability to understand. Mr Fly, after a verbal prompt from me to focus on their comprehension of Nicolas' lecture, which is not visible on the chat transcript, said, 'Umm...maybe too fast and not clear pronounce.' This, however, was a follow-up from his previous comments where he (like others in the class) had initially put the onus on himself and his (in)ability to 'hear' or to 'listen'.

Using NVivo, it is possible to run word frequency queries across data types. Isolating this one chat from the entire study, I produced a diagram (see Figure 5.17), which shows a word frequency cloud based on the responses from this chat.

According to the word frequency query, the word 'pronounce' was mentioned just once (weighted percentage of 0.41), the same number of times that 'accent' was mentioned. Words with the same frequency included 'handsome' and 'humorous', although talk was mentioned twice (0.82 per cent) and 'speak' and 'fast' were each mentioned four times (1.65 per cent). So, I was not wrong in my intuitive deduction that the students had not followed the contents of Nicolas' speech well, although Mr Charge once again demonstrated his exceptionally high ability with the following observation, based on the content of the lecture:

It was very surprised for me that PETs are recycled only 20 per cent and another 80 per cent are just trash...

He later followed this up with the observation that 'I know that more we pollute river, lake, ocean, less clean water we are supposed to drink.'

These comments came shortly after Mr Charge's first contribution to the chat, in which he expressed similar sentiments to his classmates that the topic was interesting but that it was 'difficult to hear', by which I took him to mean in terms

Figure 5.17 Word frequency of responses to classroom visitor

of comprehension and not in terms of the content being upsetting (although both meanings are quite applicable). Mr Charge's fourth and final contribution returns to the language-related features of the talk when he says simply, 'I wished he had spoken a little slowly...f(^^;'

As the visualisation makes clear, students found the lecture difficult. They focused primarily on linguistic aspects which they did not understand, but aspects of content such as Abenomics and the environment did also feature in the feedback discussion, with Ms Downtree noting that 'he knows more about Abenomics than Japanese.'

As stated at the start of the section, I had initially planned to make a questionnaire to evaluate how they felt about Nicolas' talk, specifically focusing on him as an authentic speaker and referring to the Authenticity of the Speaker activity (see Section 4.4). However, I was very pleased with what I perceived as the more in-depth and personal feedback which I collected through the chat function. However, simply using a chat room does not ensure equal participation, and some members of the class did not make much contribution to the feedback, and others did not take the discussion particularly seriously. As such, making a close comparison with the Authenticity of the Speaker activity is not possible due to having incomplete data. Although I can look at word frequency reports, they tell me little about the overall perceptions of the class and provide only a small fragment of data to suggest my own intuitions were correct, but little more can be deduced. For this reason, I feel that for such an activity, perhaps a rating task with more structure (in addition to the feedback chat) would have been a better way to understand what truly happened with the classroom visitor. This demonstrates once again the fine line and balancing act of teaching and researching. In this respect, first-hand experience really is as important for classroom research as it is for teaching practice.

5.10.3 The Snowman

The classroom visitor had been an experiment in some ways, intended as a follow-up from the Authenticity of the Speaker activity which we did at the start of spring. Bringing a real-life speaker of English as an international language who cared deeply and knew well the content we had been focusing on in class, Nicolas was a perfect person to visit us and, although listening to his lecture proved extremely challenging for the CLERAC learners, the overall experience was positive and I felt we had all benefited from our hard work. Then, for the end of this class, I wanted to introduce a Christmas element as a small treat for the group. In doing so, I was also introducing another part of myself, and a very authentic series of interactions ensued as I shared something deeply personal.

One reason that the feedback session did not take priority in the lesson was that I very specifically wanted to end the year on a high note, as this was the last lesson of 2014 and we would not see each other for two weeks over the winter break. In my audio journal I noted that

> I think we already knew how each other felt. I knew it was too difficult for them. They knew I know it was too difficult for them. It was probably because of his pronunciation. Not to do with the fact that he was French, just his way of talking. Data I collected just confirmed what I already knew!

In fact from the reflection and journal entry, I can see that my priority for the lesson was definitely watching *The Snowman*, but before we watched it, I showed the students the reply I had received from Reggie Bibbs (from the Prejudice lesson's video). I noted that students seemed impressed that we had made personal contact with Reggie (see also Vignette 3 in Section 7.4). In actual fact, Reggie had replied just under a month ago, but I had not found an appropriate time to mention it to the students as the semester unfurled.

I set up the video by explaining that *The Snowman* animation was first aired in the United Kingdom on 26 December 1982, which just so happens to be the year I was born and therefore my first ever Christmas. Students were transported into the personal significance of this movie for me, and I felt this did a good job of contextualising the video and investing the students in it. I noted that 'I got a warm, fuzzy, genuine feeling as we watched it.' Interestingly, the very day before, I had also watched the same video with my Writing Skills class for my own Department of English Literature students, but at that time I had 'felt stupid as I was watching it. Too personal. I hate Christmas and corny themed lessons [...] I felt that familiar surge of shame and embarrassment as I bared a little too much of my own soul.' There was a very marked contrast between my emotional response to watching *The Snowman* with CLERAC.

> Really connected as people. Today's class feels like hanging out. Warmth and love in the air. Ms Smallville and Ms Downtree are laughing at every little cute bit. All the students were laughing and responding. They were all nicely engaged and Christmassy. Very different from yesterday.
>
> (TRJournal 19/12/2014)

Despite this higher emotional investment in CLERAC than in other classes, one other point which I feel is important to note is that for my other classes I had already given the students most of the feedback they needed so that they could be working over the winter break. With CLERAC, I was decidedly less well organised. I even accidentally wrote some notes on the back of Ms Oldriver's Output Session score sheet, and had to print her out another one. Several of the CLERAC students were still waiting for grades from me, whereas students belonging to my own department had received their feedback on time. I will revisit this issue in Chapter 6.

We ended the class on a nice personal note in this way and wished each other Merry Christmas and Happy New Year. In my journal I recorded that 'they were all really happy and clapping and in good spirits. A real end of the year, celebratory atmosphere'. After this, I reflected on my own year and noted that I had achieved a great deal, both personally and professionally.

5.11 Wrapping up

When we returned in the new year on Wednesday 7/01/2015 (lesson 212B), I focused on wrapping up the entire course. We conducted a timeline review activity in which students worked in small groups (usually pairs) to create a timeline of everything we had studied since April 2014. This was an activity which I planned just before going into the class, and I found it very successful. As I walked around the room, each group seemed to be engaged in the activity and they were looking through their notes and the syllabus. There was a sense of achievement looking back over all the different topics we had studied, something that several of the students commented on during the classroom audio. Below are three of the reviews to compare how the students reflected on the course as a whole.

Figure 5.18 Ms Downtree and Ms Oldriver's timeline review

Ms Downtree and Ms Oldriver have included personal events in their timeline (Figure 5.18), such as turning 19, which have nothing to do with the course contents yet show that they were *people-in-context* as the course progressed. This to me communicates that they were able to personalise the course and incorporate it into their overall developing identity.

Mr Charge and Mr Fly's timeline is also interesting (Figure 5.19), as it shows a collection of their own memories and the events that most stood out to them. It is not comprehensive and certain things are picked out (such as the debate, which only took one lesson), whilst other things are left unsaid (such as essay writing or video projects). Mr Charge also remembers my 'handsome' joke from the very first lesson.

Mr Auxiliary worked with Mr Dawn, and so his timeline cannot be shown as Mr Dawn requested that his pedagogic materials be left out of the study; however, it has much in common with Ms Saltfield and Ms Redslope's timeline (Figure 5.20), which, although very nicely drawn and fun, was constructed through methodically looking back over the notes and syllabus and thus it presents mainly the facts of the course. Mr Auxiliary's and Mr Dawn's was even more so, although the most formulaic timeline was produced by Mr Po and Mr Cloud, which did not even feature any drawings. Note that in Ms Saltfield's timeline there is a reference to my joke about X university being inferior to Sophia, a recurring joke from the first lesson.

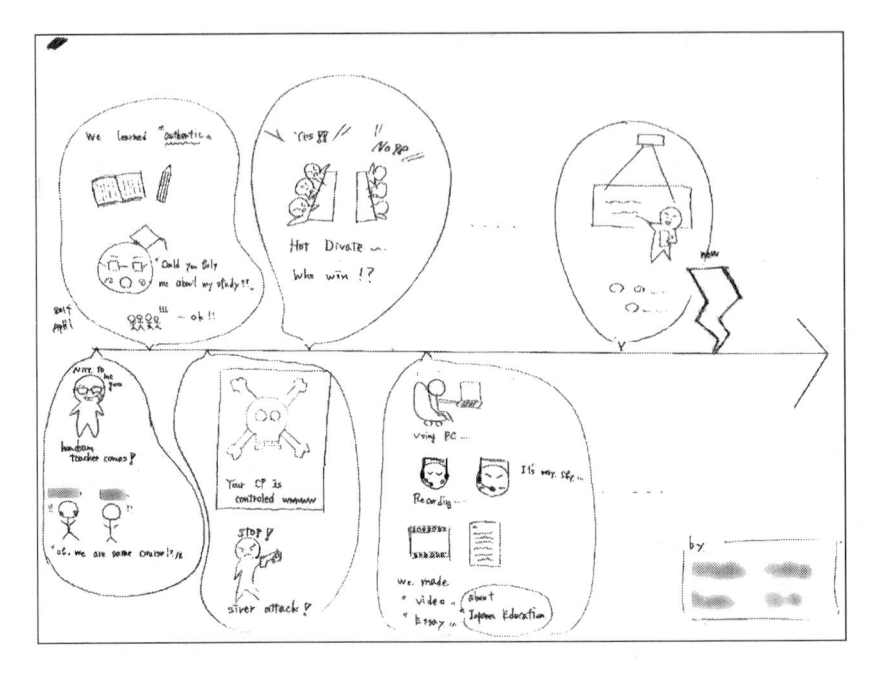

Figure 5.19 Mr Charge and Mr Fly's timeline review

Figure 5.20 Ms Saltfield and Ms Redslope's timeline review

In lesson 213A on Friday 09/01/2014, we conducted the end-of-semester review activity, again using the same format as the mid-semester autonomy exam. I also showed the students a video that I had made to thank them for their hard work and to remind them what a great course it had been. Mr Charge noted in his end-of-semester reaction paper that after watching the video I made, he

> remembered what we have done and I recognised how much topics you have prepared for us. Some was like joking, other was serious. You made us consider a lot of things. I could keep my motivation in most of topics.
>
> (20/01/2014)

Lesson 213B was cancelled due to departmental commitments, leaving just two more lessons. On Friday 13/01/2015 lesson 214A, we had our last meeting in the CALL room. During this lesson we simply worked on essays, although I noted that we had a lot of banter and the atmosphere was very relaxed, most of the assessments now being over.

5.12 The final day of the course

For the final lesson on Wednesday 21/01/2015, we repeated the activity from the first ever class and conducted our second REDs. For this lesson I provided photocopies of the students' original REDs so they could compare. The atmosphere was really amazing, and I felt everyone was synergised and connected, an extension of the timeline lesson but this time with an added sense that this was our final lesson. Ms Oldriver arrived 40 minutes late, and when she came I took the students out to the university cafeteria where I bought them all tea, coffee and doughnuts to share.

It was only when I returned and recorded my final reflection that I realised I had forgotten to collect their REDs. I emailed the students and asked them to take photos or drop off their REDs at my office, as this was obviously going to be an important part of the study and helpful in looking back at how the students' English identity and relationship to the language might have developed in the course of the year. Sadly, I was only able to retrieve six REDs in this way (Mr Cloud, Mr Mouth, Ms Redslope, Ms Downtree, Ms Lovehouse and Mr Swamp), which communicates something in itself. First, it communicates that I prioritised the experience at the end of the lesson over the data collection, and secondly, it communicates that only a small number of the students invested enough to help me in recovering the REDs.

Luckily, in listening back to the classroom audio I am able to recreate some of the REDs from my descriptions of them. I used this technique to create my own replica of Mr Auxiliary's RED, which was my favourite from the first class and which showed English as a snake and Mr Auxiliary as a frog about to be eaten. Figure 5.21 shows my recreation of the lost RED from the last day of class, which shows the same picture with a crucial difference: the frog now has a means to defend itself.

One way I gauge the student's reciprocity of my personal investment in a class is in things like taking photos of me on the last day of class and possibly uploading

Draw a diagram that shows how you see your relationship to English. Use words and pictures to explain it.

Figure 5.21 Mr Auxiliary's revised RED

them to Facebook. Also students are sometimes kind enough to send me personal emails or handwritten notes of thanks. Occasionally, I might even receive gifts. The day after the last CLERAC class, I received a box of Godiva chocolates from a student in my Integrated Skills class. I noted in my journal that the Writing Skills class, whom I had originally intended to collect data from with CLERAC, did the aforementioned things, which suggests a strong personal connection. However, the CLERAC class did not take any photographs, send me any friend requests or send me any unsolicited personal emails or letters. Of course, this is a very blunt instrument for gauging personal involvement, and yet it still deserves mention as I often felt that the CLERAC engagement was an engagement created only between 9:15 and 10:45 on a Wednesday and Friday.

I did not have a great deal to say in the reflection after the class, although the last words in my audio journal are 'I don't want to say goodbye.' However, in truth it was also a great sense of relief to finish the class, although looking back from the vantage of completing this write-up, I realise that I still had a very long quest ahead of me in order to make sense of my own practice and professional development.

Notes

1 Unlike the other topics, Prejudice was not originally part of the DCT course.
2 Abenomics is named after Japanese Prime Minister Shinzo Abe, and refers to his policies to reform the Japanese economy.

6 Bridging the gap
Synergies into praxis

> Life can only be understood backwards; but it must be lived forwards.
> Søren Kierkegaard (Journals IV A 164 [1843] 1996, p. 63 and 161)

6.1 Introduction

The main focus of the narrative, and the puzzle at the heart of this inquiry, was an examination of the gap that I perceived opening up between my students and myself as my own professional identity altered during the natural development of my career. I undertook this research using certain methodological approaches as tools in order to help me uncover how to bridge this perceived gap and ultimately how to be a better teacher and to 'grow wings' as a reflexive practitioner (Edge, 2011). As stated in Chapter 2, my instincts told me that the reason for the perceived gap was related to the construct of authenticity, and I was particularly interested in examining how this related to motivation as a complex dynamic process. What developed from this inquiry was an overall observation that my motivation seemed to be closely related to the students', and that by utilising certain techniques in my teaching I was able to facilitate a group dynamic for the CLERAC class in which most of the members were keen to work together and maintain what I originally perceived as a fairly high level of motivation towards developing their language skills and a largely positive orientation towards the class. However, in constructing the narrative, I have formed a slightly altered view, coming to see high motivation as in fact a strange attractor rather than a true attractor state as I had originally believed directly after the class ended.

The intention behind this chapter is to gather these closely interrelated ideas and to explain what practical relevance they may have in terms of language teaching and language teacher education. In tracing my own professional development in this way, it is hoped that, although no generalisations can be made, practical suggestions can be offered instead. In this way, I am seeking praxis by combining theory into practice, using the construct of authenticity as a binding agent and imagining one of the main aims of language teaching to be the achievement of positive motivational synergy between students and teachers. Striving towards praxis in this way is seen to be the ultimate goal in a developing teacher seeking to gain a deeper sense of balance. As Crookes (2009, p. 117) has asserted, language teachers 'should engage in praxis – that is, theoretically motivated practice' because by developing our philosophy of practice and marrying this with actual teaching behaviour, we can enact scholarship of teaching and authenticity together and realise our full potential as educators (Kreber, 2013).

6.2 Authenticity: developing a philosophy of practice

In this section I will discuss how background political, contextual and economic forces affect authenticity and motivational synergy in subtle ways that may not always have been clear to the students and me during the course of the teaching.

6.2.1 Japan's educational system: empathy, acceptance and congruence

Chapters 2 and 3 discussed at length the contextual background of the study, specifically making reference to the Japanese Ministry of Education's stance towards foreign/English language instruction, the very real pressures to learn and yet the rather abstract nature of English in Japan. Understanding these contextually situated currents is seen as an essential aspect of group dynamics (Dörnyei & Murphey, 2003) and to 'delimiting context in relation to the learner' (Ushioda, 2015, pp. 50–52). When I came to teach CLERAC in April 2014, I had still only been in Japan for three years (since February 2011). It was the start of my second year as a full-time employee of Sophia University, and I was very much on the early steps of a steep learning curve about Japan's educational context. Whilst this study has been a catalyst for me in terms of deepening that understanding, I am still learning more about what is an 'appropriate methodology' (Holliday, 1994, 2006) for my teaching situation broadly. As language teaching inevitably features a large amount of cross-cultural contact, sociopolitical and economic forces are ever present in the language classroom. In my case, as a teacher who may be seen to represent the 'other' culture and language (Holliday & Aboshiha, 2009; Kanno & Stuart, 2011; MacDonald, Badger, & Dasli, 2006; Susser, 1998), I have a responsibility to myself and my learners to understand as much as possible what forces are influencing my classroom practices, how they are tethered to my students' pre-existing beliefs and previous educational experiences, and to be mindful of these influences as I attempt to construct what Holliday (1994, pp. 37–40; 1999) refers to as the 'small culture' of my own classroom. Without such knowledge, it seems very unlikely that a practitioner would be able to fully empathise with his or her students. Empathy, along with acceptance and congruence (or authenticity) as posited originally by Carl Rogers (1961), are the three cornerstones of good leadership and being a *facilitator* of learning (Dörnyei & Murphey, 2003, pp. 92–93). Therefore, it seems that in order for me to cultivate a sense of authenticity within the CLERAC class it was necessary to understand where my learners were coming from and where they were headed in terms of their educational goals and social context. This could be seen as a conscious effort to increase my own emotional intelligence and understanding of my learners, something which Gkonou and Mercer (2017) have linked with more effective teaching. In their study, they found high levels of emotional intelligence to correlate with increasing experience. Throughout the course, as highlighted in the narrative, I made frequent statements in which I tried to demonstrate my understanding of the social, institutional and political context of our work together and contextually situate them in our classroom reality. For example, as discussed in the initial conditions and throughout both semesters, I often struggled with issues surrounding attendance because my situational identity as a teacher required that I keep strict attendance records, yet as I felt this to be at times inflexible and potentially damaging to rapport, I often underplayed this role or distanced myself from the responsibility. Another way that I attempted to develop empathy with the class was by continually invoking my own transportable identity as a learner of Japanese, which again seems to have been a conscious attempt at building an empathic bridge between the students and myself. Sharing such personal information is referred to as 'self-disclosures', and has been shown to be an important aspect of teacher-student relationship forming, having particular relevance for motivation (Henry & Thorsen, 2018). This could be seen as an attempt at harmonising with the class, reducing the 'otherness' that I represented and fostering convergence on a personal level. These are all elements of how motivational synergy was nurtured in the classroom through a culture of authenticity.

6.2.2 *Authenticity and beliefs about education*

Further elucidating on this point from Chapter 2, I would like to examine why authenticity in the classroom is hinged upon a shared set of values about the purpose of education. In the narrative, there were two critical strands in which divergence occurred, leading to a failing of positive motivational synergy. One of these was the relatively poor quality of the final video projects produced by students at the end of the spring semester, and the other was the damaging and continuous effect of the output sessions in autumn. In the first instance, I became dissatisfied with the class when I realised that the CLERAC students had invested much less effort in their final video projects than the 2012 English Studies students had for DCT. Despite assigning a large amount of CLERAC's class time to working on these projects (35 per cent of lessons in spring had some element), I felt that the groups had not worked together until the final moments of the course when the deadline was imminent. This, for me, was a clear indicator that the class members' expectations of themselves were divergent from my own expectations. This could be for a number of reasons. First, my own expectations were, as I stated in my journal, not as high as they had been for DCT because CLERAC was primarily made up of much lower English proficiency first years, whereas DCT had been comprised of very high proficiency students in their second and third years. Also, CLERAC was a compulsory course which was not department specific, whereas DCT was an elective for the English Studies Department. I felt I had adjusted my expectations accordingly, in terms of time invested outside of the class and the quality of the language output of the students. However, I was still expecting high-quality videos which showed the students' passion for their subjects. The disconnect here is that the DCT videos were based on topics similar to those taught to CLERAC in the autumn, not the spring. In other words, the real 'content' (about which I in particular was passionate) of the CLERAC course was not introduced until autumn, by which time I was already disenfranchised with the CLERAC groups' videos and had decided to replace the video assessment with output sessions. This again proved to be a poor decision which led to further divergence between my expectations and what the students produced. The major difference between my disappointment with the video project and the output sessions was that in the latter I blamed myself, whereas for the former I blamed the students primarily. These were major flaws in my teaching approach that are likely to have also led to losses of positive synergy, which should have been controllable had I been a more effective facilitator/teacher. The reasons underlying this are, I believe, connected to my developing 'philosophy of practice'. During the spring narrative, I presented a critical reflection that arose on 23/05/2014 (Section 4.7) about my reasons for teaching being more concerned with providing a positive experience of the language than connected to perceived learning gains in language proficiency. This stands in contrast to the focus on learning aims in defining authenticity which Gilmore (2007a, 2007b) calls for.

As a result of my prioritising personal interactions and rapport building with the CLERAC students, I feel I neglected to clearly explain and communicate my expectations for assessments. When assessments were foregrounded by the necessary forces that structure the course, and when my situational identity was likewise foregrounded, I found it difficult to manage certain conflicting beliefs that I held and different identities that I presented to the class (see Section 6.6.2.1). In this way, not only was there a gap between what I expected and what my students produced, but there was also a gap in two distinct aspects of my teaching persona. As such, it seems inevitable that synergy was negatively charged and a divergence in orientation manifested itself.

In light of this, I believe that feedback was one of the major components in determining whether positive synergy occurred.

> In its original sense in systems theory, feedback meant the exchange of data about how one part of a system is working, with the understanding that one part affects all others in the system, so that any part heading off course could be changed for the better.
>
> (Goleman, 2006, pp. 150–151)

The importance of feedback is also a common feature in the literature on Exploratory Practice. Looking back over the narrative, feedback is consistently mentioned as important, particularly in relation to moments of high positive teacher-student motivational synergy, the clearest example being the 'number one' episode. I received feedback from the students that our class was very successful, I reiterated this feedback to the class and it became a shared achievement which distinguished our group from any others, a form of group pride which contributed to its cohesiveness (Dörnyei & Murphey, 2003, pp. 62, 69). However, that very day I had fallen off my bicycle and would be unable to teach the next lesson. When I did not receive any personal indications of sympathy from the CLERAC students (in contrast to those received from students from my department), I took this *lack of feedback* as a lack of empathy or caring, which had a profoundly negative impact on positive motivational synergy. Similarly, until the end of the spring semester, the students had received very little formal feedback from me regarding their work, because most of the classroom assessments were waiting to form a 'bottle-neck' at the end of semester. When I tried to rectify this situation by introducing output sessions as a staggered form of assessment occurring in stages throughout the autumn semester, I once again failed to communicate my expectations to the students effectively, and negotiation was not used. Furthermore, it was not until later reflection that I realised that this method meant assessments were only staggered for me; the students still had to wait their turns, which simply meant some had more time than others. Conversely, times when learning outcomes were negotiated, such as self-assessments and reaction papers, seemed to have been events at which very high levels of synergy were attained (discussed further in Section 6.4). This is likely to have much in connection with Ushioda's (2014) recommendation to increase metacognition in the classroom, connecting the methodological and pedagogical aims of the teacher to practices in class and com-municating them to the students in a mutually involving way.

6.2.3 *Group dynamics and sociometrics*

As group dynamics are an essential component of the overall classroom experi-ence and, like every class, CLERAC had a 'life of its own' (Dörnyei & Murphey, 2003, p. 3), I feel it is important to expand on these ideas in more detail. The group dynamics of CLERAC were very much the main medium through which overall synergies were experienced between the class and myself. Also, as outlined in Chapter 2, group dynamics are hypothesised as both an indicator of motiv-ational synergy and as a facilitator of this synergy, or a *synaptic crossing* for teacher-student motivation. As discussed in Section 2.6.2, these crossings rely on the exchange of energy and feedback.

One way of 'disentangling complex and interwoven systems' (Caldarelli & Catanzaro, 2012, p. 41) is to examine the relationships between members of a network, or actors. In this case, actors would be participants in the class, and the relationships could be almost anything that connects the participants to one-another. Since the pioneering work of Jacob Moreno (1934), teachers have been administering questionnaires to students about their relationships to others in the class, and these are then turned into social network diagrams (or net-work sociograms) of varying complexity. As Degenne and Forsé (1999) explain, the sociogram 'is a sociometric tool used to build a record of relations among members of a group' (p. 23). Moreno's earliest sociograms still resemble those most widely used by teachers today in that they simply ask students to name two other students that they would like to work with on a task or project (Leung & Silberling, 2006). The resulting sociogram can be extremely useful for teachers to identify 'isolates', or students who may be excluded by the group, and also understand the general dynamics of the class. I did not do such a questionnaire with the CLERAC class, as I did not learn about sociograms until after I had collected the data. However, I still felt that creating a sociogram would be a useful way to visualise the complexity of the class and to recognise 'individuals as fundamentally social and relational beings' (Mercer, 2015b, p. 74). I created a sociogram based on three relationships which were known to me: members of the same department, students who regularly sat together, students who were in the same group when working on assessed projects. The network sociogram represents visually some of the relationships between the students in the class. Because of the complexity of the classroom as a context for group dynamics, I have chosen to present several different sociograms because, as Wenger (1998) points out, 'treating such configurations as single communities of practice would gloss over the discontinuities that are integral to their very structure, [thus] they can profitably be viewed as *constellations* of interconnected practices' (p. 127; emphasis in original).

The first sociogram (Figure 6.1) represents only the members of each department, and the relationships between each node are associative, meaning they are

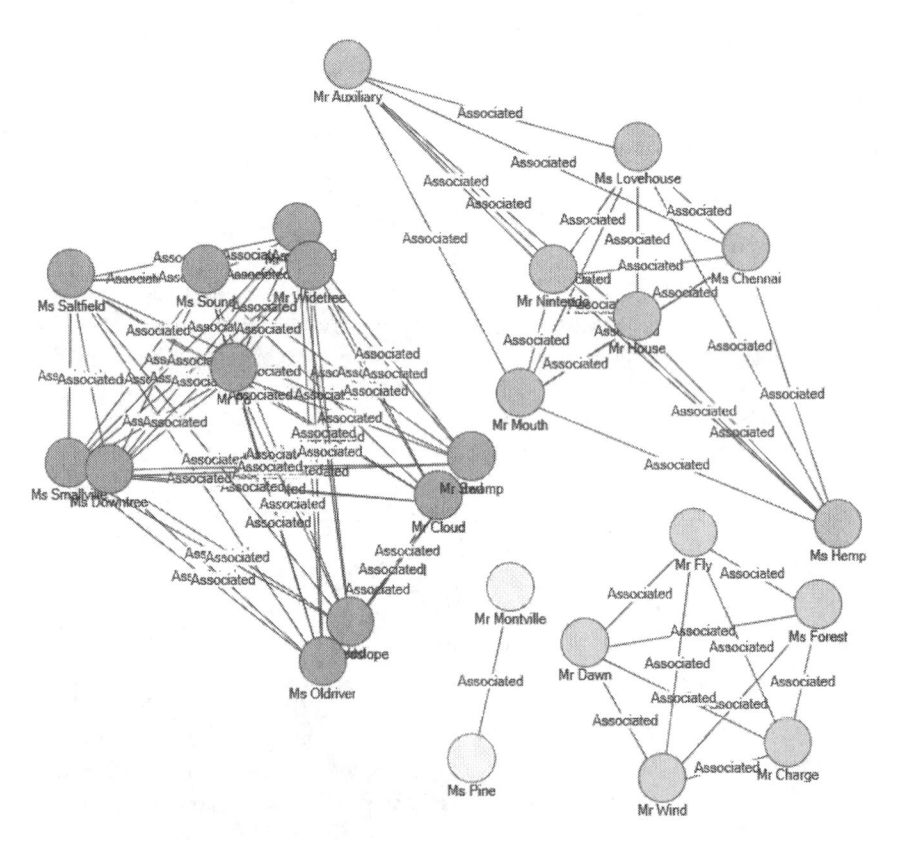

Figure 6.1 Sociogram showing department membership

neither unidirectional nor bidirectional but simply established through membership of the same department, a relationship not built on personal factors. A circle (node) represents a student participant, and a line (edge) represents a relationship between students. Node colour also indicates the degree of inness, meaning that a darker node shows that the student was generally more connected to the group. For this reason, Ms Pine and Mr Montville, the only two class members from the Department of Economics, are coloured more lightly than those in the Department of Materials and Life Sciences, which is the largest group. The other second-largest group, containing Mr Auxiliary, is the Department of Information and Communication Sciences, whilst the second smallest group is the Department of Engineering and Applied sciences, to which Mr Charge belongs.

The next sociogram (Figure 6.2) shows only the seating preferences for each student. These are the default seating patterns that the students chose when they took their seats at the start of class, so these pairings remained fairly consistent throughout the academic year. I saw this as a bidirectional relationship, although it may be that the proximity of the seating was not evenly reciprocal.

As mentioned, students did often change seats whilst working in different discussion groups or whilst working on projects, which is shown by the third relationship I plotted as a sociogram. Figure 6.3 shows which students collaborated in assessed group work, on the group video project in the spring semester. As students chose these groups, this is also seen as a bidirectional relation.

Figure 6.4 shows the output session groups.

Figure 6.5 shows the combination of both assessments.

Finally, Figure 6.6 represents all these relationships and is a full network sociogram for these three relationships in class. In this diagram, the nodes are represented by the degree of centrality, a calculation based on the number of edges and the direction of the relationship. Nodes are also sized and coloured according to the same category, meaning that a larger node suggests that this student was more active within the group, and a smaller node represents a tendency toward being an isolate. The thickness of the edge represents the number of relationships between nodes, so a thicker line means that there are more relationships between the connected students.

The sociogram presented in Figure 6.6 is barely legible due to the number of relationships it presents, and yet it does not do justice to the real complexity of the actual classroom as uncovered in the narrative. For example, Mr Auxiliary was most certainly an isolate in almost every class, and as I briefly touched upon in the autumn narrative, he seemed to lack the ability to read others' feelings based on his responses to the output sessions, which were in stark contrast with other members of the group. Furthermore, Mr Charge, despite his very strong motivational orientation to succeed in English, was also an isolate of sorts, because he was not keen to mix with other students and expressed a clear preference to either work alone or with his one friend from the class, Mr Fly. From the sociogram we can see that Mr Charge is represented by a smaller, lighter coloured node than Mr Auxiliary.

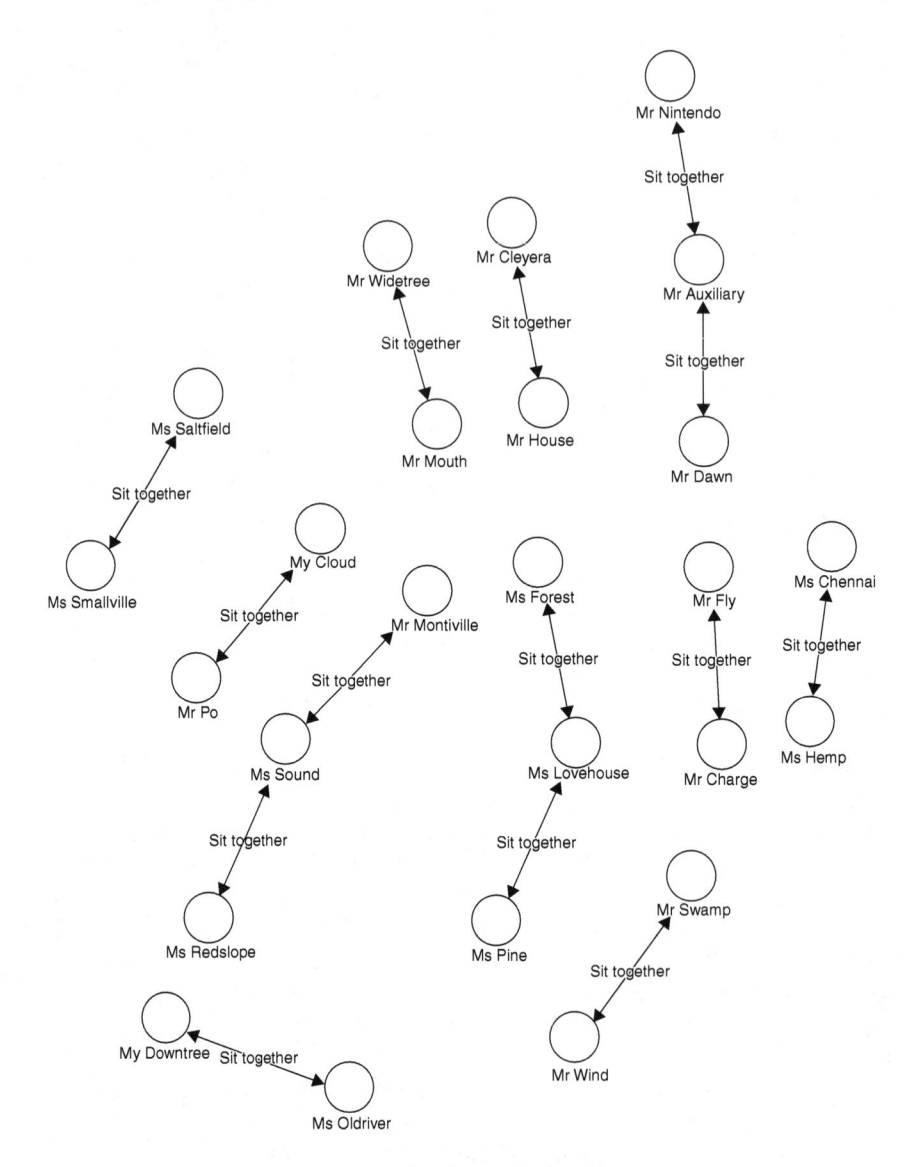

Figure 6.2 Sociogram showing seating preference

It is also possible to create egocentric sociograms, which take one group member as the central focus. Figures 6.7 and 6.8 show Mr Charge's and Mr Auxiliary's egocentric sociograms respectively.

Mr Charge's sociogram shows the relatively small number of people with whom he had a direct connection in the class. His strongest ties were to Mr Fly, with whom he has remained very close friends over the years up until the time of

Figure 6.3 Sociogram showing video project groups

writing (2017). The rest of the sociogram is made up of relatively uncommunicative students, such as Mr Auxiliary and Mr Dawn, and two students who were
on the low end of the spectrum in terms of my overall estimation of their level
of engagement (Mr Mouth and Mr Widretree). Mr Wind is interesting because,
although not a Focal Participant, Mr Wind was probably one of the most outspoken and interactive people in the group, and it is noticeable that Mr Wind and
Mr Charge were merely associated by department and never worked together
directly on projects.

Despite sitting close together in almost every class, Mr Auxiliary does not
seem to have a strong relationship with Mr Dawn as they have only one relationship. This suggests that they sat close together only as a result of both wanting
to sit at the back, perhaps because this was far from the teacher. They also shared
similar traits in terms of communicative ability and slight social awkwardness.
This lack of connection is hinted at in the narrative. When Mr Nintendo dropped
out of the class, this was met with something resembling indifference by the two

Figure 6.4 Sociogram showing output session groups

people (Mr Auxiliary and Mr Dawn) with whom he had sat for over a half a year. It is also notable that the two both liked football, but did not work together on video projects, although Mr Dawn had specifically indicated that he wanted to do a project about soccer.

Although their personalities were very different, there are similarities between Mr Charge and Mr Auxiliary in this way. A further similarity is observable in their self-report graph of their own motivation (Figures 6.9 and 6.10), collected during self-assessment 102.

Despite the marked differences in their behaviour and the way their motivation manifested itself, at least from their self-reports they seem to have much in common in that they perceived their motivation as being both high and stable.

Since teaching the course, I have learned more about group dynamics and encountered the idea that forcing students to move seats regularly and work with different members of the group is a good way of avoiding cliques within the

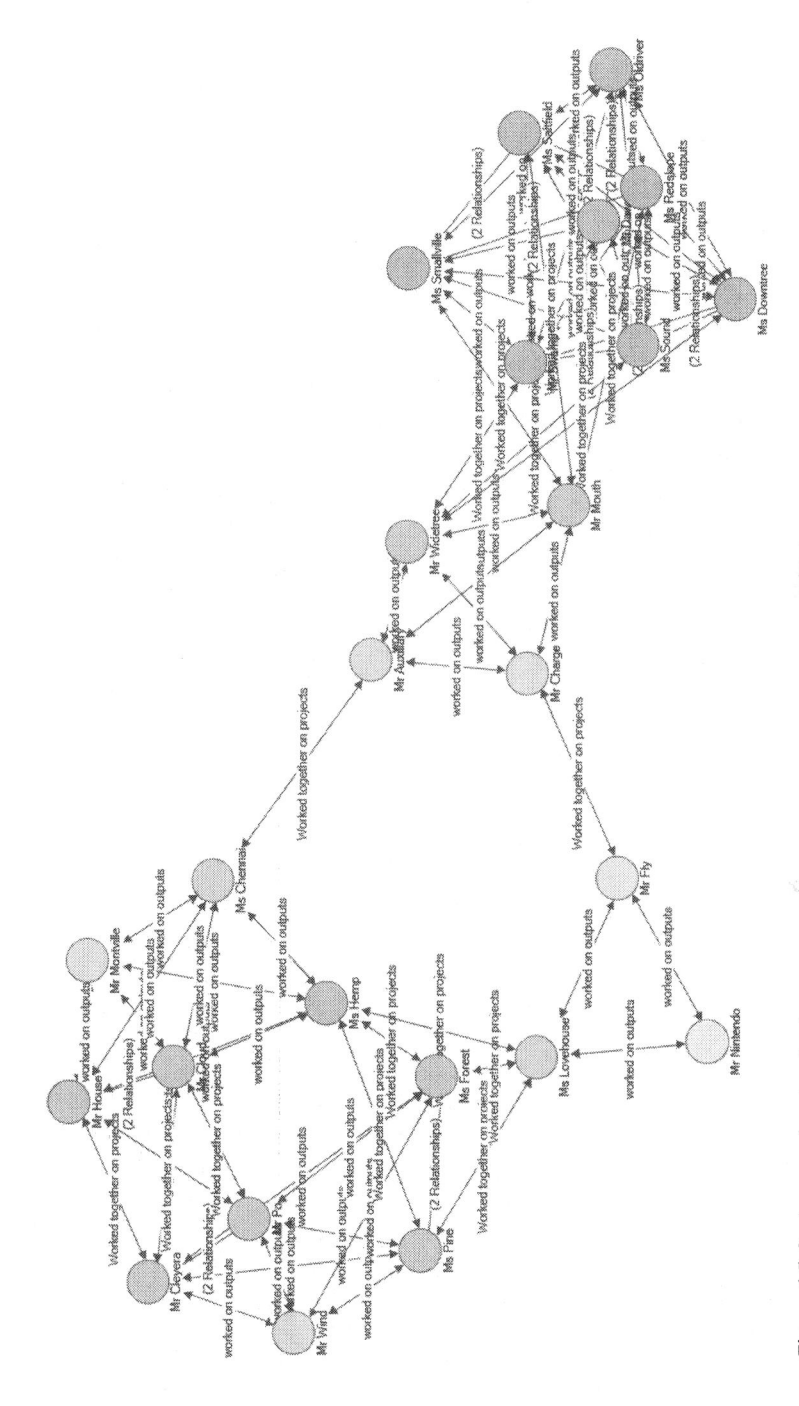

Figure 6.5 Sociogram showing both assessment groups

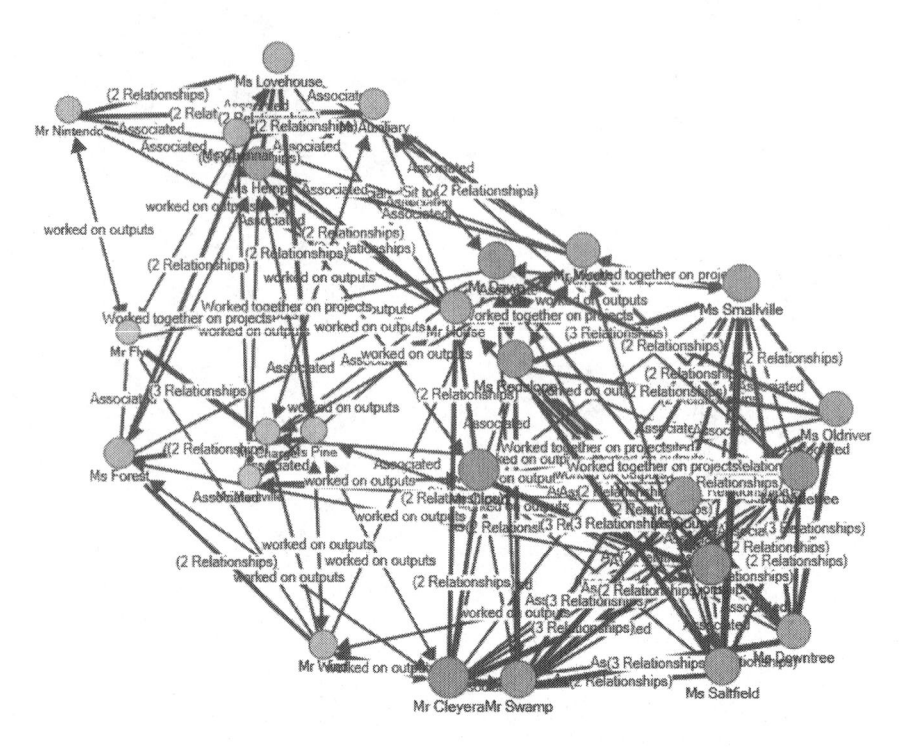

Figure 6.6 Sociogram of all plotted relationships

class and fostering better dynamics. During the CLERAC teaching phase, I did several mingling exercises, and these were especially done when students found groups to work together during assessments (videos and outputs). However, in the ordinary course of teaching I rarely forced the students to change seats and generally let them choose where to sit. I preferred not to dictate where they would sit, particularly because having a map of where each person sat initially helped me to learn all their names. In hindsight, this might have led to the solidification of isolate-type behaviour in learners such as Mr Auxiliary, Mr Dawn and Mr Nintendo, as well as Mr Charge and Mr Fly to some extent. This would certainly be something that warrants deeper inquiry in the future.

One finding from the analysis of the narrative is that my increased reflection on the class is what led me to seek a deeper understanding of group dynamics. In particular, I questioned my initial assumption that Mr Auxiliary was 'demotivated' or 'an English Hater' (Erikawa, 2009; Kikuchi, 2013) and came to a deeper understanding of Mr Auxiliary as a person-in-context. This is related to the 'Pygmalion effect', which refers to the fact that higher teacher expectations lead to greater performance. This effect is named after the Greek myth from a study conducted in 1965 (Rosenthal & Jacobson, 1992), which has relevance for L2 motivation (Dörnyei & Ushioda, 2011) and language classroom dynamics

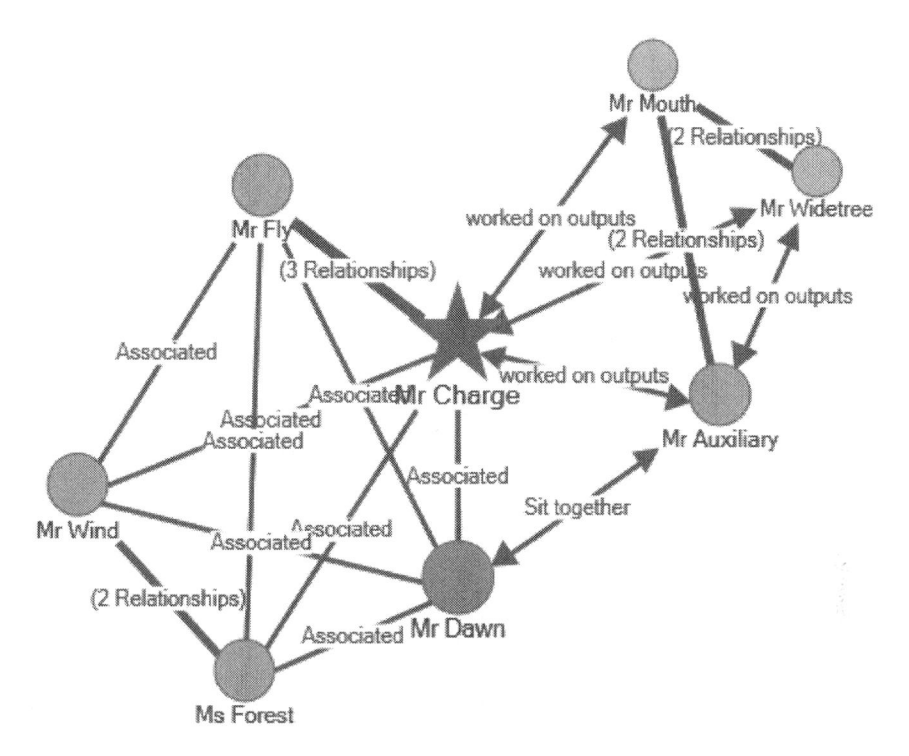

Figure 6.7 Mr Charge's egocentric sociogram

(Dörnyei & Murphey, 2003). Of course the effects can be reversed, which is often referred to as the 'Golem effect' (Babad, Inbar, & Rosenthal, 1982). As mentioned in the narrative, this is something I was aware of and tried to avoid as I taught CLERAC, which led to my questioning my assumptions about the students through deeper reflection. Rather counter-intuitively, by being more subjective about my learners as people, I believe I was actually better able to evaluate their work in class more objectively, or at least in a fairer way, which is how a rather uncommunicative student like Mr Auxiliary was still able to get a high score for the class and to be recognised as someone who was not simply lacking in motivation towards English. I believe a more thorough case study of learners such as Mr Auxiliary, who fit the profile of 'uncommunicative', would be helpful areas for future research. There are students like this in almost every class, and Mr Auxiliary seems to have much in common with Ahmad from Hanks' (2015b) study, who 'struggled with the collegial elements of EP', particularly during group work (p. 126).

The current inquiry certainly seems to lend support for the notion that group dynamics are important considerations for teachers wishing to facilitate a good environment conducive to learning. The overall levels of motivational synergy and the balance between convergent and divergent orientations seem hinged on

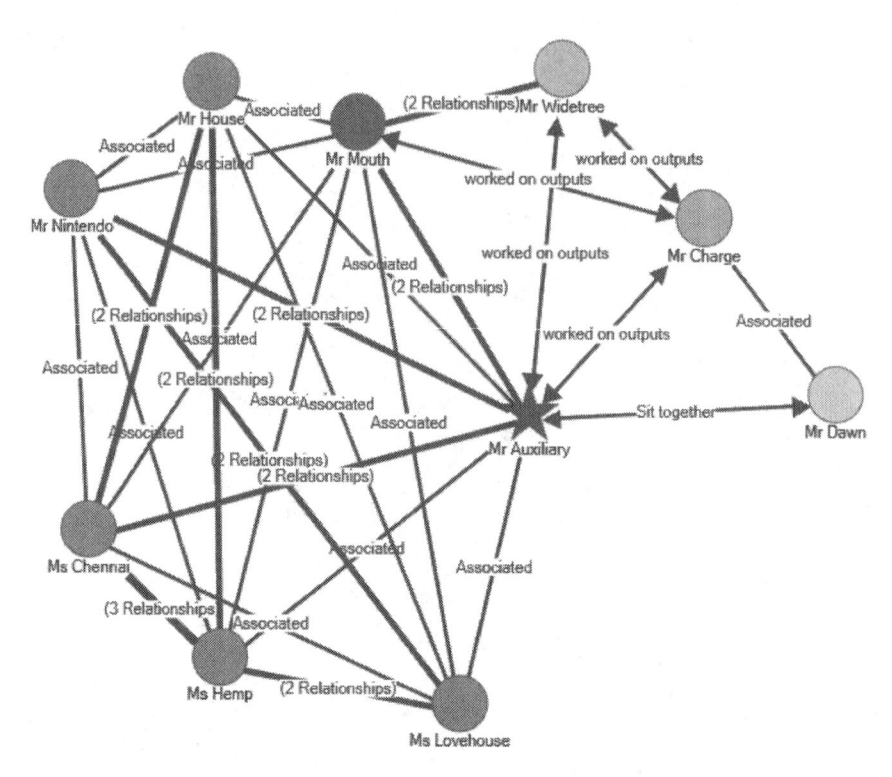

Figure 6.8 Mr Auxiliary's egocentric sociogram

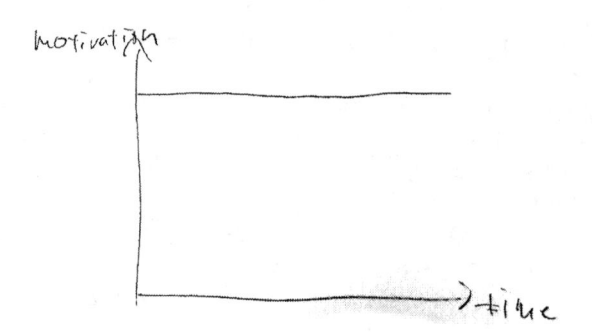

Figure 6.9 Mr Auxiliary's self-report on motivation (SA102)

classroom group dynamics. Although these sociograms were generated by specialist software (NVivo 11 plus) and can be plotted against detailed computations such as degree of in-ness, they can also usefully be drawn by hand or using free software (such as SocNet or Cytoscape), and certainly for me in terms of praxis they have been very useful in developing a deeper understanding of the

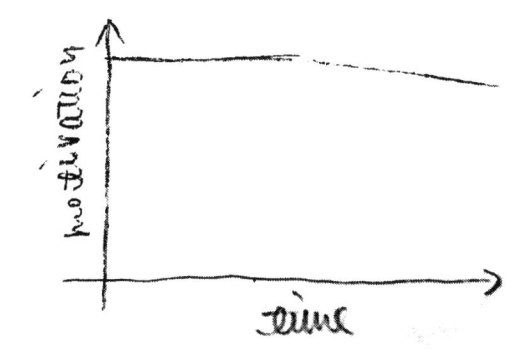

Figure 6.10 Mr Charge's self-report on motivation (SA102)

constellations of interconnected communities of practice that exist in complex groupings such as a classroom setting. This is why Holliday (1999) quite rightly refers to classrooms as 'small cultures'.

6.3 Autonomy: becoming a reflexive practitioner

I'm very reflective already but WOW what a huge and open chasm this experiment has revealed in myself. I'm changing! I can feel it. (TRJournal 18/04/2015 [very early in the semester])

I often noted in my journal that I had entered a state of 'hyper reflexivity', or a 'hyper-alert state'. Partly the reason for this was that I was simultaneously writing a book about authenticity, and thus developing my 'philosophy of teaching' and working on my own definition of authenticity, which has changed and developed several times since I began this inquiry, leading me to frequently label it a 'quest for authenticity' (see Chapter 2, also Pinner, 2016b). As I came to understand authenticity as a deeply personal state which is contextually and socially dependent, it seems inevitable that to arrive at this conclusion, I had to look deeply inside my own beliefs and to construct a deeper understanding of my own emergent teaching identity, which were both a product of and facilitated by my focus on Reflective Practice.

However, this 'hyper-reflexive' state came with certain disadvantages as well. First, it bled into my personal life and made me very conscious of any personal issues I was having. Zeroing in on such issues sometimes created tensions which I was not well equipped to deal with, and these eventually became the focus of my journaling. I often intentionally tested the boundaries between personal and professional life in trying to ascertain the boundaries of classroom authenticity and to put into practice the notion of the person-in-context relational view of motivation (Ushioda, 2009), but I feel that I took it somewhat too far at times and this resulted in divergences rather than convergences. This also explains the second downside which I observed from the hyper-reflexive state, which was that it began to eclipse the data which had arisen from the students. In other words, the main data source, as the narrative shows, was my own reflections and journal entries. Certainly during the actual teaching of CLERAC, this was even more so, and a large number of the most useful reflections to have arisen from this inquiry came too late to immediately benefit the learners from the CLERAC course. In this way, as discussed in Chapter 3, this study falls short of some of the propositions that guide Exploratory Practice put forward by Allwright and Hanks (2009). Specifically, I was not good at involving the participants in puzzling, and I have some trepidation as to whether they truly were the main beneficiaries of the research. One small consolation for this was offered to me by Ema Ushioda in a discussion on 31/05/2016, when she explained that future generations of my learners will be the main beneficiaries of this inquiry, and that this principle is not necessarily limited by the life span of the course, which this inquiry obviously extends beyond.

Another danger of the 'hyper-reflexive' state was that too much reflection can lead to paralysis, as discussed previously (see also Claxton, 2000). Perhaps this could account for some of the largest divergences between the students and me, such as my failure to properly negotiate the output sessions with them and other assessment criteria. Another example of this was lesson 208A, in which we watched *The End of Suburbia*, and my seeming inability to act upon the 'inevitable disaster' until it had already taken place, preferring to reflect deeply as it happened rather than to sidestep the problem before it manifested. In this way, I seem to have been prioritising what I *had done* in the class as opposed to what I *was doing*. This leads me on to the next section in which I will discuss planning the lessons, attempting to be flexible and generating content around students.

6.3.1 *Planning versus intuition*

The edited volume by Atkinson and Claxton (2000) has been a source of inspiration to me, especially during the actual teaching phase of this inquiry. As I will discuss further in Section 6.4 of this chapter, I have been engaged in a long process of designing and adapting my own content since moving to Japan in 2011 and moving almost entirely away from textbooks. I felt generally a dislike towards textbooks because, having selected or been assigned a textbook, teachers are often 'locked in' to the structure and content provided within (Copland & Mann, 2012; Mann & Copland, 2015). I thought that by designing my own materials I could avoid this. However, after writing several courses I soon found myself in a paradoxical situation of having designed my own textbook, and I was still 'locked in' but this time to my own content. I began to feel that I was overpreparing for lessons, something which chimed with Steve Mann's (2002) observations 'that the more I plan (for lessons or sessions), the less well I communicate' (p. 198). This is something Mann only brought to consciousness, or fully articulated (despite having strongly felt it for a number of years), during a session with colleagues with the express purpose of allowing teachers a forum to discuss their own practice and professional concerns, which were structured loosely around Cooperative

Development (Edge, 1992), and in which Mann (2002) was able to 'talk [himself] into understanding' and 'better understand [his] dialogic and reflexive relationship with [his own] teaching context' (p. 195). In other words, this was an observation facilitated by collaborative Reflective Practice. The observation that too much planning seemed to hinder teacher flexibility is something I too came across during discussions with colleagues as this inquiry unfurled.

As the course progressed, I would push this idea of 'flexibility versus planning' to the limit, sometimes walking into lessons with 'no idea' what I was going to teach, but usually going in with 'just a vague plan' which I had put together in the half hour or so between arriving at my office and starting to teach in the first period. Lack of a clear plan or failing to prepare for lessons has been shown to have a negative impact on student motivation (Kikuchi, 2009, 2013, 2015), yet my intention was to break free of my rather too rigid planning and materials-driven style of teaching and into a more personalised, responsive and learner-centric model. As the narrative shows, I was not always successful, but this effect certainly contributed to a new understanding of *the living textbook*, as I will discuss in Section 6.4.

A further element of intuition came from the research process itself. As I identified in Section 2.6.2, synaptic crossings are seen as something teachers can often recognise intuitively, as they are based on feedback and energy investment (EROI). Good or experienced teachers are 'tuned in' to their learners and, due to our ability as social organisms to empathise with one and other, we can often sense how others are reacting to us and how they might feel about us. Thus, synaptic crossings have a dual function as being indicators of synergy. This is an intuitive process, but one which I have attempted to reflect on and understand more deeply. One such example of how my unpacking of intuition led to a deepened understanding of the classroom was in my expanded perception of time and experience in the classroom.

6.3.2 Time, experience and the classroom force multiplier effect

Timescales are important to bear in mind when researching complex dynamic processes (de Bot, 2015), especially when paying particular attention to the way learners interact with and construct the contexts of their own learning.

> To make our research more manageable, we are obliged to make certain pragmatic decisions about the contextual elements to be included and excluded, and pragmatic choices about the nested levels of analysis to focus on.
> (Ushioda, 2015, p. 49)

As I mentioned in Section 6.3.2, each person in the class experiences the 90 minutes of instruction completely independently and thus for one class there is 2,340 minutes of experience (N25(+1 as the teacher) X 90). This is perhaps an important observation as it shows that we are not teaching in a vacuum, and of course no two learners will experience the lesson (or the constructs of authenticity or motivation) in the same way. Complexity theory has ways of explaining gener-alisable patterns of behaviour (referred to as attractor states; see Hiver, 2015a for more information), but this could be a reductive way of talking about a class full of people since it generally relates to systems which can be plotted mathematic-ally, which of course barely applies to complex social phenomena (see Verspoor, 2015 for further discussion). The variability of learners' experience is something already touched upon in discussions of language teaching, perhaps most famously by Dick Allwright (1984) in his discussion about 'why don't learners learn what teachers teach?'.

Acknowledging the Experience Multiplier and quantifying a 90-minute lesson as 2,340 minutes of experience was an eye-opening realisation for me. I first realised this when listening back to the CaLabo recordings of students' group discussion collected from the CALL room. The amount of class time dedicated to the discussion was about 20 minutes, but with five groups this meant that I had to listen to 100 minutes of student discussion. This realisation made me appreciate the true nature of the 'reality' of the class. Conceptualised this way, my experience of one lesson is only 4 per cent of the total (see Figure 6.11).

Having said this, the actual amount of time the learners spend with me in the class out of the entire academic year is much smaller. As detailed in Section 4.3, the class met 28 times in spring and 27 times in autumn, for a total of 4,950 minutes of contact time (90 X 55). However, the number of minutes in the period between 14 April 2014 and 21 January 2015 is 387,360, meaning the percentage of class time to out of class time is 1.28 per cent (Figure 6.12).

This realisation helped me put the class into real perspective, in terms of both time and context, and to gain a more holistic perspective on the complexity of the classroom and language learning processes (Dörnyei et al., 2015b; King, 2016c;

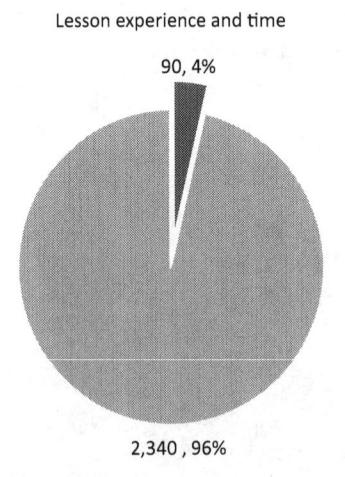

Lesson experience and time

90, 4%

2,340 , 96%

Figure 6.11 One person's experience of the lesson total

Per cent of academic year spent in class

4,950 , 1%

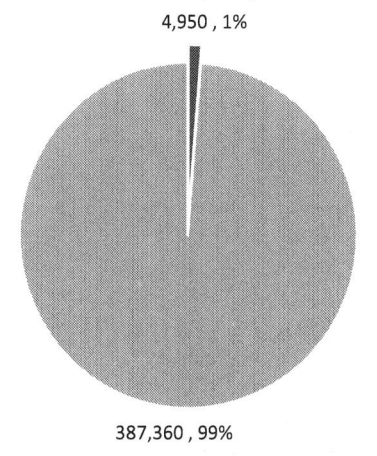

387,360 , 99%

Figure 6.12 Per cent of time spent in class

Kramsch, 2011; Larsen-Freeman, 1997; Sampson, 2016; Tudor, 2003; Ushioda, 2015). Understanding my experience as a subjective point of view on a much wider whole also helped me see the underlying ecology of the classroom, meaning the relation of agents to others within their environment (Kim, 1995; Kramsch, 2002b; Tudor, 2003; van Lier, 1998, 2000, 2002, 2006). These paradigms were discussed in Chapter 2, but here I am trying to show how they manifest themselves as a reality, certainly in terms of the Experience Multiplier. Thus, it seems imperative that learners are able to find meaning and personal value in the work, to achieve self-authenticity in order to connect this with social authentication. In such a situation, motivational synergies are bound to flourish.

This is an important realisation in terms of motivational synergy and authenticity, as it may have helped me as a practitioner gain a sense of necessary distance and step back from my own experience and understand the complexity of the class as a whole. Understanding the contextually situated nature of the class is essential in recognising complex dynamic processes and giving life to the ecology that animates the classroom over time as its identity emerges and develops. Another important aspect of creating a convergent orientation and maintaining positive motivational synergy was increasing the learner's sense of identity as speakers of English through encouraging their own self-reflection

6.3.3 Identity creation and reflective learners

Many volumes deal with the issue of reflexivity as a positive and desirable component of language teacher education (Edge, 2011; Johnson & Golombek, 2002; Kelchtermans, 2009; Mann, 2005; Richards & Lockhart, 1994; Walsh & Mann, 2015); however, these works largely concentrate on the teacher as the main reflective agent in his or her practice. In terms of learner reflection, there is of course already a much larger body of work discussing the role of leaner autonomy, yet autonomy is still quite distinct from reflection. Reflection would seem to entail a more purposeful questioning of the reasons for learning and doing, of building a balanced and developed understanding of self-as-learner and learner-as-self, which in itself would clearly lead into a developed future self-image and vision (Dörnyei, 2009; Dörnyei & Kubanyiova, 2014; Dörnyei & Ushioda, 2009; Muir & Dörnyei, 2013; Ryan & Irie, 2014).

One approach that does encourage learners to become self-reflective is Exploratory Practice, because this methodology encourages learners to develop their own puzzles, highlights the learners' agency in the research process and, 'through encouraging practitioners to set their own research agendas, makes the work directly relevant to the participants themselves' (Hanks, 2015a, p. 127). Although I felt that I had not sufficiently involved the learners in the research process as much as I perhaps could have, in terms of facilitating reflection in the learners, the study did not fall short. Throughout the year, the CLERAC students submitted numerous reflective papers and conducted both formal and informal tasks which invited them to reflect on their own learning and their own reasons for learning. This is in line with what Ushioda (2014) advocates when she speaks about the connection between metacognition and motivation.

Although the puzzling process was not made as overtly clear to the CLERAC learners as it was in, for example the study by Hanks (2015b), I believe that CLERAC was structured around the belief that learners also needed to reflect on their learning in order to become more successful, autonomous and motivated. This was one of the synapses in which positive synergy was fostered, along with negotiating content (see Section 6.4), and very much a practical product of my philosophy of teaching, which particularly relates to the authenticity continuum discussed in Chapter 2. In the following sections I will examine some of the main ways that reflection was formally engineered into the CLERAC course.

6.3.3.1 Reaction papers

As detailed in the overview of the narrative and as part of the narrative itself, the students regularly wrote short reflections on topics discussed in class in the Coffee Room, and were also asked to write more formal reaction papers which were assessed as written coursework, making up 20 per cent of the grade for the semester.

As mentioned in the spring narrative, in her end-of-semester reaction paper, Ms Redslope said that, although at first she felt that she wished I would speak Japanese more during the class to help her understand, she found the class 'very fun', and further explained that she had not only developed the confidence to study abroad, but also that her TOEFL score had risen as a result of the class.

> Thanks to you, I decided to travel the Australia in studying abroad. Because I thought I want to speak English with the many people by speaking with you. And to be honest, time to sit at the desk and study English was less

than high school student's time. But my score in TOEFL rises. I think that's because your English which is a native was heard twice a week. I'm very thankful to you. I'm going to learn many things in studying abroad.

(Ms Redslope, 14/01/2015)

This is a very positive result, especially in light of the decreasing number of students who are choosing to study abroad from Japan, and the tendency for shorter stays (MEXT, 2015). From the 24 students who completed the CLERAC course, at least four went on to study abroad, accounting for 16.7 per cent of the student body of CLERAC. This is impressive considering that only about 13 per cent of students from the English Literature Department choose to go on study abroad programs, bearing in mind that these are English majors. Study abroad has been linked with identity creation (Ryan & Irie, 2014) and the ability to 'authenticate learning' (Irie & Ryan, 2015, p. 344). However, notice also that Ms Redslope still holds a preference for 'native speaker' English, divergent from my aims for the class in the global English lessons.

In his end-of-semester reaction, Mr Auxiliary commented that he wanted to 'scold old myself who had held prejudice by trivial things' based on his deepened understanding from our study of prejudice.

Surprisingly, some of the best reaction papers and reflections came from students whom I did not expect. Mr House wrote the following reaction:

This class not a common way of studying English but studied English through various society problems or humorous subjects. I was not get sick and tire of class and always be delight by this way. For example, 'True or false' was interesting thinking that photo or other's story is true or false, 'Critical thinking' was thought us fallacy. Video project gave us sense of accomplish that finished making video, and the knowledge of unknown world that deep sea or other groups' research. Autumn semester was five problem that prejudice, consumerism, economic, environment and wildlife. They are big problem of the world, so this class was very good opportunity of thinking those problems. And session by student was also good opportunity of telling others. It is pleasant for me to attend this class. So new subject raised my motivation.

While I could also improve English skill for understanding contents. I was not good at listening and talking English, but I used English without being afraid of mistake. I think this is being authentic. Authentic means that have credibility. Actually, I feel that can trust my English skill than before because my listening and speaking skill improved. I be thankful to Richard. I think other classmates too. Because this class was number one in 98 English classes. This is trust for Richard from students. This is authentic in terms of being able to trust. Ultimately, thank you for teaching me in a year. I hope to take your lesson.

(Mr House, 13/01/2015)

Mr House shows that my research themes had clearly impacted his experience of learning English, and communicates the possibility that my aims for the class, as expressed in the narrative as I developed my philosophy of teaching, were transmitted and received through the synaptic crossing of motivational synergy produced by working towards social authentication in the classroom. As I have detailed, social authentication relied on feedback and having a mutually beneficial EROI.

In this way, the reaction papers not only enhanced students' metacognitive and reflective practices but also provided a form of feedback between myself as the teacher and the students. As I have discussed, empathy and feedback seem interconnected, and both were hypothesised to be both prerequisites for synaptic crossings of motivational synergy and retrospective indicators of synergy. These are therefore essential components in social authentication.

However, although these reaction papers reveal learner reflection and provide feedback *to* me, there is a lack of bidirectionality in this feedback. Although I did often compose personal responses to the students when I sent my feedback, this was often limited to a line or two of writing. During the class, the feedback I gave was a constant feature of my interactions with the students, but as this was informal verbal feedback, its impact is likely to have been transient and therefore limited.

I would have liked to require learners in the CLERAC class to compose regular journals in English, but I felt that doing so would both be an infringement on their privacy and create too much work, both for me to mark and for the students to compose. I also would have felt uncomfortable in assigning journal entries as homework on ideological grounds, as the rationale behind such an assignment is likely to be linked with learner autonomy, and yet doing so would actually reduce the autonomy of the task because it would become required rather than volitional.

Chiesa and Bailey (2015) advocate the use of dialogue journals, which are reciprocal exchanges between students and teachers that carry on over time. However, as I teach some nine lessons and work with approximately 200 students each week, these types of exchange seem impractical to me. Even composing just 25 such reciprocal journals for CLERAC would have been a very large amount of work each week, although no doubt very rewarding. In some ways, the lack of bidirectional feedback was filled by the use of the Coffee Room, which was the main source of written dialogue between members of the class.

6.3.3.2 Coffee Room

The Coffee Room is something that I use with all the classes I teach, although the extent to which it is taken up varies greatly from class to class. With CLERAC, the Coffee Room was one of the most vibrant places where exchanges took place, although this happened mainly in the spring semester and fell off in the autumn (see digital appendix (Appendix 5) for a summary of posts and usage). Upon reflection, I feel I could have used the Coffee Room much more effectively, as writing is a very important part of second-language identity creation, through what Kramsch and Lam (1999) label 'textual identities' that I have previously connected to the concept of authenticity (Pinner, 2016b).

In Figure 6.13, the number of replies to a post are plotted against the days since the last post.

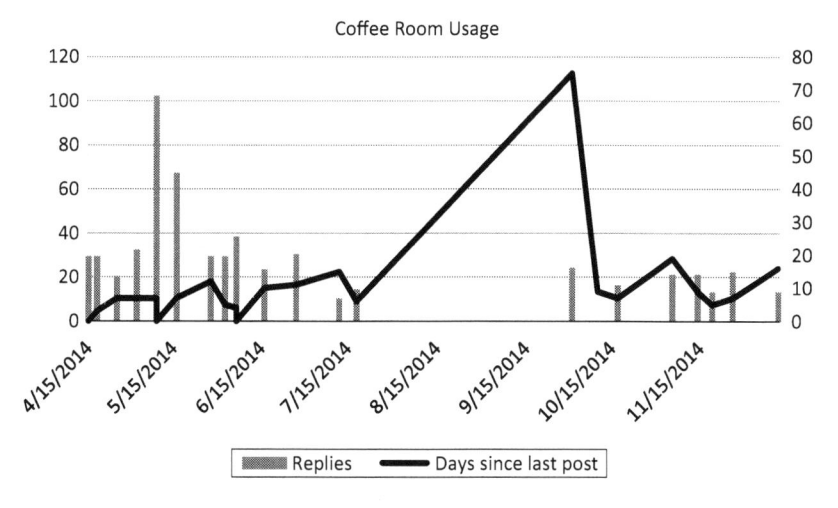

Figure 6.13 Coffee Room usage showing replies and time between posts

As the chart shows, the number of replies seems to be higher when the Coffee Room is used regularly and with only small intermissions between posts, suggesting the need to keep the momentum going. One way this was achieved was to give students the job of forum managers, as detailed in the spring narrative. For reasons now unclear to me, this practice was not carried over to the autumn, but it would certainly be a recommended way of increasing the uptake of such reflective platforms, although perhaps more guidance is needed if it is to be used specifically as a reflexive tool.

Another interesting aspect of the forum is the way it was used by individuals in the class. The most active poster was Ms Hemp, who posted 32 times in the spring when the average was 19.7 posts for the first semester.[1] This is interesting because Ms Hemp was definitely not a very outspoken member of the class, and yet she was able to balance out her participation through the creation of a textual identity in the Coffee Room forum, in much the same way that Warschauer, Turbee, and Roberts (1996) noted 20 years ago. The lowest poster was Mr Nintendo (seven posts), followed by Mr Widetree (ten posts). The most active reader was Mr Wind, who viewed 268 posts compared to the average of 163. Ms Saltfield was the lowest in terms of reading her classmates' posts, with only 84 views, followed again by Mr Widetree, with 95.

Another important reflective tool, and a way that students attempted to balance their participation, was through self-assessments.

6.3.3.3 Self-assessment

As can be seen from a simple performance indicator such as the Coffee Room, Mr Widetree was not an active participant in class. He was one of the students

I identified early as potentially 'bad' in the spring narrative (and the first time I mentioned the Pygmalion effect), and in my journal I referred to him as a 'leech' on 28/11/2014 in the audio journal. As noted, I felt Mr Widetree was 'sly' because, unlike Mr Auxiliary, who I felt was trying to work hard, although this was not always clear from a purely communicative standpoint, Mr Widetree was trying to appear like a hard worker whilst attempting to do as little as possible. He seemed not to credit me with the powers of observation to see through his 'tricks', such as looking at unrelated websites in the CALL room without seeming aware that I could still see what he was looking at from my desk, without having to walk behind him. This is relevant because Mr Widetree gave himself 100 per cent for every one of his self-assessments, as did his seating friend, Mr Mouth, a score I feel was *inauthentic*. These two students were the only two to do this, which I felt was an abuse of the system. This has much in common with another event from another class I was teaching in 2014, detailed at length in Pinner (2016c). Despite the possibilities for students to misuse my trust in them, overall I felt that the self-assessments for class participation were not only accurate (according to my own intuitive sense of their efforts in class) but also an extremely useful tool in helping the students maintain motivation throughout the semester by engaging in reflection (Pinner, 2016d). Self-assessment has been shown as one of the most powerful enhancement tools for student performance (Hattie, 2008, 2012), and it certainly seems to be a useful way to improve students' metacognitive skills in connection to L2 motivation (Ushioda, 2014).

6.3.3.4 Overall performance indicators

Although attendance, being on time for class and getting good grades for assessment do not equate directly with motivation, these are good indicators of motivation and are how teachers and students are assessed in many Japanese university English-based classes. As the spring narrative recounts, the students as a whole did not perform particularly well on their video projects, and attendance (especially lateness) were issues that plagued both semesters. As teachers are accountable and have to be very careful in record-keeping for class in order to justify the grade they will award students, it is natural that teachers will collect certain types of evidence which could be used as a rough indicator of motivation. Of course, it is dangerous to assume that these *are* indicators of motivation, but collectively such performance indicators may help contribute to a holistic picture of motivation, which is another reason why teachers are likely to be aware of their students' level of motivation (Cowie & Sakui, 2011). One interesting observation is that, in creating the narrative, I found my overall reflection of the CLERAC course shifting and beginning to change. Before composing the narrative, CLERAC had been one of the best classes I had ever taught, second only to DCT and perhaps even better in many ways. As I went back over the data and my reflections, I realised that, in terms of performance indicators, I had actually been consistently disappointed with the assessed coursework produced by the learners. Conversely, the overall grades for the students were relatively high (see digital appendix (Appendix 5) for an overview of the students' grades). This highlights the subjective nature of this inquiry, and of even such quantitative data as grades and other statistics which I have labelled performance indicators. This would suggest that language teachers would benefit from instruction on the nature of assessment, in particular focusing on validity and fairness. Grades are essential for extrinsic class motivation in Japanese universities, because many universities use the GPA system (grade point average) and this may also be reported to companies during job hunting. In general, students' motivation is greatly affected by their grades, and this also provides an important element of feedback between students and teachers, which contributes to motivational synergy and hinges on both parties being convergent in their beliefs about the purpose of the class and being congruent in terms of personal authenticity. Furthermore, grades are the most important synapse for the flow of meaningful feedback between teachers and students. Therefore, based on this inquiry I have made several attempts in my current teaching practices to improve the quality and quantity of feedback that I can give to my students. Of course, in order to be manageable, this requires lower teaching banks, smaller classes and increased contact time between teachers and students. Sadly, the overall trends seem to be in reverse of the recommendations I would make based on this finding (Altbach, 2004; Gieve & Miller, 2006; Ritzer, 1996).

6.3.4 Further down the spiral: reflexivity as a never-ending quest

As discussed at the opening of this section, in conducting this autoethnographic inquiry I entered a state of 'hyper-reflexivity' which was not always conducive to good practice, although it generally led me to deeper observations and helped me find my authentic self and become self-congruent in my philosophy of teaching. This is why complexity theory seemed the only paradigm which could encompass a study such as this. In entering such a state of reflexivity, it often becomes difficult to distinguish between personal and professional issues, or practical and theoretical concerns. It becomes hard to know when the research stops (Bell, 2011). This relates not just to data collection and focus but also to the act of teaching and developing as a balanced professional. Becoming a better teacher, I found, came to mean becoming a better person in general and involved moving towards my own ideal future self. There is also an ethical issue as the researcher must carefully consider how much of him or herself to reveal (Dashper, 2015).

In conducting this inquiry, and especially in the writing phases as I prepare to share the findings *as research*, I have revisited the CLERAC narrative many times from many different perspectives. As Ryan and Irie (2014) have discussed, the Self is constantly recreated by imagining and replaying memories. Engaging in Narrative Inquiry, reflection and autoethnography has brought to consciousness a much richer and more holistic understanding of my authentic teaching self. But although this process was facilitated by 'narrative knowledging' (Barkhuizen, 2011, 2013b; Barkhuizen et al., 2014) and 'talking into understanding' (Mann,

2002), this is an ongoing process and thus the changes to my practice are permanent and yet incomplete. This is why teacher education programs would be well served to include components that encourage narratives, journaling and other reflective tools that can facilitate professional development as an ongoing and emergent process (Farrell, 2007; Johnson & Golombek, 2002; Kelchtermans, 2009; Mann, 2005; Schön, 1983; Walsh & Mann, 2015). However, there were also negative aspects to the reflective state. As I was collecting data and living the narrative, I often wondered how sustainable such hyper-reflexivity and awareness would be in the long-term. I asked myself if it was only a feature of conducting formal research or if it could be maintained in normal teaching. More generally, in terms of teacher education, one has to ask whether this type of reflection could be effectively included in teacher education programs. It would seem impossible to *impose* such personal reflection as a course requirement and retain the levels of authenticity and self-congruence that I attained in this inquiry. This leads us to question to what extent reflexivity and self-reflection can be taught. It was only by doing this type of research that I was really able to learn how to go about conducting a study such as this. As discussed in the evolution of my design chapter, the system I used for reflecting, journaling and keeping notes progressed through several distinct phases before becoming mature, and even then there were many areas for improvement. By way of demonstration, Figure 6.13 shows the length of the audio reflection that I recorded throughout the narrative. The linear trend line shows that the length of the reflections tended to increase the longer the study continued, with a slightly steeper increase coming in around the entry for lesson 206A (05/11/2014) when I 'considerably improved' the system I used which incorporated detailed field notes. Overall the average length of the reflections more than doubled over the course of the data collection (Figure 6.14).

However, although the nature of these reflections is very introverted, personal and individual, the process of reflecting is certainly not just a solitary act. My philosophy of teaching and professional identity were co-created with my students as I engaged in the process of teaching and learning. Furthermore, all of these reflections were developed in discussions with colleagues, attendance at conferences where I participated and also presented, as well as the countless other social occasions when identity was negotiated and developed throughout the course of experience.

However, as I mentioned in Section 6.3.3.4, reflecting back on the narrative and in particular focusing on the performance indicators has discoloured my overall impression of the class. This reflection has caused me to view my initially very positive perspective on the class as being based on an illusion of success, both in terms of performance on assessments and in terms of forging a personal connection.

6.3.4.1 Strange attractor

The aforementioned illusion of success could be a result of what in complexity theory is known as a strange attractor, which is a special type of attractor state. This is a state or set of 'values that a system tends to approach over time but never

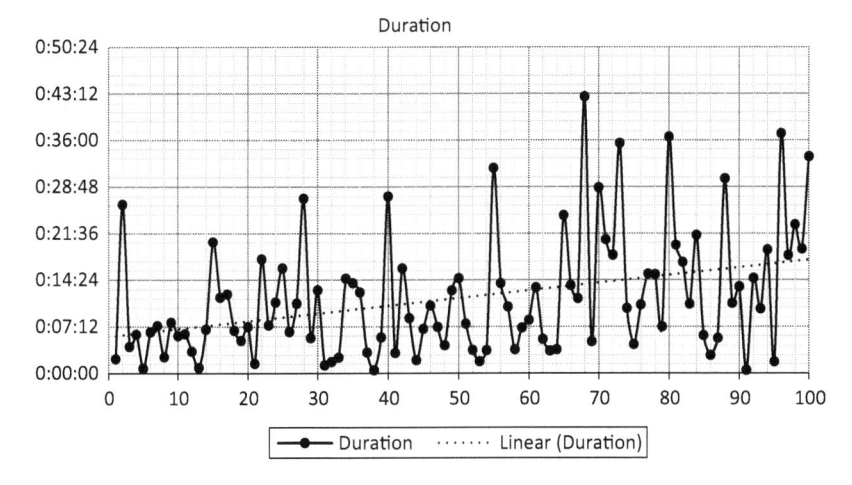

Figure 6.14 Duration of audio journal reflections

quite reaches' (Hiver, 2015a, p. 26). In other words, CLERAC wanted to be highly motivated, we often synergised *in the class* and the students tended to be convergent with me towards the same goals, and yet, as evidenced by their lack of personal interest in me *as a person*, by their rather minimal efforts in preparing for final assessments, by the frequent attendance and lateness issues and by their general lack of language proficiency improvement (presumably the result of minimal out-of-class work), they never quite seemed to reach the stage of high motivation that I have perceived from other classes, not least DCT. I should also point out that this is not the fault of the students, because the onus is on me just as much as it is on them. This was a mutual inability to synergise to the levels I had hoped for. Ironically, I think that the high levels we achieved were a result of this class being the centre of this inquiry, and yet, paradoxically, this may also account for the fact that high motivation was a strange attractor as well.

Of course, DCT made videos about topics that both they and I were passionate about (social issues) and thus there was synergy there. But the video projects in spring were about Deep Sea Creatures, Disney and Steve Jobs, which I had no involvement or investment in. In this way, there was perhaps *too much autonomy* here without there being sufficient guidance. I was not interested in their topics, and thus I perhaps offered fewer ideas and less encouragement than for DCT. By the autumn semester, when the same topics from DCT about which I was passionate were introduced, I had already abandoned the chance to redeem the video projects and moved the students in the direction of outputs, which were too high level and for which I did not explain my expectations clearly enough. These are of course highly demotivating factors that Kikuchi (2015) lists under 'teacher incompetence'. Although these failures are hard to admit and have contributed to the discolouration in my memory of the overall success of CLERAC, I feel it is important to retrospectively question my overall impression of the class and identify practical areas where I could improve my teaching. Although I was not looking for problems/solutions in my teaching, identifying areas for improvement is a necessary step in every teacher's ongoing development (Borg, 2006; Johnson & Golombek, 2016, 2002).

Realising this has added a retrospective sense of shedding the illusion that I wrapped around myself as I was teaching CLERAC. CLERAC *was* special, but perhaps only because I made it special. This inquiry has opened my eyes to the realities of my own subjectivity and highlighted the importance of evidence-based reflection rather than research that 'helps perpetuate the suspicion that [Reflective Practice] suffers unduly from individual narcissism and introspection' (Walsh & Mann, 2015, p. 353).

In defence of CLERAC, however, I would like to point out that whatever is learned in the language classroom is likely to be lost or forgotten over time if it is not put into practice on a regular basis. In other words, whatever the students learn will eventually fade if study and use are not maintained (de Bot & Hulsen, 2002). Furthermore, Gomes de Matos (2002) states that the language learner's rights involve *experience* and *humanising* qualities. Thus, in line with my philosophy of teaching, the main purpose of CLERAC was to provide a positive emotional charge in terms of motivational orientation towards the act of studying. In this respect, I still feel the CLERAC course was a success. Certainly, in terms of my own professional development as well, CLERAC will have a lasting influence on my identity as a teacher and as a researcher. One of the main influences of CLERAC was my approach to materials and the realisation that I will constantly need to revise and update my materials in order to fit each class, which I discussed previously as *the living textbook*.

6.4 Motivation: the living textbook

This section discusses how the negotiation of content and the involvement of students in the decision-making about the course is an essential way that positive motivational synergy is achieved. In particular, these instances contribute to synaptic crossings in which feedback can pass between teacher and students, allowing the course to align itself around the individuals who make up the group in an emergent way, thus leading to social authentication and motivational synergy. These crossings are facilitated by paying attention to certain issues relating to authenticity which arise in the process of negotiation, and subsequently updating materials in order to keep them alive, a way of ensuring the energy investment is on track and going in the right direction. The *living textbook* thus refers not just to materials but also to the process of building materials and content to fit around each individual class. An example of this from the narrative might be the time we watched the documentary *The End of Suburbia* in lesson 208A. This lesson was simply a disaster waiting to happen, a case of me having run out of steam and not adapting the materials to fit my learners. The energy I invested was small, which is why the energy return was also very small, leading Ms Downtree and Ms Oldriver to fall asleep. Conversely, in lesson 209B,

I found a more appropriate video to watch (overcoming *Peak Comprehension*) which was specifically aimed at the learners in CLERAC. Another way of ensuring that the content fits the learners is to allow them the autonomy to choose their own content, in a process of negotiation.

Autonomy does not equate to simply letting the students choose what to do in class. It is recommended that the teacher utilise a more *autocratic* style of leadership at first and then move towards a more democratic style as the group becomes more independent (Dörnyei & Murphey, 2003, p. 91; following Lewin, Lippitt, & White, 1939). The video projects are an example of autonomy with mixed success. A more successful (and more structured) example would be the debate class (107A), although this format was underexploited and used just once. Perhaps the best example, however, is the self-assessment for class participation, in which metacognition and reflection were built directly into the course. Overall, giving the CLERAC students more scaffolded control allowed us to synergise our learning aims and classroom behaviour, which again is how the increased metacognitive awareness combined with an Exploratory Practice framework in order to achieve a sense of praxis between my philosophy of teaching and much of my behaviour in class.

This inquiry uses a definition of authenticity which has moved away from 'materials' and 'texts' and into something far larger and more central to identity but inevitably less tangible. Nevertheless, materials are still a vital aspect of the way authenticity is constructed in the language classroom.

Just as van Lier (1996) calls for 'balanced teaching' in which lessons are made up of 'both planned and improvised elements' (p. 200), I have been experimenting with doing less planning and, somewhat in the tradition of Dogme ELT, trying to build lessons around the students in the moment of the lessons. As documented in the narrative, this was not always successful, and created a tension between my own desire to carefully plan lessons, as well as an internal conflict between intuition and reflection. It is clear from my decision to implement output sessions, as well as other areas where I felt I had let the class down, that not all of my instincts were in the best interests of the class. However, the lessons which were most successful seemed to be the ones such as the debate class using *The Economist* posters, the fallacies lessons and the work on consumerism. These lessons featured a balance of planned and improvised elements. Finding my own balance also involved gaining higher proficiency with the CALL room software and getting to know the students well enough to be able to predict what they could do and how much scaffolding they would need. This was made more difficult by the mixed levels of the class and of course the variability in their individual personalities.

As I was teaching the course, at times I felt I was caught up in a 'flow', which I described as the process of intuitively sewing serendipitous events into my work as if they belonged to a path, organically evolving of its own accord. This was the feeling I had when the hyper-aware state was in balance with my intuition and philosophy of teaching.

The complexity of negotiating content has a long history in the literature of language learning and SLA, and these issues also relate to philological issues such as *prior text* (Becker, 1984, 1995) and literary theories such as *value judgements* (Eagleton, 2008). For example, Mishan's (2005) notion of Currency developed in the narrative as a sub-facet of awareness (van Lier, 1996), as by consciously paying attention to the things happening in space and time around me, these naturally translated themselves into teaching ideas. This is why I found the term *living textbook* so appealing as it suggested an organic, emergent process of choosing what to do in the classroom based on what was important at *that time*, to those particular *individuals*, in that particular *context*. In this way, authenticity seems to be a natural aspect of ecological approaches to language learning, and complexity theory seems an appropriate paradigm for studying such contextually situated dynamic processes.

6.5 The authenticity gap

So far in this chapter, I have attempted to present some of the complexities of the discoveries from the narrative in such a way as to connect them to existing ideas in the literature and thus give them both a practical and a theoretical justification. However, in order to achieve praxis, I will need to relate them once again back to my own specific context. As stated throughout this inquiry, my search for authenticity has become a quest for my own personal beliefs and best practices which reflect who I am and who I want to be as a teacher. This has involved a process of socially mediating my identity in order to be able to fulfil the role I felt my students required of me.

During a discussion with Ema Ushioda on 30/04/2015, I realised that what I was really looking at in terms of authenticity and motivation could best be described as either a bridge or a gap. Understanding this felt like a tectonic shift had occurred in my mind, although I already *knew* about it. This was the bringing closer to consciousness or the rediscovery of my initial motives for the inquiry. As the CLERAC course progressed, and especially as I went back over the data to construct the narrative, I started looking for ways in which motivational synergy was influenced by authenticity in these two respects.

Although many separate and interrelated components make up the gaps and bridges in authenticity, I have chosen to focus on my own developing identity as I become a more experienced teacher, in other words the expanding age gap between my learners and myself, and the cultural differences between us with a particular focus on schemata, prior text, habitus and the power imbalance between the social position of teacher and students in terms of how they experience the 'small culture' of the class.

6.5.1 Gaps in self

A recent observation which has greatly influenced my teaching identity was my awareness of the growing divide between the students and myself in terms of my age and social status. Teaching in London between 2006 and 2010, I framed myself very closely as an equal to my learners, as another peer who happened to know the local culture and language. In Japan, I stand out as one of the only non-Japanese people in the classroom, a minority. Here I represent a visual stereotype of the 'native speaker' (Amin, 1999; Kubota & Lin, 2006; Liggett, 2009; see also Kubota and Lin, 2009b for edited volume), and I am also an import of English culture (Bailey, 2006, 2007). In some ways, I am perhaps a personification of the 'extrapolation techniques' which were the main crux of criticisms against culturist assumptions of authenticity (Hung & Victor-Chen, 2007; MacDonald et al., 2006; Pinner, 2016b; Seargeant, 2005). Conversely, in London I was part of the ethnic majority of Britain, but the class was very multicultural, so fewer people stood out in terms of gender or ethnicity due to the increased diversity. In Sophia University there is also about 80 per cent females to 20 per cent males, and of course a very small number of students who are non-Japanese. All of these factors contribute to how I am perceived differently in my new teaching role, and have contributed to the increasing authenticity gap and my growing need to bridge this.

6.5.2 *The culture gap*

As I have already discussed, cultural schemata, prior text and habitus are essential considerations when selecting materials to use in classrooms that aim to facilitate authenticity and motivational synergy. The fact that my students are primarily now all from one country (Japan) and are thus mainly monolingual and share the same cultural and national identity starkly contrasts with the multinational, multi-lingual and multicultural teaching context of London. Using English in a mainly monolingual class in Japan has an inherent chime of 'inauthenticity' as clearly it would be more natural to communicate in the language which comes more easily. There is a danger for the target language to become 'ritualised' (Rampton, 1999, 2002).

Whilst the multicultural setting was perhaps even more complex, the fact that most of my students are Japanese actually serves to highlight these cultural differences further by creating a clearer divide and thus a tendency to essentialise the difference between 'me' and 'them'. As I acculturate to Japan, this gap is changing in nature and I am now very sensitive to forms of 'othering', and much more likely to have shared cultural and linguistic reference points in terms of schemata and habitus, which are not only culturally specific or also age related but also highly individual. For example, my dislike of football is something that may have distanced me from Mr Auxiliary, but this is not specific to either culture or age and is simply a matter of personality. Inevitably, as I attempt to personalise the language learning process, this brings me closer to some students and distances me from others.

In London I could make a reference to a film series such as *Star Wars* and the students, for the most part, would be able to use that cultural point of reference for me to make an example to illustrate a point or make a joke or simply to build rapport. More deeply, these films have even been described as a useful schema for building an understanding of ethical issues (Baggini & Fosl, 2007, pp. 122–123).

These types of reference are drawn from my own cultural schema, and were a large part of my teaching identity because I saw myself as belonging to the same generation as my students, and they were *authentic* in the sense that they were shared social and individual points of reference. In Japan, working with 18- to 22-year-olds, I soon learned that *Star Wars* was no longer a reliable shared reference. However, in 2015 when a new *Star Wars* film was released, interestingly this series gained a great deal of currency and it was once again a shared reference point. This illustrates the complexity of these shared points and how they can contribute to the authenticity gap.

Through undertaking the study, I was able to identify early on that the reason for my interest in authenticity was that I wanted to bridge this gap by gaining a deeper understanding of the issue, so that I might replace those things which were becoming obsolete with things which would enable me to retain the highly authentic bonds of rapport around which I structured my teaching approach. In this way, I came to see a reconceptualised version of authenticity and the new types of content that I would create from this new philosophy of teaching as a bridge between my students and me.

6.6 Authenticity as a bridge

At the beginning of this inquiry, my original hypothesis was that authenticity would be at the intersection between the 'real' world and the classroom (see Figure 6.15).

However, as my understanding of the construct of authenticity has shifted away from what I have labelled as the 'classic definition' and towards a dynamic, contextually situated and socially mediated concept, my belief about authenticity in the classroom has also changed. I believe that moments of positive motivational synergy between my learners and myself were most effectively created when all of us were convergent in our beliefs about what we should do with our time together in the class. This sounds overly simplistic, but I would argue that this is actually a very complex dynamic which is hinged on a range of assumptions

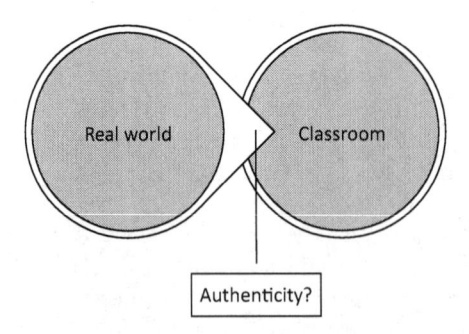

Figure 6.15 Authenticity as the intersection of the real world and the classroom

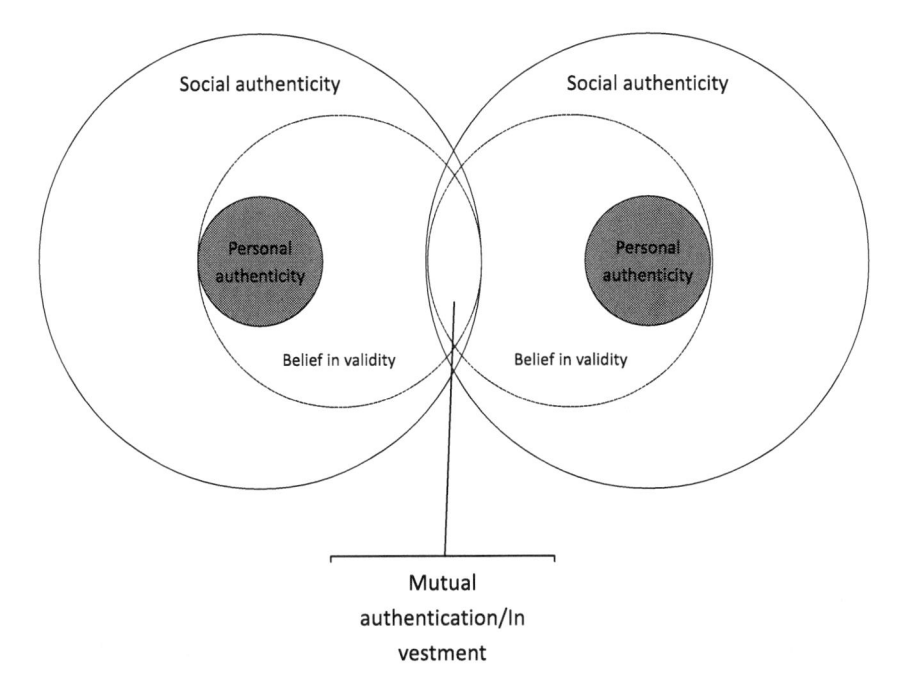

Figure 6.16 Motivational synergy as facilitated by authenticity as a bridge

and other contextual factors, as detailed in the *underpinning currents* section. For example, learners do not always consciously know what they want to get out of an individual lesson or even from a full course. The teacher may have a better idea in this sense than the learners, although the teacher must be careful not to rely on assumptions to arrive at conclusions which are not resultant from evidence-based reflections (Allwright & Hanks, 2009; Farrell, 2015; Hanks, 2015b, 2017; Walsh & Mann, 2015). This has much in common with the need for 'personal theory analysis' (Tripp, 1993, p. 51), meaning that reflection should move us away from unquestioned beliefs and invalid observations.

This inquiry has led me to view the authenticity bridge as a process of mutual validation in which motivations are aligned between individuals, and in particular between teacher and students. Figure 6.16 shows how I now view these complex factors. Social authenticity can be shared through context and through belonging to the same group (as in a class), yet it also encompasses the deeper underpinning currents behind language learning discussed in Section 6.2. Personal authenticity is more elusive and remains constantly 'grey' as it is redefined for each new social transaction as our identities shift and develop. However, a point of interaction is achievable when there is a crossover in the belief in validity about what one is doing. I would argue that language teachers can facilitate this shared sense of validity by using pedagogic tools such as reflection and negotiating content.

This process is also further dependent on the triadic relationship of authenticity, motivation and autonomy and the idea that authenticity is itself dynamically constructed along a continuum, emergent from context and social interaction.

6.6.1 Feedback

Maintaining positive motivational synergy is dependent on the presence of bidirectional feedback. As I related in the narrative, the moments of highest synergy were generally attributable to some form of feedback. For instance, learning that our class was 'number one' was a form of feedback *from* the students which I then turned into feedback *to* the students. The feeling of elation I achieved in this lesson was such that I was able to enjoy the lesson despite suffering severe pain in my back from a herniated disc, surely an example of eeudaimonia in which even severe physical pain could not hinder my enjoyment of the class. A further example came from the exchanges between Mr Charge and myself after his output session, which contrasted starkly with the almost unreadable and cryptic feedback I received from Mr Po, whose words in his email did not seem to match his actions in the classroom whilst watching other students' output sessions. Therefore, like reflection and autonomy, feedback is fraught with complexities because some feedback can be demotivating, non-constructive or even based on false observations. For an excellent summary of the importance of feedback in education and practical ways to apply it, I recommend Hattie (2012). Also, feedback is discussed more generally in terms of emotional intelligence by Goleman (2006) (see also Gkonou & Mercer, 2017). Throughout this study, feedback has been mentioned frequently. However, the key point is that feedback should be constructive, bidirectional and does not simply refer to 'grades'. Feedback is also essential in negotiating the teach/learn dichotomy.

6.6.2 Negotiating the teach/learn dichotomy

It has long been established that what teachers teach is not always the same as what learners learn (Allwright, 1984). In addition to this is the problem that what I want to teach might not always be aligned to what my learners want to learn. I have argued several times throughout this book that students and teachers need to be on the same page regarding their belief in the purpose of education in order to truly achieve positive motivational synergy. As authenticity relates to a feeling of congruence between what one is doing and what one wants to be doing, authentic experiences in language teaching are likely to depend on whether or not people are invested in the content being used for instruction. In other words, the extent to which classroom stakeholders are interested in the topic will have a large impact on learning. Too much 'authenticity' for one stakeholder could come at the expense of the other.

There is always some overlap between interests and what participants will be able to view as authentic; however, there are also areas where people are not compatible as well. For this reason, it is worth bearing in mind van Lier's caution

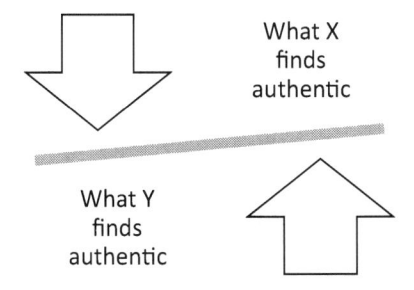

Figure 6.17 A simple representation of divergence

that authenticity cannot be experienced at the same amount for everyone at the same time (1996, p. 128). This seemed to manifest itself early on in the narrative of CLERAC when I realised that the students and I held different beliefs in regards to English and its position as an international language, something I have referred to as divergence throughout this inquiry.

This divergence could perhaps be visualised even more simply as in Figure 6.17.

Some situations will be easier for the students and teacher to *authenticate* than others. Since authenticity is a process of *personal engagement*, 'it is a goal that teachers and students have to work towards, consciously and constantly' (van Lier, 1996, p. 128). This means that what the students want to learn and what the teacher wants to teach are negotiated in order to achieve a shared level of optimum authenticity, which is probably best dynamically represented as being part of a continuum (Pinner, 2014a, 2016b).

However, this negotiation needs to be balanced. Although currently in vogue with many of my learners, as I have no interest in Lady Gaga it would be inauthentic of me to teach a lesson about her to my students, not least because I know nothing about her. However, a more authentic workaround would be to ask the learners to teach me about Lady Gaga and to attempt to alter my opinion of her. Similarly, it would be inauthentic of me to refrain from teaching my students lessons about topics of which they have no existing schematic knowledge or prior text. Holliday equates such a view with culturism.

> Children everywhere build their lives on imagining things they have never seen, from wild animals, to people in their history, to Martians. It is indeed culturalist to imagine that people can only find meaning within things with which they are familiar within their own community because it implies a bounded culture which cannot dream outside itself. Social authenticity does not therefore only relate to discourses in home society. It can also relate to the interface between home and the world – for example, the Internet, politics, tourism, globalisation, and visions of the Other.
>
> (Holliday, 2005, pp. 105–106)

In this way I have introduced students to topics of which they had no prior knowledge, won their interest and broadened their knowledge, which is intrinsically rewarding for me as a teacher. Furthermore, as the teacher represents the main catalyst for synergistic motivation, I would argue that it is more important that the teacher is interested in what he or she is teaching as this can always be transferred to the students (Csizér & Magid, 2014; Dörnyei & Ushioda, 2011).

6.6.2.1 *Banter, prioritising the experience over the results and the 'David Brent effect'*

As I discussed in the section entitled 'illusions of success', CLERAC was not as successful as I had hoped, which I now see as the result of the high motivational state we sought in class being a strange attractor state that we often moved towards and yet never managed to attain fully. The high motivational state which would have produced better final assessment results or higher input (EROI) from the students evaded us because we could never remain situated in that state space for long enough for this to become a full attractor state. Perhaps this is due to my earlier observation, cited in the narrative from 23/05/2014, that my purpose of teaching CLERAC was to focus on providing a positively charged *experience* of the language (Tomlinson & Masuhara, 2010), which meant I de-emphasised my focus on language learning gains. In some ways, this is reminiscent of the awkward fictional boss character David Brent from the UK sitcom *The Office*. Much of the black humour in this series comes from the fact that Brent sees himself primarily as an 'entertainer' and 'friend' to the staff at the office and a boss second. The irony is that Brent is heavily situated as a boss, and he is unpopular because he is incompetent, due especially to his prioritising personal relationships over professional ones. It is quite a jarring realisation for me that I might have been enacting a 'David Brent effect' on CLERAC by holding the belief that my learners' personal experience of learning English was more important than any learning gains.

One common theme to emerge from word frequency searches over my journal entries was the idea of having 'banter' with my students, which has much in common with the view of authenticity put forward by Cook (2000) in his discussion about language play.

As I have stated throughout this book, one of the main ways synergy is achieved is through teacher and students being convergent in their aims and applying the appropriate behaviour towards reaching shared goals. Early on in the narrative I was developing a philosophy of teaching that was based on a definition of authenticity that prioritised experience rather than outcomes. Although this is a perfectly good philosophy of teaching, it is not without problems as it downplays certain aspects of my job as a teacher. I have a responsibility to motivate my students (Dörnyei & Kubanyiova, 2014), and yet I also have a responsibility to help them learn. The two are linked, but if my approach is to personalise the learning, this may jar with some students who are happy to view English merely as a communicative tool in which they need only perform transactional exchanges (see for example Kubota, 2013; Matsuda, 2011). In asking such students to invest more than they are willing in the learning, I may invoke the 'David Brent' transportable identity that serves as Mr Hyde to the Dr Jekyll of my motivational teaching persona. Less elaborately, I may demotivate some slightly more withdrawn or less ambitious students simply by asking too much of them. In a discussion with a colleague on 03/09/2016 in Nagoya, a fellow teacher told me that he sees motivation as a 'choice' and a 'negotiation' of aims, because, just as the teacher in Matsuda's (2011) study phrased it, 'not everyone wants to be a star'. In this case, perhaps it is reasonable to expect a lower ratio of class motivational synergy. Working towards full synergy is perhaps closer on the spectrum to 'obsessive' rather than 'harmonious' passion for teaching (Carbonneau et al., 2008). This also connects with the common issue of teacher burnout which affects an inordinately large proportion of teachers (Dörnyei & Ushioda, 2011), and was something that has been cited as an original justification for developing Exploratory Practice as a research method (Allwright, 2003; Allwright & Hanks, 2009), even being described as a starting point and 'key factor in the lives of [...] teachers' (Allwright, 2005, p. 356). Hiver's work on teacher immunity is also relevant here, as teachers must constantly recalibrate their identities around their teaching contexts in order to survive the often very demanding realities of language teaching (Hiver, 2015b, 2017; Hiver & Dörnyei, 2017). Balancing my personal life with my full-time work and demanding research agenda was also a central justification in the research design of this project. In this way, this inquiry has helped me develop and justify my philosophy of teaching into something sustainable that I can use as a grounds for further practical inquiry. I have uncovered a much deeper understanding of the links between my motivation to teach and my students' motivation to learn, and the complexity underlying this may not be conducive to 'hard evidence' or 'scientific proof', yet it certainly provides a narrative of development which I can reflect back on as I try to move forward towards a better balance of personal and professional conduct, and to help me to retain my focus on praxis as I deepen my understanding of my own teaching.

6.7 Summary and conclusions towards praxis

This chapter has attempted to shift the focus of analytical lens used in the narrative. The data I presented in the narrative focused exclusively on my teaching and me. In trying to achieve a sense of praxis, I have attempted to turn the reflections around in a way that can highlight their relevance to others.

In the first section of this chapter I discussed the necessity of understanding the underpinning currents that contribute to our teaching contexts and the specific dynamics of any particular class. I then moved on to a discussion of the research/teaching process behind this inquiry, in particular how reflexivity was an essential component of the way my own professional identity and philosophy of teaching began to emerge and develop in the physical embodiment of my actions in and relating to the classes I teach. Finally, I discussed the importance of involving the learners in this process, whether directly by asking them or indirectly by factoring in our intuitions of their needs and abilities when choosing what to do in the class. These then became some of the components that contribute to the construct of authenticity being either a gap (divergence, negative synergy) or a bridge (convergence, positive synergy) between the students' and the teacher's motivation.

The assumption underlying these conclusions is that authenticity works as a binding agent in creating positive motivational synergy between students and teachers. Another assumption is that facilitating motivation is one of the main aims of practicing language teachers, as this is the well from which other learning springs. In attempting to present such personal findings in a way that makes sense to others, I have necessarily had to focus on certain issues at the expense of others, which is of course one of the major challenges to the complexity paradigm which I am using to frame this inquiry (Larsen-Freeman, 1997; Menezes, 2013; Tudor, 2003).

Discussing the issue of teacher motivation in their in-depth survey of the field of psychology in language learning, Dörnyei and Ryan (2015) explain that

> the ultimate aim of motivational research is always to explain student learning, and in order to associate the latter meaningfully with the motivation of teachers, we need to show first that an increase in teacher motivation leads to improved motivational practice on their behalf, which in turn promotes student motivation, which eventually results in enhanced student performance. While this chain is intuitively convincing, it is difficult to get empirical confirmation for it because of the manifold confounding variables at each connection level.
>
> (p. 101)

This is exactly the problem that I have grappled with in undertaking this study. However, although I am not able to *prove, quantify* or say unequivocally that these two are linked, I believe I have at the very least provided a window into the dynamics at the heart of this complex chain of processes. This compares with the definition of educational success (Larsen-Freeman, 2002, pp. 36–37) and teachers engaging with the 'why' value of their approach (Dörnyei & Kubanyiova, 2014, pp. 130–131). In other words, rather than providing explicit answers, I have focused on continuing my 'quest' in the search for deeper knowledge without the false pretense of ever expecting to gain a definitive answer.

Writing analyses based on observations which utilise complexity theory and Reflective Practice has been a challenge, and thus I do not feel it would be appropriate to draw conclusions that I would claim are generalisable or broadly true to other contexts. However, I would simply like to restate my intention that these observations will be of interest and perhaps useful to other teachers who are similarly engaged with a continual process of identity negotiation as we attempt to find what we can do to best help our learners and to facilitate a culture of authenticity in our language classrooms. Certainly, as a result of this inquiry, it has become one of my primary aims as a teacher to bridge the authenticity gap between my learners and myself in order to create a mutually motivating learning environment in which our aims are convergent towards synergy.

Note

1 Sadly, data were only retrievable for the first semester as I did not collect this information in time over the autumn semester and it was deleted from the system due to a server update in 2015.

7 Vignettes

Dima Yousef: I really do believe student motivation and energy is contagious. When my students are excited and engaged, I feel the lesson just flows. Also, I become motivated when students tell me that a lesson changed their mind or encouraged them to learn more about the topic... even if teachers plan amazing activities and tasks, students' lack of interest or motivation or energy will affect the flow of the lesson and the teacher.

(Comment posted to the IATEFL Research SIG's Facebook discussion in reply to my post about teacher-student motivation)

7.1 Introduction

In the previous sections I presented a narrative of my own teaching experiences over the course of an academic year, and the reflections on this experience that have influenced my practice and helped shed light on the relationship between teacher and student motivation. Following this, I would now like to present alternative perspectives on this relationship through a series of nine reflective vignettes that were elicited from colleagues and fellow practitioners around the world.

Vignettes can be 'a key part [to a] data-led approach' (Mann & Walsh, 2017, p. 2) because they foreground experience and do so in an interactional manner. Vignettes have been used primarily in psychological research, but also more recently in a number of fields such as clinical therapy and the social sciences. Often, the vignettes are actually written by the researchers:

> Vignettes are generated from a range of sources including previous research findings, [...] in collaboration with other professionals working in the field [...], or based on real-life case histories [...]. Participants are typically asked to respond to these stories with what they would do in a particular situation or how they think a third person would respond. The scenarios depicted in the stories can take the form of 'moral dilemmas'.
>
> (Hughes, 1998, p. 381; adapted with citations removed)

However, the vignettes in this book were produced by asking participants to respond to a brief, in which I first explained that my research looked at how my motivation mirrored my students' in both positive and negative ways. I foregrounded the brief by stating that it is commonly accepted that if the teacher is motivated, the students are more likely to get motivated, and I made it clear that I was looking at this dynamic relationship. Then, I asked respondents if they had any reflections on how their motivation as a teacher is reflected (or synergistic) with their students'. So, in this case, the vignettes were not hypothetical, but actually specifically requested a reflection on actual experience.

Although initially I had envisaged interspersing my own central narrative with vignettes from fellow practitioners, after compiling the reflections from colleagues I realised that, although in many ways they do support my own observations, they also bring other aspects together, and as such I felt many of them were too strong as stand-alone pieces to be merely used in support of my own narrative. As such, I include all the vignettes here in their own chapter, allowing them hopefully to speak for themselves more and thus to combine the themes from the narrative into a new configuration with its own central features. As such, these vignettes have become an additional piece of data to the central study, but also another example of how presentation and analysis are entwined in the writing of an autoethnography.

Before sharing the vignettes, a quick note on the contributors and how their vignettes were collected. After securing a contract to publish this inquiry, I decided that I would like to expand my own reflections with some narratives from other teachers. Although my aim was indeed to find further evidence to support my own findings, I was in fact just genuinely curious to know what other teachers thought about my findings. I posted a call for contributions to various online groups, mainly on Facebook, which acted as discussion forums for teachers. In addition to this, I also contacted a number of colleagues who are teaching MA courses in applied linguistics, whose students I hoped might be interested in contributing a short reflection on the relationship between teacher and student motivation.

Although I am very pleased with the nine contributions I received in this way, I must admit it was not as easy as I had first thought to persuade teachers to submit their vignettes. In retrospect, this is a limitation to this data, as I have found dialogical discussions with fellow practitioners often reveal that many teachers have strongly developed theories about the synergistic links which I have described in this book. Not all the vignettes support the observations I have put forward (for example, Caroline's in vignette 9 shows that certain students who feel they only have 'one shot' may motivate themselves quite independently and not rely on the teacher). However, all the vignettes have something to offer in terms of a deeper understanding of the ideas I have presented so far in this inquiry.

The vignettes are presented in no particular order, and each one is followed by a short analytical summary from me, in an attempt to highlight the features which I found most salient to the themes in the book. Any misrepresentations or errors in analysis are entirely my own fault, although I have taken pains to further consult with each contributor and share my analysis with them before publication.

The first vignette takes us to Moscow, Russia, where Sergey Alferov teaches business English to corporate classes.

7.2 Vignette 1: (not such) a gloomy December morning in Moscow

By Sergey Alferov, Moscow, Russia

Having started learning English at primary school in Moscow in 1990, on the brink of the Soviet Union collapse, I now teach in the same city, but in a completely different setting. The 'iron curtain' has fallen, or so one hopes, and I am currently enjoying teaching EFL to adult learners working for huge multinationals operating in the country or vibrant Russian IT companies expanding their business globally.

My students come from all over Russia, bringing a wealth of experiences to share, creating diversity, challenging each other's and my assumptions and thus making our communication genuinely interesting. Most of them have to use English at work, so there is a clear need to develop their language skills. Given the relative methodological flexibility I am currently enjoying, this sounds like a perfect learning environment.

There is only one minor disadvantage: the students learn English at their workplace, before, in the middle of or after a hard working day. Consequently, it may be quite challenging for them to focus on the language learnt instead of their sleep deprivation, impending deadlines or recent feedback from the boss. This also means that finishing my class at 9 p.m. may not prevent me from starting the next one at 8 a.m. the following morning.

In order to get a deeper insight into the interplay between the learners' and the teacher's motivation in this context, a first-person account of what it may feel like being a teacher in my morning class is given below. Some researchers would label this description 'phenomenological', meaning that the focus is on presenting the reality as it reveals itself to me, rich in detail and inevitably 'subjective'. Some more objectifying points are 'bracketed' in order to sharpen the focus on 'phenomena' (Finlay 2009).

It is 8:30 a.m. in December. The sun has just risen magnificently over the otherwise gray city. I am sitting in a meeting room, sipping hot tea and looking at the cloudy sky outside. My students are about to come, one at a time. The variables impacting their timing include Moscow traffic, nursery school timetables, parking space availability and their overall time-management skills.

When the first student arrives, he looks somewhat sleepy. We discuss his weekend and his work. The time drags a little and I am starting to wonder why either of us actually needs to be here. As far as I remember, the student's purpose is to practice speaking and listening. These are the needs I could help satisfy. But what about some more pressing needs? I suggest getting a cup of coffee to wake up and say that I assume the student has had a wonderful evening. The comment cheers him up a little, and he looks more alert. But then he needs to write a couple of quick replies to urgent messages on his phone. I wonder why it does not annoy me. Maybe I am half-asleep myself and unable to respond adequately?

By the time the next student turns up, a topic for discussion has emerged: staff motivation programmes and how they work. This is something both students can relate to. Personally, I am curious to get an update from professionals working in a totally different sphere. It is great that the students have enough language to express most of their ideas!

In the course of the discussion the third student joins the group. Her generally unsuccessful attempt at using the second conditional along with her colleagues' inability to quickly correct the mistake gives us the language focus for today. I get a lot of support from one of the learners, who regularly asks for more form-focussed instruction and revision. While my students are completing a short controlled practice task, double-checking with the rules, I feel they are challenged in a positive way: their minds start searching for optimal solutions, trying to make sure they understand the contexts and can choose the most appropriate forms. Being around people whose mental power is fully switched on gives me the feeling of purpose and inner peace.

When starting a less controlled task, I feel my students' imagination is awakening. Sometimes they lack ideas, so I need to guide them a little. By this point I have stopped asking myself why I am here, because my focus is on facilitating the learners' imaginative use of the language. Our laughter signals when ideas get an unexpected or bizarre twist and are communicated well enough for other people to get the joke.

When one of the students is struggling with words, I can feel my muscles tense as if to help their concentration. When an utterance is grammatically correct and informative from the first attempt, I feel excited as if the sports team I support has just scored a goal. If the mistake is repeated several times, my occasional playful groaning seems to give the learners an extra push to improve their accuracy here and now. It is clear that my involvement energises the learners, whereas their success empowers us all. By the time the class is about to finish, we feel wide awake, full of energy and quite happy with each other.

What is curious about my teaching experience as represented above is the fact that collaboration in class and successful learning require from both the teacher and the students getting through multiple layers of irrelevancies, distractions and inhibitions. Some learners can join (and help create) an efficient learning environment quicker than others. Some explicitly ask for 'five minutes just to listen' before they are ready to take a more active part in the work of the group if they come late. The feeling of purpose is maintained together, but the crucial part for me lies in understanding that what we do in class caters for a wide range of my students' short- and long-term needs as language users.

Reference

Finlay, L. (2009). Debating phenomenological research methods. *Phenomenology and Practice*, 3(1), 6–25.

7.2.1 Analysis

In this vignette, Sergey Alferov shows how his attitude to class goes up and down within a single lesson. The polar extremes of 'wondering why he is there' to feeling 'awake and energised' struck a chord with me, as I mentioned in Chapter 5 about my own reflections on the Prejudice class and especially the Food class, ranging from 'really exciting' and 'went well' to 'horrid' whilst reflecting on exactly the same class. This highlights the importance of perception and the need for data-driven reflections, as teachers are likely to use their fluctuating emotions to form their appraisals (Gkonou & Mercer, 2017; Mercer & Gkonou, 2017).

Sergey frames his reflective narrative first in terms of the challenges to motivation he and his students face. Noticeably, these challenges are all situated, contextual, part of the complex fabric of each person's daily life. Even the weather and the traffic are part of this backdrop. This again has been discussed in regard to group dynamics, as discussed in Chapters 4 and 5 in the main narrative and in Section 2.6.3 (see also Dörnyei & Murphey, 2003).

What strikes me as interesting about Sergey's reflection is the way that it is clearly the classroom dynamics, the shared joy of interaction and communication, that get the class moving towards positive synergy. Also fascinating was Sergey's attention to physical indicators of synergy – he mentions tensed muscles, excitement, even groaning. These are social cues that the class share in order to display their involvement. Here social authentication is worked at unconsciously, it is a natural by-product of the class's interactions, and it takes place as Sergey tries to cater for both his students' 'short- and long-term needs as language users'.

7.3 Vignette 2: why do you do it?

By Marina Gonzalez, Buenos Aires, Argentina

> When I close my eyes and try to think of the primary school where I teach, a recurrent phrase from some colleagues and a couple of images come to my mind. The phrase is: why do you teach at a state run school with all the training that you have? You should be in charge, not in the classroom! And then, the images bring me the answer that I know and that are more than enough for me, but which others may not see. I see the group hug from 5th form when I walk into the playground, smiles, kisses and shoves to be closer; the enthusiasm with which they sing and dance our songs; I see them singing the karaoke version of their favourite song in their government provided computers. I also think about my feelings before starting the school year last year because I knew I would be teaching F., a repeating student who

was overage and had a terrible attitude towards my subject and learning in general. I remember my happiness and surprise when he produced a word in English and clapping at his achievement as soon as I managed to contain the tears welling in my eyes. And most of all, I remember that at the end of his graduation ceremony, I went to congratulate his mother and we both started shouting our happiness about his having managed to finish primary school. And his big, round surprised look at those two crazy women…(which I hope was an insight about how people care about him).

Last week I was working at university. I saw one of the teachers who works in my team and he welcomed me with food, as he always does, out of love and without thinking of my increasing weight. I greeted two faculty colleagues, who are in charge of certain majors at our university. They both told me that in their new study plans they wanted English to be part of the subjects, not an external requirement. I was delighted because I knew that the students who had learnt with us were the ones to suggest this change in the study plan. And later on, working in the office, a former student walked in to say hello. I saw her wearing a rosary and felt something was wrong. She gave me a big hug and told me her mother had died a few days before and that she was very sad, but she knew she would get better. I must confess I couldn't recall her name quickly, but as we were talking I remembered everything she had shared with me in informal talks after class about her recent moving in with her boyfriend, how well they cooked, her work history, her relation with her mom. She means a lot to me, although I feel guilty about not recalling her name on the spot. But I work with around three hundred students per year…

7.3.1 Analysis

In this vignette, Marina Gonzalez shares a reflection that beautifully captures the busyness of her life, the way it is full with people who are either currently her students or have been and are now grown up. She shares with us the way people see her in her profession and often question her choice to remain a teacher and not to 'be in charge'. Her vignette captures the colour and texture of the busy emotional and social aspects of her teaching. Teaching is clearly more than just arriving for class, prepared and ready to teach. The teaching does not stop when the lesson is over, and it's an emotional burden as much as anything else, but a burden that also brings with it the greatest rewards (Gkonou & Miller, 2017). She clearly takes some form of responsibility for positive changes happening at university level, hinting that this is indirectly a result of her teaching.

For me, one of the most interesting parts comes at the end, when we see Marina talking to a person whose name she cannot recall during the time of writing. Clearly here there is a strong personal connection, but at the same time it is a professional relationship. Marina has heard this person's personal stories and consoled her during tragedies, and yet she feels guilty that she cannot recall the speaker's name. In the vignette, Marina did not mention any other names (apart from F.), so in mentioning it here she clearly wants to draw attention to a conflict. She could tell the story and omit the fact that she does not recall the ex-student's name, but she tells us in order to highlight the professionally imposed emotional pressures of her work. Shi (2002) presents a narrative in her work that highlights the importance of remembering names (also mentioned at the start of my narrative in Chapter 4). And yet, teaching around 300 students a year, Marina cannot be expected to remember all the names of her students, especially ex-students, who must number in the thousands. Conversely, it is likely that these 300 students all know Marina's name and remember details about her that she has shared during class, personal details that make them feel comfortable and ready to open up to her (Henry & Thorsen, 2018). If 300 people remember one thing, that is very different from one person remembering 300 things, not only cognitively but also emotionally. Whilst this can be a boon for us teachers in those moments when the emotional payback comes from sharing in happiness and success, or taking credit for making the world a better place, there is also a daily stipend of emotional energy that we have to pay in order to achieve these returns later on. It's an emotional gamble, and we do not always get the returns on our investments.

7.4 Vignette 3: the Film Club

By Elizabeth Bekes, Cuenca, Ecuador

> I ran a Film Club in the last semester for teacher trainees at Ecuador's only teacher training university (Chuquipata, near Azogues). For the first season, I chose inspirational films about teachers. The first one was *Pay It Forward*, the second *Freedom Writers*, and the third was the documentary on the Recycled Orchestra of Cateura titled *Landfill Harmonic*. I love all three, and I suppose that my enthusiasm might have been contagious. A group of more than 30 students gathered on each occasion, and worked with the native and non-native speaker facilitators coming from the city centre of Cuenca for these Saturday screenings.
>
> Beyond providing historical information (for example, on the Holocaust or the Freedom Riders) and scaffolding the content in other ways, too, I made a serious attempt to connect to reality what we saw on the screen.
>
> In the first instance, I encouraged teacher trainees to write up an experience when they had performed a random act of kindness. There was one that stood out: Diana's story…Her young daughter was in hospital and she shared a room with another sick baby, whose parents had not eaten for 24 hours while they were watching their child. Diana went home and cooked for them, fearing that they might refuse out of pride. But they were grateful and ate everything. They parted ways, but weeks later Diana heard that the couple's baby girl had died.
>
> With Freedom Writers, I asked my students if they had a message for Erin Gruwell and her Freedom Writers. One of the students then insisted

on sending a very personal message to Erin (which we posted on the guest Facebook page of the Freedom Writers Foundation).

As for the Recycled Orchestra, which was founded by Favio Chávez and consists of the kids of Asunción's landfill area using instruments that have been made from garbage, when we learnt that they are now building a new music school in Cateura, we did a bit of fundraising after the screening, telling the teacher trainees that the facilitators would treble the amount raised. The students, who often do not have 12 cents for the bus, donated about USD 20.00. One student, who didn't have any cash on him, gave us four brand-new coloured whiteboard markers. That we didn't treble, but the USD 60.00 has been sent off...

We have now set up a Facebook page for the Film Club, are in contact with the author of *Pay It Forward* (Catherine Ryan Hyde) and her PIF Foundation. I bought the young reader's version of the book for later use. We have also contacted the Freedom Writers Foundation and watched Favio Chávez' moving TED talk in Amsterdam.

We are now ready for the next season: *The Mission, 1492, What's Eating Gilbert Grape, Dirty Dancing* and *Slumdog Millionaire*. I will need to think about how to engage and enthuse the student audience, but judging by what has happened so far, I'm sure I'll find a way.

7.4.1 Analysis

In this vignette, Elizabeth Bekes shares her project and her passion. Under the classic definition of authenticity, the use of films in the class would be seen as utilising authentic materials, but what is most authentic in this vignette is not so much the materials used as the sentiments behind them. Elizabeth implies some knowledge of the limits of classically 'authentic' materials when she states that she made a 'serious attempt to connect to reality', which seems a kind of acknowledgement that merely watching a film is not in itself a guarantee of authenticity. Her students raising money for charity echoes the work done by my own DCT class, which I have repeatedly mentioned in this inquiry as the starting point for my puzzling process. Clearly, Elizabeth has invested a great deal of herself into the film club, and the payback from her students seems evidence that this was a worthwhile investment.

Another similarity which I noticed was when Elizabeth mentioned being in touch with Catherine Ryan Hyde, which reminded me of how I made contact with Reggie Bibbs from the Prejudice lesson with CLERAC in the autumn semester. Here again, the connection between classroom and outside world is important in creating authenticity in the classroom, and makes the language subject come alive through social interaction, as well as being an empowering use of language which makes links between our learners and influential people who have made an impact on their lives.

The story about Diana's random act of kindness is clearly very emotional, and although the vignette captures and retells the story wonderfully, we also see only a small hint of what must have been a much bigger event with many students sharing similar stories and reflecting on their own lives as they brought this into class. This focus on doing things for others and making connections of course foregrounds the issue of empathy, which I mentioned as one of the indicators of synergy.

7.5 Vignette 4: on motivation (and coaching)

By Timothy Wong, Monash University, Malaysia

The journey to motivating students begins with the teacher's own intrinsic motivation. My journey began when I left the corporate world to become a language teacher at 33. Within weeks of the new vocation I knew I was like a fish in water in the teaching profession. Everything about it sparked interest. The process was organic yet fluid. I was eager and took risks in teaching innovatively. My students lapped it up, and then they saw improvements in their own learning. It was a win-win situation. As a teacher I modelled the best I can what a life buoyed by motivation looked like.

However, as the months went by, I saw that motivation alone did not sustain the student's endeavours. I realised that teaching must go with coaching, and coaching in small scaffolded measures. Along with that I surmised that I needed to diagnose the student's weaknesses accurately in order for the coaching to be meaningful. For that to happen I needed to connect with my students and measure my students' performance objectively. One student, for example, complained that he had a speech impediment, but after diagnosis, it was found that he had a lack of confidence as his problem was triggered by his rather aggressive girlfriend who spoke well. So, more than pure diagnosis on language matters, I ventured into coaching self-esteem, social skills, leadership, and teamwork, while promoting intrinsic motivation.

As the years went by, I further learned the importance of having relatable learning checkpoints for my students. In order for students to assess themselves well on their learning, it was important to provide rubrics that helped to map out their progress. With a helpful rubric, any student can see where they are and motivate themselves to the next category of the rubrics. The rubrics too need to come with helpful examples in order for students to feel that they are capable of reaching the next point of their learning journey. The correct use of rubrics can also introduce the students to concepts of critical thinking, and allow them a language to communicate in and discuss their learning expectations. Inadvertently this would lead to the student finding their voice, an integral part of intrinsic motivation.

Nevertheless, through it all, I am aware that my own vulnerability in opening up to the student's needs opened a pathway to engage in motivational work. Without some form of self-awareness in my own learning journey, I would not be able to fuel the motivation in my students' lives. In the words of Judy Sorum Brown (2000, in her poem 'Fire'),

When we are able to build
open spaces
in the same way
we have learned
to pile on the logs,
then we can come to see how
it is fuel, and absence of the fuel
together, that make fire possible.

7.5.1 *Analysis*

Timothy Wong's vignette shows how being a teacher is about being more than just a teacher. He shows how his own development as a teacher has been part of a wider personal development, and that his focus on motivation led him to find ways to encourage more autonomous and metacognitive strategies in his work with learners, something which is advocated in motivational research that is intended to influence best practice (Ushioda, 2014, 2016).

The rubrics that Timothy uses now to help his students, take up the main thrust of the vignette, and here we see that aside from being a form of scaffolding in terms of goal setting, they are also a form of feedback for students as well, making them extremely powerful tools. This is something I touched upon in this inquiry when I mentioned the importance of working with students' ZPD (Section 5.6 of the autumn narrative), and also when I mentioned feedback as a synaptic crossing which facilitates positive motivational synergy. Here, feedback is envisaged as being primarily positive and constructive, but feedback is not always as straightforward as this, as the next vignette illustrates.

7.6 Vignette 5: teacher frustration motivates students to do better

By Sal Consoli, Warwick, UK

> This is a short report on an episode of classroom life during a pre-sessional course in a UK university. A pre-sessional is usually a short intensive programme which international students are required to complete in order to meet the language entry requirements of their programme of study at a University. The course equips students with the basic language, study and research skills to perform well within an English-speaking academic environment. On this specific summer pre-sessional I was the tutor responsible for Reading and Writing, and one of my key goals was guiding the students through the processe(s) of producing an essay which complies with a series of academic writing conventions (e.g. referencing, forming well-structured arguments). During my time with these students I also felt the responsibility to help them become critical thinkers as well as writers. Below I report on a 'critical episode' which occurred mid-course. This was critical in that it

disrupted, or perhaps shaped, the flow of the lesson and noticeably impacted on the students' learning experience. What will appear surprising, as it was for me on the day, is the unexpected synergy between my behaviour and the students' reaction. At this stage, I ought to point out that one of the key tenets of my own teaching philosophy is ensuring everyone has a 'good time' in class (both teacher and students) in such a way that my teaching may support or enhance (at times generate) learning motivation.

On that day (Thursday – mid-course), I decided to take a break from the teaching of new skills. Instead, I took stock of all the major (often basic) language mistakes that I had seen in the students' formative writing and prepared a few pair and group tasks to address these language problems. The key focus was on the usage of the present tense, the past simple and present perfect.

During the second part of this session we checked some homework and focused on the type of academic language used in the introduction of an essay. It was during this second section of the lesson that the **critical episode** occurred, and this related to the students' reluctance to answer whole-class open questions even when they had the right answers. I was audio-recording this lesson for the purposes of some research I was conducting at the time, and therefore below I report on my post-class reflections as well as specific interactions as they happened in the classroom.

I called this the 'I don't care episode' – it all started when I asked an open question to the class, and after 29 seconds of silence, which I think feels like ages for a teacher who's hoping to get a response, I intervened. Looking at Jessica who seemed to have an answer ready, I said to her: '*you answered this, right?*' and she said: '*yeah but I'm not sure*', and at that point with a smile on my face but certainly disapproval tone in my voice, I said: '*it doesn't matter!*' And continued saying:

'*I don't care if you're not sure, I don't care if it's wrong, I don't care, I don't care, I don't care, I don't care (4 seconds pause) I don't care!!!* (Students laugh). *What I DO care about is that you TRY – all of you! It doesn't matter if it's wrong. I'm happy if it's wrong because if it's wrong I can teach you – that's my job!! But if you don't talk it's a disaster!*

At this point I said: '*right, I'm going to leave the room and come back in and pretend this never happened*'. (Students laugh).

When I came back in I said, '*good morning everyone*' and went straight into the last activity we were looking at and asked an open question – I looked at Jessica, expecting her to give me an answer and with a smile on my face, but certainly a lot of expectation. She volunteered her answer, and this was a good answer; therefore, when she finished I stopped for a few seconds and said, '*that was brilliant! See? You were not even sure and that was good. Obviously there could be other alternative answers...* 'and I looked at the rest of the class and Marta volunteered some answers. Then I looked at Jessica again and said: '*but that was good so even when you're not sure it might be right so you might just as well share your thoughts with the teacher and if you're wrong that's fine, it means that there is learning that needs to happen and if you're right you are going to impress the teacher so in either case it's a win-win situation. Okay? Does that make sense for all of you?* (YES) *so I don't have to go out of the door next time I ask you a question?* (hmm smiling and laughing) *right...*'

This episode showed the level of frustration I had reached after three weeks in relation to the students' reluctance to volunteer answers to open questions or interact openly with me during class discussions. This is, in my view, one of the key skills international students need to develop in order to integrate fully and successfully within a UK university setting. I had already taken various opportunities during other lessons to explain the value of such dialogic behaviour within a small class (i.e. seminar-like) context at university, and I believe that by the time when the above episode occurred, I had reached an unbearable level of 'frustration' in this respect. However, what I found surprising was that despite my worry about 'denting' my students' motivation, with my frustrated reaction, they actually responded with plenty of laughter and approval. I realised, on reflection, that this was probably due to the friendly relationship already established with them. However, I cannot deny that I was seriously concerned, after my slightly impulsive reaction, that I may have crushed some of their motivation to study in the UK. To my surprise, when at the end of that class I asked them whether I had destroyed their motivation to learn in a UK university, Marta said: *'actually, I feel more motivated'*.

7.6.1 Analysis

In this vignette, Sal Consoli shows that as teachers who care about our students and, in particular, want them to enjoy the lesson, we have to make difficult professional choices at times when the students are not doing what we want them to do. Often, what we want them to do is to perform better, work harder, invest more, and basically we want this because we know it will produce the best results in them. This was clearly what made this incident critical to Sal, who stressed that he did what he could to ensure that both teachers and students have 'a "good time" in class', which intentionally echoes the 'quality of classroom life', which I discussed as an essential aspect of Exploratory Practice (Gieve & Miller, 2006). This sample actually comes from a larger study by Sal which utilises Exploratory Practice and Narrative Inquiry (Consoli, in preparation)

What stands out to me about this episode is, first of all, Sal's fear of damaging the hard-earned rapport with his students by expressing his genuine frustrations at their reluctance to speak in class. As Sal makes clear, this frustration is not born of his own desire to be liked by the students, but much more fundamentally by his having their best interests at heart. He knows what is required of them in the university situation for which they are preparing, he knows what challenges lie ahead of them, and he feels that his class must reflect those same realities. This shows that he is using his knowledge of the language use domain to invoke a type of assessment authenticity in his class, intended to prepare his students for the next stage in their studies for which his class is designed.

The outcome of his expressing an 'unbearable level of "frustration"', interestingly, is not to demotivate the students, but in fact the opposite. Notice also that Sal did not simply lose his temper, but actually this was a calculated and controlled expression of emotion, albeit one he would rather not have had to do. My own reflection on this is that perhaps, in seeing Sal 'get serious' or use his authority to push the students, he communicates to them his care and investment in their future. This is somewhat ironic, as he labelled this the 'I don't care episode', but in fact clearly he *did* care about the students, and I think his show of emotion seems to have communicated this concern effectively. As teachers, it is often easier to just pass a student than to fail them. If we fail them, we need to have them resubmit. We may need to work with them more to help them get their work up to the standard required to pass. Just assigning a low grade means that the student can pass but may not receive the extra help they truly need. Likewise, it is easier to be nice to students than to vent our frustrations and ask them to work harder. As I have mentioned earlier, the language classroom is intrinsically a face-threatening situation (van Dam, 2002), and yet in demonstrating his frustration Sal showed that he really did care about the students, that his class was really a serious environment where he had professional expectations developed around the aims of the course and with the students' best interests at heart.

7.7 Vignette 6: Thursday afternoons

By Erkan Külekçi, Kastamonu, Turkey

> After all the years I have spent on language teaching and teacher education, I consider myself an English language teacher who is well aware of the importance of making lessons engaging and students motivated. However, I should admit that I sometimes overlook this awareness in the hustle and bustle of daily life. At this point, I do not separate daily life from professional life because I think the fine line between my personal life and professional life often gets blurry under long hours of teaching, supervision, administrative work and my attempts to conduct research. I teach an English for general purposes course to first-year undergraduate students in the Faculty of Education at a state university in Turkey, and I would like to tell you about a particular classroom where I followed a different, but already known, path to make the lessons more 'bearable' and engaging.
>
> I used the word 'bearable' as I had this class on Thursday afternoons after 22 hours of teaching in a week. In addition to my own physical tiredness, I often got a couple of students yawning and making scribbles on their textbooks during the lessons. At the beginning of the semester, I did try to ignore those students and continue my lesson since their behaviour could affect my mood in a negative way and ignoring them would seem a kind of coping strategy to help myself feel energetic and motivated enough for

the lesson. However, after two or three lessons, I decided to talk with the students frankly and explain the situation to them because I felt that I really did not want to enter the classroom and do any lessons. I told them that I was aware of the fact that most of us were tired in this class, but to some extent our 'expression of tiredness' could affect each other's motivation and energy to continue the lesson. Indeed, I mentioned that this could turn into a vicious circle where we might keep playing our roles of 'teachering' and 'studenting' without being truly involved in the lesson. That is, while whining and yawning, we could complete the activities on the pages and finish the lesson hours just for the sake of doing a lesson. At this point, some of the students blamed the textbook and my tendency to follow the text-book activities step by step without any signs of flexibility. I did not inter-rupt them or defend myself, but merely listened to them. Then some of the students talked about their course load during the week and the amount of assignments they had to do. Some of them mentioned that they had studied English for around eight years and that apparently they were not capable of understanding English lessons. At the end, one of the students asked me, 'What about you? Why do you look tired in this lesson?' I had several answers in my mind; however, I only said 'mainly because of my work load' and told them about the courses I was teaching during the week and the number of exam papers I needed to grade. It was interesting to see that we were kind of having empathy for each other. In fact, I realised that I had never asked how their week was going before starting my lessons (I often asked, 'How are you today?' and wanted them to open their textbooks before the lessons as soon as I heard 'Fine'). In that lesson, I also encouraged them to share their ideas about what kind of activities they wanted to do in the lessons and how we could make the lessons more engaging. Their ideas reminded me of one of the personal principles I tried to follow in the days of my early career: being flexible within pre-set and clear goals of each lesson.

After that talk with the students (by the way, it was in their first language – Turkish), I paid more attention to starting my lessons by asking how their week was going and listening to their answers even if it took around ten minutes each week, and to using different resources (mostly online ones on the smart board, because they could be very fun and time saving) in order to keep the students engaged. In the following weeks, there was no yawning in this class, and I could see that the students could bear the Thursday after-noon lesson hours and got more involved in the lessons.

7.7.1 Analysis

In this vignette, Erkan Külekçi shares with us a truly eye-opening moment from his classroom which I hope many of us can recognise from our own practice. Namely, once we actually talk to the students about their lives, the factors influen-cing their behaviour in the classroom that come from outside, then we see them as people. Erkan moved beyond 'how are you?' and 'Fine' to actually genuinely ask the students how they felt and what was up. They responded the same, and this created an empathic connection between the two. Mercer (2016) has discussed the importance of empathy for language teaching and SLA, due to the centrality of relationships, our role as relational beings and the importance of interconnectedness, all of which are particularly salient in the work we do as language educators due to the role language plays in society. I also posited that empathy is an indicator of synergy and discussed its importance throughout this study.

What is most striking about this vignette is the way Erkan is clearly not merely busy but actually at the point where his lessons are causing him to be physically tired, and lessons towards the end of the week need to be 'bearable' for him and students. In other words, he is trying to survive in the face of a very demanding workload, and thus his expectations of himself and of his students are inevitably affected. He shows the disconnect between what he knows from his teacher education courses and what he is physically able to achieve in the class. What he also shows is his great resilience and resourcefulness. Like the teachers in Hiver's work (2015b, 2017), Erkan shows how he has developed his *teacher immunity* in order to survive and to continue working as a teacher. Hiver (2015b) states that 'teacher immunity acts as a line of defence to the demands placed on teachers, and the often traumatic experiences they encounter that result in emotional exhaustion and burnout' (p. 226), and clearly in Erkan's vignette we see that one strategy for developing this immunity and for strengthening his own resolve is to talk to the students as people (Ushioda, 2009), whilst presenting himself as a teacher as a person (Glatthorn, 1975). These two humanising aspects of the language learning classroom are something I discussed as one of the essential aspects of constructing a culture of authenticity and forging valuable bonds between learners and teachers (Pinner, 2016b). Talking directly to students when we are confused about their behaviour is also something I have personal experience of (Pinner, 2016c), and, like Erkan, I found that discussing the problems face-to-face led to a harmonising of understanding. In this way, empathy is one of the composite materials for constructing the bridge of authenticity between learners and teachers.

7.8　Vignette 7: passion is contagious

By Bushra Ahmed Khurram, Karachi, Pakistan

> When I try to recall when I decided to become a teacher, I realize that perhaps I made this decision when I was in kindergarten. I remember that my favourite pastime as a five-year-old was imagining that I was my English teacher. Throughout my childhood nothing gave me more pleasure than to teach to an imaginary class of students situated in my bedroom. Over the years, the more I taught different imaginary groups of learners, the more closely I observed my teachers and imitated the English Language lessons they taught us. During my postgraduate studies I also started attending international ELT conferences held in Pakistan. This presented me with opportunities to learn the best practices for teaching English right from the ELT

experts around the globe. Some of them went on to become my friends, which further nurtured my passion to become an ELT teacher.

On completion of my Master's degree, I was offered a teaching position at a state-run university. I was also informed that students of this particular university generally lacked enthusiasm and commitment towards the English lessons held at the university. This was manifested in their classroom behaviours such as a lack of attention and a low level of participation in the lessons, [and] irregular and low attendance rates. This attitude of students towards their English lessons prompted me to engage in some motivation-enhancing practices to positively influence the students' interest in the lessons. For this purpose, I took several measures to stimulate and engage the students in my lessons. One of the steps that I took was that students were informed that I was available and keen to scaffold them by providing help in understanding the tasks, both in and outside the class. Moreover, students were specifically told that I would be available for one-to-one discussions 15 to 20 minutes prior to the class (some teachers in my context neither reach the class on time nor are available for discussions outside the lessons). I hoped that the act of reaching the classroom before time and making myself accessible would communicate to the students that I am enthusiastic about English language teaching and take it seriously. I hoped that this would increase the students' interest in the lessons as the literature indicates that 'student attitudes and orientations towards learning are, to a large extent, modelled after their teachers both in terms of effort expenditure and orientations of interest in the subject' (Dörnyei, 1994, p. 278). In this regard, Dörnyei (2001, p. 34) also states that 'if you show commitment towards the students' learning and progress, there is a very good chance that they will do the same thing'. During the lessons I noticed an increase in the students' engagement in the lessons, which was evident from the fact that they started coming to the class regularly and early. Moreover, students often got engaged in useful discussion before the start of the lessons. Most of the students also started actively participating in classroom activities. This experience taught me that motivation and passion for a subject are indeed contagious!

References

Dörnyei, Z. (2001). *Motivation strategies in the language classroom.* Stuttgart: Ernst Klett Sprachen.

Dörnyei, Z. (1994). Motivation and motivating in the foreign language classroom. *The Modern Language Journal*, 78(3), 273–284.

7.8.1 Analysis

Bushra's narrative not only finds support for her observations in the research literature, but it also provides a very strong personal narrative about how one teacher's strong vision can fill classroom after classroom with positive learning experiences, despite the potential 'Golem' effect of her colleague's warning about students' lack of enthusiasm. Although I have only met Bushra a handful of times, we have known each other now for several years, and one thing which has always struck me about her (and inspired me to elicit a vignette from her) is her resilience, energy and attractive self-confidence. I have no problem believing that Bushra walks into classrooms year after year and converts a primarily divergent classroom culture into a primarily convergent one in a short space of time with her natural charisma.

Bushra takes charge of a potentially difficult situation by identifying its likely cause right at the start. She realises that this lack of investment from students could be due to a lack of reciprocal investment from the teachers, and she takes pains to show that she is available for her students, that she will make time for them, that she *cares* for them and has empathy, trust and support (she specifically mentions scaffolding, and this is something I happen to know Bushra has a deep knowledge of). Bushra clearly shows that she has decided to make motivation a conscious focus for herself and her students, and right at the start she utilises the introduction of metacognitive strategies in order to facilitate a convergent classroom culture and positive motivational synergy.

7.9 Vignette 8: digital storytelling

By Dima Yousef, Dubai, UAE

After attending a conference on exploring new ways of storytelling in the world of media and digital technology and reading more on how this could actively engage students, I decided to introduce digital storytelling to my students as their final project. As a lead-in activity, the students watched Chimamanda Ngozi Adichie's TED talk on the dangers of single stories as they can create stereotypes and take away the dignity of people. She also talks about how personal narratives empower individuals as they share their stories and experiences. I asked students to reflect on these powerful statements and think of a story they would like to share with the world and how this would change how others think of them. Stemming from my belief that perfect lessons and activities are not sufficient to engage students, I wanted the students to relate and connect to the concept of storytelling before we began the project.

After the introductions, I announced the task: as a group, they would create a two- to three-minute video story that included still images, video, voice-over narrative and music and/or other sound effects. I shared with them the elements of digital storytelling and focused on the 'gift of voice'. I also provided them with a few questions to consider while brainstorming ideas for their video. For example, what is your connection to this topic? Is it motivating to an audience? Can you tell this story in just a few minutes? What makes your story unique? What do you hope your audience will do, think or feel after watching your video?

Their engagement was a direct reflection of my attitude toward the whole project. I was so excited about the whole concept of digital storytelling, and the students could detect that. Students were engaged throughout the planning, designing and presenting of their stories. The students' excitement and positive attitude towards the project successfully increased [their] engagement. I was not worried about work completion, participation, distractions or even absences. Students' motivation throughout the stages of completing their videos infused me with energy, confidence to explore new project ideas and patience while the students are learning new techniques and tools to produce creative videos.

Another component of the project was to write a short reflective essay responding to the following:

- Explain the activity. What was your topic and purpose? How did you come up with your ideas for your project?
- Identify the challenges and difficulties while working on this group project.
- What did you learn about yourself as you worked on this project?

Student engagement was easily assessed and identified in the responses. Although the task was unexpectedly challenging, they felt empowered because they were given a choice, a voice and a space to share their ideas. They were pushed out of their comfort zone. Reflecting on the project, I realize how important it is for a teacher to be motivated and engaged throughout the learning process. Preparing and planning a lesson or an activity is one element contributing to its success. As teachers, we should focus on cognitive and emotional engagement: involve students in the process, challenge students and ourselves. Indeed, this deeper form of engagement will provide our students and us with better learning experiences.

7.9.1 *Analysis*

In Dima's vignette, she shows how her decision to try something new and innovative in the classroom led to great results and a high point in her teaching. Although the project is very much facilitated and introduced by Dima, it is her students who make the project successful. This, according to Dima, comes from various factors, such as her enabling them to 'relate and connect' to the concepts and get involved in the content. From the outset, Dima makes it clear that this was not a project with specific linguistic focus or language aims, but a chance for her learners to share 'personal narratives', to empower her learners as authentic speakers of the target language 'as they share their stories and experiences'. In this way, the project was mainly for the students, about the students, and this is likely to be a large contributor to its success. These are likely to have greatly contributed to the fact that it was a project which seems to have facilitated much congruent positive motivational synergy. Clearly, though, the project is not apolitical or neutral. It is not a flavourless project where the students are expected to do whatever they want. Dima hints at how she imparts some of her own values, ideas and beliefs to the students (for example, framing the task with Chimamanda Ngozi Adichie's TED talk, which communicates a strong message about certain prejudicial judgements and the cultural capital of stories), which is probably why the task was challenging. However, this is also very likely to be why Dima also invested so much of herself into the task, to which the students responded and their enthusiasm was a 'direct reflection' of her own. In this way also, the digital storytelling task seems to incorporate many aspects from Mishan's (2005) 3Cs of authenticity (culture, currency and challenge).

Finally, Dima's awareness of her students' engagement hints at her own implicit knowledge of indicators. She utilises a reflective essay (showing also her ability to incorporate metacognitive tasks), which she clearly uses to assess their engagement through these assignments. Other indicators she seems to utilise are on-task engagement and, of course, the final product of their work.

7.10 Vignette 9: FeLT NYC

By Caroline McKinnon, New York, USA

> Throughout my career I have taught students from every economic and social background. This has given me a lot of food for thought when it comes to motivation and student-teacher interaction. The general consensus is that teacher and student motivation are co-dependent and equal.
>
> A highly motivated student can transcend stressful and negative situations, including an unmotivated teacher. However, it does add a burden to the student's learning experience. An unmotivated teacher is less likely to personalize material, spend time to plan effectively or with meaningful purpose, or find out the reasons for learning. In my experience, it is essential that a teacher understand what brought a student to the class. For example, a student funded by parents who believe English will add to their economic value has a completely different motivation from a refugee learning English to survive in a new country.
>
> For years, I taught in private schools and colleges and became accustomed, rightly or wrongly, to attributing motivation to the nationality or financial independence of the student. I would say things such as 'This student is paying for their own education, so they want it more.' I now accept that this is an oversimplistic and often erroneous viewpoint, that finances and motivation are intertwined the way I had assumed.
>
> A few years ago I launched a non-profit organization called FeLT NYC. The education we provide to immigrant and refugee women is free. Also, there is no formal testing, and goals are personalized and not scaled to a level. Our students are often illiterate and/or have very little education from their

home countries, where education is expensive and for the privileged. They may come from war-torn countries, have experienced political oppression and severe economic disadvantages, and have found themselves resettled in a country that isn't necessarily 'friendly' to them or their culture. What is their motivation?

I have found that in many ways immigrants or refugees are less susceptible to codependent motivation. This is because they tend to feel that they have one shot at learning and must do everything to show appreciation. I am not saying that teacher motivation isn't important, just not always symbiotic.

On the other hand, a teacher who has experienced, first-hand, immigration or refugee status (either in person or in their close circle) often brings a level of motivation to make sure that their students have an easier path. My students are vulnerable. They are looking for reassurance when learning. It is essential that the teacher maintain a positive attitude and a strong desire to ease their learning path. This means motivating them when outside forces seem to be stacking up against them. I have found that a student struggling with adequate housing or immigration worries performs better if the teacher motivates them through addressing the issue as a teaching moment. I know my own students are motivated by my own journey as an immigrant. I may have the advantage of language over them, but we can bond over shared wonder or issues faced by all newcomers to the country. I am motivated to teach them practical and meaningful language, not just predetermined language from a 'one size fits all' textbook. I know that this method creates a level of trust and understanding.

I believe that teacher-training courses tend to steer away from including motivation. I believe that it is integral to arm a teacher with a) the skills to keep them motivated and b) the methods to incorporate motivation into the classroom.

7.10.1 Analysis

In this vignette, Caroline McKinnon throws a dose of much-needed water on my idea of motivational synergy, by reminding us that sometimes motivation can be one-directional. There are students and teachers who have such a passion for what they are doing that they can keep going by the force of their own will. As Caroline's reflection makes clear, however, this may well be due to extenuating circumstances. In terms of having a more sustainable experience, Caroline's narrative still strongly supports the idea of motivational synergy because she shows how people helping one another creates a strong bond and thus a personal investment with the language. The struggles that Caroline faces in working with immigrants in the United States, especially in light of growing right-wing sentiment and the polarisation of the US media (Levendusky, 2013), shows also the importance of her own teacher immunity (Hiver, 2015b, 2017), which (as I know from being personal friends with Caroline) is a strength of commitment that is fuelled by her strong ethical and philosophical principles, and which are so clearly made manifest in her work as the founder of FeLT NYC (https://www. feltnyc.org). It is no coincidence that on the FeLT NYC website it states, 'We are firm believers of love's ability to trump hate', and although Caroline does not use the word 'love' in her vignette, it is clearly love that drives her to charitably dedicate her time and energy to such an important cause at great personal expense. Whilst some may argue that 'love' is an inappropriate emotion between teachers and students, or that strong emotions have no place in a professional relationship, Barcelos and Coelho (2016) present an excellent justification for love. They argue that love is essential in creating a passion for teaching, that it serves as a motivational fuel and source of energy for being attentive to others, and that love can create a 'positivity resonance' in the classroom. They even state that love is essential in facilitating spiritual and mental growth with our students, although I know Caroline would say that she receives just as much spiritual growth facilitation from her students. Caroline also demonstrates the importance of empathy as a synaptic crossing, by positioning herself as an immigrant female, which she states is vital in being able to 'bond over shared wonder or issues'.

Astonishingly, Caroline's work with immigrant women and her passion for this great cause has actually led to her receiving various types of personal abuse from less-enlightened individuals who are threatened by her open-mindedness and seem unable to contemplate her motivations for trying to help people to integrate into a new culture and society. This again shows the need for a strong teacher immunity, but also once again demonstrates that the teacher and the person are one and the same, and that our personal identities as teachers are often very much an extension of our personal identities, and as such our own beliefs and philosophy of practice are essential for us to find authenticity as we strive for a sense of congruence between our actions and our beliefs (see Bullough, 2009; Bullough & Pinnegar, 2009; Dörnyei et al., 2016; Vannini & Burgess, 2009 for more on the importance of congruence in motivating teachers and maintaining authenticity).

Clearly, Caroline believes that motivation extends beyond the reaches of a single class and goes further than one activity. Her teaching is about empowering her learners so that they can live a better life and survive their difficult situation with dignity. It is for this reason that I fully agree with Caroline that more teachers should learn about motivation and find strategies to maintain both their own motivation to teach and their learners' motivation to learn, and I would argue that finding the link between these two is one of the most enriching aspects of working as a language teacher.

7.11 Summary

This section has presented nine vignettes from a diverse sample of teachers working in different contexts, with different learners and different needs. Although each vignette presents a very different view of motivational synergy and the relationship between teacher and student motivation, each one provides us with further rich insights into the working principles of passionate teachers and what motivates their practice. We have seen both the struggles and the rewards of their work here, and all that remains is for me to thank each and every one of these contributors for sharing their stories and to hope that these stories further resonate with readers to continue their own quest for authenticity in the language classroom and to continue to work at building bridges between us and our learners.

8 Conclusions

> When you look closely at anything familiar, it transmogrifies into something unfamiliar.
>
> Alexandra Horowitz (2014)

Ultimately, this study is primarily written for people who are interested in the development of teachers' professional identities and who benefit from hearing stories from practitioners' classrooms, whether they are interested in motivation, authenticity or teacher research more generally. The reasons for wishing to hear such stories are deeply personal, but of course we can imagine that in reading a narrative of development, the reader may question his or her own experiences. As Riessman (2008) has noted, 'individuals and groups construct identities through storytelling' (p. 8), although the way narratives work for individuals or groups is different. A large part of the purpose of this inquiry is to construct my own identity, and it is hoped that reading this narrative will also help others in personal ways. Writing up research and publishing provides academics 'with the means to demonstrate a competent persona and the right to be heard so that, in constructing their texts, writers also construct themselves as academics' (Hyland, 2015, p. x). This is my attempt at becoming a better teacher and a researcher and 'constructing myself as an academic'.

8.1 The quest for authenticity

In many ways this book is a quest for authenticity. It has led me down many paths, some of them dead ends, some rewarding. If someone were to ask me, 'what is authenticity?' I would have to reply that the simple answer is there is no simple answer. Authenticity is heavily reliant on context and individual factors, but it is also tethered to much larger social constructs as well. It is a vital aspect of language learning, and part of my aim in this inquiry has been to try and make sense of that and to explain it back in practical terms without getting lost in the stratosphere of cloudy and bewildering concepts which, like the weather, are all components in a complex dynamic system.

Applied linguistics and SLA are undergoing something of a theoretical renaissance based on insights from complexity theory (Larsen-Freeman, 1997;

Larsen-Freeman & Cameron, 2008a; Menezes, 2013; Tudor, 2003) and dynamic systems approaches (de Bot, 2008; Verspoor et al., 2011). These fields are influencing research methods and urging a move to more qualitative methods of inquiry, whereas before quantitative methods were by and large the majority of published studies (Larsen-Freeman & Cameron, 2008b; Ushioda, 2009, 2013c; Ushioda & Dörnyei, 2009). With theories and research methods shifting in this way, and from re-evaluating the landscape of language acquisition, now seems like a very good time to also look at concepts which are central to what goes on in the classroom in terms of materials, in terms of teacher-student interaction and in terms of identity in language learning. It is for this reason that I believe my quest so far has been worthwhile. By making this a personal quest with a longitudinal aspect, I hoped that I could somehow make sense of the puzzle at the heart of this inquiry, or at least report my attempt with as much depth as I can afford.

Overall, I felt that the classes went very well, and I became strongly attached to the class and certain members. I quickly learned all their names, and I got excellent feedback from the students, both directly and from the anonymous institutional mid-semester and end of course evaluations. I have no doubt that this was largely due to the immense amount of energy I invested in the class. However, I cannot deny that one reason for my investment in the CLERAC course was precisely because I knew this would be the class which would be the focus of this inquiry. In other words, by looking for authenticity, I actually created it. In some ways, this might contradict the established existential notion of authenticity cited at the start of this book, in which it was suggested that searching for authenticity leads to inauthentic behaviour (Sartre, 1992; van Lier, 1996), and of course this is something I have tried to address in my justification of this study. However, one of the findings of this inquiry is that creating a culture of authenticity in the language classroom requires a conscious effort, constantly negotiating and acclimatising to the developing identity of the individuals in the classroom.

For most classes, I felt a kind of excitement about my work and I looked forward to seeing my students' faces. I felt a great sense of duty to them, and I felt they would always be important to me as I 'immortalised' them (at least in my own personal experience as a teacher) in this inquiry. They were helping me probably more than I was helping them, so I wanted to work hard to create a good personal rapport with each student, to set reasonable amounts of coursework and to give prompt, accessible and good-quality feedback on all their work. I also knew, however, that anything they did in the class could be used as data, and so I did things which I knew would be fruitful as PEPAs. However, quite often, these tasks proved to be very valuable for the students (and little used by me in my analysis), and so I feel that this ended up balancing itself out, and as such the 'quality of classroom life' was still the main concern throughout the inquiry. However, the main difficulty with this study was that everything was recorded and everything was relevant, even though it did not always seem so at the time.

> Construed as an 'authentic practice', the scholarship of teaching emerges as an activity that is guided by certain standards of excellence, virtues and values.

Fundamental to the pursuit of certain virtues and values is critical reflect-ivity, a quintessential aspect of scholarship (Anderson, 2000). Engagement in this practice furthers the authenticity of teachers and ultimately is aimed at serving the important interest of students. The important interests of students [...] is the students' own authenticity. Both teachers and students are thus implicated in a process of transformative learning, of objective and subjective reframing, of redefinition and reconstruction, in short a process of *becoming*.

(Kreber, 2013, p. 5; emphasis in original)

Fundamentally, I think that to understand authenticity you have to understand yourself. You have to know what you believe, why you believe it, what you are interested in and have a strong hold on your philosophy of teaching. It requires a great deal of reflexivity, and at the same time, you cannot be too inward looking. Authenticity cannot come from simple navel-gazing. One must simultaneously strive for an understanding of one's own context, surrounding society and people. In the classroom context this means making a connection with each group and with the individuals who make up that group. It is no small task, especially when one factors in the complexity and difficulty of classroom teaching. Another aspect is about being reasonable and setting realistic goals about the level of authentic engagement you can achieve with the situation, context and materials. If you are not able to choose your own materials, for example, and have to use a dry old text which was selected by your country's Ministry of Education, you need to recognise that authenticity can still be a living and organically emergent part of your teaching and learning experience. Not everyone will have the time or opportunity (or even inclination) as I have to look so inwardly at my own practice whilst receiving the guidance I needed to try and connect that personal insight with others in my community of prac-tice and sphere of experience. Therefore, I wanted to present the findings I have made as engagingly as possible, and stress that this is about a process, not the individual components.

8.2 So what?

At this point, the most pressing issue that I must address is the 'so what?' question, often posited by Dick Allwright in his endeavour to highlight the prac-tical implications of his work. It may seem a harsh question, but this is often what people ask (directly or indirectly) when I explain that I am conducting Narrative Inquiry or autoethnographic research on my own self. Fundamentally, how is this generalisable, or useful to other practitioners? One simple answer to the question of generalisability is that this study is not intended to be generalis-able, at least not in the traditional sense. This study is obviously very personal, and as a result it is both situationally and contextually unique. It could not be copied or replicated. However, that is not to say that this study should not be useful to other practitioners.

As stated in Section 3.2, the purpose of this inquiry was to make sense of my own development, to gain a better understanding of why the DCT course was so successful and to see if I could recreate those conditions in another class, specifically one made up of non-English majors. I also wanted to examine to what extent any such findings could be turned into practical lessons for teacher education and techniques to empower students in their own learning, following some of the main principles from Exploratory Practice. Although these are not insignificant questions, they are of course quite personal to my own development and thus one might be forgiven in asking 'so what'?

Throughout this inquiry, I have made it clear that the main focus was on the synergistic relationship between teacher and student motivation, and how the concept of authenticity is an aspect of this dynamic process. From these elusive and complex interactions, I have been able to distil what I believe are genuinely practical insights into the nature of classroom interactions at both an individual and a group level, paying particular attention to context. What this means for other practitioners, language teacher educators and researchers is a deeper understanding of language teacher identity and a rare and hard-to-find cross section of a single language course spanning a year of twice-a-week instruction. In that sense, this study is quite important in that it allows the reader a deep and personal account of these vital processes, which I have argued are central to the authentic experience of language teaching and learning.

In terms of relevance to others, for motivational research I feel the insights regarding social authentication, synaptic crossings and indictors of synergy are likely to be the most useful contribution overall. These are not only quite tangible and operationalisable in terms of research, but they are also practical and fairly easy to understand from a practitioner's point of view. In terms of linking motivation with authenticity, I hope my discussion of the authenticity continuum and the language impetus triad will also be seen as making a useful contribution.

In terms of practice, one of the most useful aspects from this inquiry is hopefully the story itself as a potential dialogue of development. In reading such a story, hopefully this invites a form of participatory reflection as well, thus starting a dialogue of sorts between myself and other teacher/researchers. As Bell (2011) has noted, 'narrative work resonates well with its audience and appears to be well remembered as a result' (p. 582), and thus it is more appropriate for generating discussions of practice and teacher development, especially professional dialogues which seek to enhance reflective practice. Also, the research method which I have used could also be seen as a contribution, and I hope that other studies in the future might choose to adopt similar, evidence-based approaches to practitioner research. I think autoethnography and Exploratory Practice are natural cousins in terms of research aims and the types of ethical considerations around which they are structured, so again I hope that having combined the two is seen as a good thing rather than a deviation from the mainstream of Exploratory Practice research.

Overall, I personally feel this inquiry has been extremely useful for me on an individual basis. If I were to read another article like this (and in preparation for this inquiry, I have read many other such personal accounts), I think I would find it very useful in terms of reflecting on my own teaching. In that sense, I hope that this inquiry makes a useful contribution both in terms of theory and practice. Recent publications that feature collected vignettes of practitioners' first-hand accounts, such as Copland et al. (2016), Hanks (2017) and Mann and Walsh (2017), attest to the usefulness of narratives like this and their validity as a form of empirical data with practical implications.

In terms of a larger contribution, Riessman (2008) argues that 'narratives do political work. The social role of stories – how they are connected to the flow of power in the wider world – is an important facet of narrative theory' (p. 8). Simply in terms of a literature review and as a summary of current thought, this inquiry presents a great deal of in-depth reading and tries to make practical connections from a wide range of sources. In this way the study may be useful in bringing to light areas previously not considered by practitioners.

I hope it is clear from reading this inquiry how much effort and hard work has gone into it. Of course, I am not just referring to myself as the author but also to my students as participants, as well as my colleagues and supervisors as collaborative contributors. Quite simply, I do not think so much work would have gone into this study if it were not going to serve some practical use and make a significant contribution to our field.

Fundamentally, autoethnographies are about empowering people, as I have explained throughout this inquiry. The idea that teachers can do research is no longer controversial, but the idea that they can do serious research which will be accepted as good-quality research done *by* teachers *for* teachers and yet able to sit alongside more established forms of SLA and applied linguistic research in academic circles is still much contested. In completing a study such as this, which attempts to be both academically rigorous and yet ultimately based on practice and intended to achieve praxis (that is, to inform practice through theoretical insights), it is my attempt at empowering such forms of practitioner research, and thus empowering teachers. This study was my attempt to challenge the often-perceived gap between theory and practice, which I have decried numerous times throughout this book. In practical terms, practitioners who are aware of this study will notice that the bulk of the data were collected by basically doing my job as a teacher, reflecting on it and presenting it as a story. I hope that practitioners who read this will feel empowered that they, too, could do something similar. Indeed, I have been able to encourage several of my colleagues to embark on practitioner-based inquiries that focus on their teaching. In Japan, where I work and where this study was conducted, many university teachers face uncertain career prospects due to government pressure for all those working at university to hold doctorates and to publish research on top of a heavy teaching load (see Chapter 7 for nine vignettes, most notably Vignette 6, which further elaborated on teachers' workloads). In other contexts, too, teachers are generally encouraged to publish and share their research findings, not just because such research can benefit others but also because doing research and disseminating findings is a form of professional development which is likely to lead to improved practice (Banegas, 2017; Banegas, Pavese, Velázquez, & Vélez, 2013). So, I genuinely feel this study is empowering for language teachers, but perhaps specifically teachers working in universities, or others wishing to gain further career prospects by engaging in academic work whilst still engaging in teaching.

8.3 Final words

Like many qualitative studies, this inquiry unearths more questions than it is able to answer. I do not see this as a failing or a bad thing. Rather, I see this inquiry as simultaneously a small step and a giant leap in the direction of authenticity research and its relation to L2 motivation and identity. This inquiry is a first, small and tentative step into the research arena as well as a giant personal step for me as both a teaching professional and a researcher. This inquiry has been rather like the mythical hydra beast which grows two new heads for each one lost. Every finding produces more and more avenues for further inquiry, and thus my research agenda seems limitless and daunting. Authenticity truly is a quest, a journey rather than a destination.

> So by all means, let us reflect, and articulate a rationale. Though let us carefully scrutinize the initial sets of ideas we call our philosophy of teaching for what is missing, and above all for what we have accepted, perhaps unconsciously, without asking where it came from and what baggage it brings with it. That done, let us identify our aims and set course.
>
> (Crookes, 2009, p. 239)

In summary, I have been able to understand more about the synergistic relationship between my own (the teacher) and the students' motivation. My evidence for this is based on my perception of the students' motivation and triangulated with practical and pedagogically useful instruments such as the end of course evaluation feedback and other data produced by the students through the natural course of teaching. I was warned against using words like 'prove', since this was never my intention, and indeed my approach to research as a social constructivist means that I would always question what it means to prove anything, since knowledge is constantly being constructed. Therefore, I have gained deeper understandings but also arrived at further areas for inquiry.

I feel I have made an important link between authenticity and motivation, but this is more due to the way I conceptualise these constructs than any particular piece of evidence. This is, nonetheless, useful to the field, as it brings us a little closer to understanding these elusive concepts and provides a detailed motivational cross section of the inside of a language classroom. The other findings in this inquiry are likely to be of relevance to language teacher education and research methodology within this discipline. I have shown that evidence-based reflection leads to insights which are vital to my own professional development, and I intend to examine closely how an understanding of the authenticity gap/ bridge enabled me to create a culture of authenticity which helped my students maintain motivation. I have unpacked the dynamic processes involved in the creation and nurturing of the small culture of the classroom, and I think that, although very personal in nature, this inquiry might be useful to others in that it adds to the pool of shared experiences from which practitioners build their expertise and knowledge. In this sense, I feel that my narrative tries to give a valid account of my experience, and as such it provides a window on the interactions that take place between my students and myself, as I attempted to make the learning process both personal and meaningful in an overt attempt to create a motivating authentic culture within the language learning classroom.

Afterword

In the spring semester of 2016, I was teaching a new elective course for CLER called Environmental Issues in English (CLEREnv), which was not going particularly well. There were only six students, and the course was a bit of a nonstarter. Then, in the autumn semester (October 2016), I printed my register for the class and instantly recognised Mr Swamp's name from CLERAC. He had optionally signed up to take one of my lessons! Although Mr Swamp was not a particularly outstanding student, his name on my register made me very happy.

On the first day of CLEREnv, we had 12 students, and a much more upbeat atmosphere than the previous semester. I could tell from Mr Swamp and his friends' reactions that they had been wondering if I would remember him. He seemed very happy when I greeted him by name as soon as I saw him. We sat in circles straightaway and went around the class in turn asking, 'why did you choose this elective class?' The first of the six new students said basically that Mr Swamp had recommended me as a teacher, and so they took this course. The second new student said the same, as did the third and fourth and so on. It became quite embarrassing, actually, and when it was finally Mr Swamp's turn to speak, he said that he had chosen the class because he had so much fun in CLERAC and wanted to practise his English again (now that his compulsory English education was over).

I kept detailed journals throughout of Mr Swamp, making note of anything that might be useful, although it was too late to add to the main body of the inquiry. What stood out the most was the fact that Mr Swamp seemingly had no memory of anything we studied in the CLERAC class. This is fortunate, as I was recycling (excuse the pun) much of the content from CLERAC and DCT in this environmental-themed class. Mr Swamp *could not remember* having made a video project. After a while, it became the kind of 'class joke' that even though Mr Swamp loved my course so much that he brought all his friends along, he could barely recall any details of the contents we covered. This merely confirms my previous statements about prioritising the experience over the learning gains. This is, of course, not applicable to all teaching contexts, but it certainly has become a central part of my philosophy of teaching.

After completing the first full draft of the book, I started teaching again in October and found that I was transformed. I did much more work on group dynamics, I put much more emphasis on *the class* as a group and yet at the same time I had a better understanding of the individuals. I made time to speak to each member in turn and allowed more opportunities for the class to sit in large circles or present in front of groups. I also did more mingling activities, although I made them appropriate to the university setting and tried to avoid the childish or *mendokusai* (tiring) activities that I had previously found off-putting about such activities. Furthermore, I reapplied Exploratory Practice, and this time I actively got the students to create their own puzzles, which usually became the focus for their assessments.

However, there is also a downside which I have noticed. Now that I have moved further along in terms of my academic career than the undergraduate students I work with, I find that I am no longer as close to them in terms of age and career path as I was when I first became a teacher. This has contributed and is contributing to the authenticity gap between them and myself. I find that, whereas once I was quite forgiving and tolerant of sloppy essays or poorly researched papers, being merely content that the students had tried to write in English, now I react strongly and strictly to poor-quality academic essays. Analysing and reflecting on this, I realised it was because I now see myself as much higher up in terms of the type of academic writing I produce and hence the type of academic writing I want to be exposed to. These are, perhaps, natural by-products of attaining such a high-level academic degree, and certainly an aspect of habitus.

Also, having invested such a huge amount of time, money, energy and personal identity into academic writing, it is natural that I would distance myself from anyone who seems not to see the validity of academic writing. In other words, a student's passive attitude to their own essay is almost an affront to my own career, as a teacher and as a writer. Naturally, I distance myself from such individuals and become strict in my marking, get easily frustrated, perhaps even begin to harbour resentment. As cohort after cohort of student comes to my classroom, I must challenge this attitude before it takes me down the road to bitterness and teacher burnout.

This inquiry has allowed me to self-analyse to such an extent that I am now confident I can recognise these authenticity gaps and begin using empathy and other strategies to build synaptic crossing in order to foster positive motivational synergy. This inquiry *has* changed me, and undertaking it has built many bridges but also created new gaps. My understanding of the topic has grown immensely, and yet there is still much for me to learn. I would like to thank you for reading and for hearing my story.

Appendix 1: Spring semester syllabus

Class dates	Course topic	Assignments
L101A (16/04/ 2014)	Introduction and course overview. Detailed explanation of assessment procedure, demonstration of eLearning resources. Student needs analysis in which a short questionnaire will be administered.	
L101B (CALL) (18/04)	Begin Research Project 1: World English	
L1.2A (23/04)	Research Project 1: Study Skills Workshop	Online research tasks
L102B (CALL) (25/04)	Begin Research Project 2: Online Security	
L103A (30/04)	Research Project 1: Study Skills Workshop	Online research tasks
L103B (CALL) (02/05)	Begin Research Project 3: Adventure Travel	
L104A (07/05)	Research Project 1: Study Skills Workshop	Online research tasks
L104B (CALL) (09/05)	Begin Research Project 4: Real or Fake?	
L105A (14/05)	Research Project 1: Study Skills Workshop	Online research tasks
L105B (CALL) (16/05)	Begin Research Project 5: Fallacies	Class Participation 1/3
L106A (21/05)	Research Project 1: Study Skills Workshop	Online research tasks
L106B (CALL) (23/05)	Begin Research Project 6: Energy Projects	
L107A (28/05)	Research Project 1: Study Skills Workshop	Online research tasks
L107B (CALL) (30/05)	Begin Research Project 7: Technology Projects	
L108A (04/06)	Research Project 1: Study Skills Workshop	Online research tasks
L108B (CALL) (06/06)	Mid semester Review activity	Need analysis. Reaction Paper (20%)
L109A (11/06)	Final Presentations workshop	Group video project work
L109B (CALL) (13/06)	Final Presentations workshop (video)	Group video project work
L110A (18/06)	Final Presentations workshop	Group video project work

Class dates	Course topic	Assignments
L110B (CALL) (20/06)	Final Presentations workshop (video)	Group video project work
L111A (25/06)	Watch Final Project Presentation Videos in class	Class Participation 2/3
L111B (CALL) (02/07)	Essay Workshop (citing and referencing)	
L112A (04/07)	Essay Workshop (writing)	
L112B (CALL) (09/07)	Essay Workshop (formatting)	
L113A (11/07)	Finish Essay	Hand in Final Essay (20%)
L113B (CALL) (12/07)	Exam Strategies Workshop	
L114A (16/07)	Final Exam in class (60 mins) Feedback and evaluation	Final Exam (10%) based on TOEFL reading and listening sections
L114B (CALL) (18/07)	Wrap-up and Review	Class Participation Round-up 3/3

Appendix 2: Autumn semester syllabus

Class dates	Course topic	Assignments
L201A (01/10)	Introduction and course overview. Detailed explanation of assessment procedure, demonstration of eLearning resources. Student needs analysis in which a short questionnaire will be administered.	
L201B (CALL) (03/10)	Begin Research Project: **Prejudice**	
L202A (08/10)	Research Project: Study Skills Workshop	Online research tasks
L202B (CALL) (10/10)	Finish Research Project	
L203A (15/10)	Student led output session: Prejudice	Output session (presentation)
L203B (CALL) (17/10)	Begin Research Project: **Food**	
L204A (22/10)	Research Project: Study Skills Workshop	Online research tasks
L204B (CALL) (24/10)	Finish Research Project	
L205A (CALL) (Tues 28/10, Virtual Friday)	Student led output session: Food	Output session (presentation)
L205B (29/10)	Begin Research Project: **Consumerism**	Class Participation 1/3
L206A (05/11)	Research Project: Study Skills Workshop	Online research tasks
L206B (CALL) (07/11)	Finish Research Project	
L207A (12/11)	Student led output session: Consumerism	Output session (presentation)
L207B (CALL) (14/11)	Begin Research Project: **Economics and Oil**	
L208A (19/11)	Research Project: Study Skills Workshop	Online research tasks
L208B (CALL) (21/11)	Mid semester Review activity	Need analysis. Reaction Paper (20%)

Class dates	Course topic	Assignments
L209A (26/11)	Finish Research Project	
L209B (CALL) (28/11)	Student led output session: Economics and Oil	Output session (presentation)
L210A (05/12)	Begin Research Project: The Environment and Wildlife	
L210B (CALL) (10/12)	Research Project: Study Skills Workshop	
L211A (12/12)	Finish Research Project	Class Participation 2/3
L211B (CALL) (17/12)	Student led output session: The Environment and Wildlife	Output session (presentation)
L212A (19/12)	Essay Workshop (citing and referencing)	
L212B (CALL) (07/01/15)	Essay Workshop (writing and formatting)	Hand in Final Essay (20%)
L213A (09/01/15	Final Presentations workshop (video)	Group video project work
L213B (CALL) (14/01/15) (cancelled)	Final Presentations workshop (video)	Group video project work
L214A (16/01/15)	Watch Final Project Presentation Videos in class Feedback and evaluation	Class Participation Round-up 3/3
L214A (CALL) (21/01/15)	Wrap-up and Review	

Appendix 3: Transcription conventions

Based on Du Bois, Schuetze-Coburn, Cumming, and Paolino (1993) and Walsh and Mann (2015)

RICHARD : MR.CHRG :	Speaker attribution. Pseudonyms are used for all students, the teacher researcher is referred to as RICHARD. When the whole class speaks or reacts the word CLASS is used. Names are usually abbreviated by omitting vowels.
MS.DWNTR?:	indicates that the identity of the speaker is uncertain. Where possible, the alternative candidate for the turn is provided as follows: MS.DWN/MS.OLDR?;
@	indicates laughter. Sometimes a further description of the type of laughter is explained in square brackets.
…	shows a short, untimed pause of less than three seconds.
((……6))	shows a longer, timed pause. The number of dots indicates one second of a pause, the duration is then given in seconds. The example shows a six second pause.
,	shows a continuation of tone
.	shows naturally falling intonation
?	shows naturally rising intonation
::	shows extended vowel. The number of colons roughly represents the length of the extension.
Nihongo	Words in italics are Japanese with the translation in double parenthesis afterwards ((Japanese language)).
[	shows the point at which an overlap starts
]	shows the point at which the overlap begins with the other speaker
[show of hands]	shows non-speech descriptions of movement. As the transcripts are based on audio recordings, these are often recalled from memory or according to field notes.
(?actually)	uncertain words or unclear words
Eng-	a word started but not completed
Er, um, ah, oh	onomatopoeic representation of exclamation sounds
AND	Words all in capitals show the word was stressed for particular effect.
!	Intentionally spoken in a humorous way with raising intonation and pitch
\	Spoken with exaggerated lowering intonation
/	Spoken with exaggerated rising intonation.

Appendix 4: CaLabo transcript

1.	MS OLDR:	*Yoroshiku onegaishimasu* (([polite] if you please))
2.	MR HOUSE:	*Onegaishima:su* ((if you please))
3.	MR AUX:	*Onegaishimasu* ((if you please))
4.	MR WIDE:	*Kore nani yaru no?* ((what should we do?))
5.	MS OLDR:	Ah.. Ah... what did you find... find*o*? Research... topic*u*?
6.		@
7.	MR HOUSE:	Ah *nani shirabeta* ((what did you research))
8.	MR WIDE:	*Ore shirabeta jikan hanbun* ((I only had half the time to research))
9.	MS OLDR:	*Ja watashi kara ikemasu...*((Okay, I'll go)) I researched topic about music in English. I like Ayana Grande, she is so cute and she is big big big artist. Ah *nandaro ski no kyoku to ii no.. nandaro... wakaranai yo* ((hmmm, a song I like. What should I say. I don't know)). Ah. I ... I have her (ah her ka?) her album. Ah Has album (...) all. *Eh, nanitsute iin daro nanisetsume shitai ga iin daro....* ((Eh, what should I say, how should I explain)) I want you to listen the music. Thank you. *Dozo sugi no hito* ((okay next person)).
10.	MR AUX:	*Ja, ikiimasu* ((Okay I will go)).
11.	MR HOUSE:	*Hai onegaishimasu* ((Yes, if you please))
12.	MR AUX:	My way is reading article of soccer (?written) in English. There are verb and the adjectives that has not looked so far and the contents are interesting. I think that it is so... it is to spended profit when I read sports article a lot. *Ijo desu* ((that is all)).
13.	MR HOUSE:	Thank you
14.		Thank you
15.	MR HOUSE:	*Ja, sugi (...) yarimasu* ((Okay, I will (...) do it [next])).
16.		*Hai* ((Yes))
17.		*Hai* ((Yes))
18.	MR HOUSE:	Uhh. I researched topic um movie in English. Ah. English is ah I think helped my studying English ah: many case English movie that is sold in Japan be able to set subtitle and up voice. I think this option is very good. Ah When we set that subtitle is Japanese and voice is English we compare Japanese and English no interval. Moreover, when subtitle is set to English we can study word grammar and pronouncing. I think movie is best tool of studying English while enjoying. Thank you. *Owari desu* ((finished))

19.		Thank you:
20.		Thank you:
21.	MR WIDE:	*Eh to desune. Choto kanashi […] shirabeta ga chigau* ((So, erm… unfortunately […] I researched the wrong thing))
22.		[…] [this sequence of turns is omitted]
23.	MR WIDE:	How to learn English. One, remember word. Two, understand grammar, three listening some video in English. Four, living in English country. Five, communicate with foreigner. Six do not be afraid to speak English. *Konna kanji? Nanka sumimasen* ((that kind of thing? Sorry, excuse me)).
24.	MS OLDR:	*Owachita* ((Oh no, we finished)).
25.		*Doushiyou* ((what should we do))
26.	MS OLDR:	Ah… Uh: haha. (………….) Ah.. uhuhuh….. (….) *Nandaro. Owa[chita* ((What to say, we finished))[
27.		]Doushiy[ou ((What shall we do))
28.	MS OLDR:	]Do you like English?
29.	MR HOUSE:	I like English, but I don't speak English well
30.	MS OLDR:	H; haha. Uh, *nandaro na* ((what to say, huh))… Ah. Me to I like English but I can't [sniffs] speak English well. I'm (…) so sad. @
31.		(…… [long pause again])
32.	MR HOUSE:	*Doushiyou* ((what should we do))
33.		@
34.	MS OLDR:	ah *nandaro.* Ah: *nandaro na* ((what should we say. What to say)) (…..) Ah; Wha. What do you recommend (…) *nandaro, shirabeta naka de* ((how to say, what did you research))
35.	MR HOUSE:	Ah, eh to. I recommend how to learn English is living in *ano* ((like)) English country. Living in another country is the most most*u* (.,…) *nandarao, ichiban hayai houho.*((how to say the fastest way)).
36.	MS OLDR:	Fast*o*? Fast way?
37.		@
38.	MR HOUSE:	fast way I think
39.	MS OLDR:	Ah: Ah:
40.	MR HOUSE:	Eh how how about you
41.	MS OLDR:	I think, I think *nandaro* ((how to say)) listening the music is *nandaro*, fast way *da ne* ((isn't it))?
42.		@
43.	MS OLDR:	listening the music is best way. (@). Do you (…) *nandake* ((how to say))? (…) *do omoiymasuka* ((what do you think))? Do you think
44.	MR HOUSE:	I think listening English music is good way.
45.		@
46.	MS OLDR:	oh thank yo[u
47.	MR HOUSE:	]but I remember music tone, phrase, I remember phrase but I don't remember English mea[nings
48.	MS OLDR:	]ah, ooh, *tashikan ni* ((that's true))
49.	MR HOUSE:	so listening to music is not good way for me
50.		[….]
51.	MR HOUSE:	I think best way is watching movie in English. Movie is not only phrase… ah I understand meaning. I can understand meaning. It's point is good point

52.	MR WIDE:	I think too
53.	MR HOUSE:	good good
54.	MS OLDR:	How many? How many do you watch the movie in a month?
55.	MR HOUSE:	u:n. (…)
56.		*Dai tai de ii yo* ((roughly is ok))
57.		Tekito no
58.		*Nand-* avengers *do ka*
59.		Oooh
60.		(…)
61.	MS OLDR:	How. How. How is it?
62.		It's very fun
63.		@ Oh.
64.		(…)
65.	MS OLDR:	Ahhh: *Nandaro* ((what to say)) (…)
66.	ALL	Ummmm…
67.	MS OLDR:	*mina ne? Mina* ((everyone, right. Everyone)). What what do you like (…) the mo[vie
68.	MR HOUSE:	]what movi[e
69.	MS OLDR:	]what, how *ka*[*na* ((maybe))
70.	MR HOUSE:	]I like the fantasy movie, like Harry Potter
71.	MR WIDE:	Ah!
72.	MS OLDR:	Ah, me too, I like the fantasy movie, for example Disney Fantasy, in English. I like the Beat and Beauty. Ah, ya so(?rry). .(….) I don't know. (?Genre)
73.		(…)
74.		@
75.		[Long pause]
76.	ALL	Ummmm…..
77.	MS OLDR:	Thank you
78.		Thank you
79.		Owachita
80.	RICHARD	(At this point I came into the conversation, but my voice is not picked up. I mention Genre and go out, then they ask in Japanese how I can hear them and Ms Oldriver says I can 'lock on'. When I leave, they pick up the conversation)
81.	MR WIDE:	I like fantasy movie, like Back to the Future
82.	MS OLDR:	I watch the movie, so fantastic
83.	MR HOUSE:	I didn't watch it.
84.	MS OLDR:	Oh, let's watch the mov[ie
85.	MR HOUSE:	]yeah, ok.
86.		(…)
87.	MS OLDR:	Are, [smiling voice] *mouu hitori nakata dozo* ((one other friend go ahead)) ha ha
88.	MR AUX:	Ah…. *Ski na eiga* ((a film I like))?
89.	MS OLDR:	*Mita koto aru yatsu* ((I film you have seen))
90.	MR AUX:	*Eigo na yatsu dake* ((Only an English one))?
91.	MS OLDR:	Yes, in English @ ah, *ma nai ka* ((maybe there isn't one))
92.	MR AUX:	Avatar
93.	ALL:	Ooooh
94.	MR AUX:	*Sono gurai kana* ((something like that))
95.	MS OLDR:	What do you think the movie?

96.	MR AUX:	It's very fantastic
97.	MS OLDR:	Fantastic? A:::[h?
98.	?MRHOUSE:	]Huh
99.	MS OLDR:	Battle, battle movie
100.	MR AUX:	*Uchiy o sukoshi battle ga aru* ((there is a kind of battle in space))
101.	MS OLDR:	eh, what category
102.	MR AUX:	Fan-...fantasy. SF *kana* ((maybe))?
103.	ALL:	Hmmm
104.	MS OLDR:	Eh, where do you watch, Ah where did you watch the movie (...) where. *Eigaka. Nantute Eiga-* ((Cinema, did you say the film-))?. Cinema? Home?
105.	MR AUX:	Yes
106.		Laughter @
107.	MS OLDR:	*Dochi* ((which))
108.	MR AUX:	*Eigaka* ((cinema))
109.	MS OLDR:	eh, 3D?
110.	MR AUX:	Ah so so. Yes
111.	?ALL:	Ehhh
112.		(....) [long pause]
113.	MS OLDR:	*Nandaro na* ((what to say huh)).
114.		(...)
115.	MS OLDR:	*Owachita* ((oh no we finished)) *U:nn. U:n.* (...) *Nandaro na* ((what to do)). (...) *Nanka aru kana* ((I wonder if there is anything else)) (...)
116.		(...) [long pause. Someone can be heard typing again]
117.	MS OLDR:	*Owach[ita* ((we finished)). [
118.	?MRHOUSE:	[*doushiyou* ((what shall we do))
119.	MS OLDR:	*Nanka aru* ((is there anything))
120.	?MRHOUSE:	what music do you like? What types of music
121.	MS OLDR:	Music? Ah: I like dance music, eh, because I (..) like (?uh) I like to dance. And I like rock music too.
122.	MR WIDE:	Oh ho ho
123.	MR HOUSE:	*Jibun no kita wa yoku wakaranai* ((I don't really know what to [?listen to]))
124.	MS OLDR:	For example (....)
125.		[Teacher can be heard ending the task and instructing people to wind down. Headsets can be heard being taken off. Conversation ends.]

Appendix 5: Digital appendix

Please visit my Warwick Portfolio for details of Performance Indicators and classroom results, such as a summary of grades and details about the Coffee Room forum usage and uptake.

http://www2.warwick.ac.uk/study/csde/gsp/eportfolio/directory/pg/live/elrmaj/digitalappendix/

References

Adams, M. (2006). Hybridizing habitus and reflexivity. *Sociology, 40*(3), 511–528. doi:10.1177/003803850663672

Akyazı, K. (2016). Exploring authenticity in (outside) an EFL classroom using TED talks and YouTube. In K. Dikilitaş, M. Wyatt, J. Hanks, & D. Bullock (Eds), *Teachers engaging in research* (pp. 191–206). Kent: IATEFL.

Allwright, D. (1984). Why don't learners learn what teachers teach? The interaction hypothesis. In D. M. Singleton & D. G. Little (Eds), *Language learning in formal and informal contexts* (pp. 3–18). Dublin: IRAAL.

Allwright, D. (1993). Integrating 'research' and 'pedagogy': Appropriate criteria and practical possibilities. In J. Edge & K. Richards (Eds), *Teachers develop teachers research* (pp. 125–135). Oxford: Heinemann.

Allwright, D. (2003). Exploratory practice: Rethinking practitioner research in language teaching. *Language Teaching Research, 7*(2), 113–141.

Allwright, D. (2005). Developing principles for practitioner research: The case of exploratory practice. *The Modern Language Journal, 89*(3), 353–366.

Allwright, D. (2006a). Practitioner research. *Language Teaching Research, 10*(4), 435. doi:10.1191/1362168806lr205pr

Allwright, D. (2006b). Six promising directions in applied linguistics. In S. Gieve & I. K. Miller (Eds), *Understanding the language classroom* (pp. 11–17). Basingstoke: Palgrave Macmillan.

Allwright, D., & Bailey, K. M. (1991). *Focus on the language classroom: An introduction to classroom research for language teachers.* Cambridge: Cambridge University Press.

Allwright, D., & Hanks, J. (2009). *The developing language learner: An introduction to exploratory practice.* Basingstoke: Palgrave Macmillan.

Alseweed, M. A. (2012). University students' perceptions of the influence of native and non-native teachers. *English Language Teaching, 5*(12), 42–53.

Altbach, P. G. (2004). Globalisation and the university: Myths and realities in an unequal world. *Tertiary Education and Management, 10*(1), 3–25. doi:10.1080/13583883.2004.9967114

Amin, N. (1999). Minority women teachers of ESL: Negotiating white English. In G. Braine (Ed), *Non-native educators in English language teaching* (pp. 93–104). New York, NY: Lawrence Erlbaum.

Anderson, B. (2006). *Imagined communities: Reflections on the origin and spread of nationalism* (Revised ed.). London: Verso.

Animal Rights Center. (2015). エシカルライフスタイル情報サイト*Hachidory(*ハチドリィ)をオープン [Ethical life style information site open 'Hachidory']. Retrieved 11 April 2019, from www.arcj.org/information/00/id=560

Apple, M. T., Da Silva, D., & Fellner, T. (Eds). (2013). *Language learning motivation in Japan* (vol. 71). Bristol: Multilingual Matters.

Ariely, D., Gneezy, U., Loewenstein, G., & Mazar, N. (2005). *Large stakes and big mistakes.* Federal Reserve Bank of Boston. Retrieved 11 April 2019, from www.bostonfed. org/publications/research-department-working-paper/2005/large-stakes-and-big-mistakes.aspx

Atkinson, D. (1997). A critical approach to critical thinking in TESOL. *TESOL Quarterly, 31*(1), 71–94.

Atkinson, D. (2010). Sociocognition: What it can mean for second language acquisition. In R. Batstone (Ed), *Sociocognitive perspectives on language use and language learning.* Oxford: Oxford University Press.

Atkinson, D. (Ed). (2011). *Alternative approaches to second language acquisition.* London: Routledge.

Atkinson, T., & Claxton, G. (Eds). (2000). *The intuitive practitioner: On the value of not always knowing what one is doing.* Bristol: Taylor & Francis.

Babad, E. Y., Inbar, J., & Rosenthal, R. (1982). Pygmalion, Galatea, and the golem: Investigations of biased and unbiased teachers. *Journal of Educational Psychology, 74*(4), 459–474.

Bachman, L. F. (1990). *Fundamental considerations in language testing.* Oxford: Oxford University Press.

Bachman, L. F., & Palmer, A. S. (1996). *Language testing in practice: Designing and developing useful language tests.* Oxford: Oxford University Press.

Baggini, J., & Fosl, P. S. (2007). *The ethics toolkit: A compendium of ethical concepts and methods.* Oxford: Blackwell.

Bailey, K. (2006). Marketing the eikaiwa wonderland: Ideology, akogare, and gender alterity in English conversation school advertising in Japan. *Environment and Planning D: Society and Space, 24*(1), 105–130.

Bailey, K. (2007). Akogare, ideology, and 'charisma man' mythology: Reflections on ethnographic research in English language schools in Japan. *Gender, Place & Culture, 14*(5), 585–608. doi:10.1080/09663690701562438

Bandura, A. (2001). Social cognitive theory: An agentic perspective. *Annual Review of Psychology, 52*(1), 1–26.

Banegas, D. L. (2013). The integration of content and language as a driving force in the EFL lesson. In E. Ushioda (Ed), *International perspectives on motivation* (pp. 82–97). London: Palgrave Macmillan.

Banegas, D. L. (Ed) (2017). *Initial English language teacher education: International perspectives on research, curriculum and practice.* London: Bloomsbury.

Banegas, D. L., Pavese, A., Velázquez, A., & Vélez, S. M. (2013). Teacher professional development through collaborative action research: Impact on foreign English-language teaching and learning. *Educational Action Research, 21*(2), 185–201. doi:10.1080/09650792.2013.789717

Barcelos, A. M. F., & Coelho, H. S. H. (2016). Language learning and teaching: What's love got to do with it. In P. D. MacIntyre, T. S. Gregersen, & S. Mercer (Eds), *Positive psychology in SLA* (vol. 97, pp. 130–144). Bristol: Multilingual Matters.

Barkhuizen, G. (2011). Narrative knowledging in TESOL. *TESOL Quarterly, 45*(3), 391–414.

Barkhuizen, G. (2013a). Introduction: Narrative research in applied linguistics. In G. Barkhuizen (Ed), *Narrative research in applied linguistics* (pp. 1–16). Cambridge: Cambridge University Press.

Barkhuizen, G. (Ed) (2013b). *Narrative research in applied linguistics.* Cambridge: Cambridge University Press.

Barkhuizen, G., Benson, P., & Chik, A. (2014). *Narrative inquiry in language teaching and research*. New York, NY: Routledge.

Barkhuizen, G., & Wette, R. (2008). Narrative frames for investigating the experiences of language teachers. *System, 36*(3), 372–387.

Batstone, R. (Ed) (2010). *Sociocognitive perspectives on language use and language learning*. Oxford: Oxford University Press.

Becker, A. L. (1984). Toward a post-structuralist view of language learning: A short essay. *Language Learning, 33*(5), 217–220. doi:10.1111/j.1467-1770.1984.tb01330.x

Becker, A. L. (1995). *Beyond translation: Essays toward a modern philology*. Ann Arbor, MI: University of Michigan Press.

Bell, J. S. (2011). Reporting and publishing narrative inquiry in TESOL: Challenges and rewards. *TESOL Quarterly, 45*(3), 575–584. doi:10.5054/tq.2011.256792

Benson, P. (2013a). Narrative writing as method: Second language identity development in study abroad. In G. Barkhuizen (Ed), *Narrative research in applied linguistics* (pp. 244–263). Cambridge: Cambridge University Press.

Benson, P. (2013b). *Teaching and researching: Autonomy in language learning*. London: Routledge.

Benson, P., & Cooker, L. (Eds). (2013). *The applied linguistic individual*. Bristol: Equinox.

Bernat, E. (2008). Towards a pedagogy of empowerment: The case of 'impostor syndrome' among pre-service non-native speaker teachers in TESOL. *English Language Teacher Education and Development, 11*(1), 1–8.

Berwick, R., & Ross, S. (1989). Motivation after matriculation: Are Japanese learners of English still alive after exam hell? *JALT Journal, 11*(2), 193–210.

Bess, J. L. (1997). Introduction. In J. L. Bess (Ed), *Teaching well and liking it: Motivating faculty to teach effectively* (pp. ix–xv). Baltimore, MD: Johns Hopkins University Press.

Block, D. (2003). *The social turn in applied linguistics*. Edinburgh: Edinburgh University Press.

Block, D. (2007). *Second language identities* (Bloomsbury classics in linguistics ed.). London: Bloomsbury.

Block, D. (2014). *Social class in applied linguistics*. London: Routledge.

Blommaert, J. (2005). *Discourse: A critical introduction.* Cambridge: Cambridge University Press.

Blommaert, J. (2010). *The sociolinguistics of globalization*. Cambridge: Cambridge University Press.

Blommaert, J., & Rampton, B. (2012). Language and superdiversity. MMG Working Paper (Max Planck Institute for the Study of Religious and Ethnic Diversity), *WP 12-09*(5). Retrieved 11 April 2019, from www.mmg.mpg.de/publications/working-papers

Blommaert, J., & Varis, P. (2011). Enough is enough: The heuristics of authenticity in superdiversity. In *Working papers in urban language & literacies* (vol. 76): King's College, London. Retrieved 11 April 2019, from www.kcl.ac.uk/ecs/research/Research-Centres/ldc/publications/workingpapers/abstracts/WP076-Enough-is-enough-The-heuristics-of-authenticity-in-superdiversity

Boo, Z., Dörnyei, Z., & Ryan, S. (2015). L2 motivation research 2005–2014: Understanding a publication surge and a changing landscape. *System, 55*, 145–157.

Borg, S. (2006). *Teacher cognition and language education: Research and practice*. London: Bloomsbury Publishing.

Bourdieu, P. (1991). *Language and symbolic power* (G. Raymond & M. Adamson, Trans.). Cambridge, MA: Harvard University Press.

Bowles, S. (2009). Did warfare among ancestral hunter-gatherers affect the evolution of human social behaviors? *Science, 324*(5932), 1293–1298. doi:10.1126/science.1168112

Boylorn, R. M., & Orbe, M. P. (Eds). (2014). *Critical autoethnography: Intersecting cultural identities in everyday life*. London: Routledge.

Braine, G. (1999). From the periphery to the center: One teacher's journey. In G. Braine (Ed), *Non-native educators in English language teaching* (pp. 15–28). New York, NY: Lawrence Erlbaum.

Braine, G. (2010). *Nonnative speaker English teachers: Research, pedagogy, and professional growth*. London: Routledge.

Breen, M. P. (1985). Authenticity in the language classroom. *Applied Linguistics, 6*(1), 60–70. doi:10.1093/applin/6.1.60

Brutt-Griffler, J., & Samimy, K. K. (1999). Revisiting the colonial in the postcolonial: Critical praxis for nonnative-English-speaking teachers in a TESOL program. *TESOL Quarterly, 33*(3), 413–431.

Bullough, R. V. (2009). Seeking eudaimonia: The emotions in learning to teach and to mentor. In P. Schutz & M. Zembylas (Eds), Advances in teacher emotion research: The emotions in learning to teach and to mentor (pp. 33–53). Boston, MA: Springer.

Bullough, R. V., & Pinnegar, S. (2009). The happiness of teaching (as eudaimonia): Disciplinary knowledge and the threat of performativity. *Teachers and Teaching: Theory and Practice, 15*(2), 241–256.

Caldarelli, G., & Catanzaro, M. (2012). *Networks: A very short introduction* (vol. 335). Oxford: Oxford University Press.

Campbell, G. J. (2014). Toilets tell truth about people: 150 years of plumbing for 'Real Japan'. In R. Cobb (Ed), *The Paradox of Authenticity in a Globalized World* (pp. 103–122). New York, NY: Palgrave Macmillan.

Canagarajah, A. S. (1993). Critical ethnography of a Sri Lankan classroom: Ambiguities in student opposition to reproduction through ESOL. *TESOL Quarterly, 27*(4), 601–626. doi:10.2307/3587398

Canagarajah, A. S. (2005). *Reclaiming the local in language policy and practice*. London: Routledge.

Canagarajah, A. S. (2012). Teacher development in a global profession: An autoethnography. *TESOL Quarterly, 46*(2), 258–279. doi:10.1002/tesq.18

Canagarajah, A. S. (2013). *Translingual practice: Global Englishes and cosmopolitan relations*. New York, NY: Routledge.

Carbonneau, N., Vallerand, R. J., Fernet, C., & Guay, F. (2008). The role of passion for teaching in intrapersonal and interpersonal outcomes. *Journal of Educational Psychology, 100*(4), 977–987.

Castro-Vázquez, G. (2013). *Language, education and citizenship in Japan*. London: Routledge.

CEFR. (2016). European Language Portfolio (ELP). *Common European Framework*. Retrieved 11 April 2019, from www.coe.int/en/web/portfolio

Chambers, G. N. (1999). *Motivating language learners*. Bristol: Multilingual Matters.

Chang, H. (2008). *Autoethnography as method*. London: Routledge.

Chiesa, D. L., & Bailey, K. M. (2015). Dialogue journals: Learning for a lifetime. In D. Nunan & J. C. Richards (Eds), *Language learning beyond the classroom* (pp. 53–62). London: Routledge.

Clandinin, D. J., & Connelly, F. M. (2000). *Narrative inquiry: Experience and story in qualitative research* (vol. 6). San Francisco: Jossey-Bass.

Clark, E., & Paran, A. (2007). The employability of non-native-speaker teachers of EFL: A UK survey. *System, 35*(4), 407–430.

Claxton, G. (2000). The anatomy of intuition. In T. Atkinson & G. Claxton (Eds), *The intuitive practitioner: On the value of not always knowing what one is doing* (pp. 32–52). Bristol: Taylor & Francis.

Cobb, R. (Ed) (2014). *The paradox of authenticity in a globalized world*. New York, NY: Palgrave Macmillan.

Consoli, S. (in preparation). *EAP in the UK: An investigation of the trajectory of students' motivation to learn in a UK university*. (PhD doctoral dissertation). University of Warwick, Coventry, UK.

Cook, G. (2000). *Language play, language learning*. Oxford: Oxford University Press.

Copland, F., Garton, S., & Mann, S. (Eds). (2016). *LETs and NESTs: Voices, views and vignettes*. London: British Council.

Copland, F., & Mann, S. (2012). *The coursebook and beyond: Choosing, using and teaching outside the text*. Tokyo: Abax.

Cortazzi, M. (2001). Narrative analysis in ethnography. In P. Atkinson, A. Coffey, S. Delamont, J. Lofland, & L. Lofland (Eds), *Handbook of ethnography* (pp. 384–394). London: Sage.

Costanza, R. (2013). Energy return on investment (EROI). *The encylopedia of life*. Retrieved 11 April 2019, from http://editors.eol.org/eoearth/wiki/EROI

Cowie, N., & Sakui, K. (2011). Crucial but neglected: English as a foreign language teachers' perspectives on learner motivation. In M. Garold, X. Gao, & T. E. Lamb (Eds), *Identity, motivation and autonomy in language learning* (vol. 54, pp. 212–228). Bristol: Multilingual Matters.

Coyle, D., Hood, P., & Marsh, D. (2010). *CLIL: Content and Language Integrated Learning*. Cambridge: Cambridge University Press.

Creese, A., Blackledge, A., & Takhi, J. K. (2014). The ideal 'native speaker' teacher: Negotiating authenticity and legitimacy in the language classroom. *The Modern Language Journal, 98*(4), 937–951. doi:10.1111/modl.12148

Crookes, G. V. (2009). *Values, philosophies, and beliefs in TESOL: Making a statement*. Cambridge: Cambridge University Press.

Crookes, G. V. (2013). *Critical ELT in action: Foundations, promises, praxis*. London: Routledge.

Crookes, G. V., & Schmidt, R. W. (1991). Motivation: Reopening the research agenda. *Language Learning, 41*(4), 469–512. doi:10.1111/j.1467-1770.1991.tb00690.x

Crystal, D. (2003). *English as a global language*. Cambridge: Cambridge University Press.

Csikszentmihalyi, M. (1990). *Flow: The psychology of optimal experience*. New York, NY: Harper & Row.

Csikszentmihalyi, M. (1997a). *Finding flow: The psychology of engagement with everyday life*. New York, NY: Basic Books.

Csikszentmihalyi, M. (1997b). Intrinsic motivation and effective teaching. In J. L. Bess (Ed), *Teaching well and liking it: Motivating faculty to teach effectively* (pp. 72–89). Baltimore, MD: John Hopkins University Press.

Csikszentmihalyi, M. (2013). *Flow: The psychology of happiness*. New York, NY: Random House.

Csizér, K., & Magid, M. (Eds). (2014). *The impact of self-concept on language learning*. Bristol: Multilingual Matters.

Dalton-Puffer, C. (2007). *Discourse in content and language integrated learning (CLIL) classrooms* (vol. 20). Philadelphia, PA: John Benjamins.

Dam, L., & Legenhausen, L. (2001). Case studies of individual learners in an autonomous language classroom – beginners' level. In L. Karlsson, F. Kjisik, & J. Nordlund (Eds), *All together now: Papers from the 7th Nordic conference and workshop on autonomous language* (pp. 65–84). Helsinki: University of Helsinki Language Centre.

Dashper, K. (2015). Revise, resubmit and reveal? An autoethnographer's story of facing the challenges of revealing the self through publication. *Current Sociology, 63*(4), 511–527. doi:10.1177/0011392115583879 de Bot, K. (2008). Introduction: Second language development as a dynamic process. *The Modern Language Journal, 92*(2), 166–178.

de Bot, K. (2015). Rates of change: Timescales in second language development. In Z. Dörnyei, P. MacIntyre, & A. Henry (Eds), *Motivational dynamics in language learning* (pp. 29–37). Bristol: Multilingual Matters.

de Bot, K., & Hulsen, M. (2002). Language attrition: Tests, self-assessments and perceptions. In V. Cook (Ed), *Portraits of the L2 user* (pp. 253–274). Bristol: Multilingual Matters.

de Bot, K., & Larsen-Freeman, D. (2011). Researching second language development from a dynamic systems theory perspective. In M. Verspoor, K. de Bot, & W. Lowie (Eds), *A dynamic approach to second language development: Methods and techniques* (vol. 29, pp. 5–23). Amsterdam: John Benjamins Publishing.

de Swaan, A. (2001). *Words of the world: The global language system.* Cambridge: Polity Press.

Deci, E. L., Kasser, T., & Ryan, R. M. (1997). Self-determined teaching: Opportunities and obstacles. In J. L. Bess (Ed), *Teaching well and liking it: Motivating faculty to teach effectively* (pp. 57–71). Baltimore, MD: Johns Hopkins University Press.

Deci, E. L., & Ryan, R. M. (1985). *Intrinsic motivation and self-determination in human behavior.* New York, NY: Plenum.

Degenne, A., & Forsé, M. (1999). *Introducing social networks* (A. Borges, Trans.). London: Sage.

Denzin, N. K. (2006). Analytic autoethnography, or déjà vu all over again. *Journal of Contemporary Ethnography, 35*(4), 419–428. doi:10.1177/0891241606286985

Denzin, N. K. (2014). *Interpretive autoethnography* (2nd ed., vol. 17). London: Sage.

Dewey, J. (1897). My pedagogic creed. *The School Journal, LIV*(3), 77–80.

Dewey, J. (1916). *Democracy and education.* New York, NY: Macmillan.

Dewey, J. (1938). *Experience and education* (Touchstone ed.). New York, NY: Simon and Schuster.

Dinham, S., & Scott, C. (2000). Moving into the third, outer domain of teacher satisfaction. *Journal of Educational Administration, 38*(4), 379–396.

Dörnyei, Z. (1994). Understanding L2 motivation: On with the challenge! *The Modern Language Journal, 78*(4), 515–523.

Dörnyei, Z. (1997). Psychological processes in cooperative language learning: Group dynamics and motivation. *The Modern Language Journal, 81*(4), 482–493. doi:10.1111/j.1540–4781.1997.tb05515.x

Dörnyei, Z. (1998). Motivation in second and foreign language learning. *Language Teaching, 31*(3), 117–135.

Dörnyei, Z. (2001a). *Motivational strategies in the language classroom.* Cambridge: Cambridge University Press.

Dörnyei, Z. (2001b). *Teaching and researching motivation* (1st ed.). Harlow: Pearson Education.

Dörnyei, Z. (2005). *The psychology of the language learner: Individual differences in second language acquisition.* London: Routledge.

Dörnyei, Z. (2009). The L2 motivational self system. In Z. Dörnyei & E. Ushioda (Eds), *Motivation, language identity and the L2 self* (pp. 9–42). Bristol: Multilingual Matters.

Dörnyei, Z., & Csizér, K. (1998). Ten commandments for motivating language learners: Results of an empirical study. *Language Teaching Research, 2*(3), 203–229.

Dörnyei, Z., & Csizér, K. (2006). *Motivation, language attitudes and globalisation: A Hungarian perspective* (vol. 18). Bristol: Multilingual Matters.

Dörnyei, Z., Henry, A., & Muir, C. (2016). *Motivational currents in language learning: Frameworks for focused interventions.* London: Routledge.

Dörnyei, Z., & Kubanyiova, M. (2014). *Motivating learners, motivating teachers: Building vision in the language classroom.* Cambridge: Cambridge University Press.

Dörnyei, Z., MacIntyre, P., & Henry, A. (2015a). Introduction: Applying complex dynamic systems principles to empirical research on L2 motivation. In Z. Dörnyei, P. MacIntyre, & A. Henry (Eds), *Motivational dynamics in language learning* (pp. 1–7). Bristol: Multilingual Matters.

Dörnyei, Z., MacIntyre, P., & Henry, A. (Eds). (2015b). *Motivational dynamics in language learning*. Bristol: Multilingual Matters.

Dörnyei, Z., & Murphey, T. (2003). *Group dynamics in the language classroom*. Cambridge: Cambridge University Press.

Dörnyei, Z., & Ryan, S. (2015). *The psychology of the language learner revisited*. London: Routledge.

Dörnyei, Z., & Ushioda, E. (2011). *Teaching and researching: Motivation* (2nd ed.). Harlow: Longman Pearson.

Dörnyei, Z., & Ushioda, E. (Eds). (2009). *Motivation, language identity and the L2 self*. Bristol: Multilingual Matters.

Dubner, S. J., & Levitt, S. D. (2005). *Freakonomics: A rogue economist explores the hidden side of everything*. London: Penguin.

Eagleton, T. (2008). *Literary theory: An introduction* (25th Anniversary ed.). Minneapolis, MN: University of Minnesota Press.

Edge, J. (1988). Natives, speakers, and models. *JALT Journal, 9*(2), 153–157.

Edge, J. (1992). Co-operative development. *ELT Journal, 46*(1), 62–70. doi:10.1093/elt/46.1.62

Edge, J. (2011). *The reflexive teacher educator in TESOL: Roots and wings*. London: Routledge.

Egbert, J. (2003). A study of flow theory in the foreign language classroom. *The Modern Language Journal, 87*(4), 499–518. doi:10.1111/1540–4781.00204

Ellis, C., Adams, T. E., & Bochner, A. P. (2011). Autoethnography: An overview. *Historical Social Research/Historische Sozialforschung, 36*(4), 273–290.

Ellis, R. (2012). *Language teaching research and language pedagogy*. Sussex: Wiley-Blackwell.

Erikawa, H. (2009). *Eigo kyoiku no politics* [Politics in English education]. Tokyo: Sanyusha Shuppan.

Fabbro, F. (2001). The bilingual brain: Bilingual aphasia. *Brain and Language, 79*(2), 201–210. doi:http://dx.doi.org/10.1006/brln.2001.2480

Fairclough, N. (2015). *Language and power* (3rd ed.). London: Routledge.

Farrell, T. S. C. (2007). Failing the practicum: Narrowing the gap between expectations and reality with reflective practice. *TESOL Quarterly, 41*(1), 193–201. doi:10.1002/j.1545-7249.2007.tb00049.x

Farrell, T. S. C. (2008). Critical incidents in ELT initial teacher training. *ELT Journal, 62*(1), 3–10. doi:10.1093/elt/ccm072

Farrell, T. S. C. (2011). Exploring the professional role identities of experienced ESL teachers through reflective practice. *System, 39*(1), 54–62. doi:http://dx.doi.org/10.1016/j.system.2011.01.012

Farrell, T. S. C. (2015). *Promoting teacher reflection in second language education: A framework for TESOL professionals*. London: Routledge.

Finch, A. (2010). Critical incidents and language learning: Sensitivity to initial conditions. *System, 38*(3), 422–431. doi:http://dx.doi.org/10.1016/j.system.2010.05.004

Fulcher, G. (2013). *Practical language testing*. London: Routledge.

Gallois, C., & Giles, H. (2015). Communication accommodation theory. In K. Tracy, T. Sandel and C. Ilie (Eds), *The international encyclopedia of language and social interaction*. Hoboken, NJ: John Wiley & Sons, Inc.

Gao, X., & Lamb, T. (2011). Exploring links between identity, motivation and autonomy. In M. Garold, X. Gao, & T. E. Lamb (Eds), *Identity, motivation and autonomy in language learning* (vol. 54, pp. 1–8). Bristol: Multilingual Matters.

Gersch, K. (2013, 21 August). Google's best new innovation: Rules around '20% time'. *Forbes.* Retrieved 6 September 2016, from http://www.forbes.com/sites/johnkotter/2013/08/21/googles-best-new-innovation-rules-around-20-time/#231c612468b8

Gieve, S., & Miller, I. K. (2006). What do we mean by 'quality of classroom life'? In S. Gieve & I. K. Miller (Eds), *Understanding the language classroom* (pp. 18–46). Basingstoke: Palgrave Macmillan.

Giles, H., Coupland, J., & Coupland, N. (Eds). (1991). *Contexts of accommodation: Developments in applied sociolinguistics.* Cambridge: Cambridge University Press.

Gilmore, A. (2007a). Authentic materials and authenticity in foreign language learning. *Language Teaching, 40*(02), 97–118. doi:10.1017/S0261444807004144

Gilmore, A. (2007b). *Getting real in the language classroom: Developing Japanese students' communicative competence with authentic materials.* (PhD doctoral dissertation). University of Nottingham, Nottingham.

Gilmore, A. (2011). "I prefer not text": Developing Japanese learners' communicative competence with authentic materials. *Language Learning, 61*(3), 786–819.

Gilmore, A. (2016). Language learning in context: Complex dynamic systems and the role of mixed methods research. In J. King (Ed), *The dynamic interplay between context and the language learner* (pp. 194–224). Basingstoke: Palgrave Macmillan.

Gkonou, C., & Mercer, S. (2017). Understanding emotional and social intelligence among English language teachers. *ELT Research Papers, 17*(03). London: British Council.

Gkonou, C., & Miller, E. R. (2017). Caring and emotional labour: Language teachers' engagement with anxious learners in private language school classrooms. *Language Teaching Research, Online first.* doi:10.1177/1362168817728739

Glatthorn, A. A. (1975). Teacher as person: The search for the authentic. *English Journal, 64*(9), 37–39.

Glatthorn, A. A. (1999). *Performance standards and authentic learning.* New York, NY: Eye on Education.

Goffman, E. (1959). *The presentation of self in everyday life.* New York, NY: Anchor.

Goleman, D. (2006). *Emotional intelligence.* New York, NY: Bantam.

Golomb, J. (1995). *In search of authenticity: Existentialism from Kierkegaard to Camus.* London: Routledge.

Gomes de Matos, F. (2002). Second language learner's rights. In V. Cook (Ed), *Portraits of the L2 user* (pp. 305–323). Bristol: Multilingual Matters.

González, O. G. (1990). *Teaching language and culture with authentic materials.* (Unpublished doctoral dissertation). West Virginia University, Morgantown, WV. Retrieved 11 April 2019, from http://worldcat.org /z-wcorg/ database. (UMI-DA9121862)

Goto Butler, Y. (2007). How are nonnative-English-speaking teachers perceived by young learners? *TESOL Quarterly, 41*(4), 731–755. doi:10.1002/j.1545-7249.2007.tb00101.x

Gottschall, J. (2012). *The storytelling animal: How stories make us human.* New York, NY: Houghton Mifflin Harcourt.

Graddol, D. (2003). The decline of the native speaker. In G. Anderman & M. Rogers (Eds), *Translation today: Trends and perspectives* (pp. 152–167). Clevedon: Multilingual Matters.

Graddol, D. (2006). *English next: Why global English may mean the end of 'English as a foreign language'.* London: British Council.

Greene, B. (2011). *The hidden reality: Parallel universes and the deep laws of the cosmos.* New York, NY: Vintage.

Gregersen, T., & MacIntyre, P. (2015). 'I can see a little bit of you on myself': A dynamic systems approach to the inner dialogue between teacher and learner selves. In Z. Dörnyei, P. MacIntyre, & A. Henry (Eds), *Motivational dynamics in language learning* (pp. 83–94). Bristol: Multilingual Matters.

Hadfield, J. (1992). *Classroom dynamics.* Oxford: Oxford University Press.

Hanks, J. (2015a). 'Education is not just teaching': Learner thoughts on exploratory practice. *ELT Journal, 69*(2), 117–128. doi:10.1093/elt/ccu063

Hanks, J. (2015b). Language teachers making sense of exploratory practice. *Language Teaching Research, 19*(5), 612–633.

Hanks, J. (2016). What might research AS practice look like? In K. Dikilitaş, M. Wyatt, J. Hanks, & D. Bullock (Eds), *Teachers engaging in research* (pp. 19–30). Kent: IATEFL.

Hanks, J. (2017). *Exploratory practice in language teaching: Puzzling About principles and practices.* London: Palgrave Macmillan.

Harmer, J. (2008). *The practice of English language teaching* (4th ed.). London: Pearson/ Longman.

Hatfield, E., Cacioppo, J. T., & Rapson, R. L. (1993). Emotional eontagion. *Current Directions in Psychological Science, 2*(3), 96–100. doi:10.1111/1467-8721.ep10770953

Hattie, J. (2008). *Visible learning: A synthesis of over 800 meta-analyses relating to achievement.* London: Routledge.

Hattie, J. (2012). *Visible learning for teachers: Maximizing impact on learning.* London: Routledge.

Haugh, M. (2010). Jocular mockery, (dis)affiliation, and face. *Journal of Pragmatics, 42*(8), 2106–2119. doi:http://dx.doi.org/10.1016/j.pragma.2009.12.018

Hawley Nagatomo, D. (2012). *Exploring Japanese university English teachers' professional identity.* Bristol: Multilingual Matters.

Hedge, T. (2000). *Teaching and learning in the language classroom.* Oxford: Oxford University Press.

Heinberg, R. (2005). *The party's over: Oil, war and the fate of industrial societies* (2nd ed.). Sussex: Clairview books.

Heinrich, P. (2012). *The making of monolingual Japan: Language ideology and Japanese modernity.* Bristol: Multilingual Matters.

Henry, A. (2013). Digital games and ELT: Bridging the authenticity gap. In E. Ushioda (Ed), *International perspectives on motivation* (pp. 133–155). London: Palgrave Macmillan.

Henry, A., & Cliffordson, C. (2015). The impact of out-of-school factors on motivation to learn English: Self-discrepancies, beliefs, and experiences of self-authenticity. *Applied Linguistics, 38*(5). doi:10.1093/applin/amv060

Henry, A., & Thorsen, C. (2018). Teachers' self-disclosures and influences on students' motivation: A relational perspective. *International Journal of Bilingual Education and Bilingualism,* 1–15. doi:10.1080/13670050.2018.1441261

Hillier, J., & Rooksby, E. (Eds). (2005). *Habitus: A sense of place* (2nd ed.). London: Routledge.

Hiver, P. (2015a). Attractor states. In Z. Dörnyei, P. MacIntyre, & A. Henry (Eds), *Motivational dynamics in language learning* (pp. 20–28). Bristol: Multilingual Matters.

Hiver, P. (2015b). Once burned, twice shy: The dynamic development of system immunity in teachers. In Z. Dörnyei, P. MacIntyre, & A. Henry (Eds), *Motivational dynamics in language learning* (pp. 214–237). Bristol: Multilingual Matters.

Hiver, P. (2017). Tracing the signature dynamics of language teacher immunity: A retroductive qualitative modeling study. *The Modern Language Journal, 101*(4), 669–690. doi:10.1111/modl.12433

Hiver, P., & Dörnyei, Z. (2017). Language teacher immunity: A double-edged sword. *Applied Linguistics, 38*(3), 405–423. doi:10.1093/applin/amv034

Hodgkinson, G. P., Langan-Fox, J., & Sadler-Smith, E. (2008). Intuition: A fundamental bridging construct in the behavioural sciences. *British Journal of Psychology*, *99*(1), 1–27.

Holliday, A. (1994). *Appropriate methodology and social context*. Cambridge: Cambridge University Press.

Holliday, A. (1999). Small cultures. *Applied Linguistics*, *20*(2), 237–264.

Holliday, A. (2005). *The struggle to teach English as an international language*. Cambridge: Cambridge University Press.

Holliday, A. (2006). What happens between people: Who we are and what we do. In S. Gieve & I. K. Miller (Eds), *Understanding the language classroom* (pp. 47–63). Basingstoke: Palgrave Macmillan.

Holliday, A., & Aboshiha, P. (2009). The denial of ideology in perceptions of 'non-native speaker' teachers. *TESOL Quarterly*, *43*(4), 669–689. doi:10.1002/j.1545-7249.2009.tb00191.x

Horowitz, A. (2014, 27 June). The art of looking: How to live with presence, break the tyranny of productivity, and learn to see our everyday wonderland. Interviewer: M. Popova. *The Dish*, The Book Club, New York. Retrieved 11 April 2019, from www.brainpickings.org/2014/06/27/on-looking-alexandra-horowitz-interview/

Houghton, S. A., & Rivers, D. J. (Eds). (2013). *Native-speakerism in Japan: Intergroup dynamics in foreign language education* (vol. 151). Bristol: Multilingual Matters.

Hughes, R. (1998). Considering the vignette technique and its application to a study of drug injecting and HIV risk and safer behaviour. *Sociology of Health & Illness*, *20*(3), 381–400. doi:10.1111/1467-9566.00107

Hung, D., & Victor-Chen, D. (2007). Context–process authenticity in learning: Implications for identity enculturation and boundary crossing. *Educational Technology Research and Development*, *55*(2), 147–167. doi:10.1007/s11423-006-9008-3

Hyland, K. (2015). *Academic publishing: Issues and challenges in the construction of knowledge*. Oxford: Oxford University Press.

Iacoboni, M. (2009). *Mirroring people: The science of empathy and how we connect with others*. New York, NY: Picador.

Ikeda, M. (2013). Does CLIL work for Japanese secondary school students? Potential for the 'weak' version of CLIL. *International CLIL Research Journal*, *2*(1), 31–43.

Ikeda, M., Pinner, R. S., Mehisto, P., & Marsh, D. (2013). Editorial: CLIL in Japan. *International CLIL Research Journal*, *2*(1), 1–3.

Irie, K., & Brewster, D. R. (2014). Investing in experiential capital: Self-efficacy, imagination and development of ideal L2 selves. In K. Csizér & M. Magid (Eds), *The impact of self-concept on language learning* (vol. 79, pp. 171–188). Bristol: Multilingual Matters.

Irie, K., & Ryan, S. (2015). Study abroad and the dynamics of change in learner L2 self concept. In Z. Dörnyei, P. MacIntyre, & A. Henry (Eds), *Motivational dynamics in language learning* (pp. 343–366). Bristol: Multilingual Matters.

Izumi, S., Watanabe, Y., & Ikeda, M. (Eds). (2012). *CLIL: New challenges in foreign language education at Sophia University* (vol. 2: Practice and Applications). Tokyo: Sophia University Press.

Jelsma, B. M. (1982). *Adult control behaviours: The interaction between orientation toward control in women and activity level of children*. (PhD doctoral dissertation). University of Rochester, Rochester.

Jenkins, J. (2002). A sociolinguistically based, empirically researched pronunciation syllabus for English as an international language. *Applied Linguistics*, *23*(1), 83–103.

Jenkins, J. (2006). Current perspectives on teaching world Englishes and English as a lingua franca. *TESOL Quarterly*, *40*(1), 157–181.

Johnson, K. E., & Golombek, P. R. (2016). *Mindful L2 teacher education: A sociocultural perspective on cultivating teachers' professional development*. London: Routledge.

Johnson, K. E., & Golombek, P. R. (Eds). (2002). *Teachers' narrative inquiry as professional development*. Cambridge: Cambridge University Press.

Kachru, B. B. (1988). The sacred cows of English. *English Today*, *4*(04), 3–8. doi:10.1017/S0266078400000973

Kamiya, T. (1995). *Tuttle new dictionary of loanwords in Japanese: A user's guide to Gairaigo*. Tokyo: Tuttle Language Library.

Kanno, Y., & Norton, B. (2003). Imagined communities and educational possibilities: Introduction. *Journal of Language, Identity & Education*, *2*(4), 241–249. doi:10.1207/S15327701JLIE0204_1

Kanno, Y., & Stuart, C. (2011). Learning to become a second language teacher: Identities-in-Practice. *The Modern Language Journal*, *95*(2), 236–252. doi:10.1111/j.1540-4781.2011.01178.x

Kelchtermans, G. (2009). Who I am in how I teach is the message: Self-understanding, vulnerability and reflection. *Teachers and Teaching*, *15*(2), 257–272. doi:10.1080/13540600902875332

Kelsky, K. (1999). Gender, modernity, and eroticized internationalism in Japan. *Cultural Anthropology*, *14*(2), 229–255.

Kelsky, K. (2001). Who sleeps with whom, or how (not) to want the West in Japan. *Qualitative Inquiry*, *7*(4), 418–435. doi:10.1177/107780040100700402

Kiczkowiak, M. (2015). Native speakers only. *IATEFL Voices, March-April*(243), 8–9.

Kienbaum, B. E., Russell, A. J., & Welty, S. (1986). *Communicative competence in foreign language learning with authentic materials. Final project report*. Retrieved from Retrieved 11 April 2019, from http://files.eric.ed.gov/fulltext/ED275200.pdf

Kierkegaard, S. (1996). *Papers and journals: A selection* (A. Hannay, Trans. and Ed.). London: Penguin.

Kikuchi, K. (2009). Listening to our learners' voices: What demotivates Japanese high school students? *Language Teaching Research*, *13*(4), 453–471.

Kikuchi, K. (2013). Demotivators in the Japanese EFL context. In M. T. Apple, D. Da Silva, & T. Fellner (Eds), *Language learning motivation in Japan* (pp. 206–224). Bristol: Multilingual Matters.

Kikuchi, K. (2015). *Demotivation in second language acquisition: Insights from Japan*. Bristol: Multilingual Matters.

Kikuchi, K., & Browne, C. (2009). English educational policy for high schools in Japan ideals vs. reality. *RELC Journal*, *40*(2), 172–191.

Kim, H.-K. (2011). Native-speakerism affecting nonnative English teachers' identity formation: A critical perspective. *English Teaching*, *66*(4), 53–71.

Kim, U. (1995). *Individualism and collectivism: A psychological, cultural and ecological analysis* (8787062194). Retrieved 11 April 2019, from www.diva-portal.org/smash/get/diva2:842739/FULLTEXT01.pdf

King, J. (2013a). *Silence in the second language classroom*. London: Palgrave Macmillan.

King, J. (2013b). Silence in the second language classrooms of Japanese universities. *Applied Linguistics*, *34*(3), 325–343. doi:10.1093/applin/ams043

King, J. (2016a). Introduction to the dynamic interplay between context and the language learner. In J. King (Ed), *The dynamic interplay between context and the language learner* (pp. 1–10). Basingstoke: Palgrave Macmillan.

King, J. (2016b). 'It's time, put on the smile, it's time!': The emotional labour of second language teaching within a Japanese university. In C. Gkonou, D. Tatzl, & S. Mercer (Eds), *New directions in language learning psychology* (pp. 97–112). Cham: Springer International Publishing.

King, J. (Ed). (2016c). *The dynamic interplay between context and the language learner*. Basingstoke: Palgrave Macmillan.

Kramsch, C. (2000). Social discursive constructions of self in L2 learning. In J. P. Lantolf (Ed), *Sociocultural theory and second language learning* (pp. 133–154). Oxford: Oxford University Press.

Kramsch, C. (2002a). Introduction: How can we tell the dancer from the dance? In C. Kramsch (Ed), *Language acquisition and language socialization: Ecological perspectives* (pp. 1–30). London: Continuum.

Kramsch, C. (2011). Why is everyone so excited about complexity theory in applied linguistics? *Melanges CRAPEL, 2*(33), 9–24.

Kramsch, C. (2012). Authenticity and legitimacy in multilingual SLA. *Critical Multilingualism Studies, 1*(1), 107–128.

Kramsch, C. (Ed). (2002b). *Language acquisition and language socialization: Ecological perspectives*. London: Continuum.

Kramsch, C., & Lam, W. S. E. (1999). Textual identities: The importance of being nonnative. In G. Braine (Ed), *Non-native educators in English language teaching* (pp. 57–72). London: Routledge.

Krashen, S. (2003). 'English: The world's second language'. Paper presented at The Proceedings of Twelfth International Symposium on English Teaching.

Kreber, C. (2013). *Authenticity in and through teaching in higher education: The transformative potential of the scholarship of teaching*. London: Routledge.

Kubota, R. (1998). Ideologies of English in Japan. *World Englishes, 17*(3), 295–306. doi:10.1111/1467-971X.00105

Kubota, R. (1999). Japanese culture constructed by discourses: Implications for applied linguistics research and ELT. *TESOL Quarterly, 33*(1), 9–35. doi:10.2307/3588189

Kubota, R. (2013). 'Language is only a tool': Japanese expatriates working in China and implications for language teaching. *Multilingual Education, 3*(1), 1–20.

Kubota, R., & Lin, A. (2006). Race and TESOL: Introduction to concepts and theories. *TESOL Quarterly, 40*(3), 471–493. doi:10.2307/40264540

Kubota, R., & Lin, A. (2009a). Race, culture, and identities in second language education: Introduction to research and practice. In R. Kubota & A. Lin (Eds), *Race, culture, and identities in second language education: Exploring critically engaged practice* (pp. 1–24). London: Routledge.

Kubota, R., & Lin, A. (Eds). (2009b). *Race, culture, and identities in second language education: Exploring critically engaged practice*. London: Routledge.

Külekçi, E. (2015). *'Authenticity' in English language teaching and learning: A case study of four high school classrooms in Turkey*. (PhD dissertation). University of Warwick, Coventry, UK.

Kumaravadivelu, B. (2012). *Language teacher education for a global society: A modular model for knowing, analyzing, recognizing, doing, and seeing*. London: Routledge.

Kumaravadivelu, B. (2016). The decolonial option in English teaching: Can the subaltern act? *TESOL Quarterly, 50*(1), 66–85. doi:10.1002/tesq.202

Labov, W. (1972). Some principles of linguistic methodology. *Language in Society, 1*(1), 97–120.

Lamb, M. (2013). Cultural challenges, identity and motivation in state school EFL. In E. Ushioda (Ed), *International perspectives on motivation* (pp. 18–34). London: Palgrave Macmillan.

Lantolf, J. P. (2000a). Introducing sociocultural theory. In J. P. Lantolf (Ed), *Sociocultural theory and second language learning* (pp. 1–26). Oxford: Oxford University Press.

Lantolf, J. P. (Ed). (2000b). *Sociocultural theory and second language learning*. Oxford: Oxford University Press.

Larsen-Freeman, D. (1997). Chaos/complexity science and second language acquisition. *Applied Linguistics, 18*(2), 141–165.

Larsen-Freeman, D. (2002). Language acquisition and language use from a chaos/complexity theory perspective. In C. Kramsch (Ed), *Language acquisition and language socialization: Ecological perspectives* (pp. 33–46). London: Continuum.

Larsen-Freeman, D. (2011). A complexity theory approach to second language development/acquisition. In D. Atkinson (Ed), *Alternative approaches to second language acquisition* (pp. 48–72). London: Routledge.

Larsen-Freeman, D. (2015). Ten 'lessons' from complex dynamic systems theory. In Z. Dörnyei, P. MacIntyre, & A. Henry (Eds), *Motivational dynamics in language learning* (pp. 11–19). Bristol: Multilingual Matters.

Larsen-Freeman, D., & Cameron, L. (2008a). *Complex systems and applied linguistics.* Oxford: Oxford University Press.

Larsen-Freeman, D., & Cameron, L. (2008b). Research methodology on language development from a complex systems perspective. *The Modern Language Journal,* 92(2), 200–213.

Lasagabaster, D., & Sierra, J. M. (2002). University students' perceptions of native and non-native speaker teachers of English. *Language Awareness, 11*(2), 132–142.

Legenhausen, L. (1999). Autonomous and traditional learners compared: The impact of classroom culture on attitudes and communicative behaviour. In C. Edelhoff & R. Weskamp (Eds), *Autonomes Fremdsprachenlernen* (pp. 166–182). Munich: Max Hueber Verlag.

Lemke, J. L. (1992). Intextuality and educational research. *Linguistics and Education, 4*(3), 257–267. doi:http://dx.doi.org/10.1016/0898-5898(92)90003-F

Leung, B. P., & Silberling, J. (2006). Using sociograms to identify social status in the classroom. *The California School Psychologist, 11*(1), 57–61.

Levendusky, M. (2013). *How partisan media polarize America.* Chicago, IL: University of Chicago Press.

Levi, D. (2017). *Group dynamics for teams* (5th ed.). London: Sage.

Lewin, K., Lippitt, R., & White, R. K. (1939). Patterns of aggressive behavior in experimentally created 'social climates'. *The Journal of Social Psychology, 10*(2), 269–299. doi:10.1080/00224545.1939.9713366

Li, N. (2006). Researching and experiencing motivation: A plea for 'balanced research'. *Language Teaching Research, 10*(4), 437–456. doi:10.1191/1362168806lr206pr

Li, N. (2007). *Practitioner research on task motivation in a Chinese university context: Integrating macro and micro perspectives.* (PhD dissertation). Centre for English Language Teacher Education. University of Warwick. Retrieved 11 April 2019, from http://wrap.warwick.ac.uk/id/eprint/2394

Lieberman, M. D. (2000). Intuition: A social cognitive neuroscience approach. *Psychological Bulletin, 126*(1), 109–137.

Lieberman, M. D., Jarcho, J. M., & Satpute, A. B. (2004). Evidence-based and intuition-based self-knowledge: An FMRI study. *Journal of Personality and Social Psychology, 87*(4), 421–435.

Liggett, T. (2009). Unpacking white racial identity in English language teacher education. In R. Kubota & A. Lin (Eds), *Race, culture, and identities in second language education: Exploring critically engaged practice* (pp. 27–43). London: Routledge.

Lindholm, C. (2008). *Culture and authenticity.* Oxford: Wiley-Blackwell.

Littlewood, W. (2000). Do Asian students really want to listen and obey? *ELT Journal, 54*(1), 31–36. doi:10.1093/elt/54.1.31

Longhofer, W., & Winchester, D. (2016). Networks of capital: Dimensions of global capitalism. In W. Longhofer & D. Winchester (Eds), *Social theory re-wired: New connections to classical and contemporary perspectives.* London: Routledge.

Lowe, R., & Pinner, R. S. (2016). Finding the connections between native-speakerism and authenticity. *Applied Linguistics Review, 7*(1), 27–52. doi:10.1515/applirev-2016-0002

MacDonald, M. N., Badger, R., & Dasli, M. (2006). Authenticity, culture and language learning. *Language and Intercultural Communication, 6*(3–4), 250–261.

Maehr, M. L., & Braskamp, L. A. (1986). *The motivation factor: A theory of personal investment.* Lanham, MD: Lexington Books.

Mahboob, A., & Golden, R. (2013). Looking for native speakers of English: Discrimination in English language teaching job advertisements. *Voices in Asia Journal, 1*(1), 72–81.

Mahboob, A., Uhrig, K., Newman, K. L., & Hartford, B. S. (2004). Children of a lesser English: Status of nonnative English speakers as college-level English as a second language teachers in the United States. In L. D. Kamhi-Stein (Ed), *Learning and teaching from experience: Perspectives on nonnative English-speaking professionals* (pp. 100–120). Ann Arbor, MI: University of Michigan Press.

Makino, S., & Tsutsui, M. (1986). *A dictionary of basic Japanese grammar.* Tokyo: The Japan Times.

Mann, S. (2002). Talking ourselves into understanding. In K. E. Johnson & P. R. Golombek (Eds), *Teachers' narrative inquiry as professional development* (pp. 195–209). Cambridge: Cambridge University Press.

Mann, S. (2005). The language teacher's development. *Language Teaching, 38*(03), 103–118. doi:10.1017/S0261444805002867

Mann, S., & Copland, F. (2015). *Materials development.* Alexandria, VA: TESOL Press.

Mann, S., & Walsh, S. (2017). *Reflective practice in English language teaching: Research-based principles and practices.* London: Routledge.

Marsh, D. (2002). *CLIL/EMILE: The European dimension: Actions, trends and foresight potential.* Retrieved 11 April 2019, from https://jyx.jyu.fi/bitstream/handle/123456789/47616/david_marsh-report.pdf?sequence=1&isAllowed=y

Martin, A. J. (2006). The relationship between teachers' perceptions of student motivation and engagement and teachers' enjoyment of and confidence in teaching. *Asia-Pacific Journal of Teacher Education, 34*(1), 73–93. doi:10.1080/13598660500480100

Matsuda, A. (2002). Representation of users and uses of English in beginning Japanese EFL textbooks. *JALT Journal, 24*(2), 182–200.

Matsuda, A. (2003). The ownership of English in Japanese secondary schools. *World Englishes, 22*(4), 483–496.

Matsuda, A. (2011). 'Not everyone can be a star': Students' and teachers' beliefs about English teaching in Japan. In P. Seargeant (Ed), *English in Japan in the era of globalization* (pp. 38–59). Basingstoke: Palgrave Macmillan.

McCarthy, M., & Carter, R. (1994). *Language as discourse: Perspectives for language teaching.* Harlow: Pearson Education.

McCulloch, E. (2012). *Taking humour seriously: An analysis of the use of humour in the English as a foreign language classroom.* (Unpublished master's thesis). Birkbeck, University of London, London.

McGrath, I. (2013). *Teaching materials and the roles of EFL/ESL teachers: Practice and theory.* London: Bloomsbury.

McVeigh, B. J. (2002). *Japanese higher education as myth.* London: Routledge.

Meddings, L., & Thornbury, S. (2009). *Teaching unplugged: Dogme in English language teaching.* Surrey: Delta Publishing.

Medgyes, P. (2002). *Laughing matters: Humour in the language classroom.* Cambridge: Cambridge University Press.

Medhurst, A. (2007). *A national joke: Popular comedy and English cultural identities.* London: Routledge.

Menezes, V. (2013). Chaos and the complexity of second language acquisition. In P. Benson & L. Cooker (Eds), *The applied linguistic individual* (pp. 59–74). Bristol: Equinox.

Mercer, S. (2015a). Dynamics of the self: A multilevel nested systems approach. In Z. Dörnyei, P. MacIntyre, & A. Henry (Eds), *Motivational dynamics in language learning* (pp. 139–163). Bristol: Multilingual Matters.

Mercer, S. (2015b). Social network analysis and complex dynamic systems. In Z. Dörnyei, P. MacIntyre, & A. Henry (Eds), *Motivational dynamics in language learning* (pp. 73–82). Bristol: Multilingual Matters.

Mercer, S. (2016). Seeing the world through your eyes: Empathy in language learning and teaching. In P. D. MacIntyre, T. Gregersen, & S. Mercer (Eds), *Positive psychology in SLA* (pp. 91–111). Bristol: Multilingual Matters.

Mercer, S., & Gkonou, C. (2017). Teaching with heart and soul. In T. S. Gregersen & P. D. MacIntyre (Eds), *Innovative practices in language teacher education: Spanning the spectrum from intra- to inter-personal professional development* (pp. 103–124). Cham: Springer International Publishing.

Mercer, S., & Williams, M. (Eds). (2014). *Multiple perspectives on the self in SLA*. Bristol: Multilingual Matters.

MEXT. (2012). *Higher education in Japan*. Retrieved 11 April 2019, from www.mext. go.jp/english/highered/__icsFiles/afieldfile/2012/06/19/1302653_1.pdf

MEXT. (2015). *The number of Japanese nationals studying overseas and the Annual Survey of International Students in Japan*. Retrieved 11 April 2019, from www.mext.go.jp/english/topics/__icsFiles/afieldfile/2015/05/08/1357495_01.pdf

Mintel. (2014). *Number of global vegetarian food and drink product launched doubles between 2009 and 2013*. Retrieved 11 April 2019, from www.mintel.com/press-centre/food-and-drink/number-of-global-vegetarian-food-and-drink-product-launches-doubles-between-2009-and-2013

Mishan, F. (2005). *Designing authenticity into language learning materials*. Bristol: Intellect Books.

Mishan, F. (2011). Whose learning is it anyway? Problem-based learning in language teacher development. *Innovation in Language Learning and Teaching, 5*(3), 253–272.

Mitchell, R., Myles, F., & Marsden, E. (2013). *Second language learning theories* (3rd ed.). London: Routledge.

Montalvo, G. P., Mansfield, E. A., & Miller, R. B. (2007). Liking or disliking the teacher: Student motivation, engagement and achievement. *Evaluation & Research in Education, 20*(3), 144–158.

Moreno, J. L. (1934). *Who shall survive?* (digital, available from archive.org ed.). Washington, DC: Nervous and Mental Disease Publishing Co.

Moussu, L., & Llurda, E. (2008). Non-native English-speaking English language teachers: History and research. *Language Teaching, 41*(03), 315–348.

Muir, C., & Dörnyei, Z. (2013). Directed motivational currents: Using vision to create effective motivational pathways. *Studies in Second Language Learning and Teaching, 3*(3), 357–375.

Murphey, T., Falout, J., Fukada, Y., & Fukuda, T. (2012). Group dynamics: Collaborative agency in present communities of imagination. In S. Mercer, S. Ryan, & M. Williams (Eds), *Psychology for language learning: Insights from research, theory and practice* (pp. 220–238). London: Palgrave Macmillan.

Myhill, J. (2003). The native speaker, identity, and the authenticity hierarchy. *Language Sciences, 25*(1), 77–97.

New, J., Cosmides, L., & Tooby, J. (2007). Category-specific attention for animals reflects ancestral priorities, not expertise. *Proceedings of the National Academy of Sciences, 104*(42), 16598–16603. doi:10.1073/pnas.0703913104

Newmann, F. M., & Wehlage, G. G. (1993). Five standards of authentic instruction. *Educational Leadership, 50*(7), 8–12.

Newmann, F. M., & Wehlage, G. G. (1995). *Successful school restructuring: A report to the public and educators* (R117Q00005-95). Retrieved 11 April 2019, from http://files.eric.ed.gov/fulltext/ED387925.pdf

Niemiec, C. P., & Ryan, R. M. (2009). Autonomy, competence, and relatedness in the classroom: Applying self-determination theory to educational practice. *Theory and Research in Education, 7*(2), 133–144. doi:10.1177/1477878509104318

Nitta, R., & Baba, K. (2015). Self-regulation in the evolution of the ideal L2 self: A complex dynamic systems approach to the L2 motivational self system. In Z. Dörnyei, P. MacIntyre, & A. Henry (Eds), *Motivational dynamics in language learning* (pp. 367–396). Bristol: Multilingual Matters.

Noels, K. A., Pelletier, L. G., Clément, R., & Vallerand, R. J. (2003). Why are you learning a second language? Motivational orientations and self-determination theory. *Language Learning, 53*(S1), 33–64. doi:10.1111/1467–9922.53223

Norton, B. (2001). Non-participation, imagined communities and the language classroom. In M. P. Breen (Ed), *Learner contributions to language learning: New directions in research* (pp. 159–171). London: Routledge. (Reprinted from: 2014).

Norton, B. (2013). *Identity and language learning: Extending the conversation* (2nd ed.). Bristol: Multilingual matters.

Norton, B., & Pavlenko, A. (2004). Gender and English language learners: Challenges and possibilities. In B. Norton and A. Pavlenko (Eds), *Gender and English language learners* (pp. 1–12). Alexandria, VA: TESOL Publications.

Norton Peirce, B. (1995). Social identity, investment, and language learning. *TESOL Quarterly, 29*(1), 9–31. doi:10.2307/3587803

Nunan, D. (2003). The impact of English as a global language on educational policies and practices in the Asia-Pacific region. *TESOL Quarterly, 37*(4), 589–613.

Oscarson, M. (1989). Self-assessment of language proficiency: Rationale and applications. *Language Testing, 6*(1), 1–13. doi:10.1177/026553228900600103

Palfreyman, D., & Smith, R. C. (Eds). (2003). *Learner autonomy across cultures: Language education perspectives.* New York, NY: Palgrave Macmillan.

Peacock, M. (1996). *The motivation of adult EFL learners with authentic materials and artificial materials.* (PhD dissertation), University of Essex.

Peacock, M. (1997). The effect of authentic materials on the motivation of EFL learners. *ELT Journal, 51*(2), 144–156. doi:10.1093/elt/51.2.144

Peacock, M. (1998). Usefulness and enjoyableness of teaching materials as predictors of on-task behavior. *TESL-EJ, 3*(2), 2–8.

Pelletier, L. G., Séguin-Lévesque, C., & Legault, L. (2002). Pressure from above and pressure from below as determinants of teachers' motivation and teaching behaviors. *Journal of Educational Psychology, 94*(1), 186–196.

Pelletier, L. G., & Sharp, E. C. (2009). Administrative pressures and teachers' interpersonal behaviour in the classroom. *Theory and Research in Education, 7*(2), 174–183. doi:10.1177/1477878509104322

Petraglia, J. (1998). *Reality by design: The rhetoric and technology of authenticity in education.* London: Routledge.

Phoenix, C., & Sparkes, A. C. (2009). Being Fred: Big stories, small stories and the accomplishment of a positive ageing identity. *Qualitative Research, 9*(2), 219–236. doi:10.1177/1468794108099322

Pink, D. H. (2009). *Drive: The surprising truth about what motivates us.* New York, NY: Riverhead Books.

Pinner, R. S. (2012a). Examining authenticity and motivation from an international perspective. *JACET ESP Annual Report, 14*, 26–35.

Pinner, R. S. (2012b). Unlocking literature through CLIL. In S. Izumi, M. Ikeda, & Y. Watanabe (Eds), *CLIL: New challenges in foreign language education* (vol. 2, pp. 91–129). Tokyo: Sophia University Press.

Pinner, R. S. (2013a). Authenticity and CLIL: Examining authenticity from an international CLIL perspective. *International CLIL Research Journal, 2*(1), 44–54.

Pinner, R. S. (2013b). Authenticity of purpose: CLIL as a way to bring meaning and motivation into EFL contexts. *Asian EFL Journal, 15*(4), 138–159.

Pinner, R. S. (2014a). The authenticity continuum: Empowering international voices. *English Language Teacher Education and Development, 16*(1), 9–17.

Pinner, R. S. (2014b). The authenticity continuum: Towards a definition incorporating international voices. *English Today, 30*(4), 22–27. doi:10.1017/S0266078414000364

Pinner, R. S. (2015). Authenticity in a global context: Learning, working and communicating with L2 teachers of English. In J. Angouri, T. Harrison, S. Schnurr, & S. Wharton (Eds), *Learning, working and communicating in a global context* (pp. 135–139). London: Scitsiugnil Press for the British Association for Applied Linguistics.

Pinner, R. S. (2016a). The nature of authenticity in English as a foreign language: A comparison of eight inter-related definitions. *ELTWO Journal, 9*(1), 78–93.

Pinner, R. S. (2016b). *Reconceptualising authenticity for English as a global language*. Bristol: Multilingual Matters.

Pinner, R. S. (2016c). Trouble in paradise: Self-assessment and the Tao. *Language Teaching Research, 20*(2), 181–195. doi:10.1177/1362168814562015

Pinner, R. S. (2016d). Using self-assessment to maintain motivation in a dynamic classroom environment: An exploratory practice inquiry of one Japanese university speaking course. *Asian Journal of Applied Linguistics, 3*(1), 27–40.

Pinner, R. S. (2018a). Authenticity and ideology: Creating a culture of authenticity through reflecting on purposes for learning and teaching. *Argentinian Journal of Applied Linguistics, 6*(1), 7–24.

Pinner, R. S. (2018b). Re-learning from experience: Using autoethnography for teacher development. *Educational Action Research, 26*(1), 91–105. doi:10.1080/09650792.2017.1310665

Plummer, K. (2001). The call of life stories in ethnographic research. In P. Atkinson, A. Coffey, S. Delamont, J. Lofland, & L. Lofland (Eds), *Handbook of ethnography* (pp. 395–406). Thousand Oaks, CA: Sage.

Polkinghorne, D. E. (1988). *Narrative knowing and the human sciences*. Albany, NY: State University of New York Press.

Polkinghorne, D. E. (2007). Validity issues in narrative research. *Qualitative Inquiry, 13*(4), 471–486. doi:10.1177/1077800406297670

Rampton, B. (1999). Dichotomies, difference, and ritual in second language learning and teaching. *Applied Linguistics, 20*(3), 316–340. doi:10.1093/applin/20.3.316

Rampton, B. (2002). Ritual and foreign language practices at school. *Language in Society, 31*(4), 491–525. doi:10.1017/S0047404502314015

Rear, D. (2010). A systematic approach to teaching critical thinking through debate. *ELTWO Journal, 2*(1), 1–10.

Rear, D. (2011). Mixed messages: Discourses of education in policy speeches to the Japanese Diet. *Asia Pacific Journal of Education, 31*(2), 129–142. doi:10.1080/02188791.2011.566985

Reeve, J. (2009). Why teachers adopt a controlling motivating style toward students and how they can become more autonomy supportive. *Educational Psychologist, 44*(3), 159–175.

Reves, T., & Medgyes, P. (1994). The non-native English speaking EFL/ESL teacher's self-image: An international survey. *System, 22*(3), 353–367.

Richards, J. C. (2001). *Curriculum development in language teaching.* Cambridge: Cambridge University Press.

Richards, J. C., & Lockhart, C. (1994). *Reflective teaching in second language classrooms.* Cambridge: Cambridge University Press.

Richards, J. C., & Schmidt, R. W. (2013). *Longman dictionary of language teaching and applied linguistics.* Harlow: Routledge.

Richards, K. (2003). *Qualitative inquiry in TESOL.* Basingstoke: Palgrave Macmillan.

Richards, K. (2006). 'Being the teacher': Identity and classroom conversation. *Applied Linguistics, 27*(1), 51–77.

Richards, K., Ross, S., & Seedhouse, P. (2012). *Research methods for applied language studies.* London: Routledge.

Richardson, P. W., & Watt, H. M. (2006). Who chooses teaching and why? Profiling characteristics and motivations across three Australian universities. *Asia-Pacific Journal of Teacher Education, 34*(1), 27–56.

Riessman, C. K. (2008). *Narrative methods for the human sciences.* London: Sage.

Ritzer, G. (1996). McUniversity in the postmodern consumer society. *Quality in Higher Education, 2*(3), 185–199.

Rodriguez, N. M., & Ryave, A. (2002). *Systematic self-observation: A method for researching the hidden and elusive features of everyday social life* (vol. 49). London: Sage.

Rogers, C. (1961). *On becoming a person: A therapist's view of psychotherapy.* New York, NY: Houghton Mifflin Harcourt.

Rosenthal, R., & Jacobson, L. (1992). *Pygmalion in the classroom: Teacher expectation and pupils' intellectual development* (2nd ed.). Berkeley, CA: Irvington & Crown House.

Roth, G., Assor, A., Kanat-Maymon, Y., & Kaplan, H. (2007). Autonomous motivation for teaching: How self-determined teaching may lead to self-determined learning. *Journal of Educational Psychology, 99*(4), 761–774.

Rukeyser, M. (1968, 2006). *The speed of darkness.* Retrieved 11 April 2019, from www.poetryfoundation.org/poem/245984

Ryan, S. (2006). Language learning motivation within the context of globalisation: An L2 self within an imagined global community. *Critical Inquiry in Language Studies, 3*(1), 23–45.

Ryan, S. (2009). Self and identity in L2 motivation in Japan: The ideal L2 self and Japanese learners of English. In Z. Dörnyei & E. Ushioda (Eds), *Motivation, language identity and the L2 self* (pp. 120–143). Bristol: Multilingual Matters.

Ryan, S., & Irie, K. (2014). Imagined and possible selves: Stories we tell ourselves about ourselves. In S. Mercer & M. Williams (Eds), *Multiple perspectives on the self in SLA* (pp. 109). Bristol: Multilingual Matters.

Saito, A. (2012). Is English our lingua franca or the native speaker's property? The native speaker orientation among middle school students in Japan. *Journal of Language Teaching and Research, 3*(6), 1071–1081.

Sampson, R. J. (2012). The language-learning self, self-enhancement activities, and self perceptual change. *Language Teaching Research, 16*(3), 317–335.

Sampson, R. J. (2015). Tracing motivational emergence in a classroom language learning project. *System, 50,* 10–20.

Sampson, R. J. (2016). *Complexity in classroom foreign language learning motivation: A practitioner perspective from Japan.* Bristol: Multilingual Matters.

Sartre, J.-P. (1992). *Notebooks for an ethics.* Chicago, IL: University of Chicago Press.

Sasayama, S. (2013). Japanese college students' attitudes towards Japan English and American English. *Journal of Multilingual and Multicultural Development, 34*(3), 264–278.

Sato, R. (2015). The case against the case against holding English classes in English. *The Language Teacher, 39,* 15–18.

Scheuer, J. (2003). Habitus as the principle for social practice: A proposal for critical discourse analysis. *Language in Society, 32*(2), 143–175.

Schön, D. A. (1983). *The reflective practitioner: How professionals think in action.* New York: Basic Books.

Schön, D. A. (1987). *Educating the reflective practitioner: Toward a new design for teaching and learning in the professions.* San Francisco, CA: Jossey-Bass.

Schreiber, M. (2013, 12 October). Tabloids brimming with anti-Korea diatribes. *The Japan Times.*

Schwartz, B. (2004). *The paradox of choice.* New York, NY: Harper Perennial.

Seargeant, P. (2005). 'More English than England itself': The simulation of authenticity in foreign language practice in Japan. *International Journal of Applied Linguistics, 15*(3), 326–345.

Seargeant, P. (2009). *The idea of English in Japan: Ideology and the evolution of a global language.* Bristol: Multilingual Matters.

Seargeant, P. (Ed) (2011). *English in Japan in the era of globalization.* Basingstoke: Palgrave Macmillan.

Seidlhofer, B. (2005). English as a lingua franca. *ELT Journal, 59*(4), 339.

Selvi, A. F. (2010). All teachers are equal, but some teachers are more equal than others: Trend analysis of job advertisements in English language teaching. *WATESOL NNEST Caucus Annual Review, 1,* 156–181.

Shi, L. (2002). A tale of names. In K. E. Johnson & P. R. Golombek (Eds), *Teachers' narrative inquiry as professional development* (pp. 136–149). Cambridge: Cambridge University Press.

Siegel, A. (2014). What should we talk about? The authenticity of textbook topics. *ELT Journal, 68*(4), 363–375. doi:10.1093/elt/ccu012

Silverman, D. (2013). *Doing qualitative research: A practical handbook*: SAGE Publications Limited.

Straub, J. (Ed). (2012). *Paradoxes of authenticity: Studies on a critical concept.* London: Transaction.

Sugimoto, Y. (2010). *An introduction to Japanese society* (3rd ed.). Cambridge: Cambridge University Press.

Susser, B. (1998). EFL's Othering of Japan: Orientalism in English language teaching. *JALT Journal, 20*(1), 49–82.

Swann, A., Aboshiha, P., & Holliday, A. (Eds). (2015). *(En)Countering native-speakerism: Global perspectives.* Basingstoke: Palgrave Macmillan.

Takahashi, K. (2013). *Language learning, gender and desire: Japanese women on the move* (vol. 16). Bristol: Multilingual Matters.

Takeda, A., Choi, E.-S., Mochizuki, N., & Watanabe, Y. (2006). Analysis and comparison of the junior and senior high school level English textbooks for Japan and Korea. *Second Language Studies, 25*(1), 53–82.

Takizawa, T. (2010). The three core values Sophia University strives to achieve: Message from The President. Retrieved 11 April 2019, from www.sophia.ac.jp/eng/aboutsophia/message/president2

Tamaki, T. (2004). Taking the 'taken-for-grantedness' seriously: Problematizing Japan's perception of Japan–South Korea relations. *International Relations of the Asia-Pacific, 4*(1), 147–169. doi:10.1093/irap/4.1.147

Tannen, D. (1991). *You just don't understand: Women and men in conversation.* London: Virago.

Tardy, C. M., & Snyder, B. (2004). 'That's why I do it': Flow and EFL teachers' practices. *ELT Journal, 58*(2), 118–128.

Tomlinson, B., & Masuhara, H. (2010). Applications of the research results for second language acquisition theory and research. In B. Tomlinson & H. Masuhara (Eds), *Research for materials development in language learning: Evidence for best practice* (pp. 399–409). London: Continuum.

Tong, J. W. M. (2002). *Filial piety: A barrier or a resource?; a qualitative case study of classroom culture in Hong Kong secondary schools.* (PhD dissertation), Canterbury Christ Church University, Canterbury, UK.

Torikai, K. (2011). 国際共通語としての英語 *[English as a common language]*. Tokyo: Kodansha.

Trilling, L. (1972). *Sincerity and authenticity: The Charles Eliot Norton lectures, 1969–1970.* Cambridge, MA: Harvard University Press.

Tripp, D. (1993). *Critical incidents in teaching: Developing professional judgement* (Education Classic ed.). London: Routledge.

Tudor, I. (2001). *The dynamics of the language classroom.* Cambridge: Cambridge University Press.

Tudor, I. (2003). Learning to live with complexity: Towards an ecological perspective on language teaching. *System, 31*(1), 1–12.

Ushioda, E. (1993). Redefining motivation from the L2 learner's point of view. *TEANGA (Journal of the Irish Association of Applied Linguistics), 13*, 1–12.

Ushioda, E. (1996). Developing a dynamic concept of L2 motivation. In T. Hickey & J. Williams (Eds), *Language, education and society in a changing world* (pp. 239–245). Clevedon: Multilingual Matters.

Ushioda, E. (1998). Effective motivational thinking: A cognitive theoretical approach to the study of language learning motivation. E. Alcón Soler, and V. Codina Espurz (Eds), *Current issues in English language methodology* (pp. 77–89). Castelló de la Plana, Spain: Publicacions de la Universitat Jaume I.

Ushioda, E. (2009). A person-in-context relational view of emergent motivation, self and identity. In E. Ushioda & Z. Dörnyei (Eds), *Motivation, language identity and the L2 self* (pp. 215–228). Bristol: Multilingual Matters.

Ushioda, E. (2011a). Language learning motivation, self and identity: Current theoretical perspectives. *Computer Assisted Language Learning, 24*(3), 199–210. doi:10.1080/09588221.2010.538701

Ushioda, E. (2011b). Motivating learners to speak as themselves. In G. Murray, X. Gao, & T. E. Lamb (Eds), *Identity, motivation and autonomy in language learning* (pp. 11–25). Bristol: Multilingual Matters.

Ushioda, E. (2013a). Foreign language motivation research in Japan. In M. T. Apple, D. Da Silva, & T. Fellner (Eds), *Language learning motivation in Japan* (pp. 1–14). Bristol: Multilingual Matters.

Ushioda, E. (2013b). Motivation and ELT: Global issues and local concerns. In E. Ushioda (Ed), *International perspectives on motivation: Language learning and professional challenges* (pp. 1–19). New York, NY: Palgrave Macmillan.

Ushioda, E. (2014). Motivation, autonomy and metacognition: Exploring their interactions. In D. Lasagabaster, A. Doiz, & J. M. Sierra (Eds), *Motivation and foreign language learning: From theory to practice* (pp. 31–49). Amsterdam: John Benjamins.

Ushioda, E. (2015). Context and complex dynamic systems theory. In Z. Dörnyei, P. MacIntyre, & A. Henry (Eds), *Motivational dynamics in language learning* (pp. 47–54). Bristol: Multilingual Matters.

Ushioda, E. (2016). Language learning motivation through a small lens: A research agenda. *Language Teaching, 49*(4), 564–577. doi:10.1017/S0261444816000173

Ushioda, E. (Ed) (2013c). *International perspectives on motivation: Language learning and professional challenges.* New York, NY: Palgrave Macmillan.

Ushioda, E., & Dörnyei, Z. (2009). Motivation, language identities and the L2 self: A theoretical overview. In Z. Dörnyei & E. Ushioda (Eds), *Motivation, language identity and the L2 self* (pp. 1–8). Bristol: Multilingual Matters.

Ushioda, E., Smith, R., Mann, S., & Brown, P. (2011). Promoting teacher–learner autonomy through and beyond initial language teacher education. *Language Teaching*, *44*(01), 118–121. doi:10.1017/S026144481000039X

van Dam, J. (2002). Ritual, face, and play in a first English lesson: Bootstrapping a class-room culture. In C. Kramsch (Ed), *Language acquisition and language socialization: Ecological perspectives* (pp. 237–265). London: Continuum.

van Lier, L. (1988). *The classroom and the language learner: Ethnography and second-language classroom research*. London: Longman.

van Lier, L. (1996). *Interaction in the language curriculum: Awareness, autonomy and authenticity*. London: Longman.

van Lier, L. (1998). The relationship between consciousness, interaction and language learning. *Language Awareness*, *7*(2–3), 128–145. doi:10.1080/09658419808667105

van Lier, L. (2000). From input to affordance: Social-interactive learning from an eco-logical perspective. In J. P. Lantolf (Ed), *Sociocultural theory and second language learning* (pp. 245–259). Oxford: Oxford University Press.

van Lier, L. (2002). An ecological-semiotic perspective on language and linguistics. In C. Kramsch (Ed), *Language acquisition and language socialization: Ecological perspectives* (pp. 140–164). London: Continuum.

van Lier, L. (2006). *The ecology and semiotics of language learning: A sociocultural perspec-tive*. New York, NY: Kluwer Academic Publishers.

van Lier, L. (2007). Action-based teaching, autonomy and identity. *Innovation in Language Learning and Teaching*, *1*(1), 46–65. doi:10.2167/illt42.0

Vannini, P., & Burgess, S. (2009). Authenticity as motivation and aesthetic experience. In P. Vannini & J. P. Williams (Eds), *Authenticity in culture, self, and society* (pp. 103–120). Surrey: Ashgate Publishing.

Verspoor, M. (2015). Initial conditions. In Z. Dörnyei, P. MacIntyre, & A. Henry (Eds), *Motivational dynamics in language learning* (pp. 38–46). Bristol: Multilingual Matters.

Verspoor, M., de Bot, K., & Lowie, W. (Eds). (2011). *A dynamic approach to second lan-guage development: Methods and techniques* (Vol. 29). Amsterdam: John Benjamins Publishing.

Vertovec, S. (2007). Super-diversity and its implications. *Ethnic and Racial Studies*, *30*(6), 1024–1054. doi:10.1080/01419870701599465

Vygotsky, L. S. (1964). *Thought and language* (E. Hanfmann, G. Vakar, & A. Kozulin, Trans.; A. Kozulin, Ed.). Cambridge, MA: MIT Press.

Vygotsky, L. S. (1978). *Mind in society: The development of higher psychological processes* (A. Luria, R. & M. Lopez-Morollas, Trans.; V. John-Steiner & M. Cole, Eds) (Revised ed.). Cambridge, MA: Harvard University Press.

Walsh, S., & Mann, S. (2015). Doing reflective practice: A data-led way forward. *ELT Journal*, *69*(4), 351–362. doi:10.1093/elt/ccv018

Wardhaugh, R. (2006). *An introduction to sociolinguistics* (5th ed.). Oxford: Blackwell.

Warschauer, M., Turbee, L., & Roberts, B. (1996). Computer learning networks and stu-dent empowerment. *System*, *24*(1), 1–14.

Waskul, D. D. (2009). The importance of insincerity and inauthenticity for self and society: Why honesty is not the best policy. In P. Vannini & J. P. Williams (Eds), *Authenticity in culture, self, and society* (pp. 51–64). Surrey: Ashgate Publishing.

Watanabe, Y. (1997). *The washback effects of the Japanese university entrance examinations of English: Classroom-based research* (PhD Dissertation), University of Lancaster,

Watanabe, Y., Ikeda, M., & Izumi, S. (Eds). (2011). *CLIL: New challenges in foreign language education at Sophia University* (vol. 1: Principles and Methodology). Tokyo: Sophia University Press.

Weigert, A. J. (2009). Self authenticity as master motive. In P. Vannini & J. P. Williams (Eds), *Authenticity in culture, self, and society* (pp. 37–50). Surrey: Ashgate Publishing.

Wenger, E. (1998). *Communities of practice: Learning, meaning, and identity* (2003 ed.). Cambridge: Cambridge University Press.

Widdowson, H. G. (1978). *Teaching language as communication.* Oxford: Oxford University Press.

Widdowson, H. G. (1979). *Explorations in applied linguistics* (Vol. 2). Oxford: Oxford University Press.

Widdowson, H. G. (1990). *Aspects of language teaching.* Oxford: Oxford University Press.

Widdowson, H. G. (1994). The ownership of English. *TESOL Quarterly, 28*(2), 377–389. doi:10.2307/3587438

Widdowson, H. G. (1996). Comment: Authenticity and autonomy in ELT. *ELT Journal, 50*(1), 67–68. doi:10.1093/elt/50.1.67

Wild, T. C., Enzle, M. E., & Hawkins, W. L. (1992). Effects of perceived extrinsic versus intrinsic teacher motivation on student reactions to skill acquisition. *Personality and Social Psychology Bulletin, 18*(2), 245–251. doi:10.1177/0146167292182017

Williams, M., & Burden, R. L. (1997). *Psychology for language teachers.* Cambridge: Cambridge University Press.

Wu, K.-h., & Ke, C. (2009). Haunting native speakerism? Students' perceptions toward native speaking English teachers in Taiwan. *English Language Teaching, 2*(3), 44–52.

Wu, Z. (2006). Understanding practitioner research as a form of life: An Eastern interpretation of Exploratory Practice. *Language Teaching Research, 10*(3), 331–350.

Yano, Y. (2011). English as an international language and 'Japanese English'. In P. Seargeant (Ed), *English in Japan in the era of globalization* (pp. 125–142). Basingstoke: Palgrave Macmillan.

Yoshida, K. (2001). The need for a qualitative change in the teaching of English in Japan in the 21st century. In A. Furness, G. Wong, & L. Wu (Eds), *Penetrating discourse: Integrating theory and practice in second language teaching* (pp. 159–172). Hong Kong: Hong Kong University of Science and Technology.

Yoshida, K. (2003). Language education policy in Japan: The problem of espoused objectives versus practice. *The Modern Language Journal, 87*(2), 290–292. doi:10.2307/1193041

Yoshida, K. (2008). *TEFL in Japan: An overview.* Paper presented at the World Congress of Applied Linguistics. Essen, Germany.

Yoshida, K. (2009). The new course of study and the possibilities for change in Japan's English education. In K. Namai & Y. Fukuda (Eds), *Toward the fusion of language, culture and education from the perspectives of international and interdisciplinary research [言語・文化・教育の融合を目指して—国際的・学際的研究の視座から]* (pp. 387–398). Tokyo: Kaitakushya.

Yoshida, K. (2013). *Reconsidering Japan's English education based on the principles of plurilingualism (2013).* Paper presented at the Twenty-second International Symposium on English Teaching, Taipei, Taiwan.

Yuasa, K. (2010). English textbooks in Japan and Korea. *Journal of Pan-Pacific Association of Applied Linguistics, 14*(1), 147–158.

Zhang, R. (2004). Using the principles of exploratory practice to guide group work in an extensive reading class in China. *Language Teaching Research, 8*(3), 331–345.

Zimmerman, D. H. (1998). Identity, context and interaction. In C. Antaki & S. Widdicombe (Eds), *Identities in talk* (pp. 87–106). London: Sage.

Index

ability 13, 28, 30, 33, 35–36, 42, 78, 84, 97–98, 104, 109–111, 116, 129, 138, 147, 150, 170–171, 175–176, 178, 180–181, 188, 191, 205, 207, 215, 219, 236, 256, 258; ability for empathy 176; ability to be objective 13; ability to be reflexive 84; ability to comprehend (*see* comprehension); ability to express 98; ability with English 97
ability to teach 33
absence (*see* attendance)
accent 23, 31, 110, 112, 188, 191–192
acclimatising 261
accommodation 38, 64
accommodation theory 38
accuracy 129, 241
achievement 7, 9, 13, 17–18, 27, 30, 32, 37, 48, 52, 60, 73, 104, 112, 134, 146, 194, 199, 202, 217, 227–228, 232–233, 235, 243–244, 252, 262, 264
acquisition 1, 15–16, 23, 25, 64, 129, 261
activities 2, 8, 16, 20, 36, 67, 69, 79, 148, 238, 251, 253–254, 268
Adams, M. 15–16
Ad-Hoc interviews 69, 73, 84–85, 87, 97, 99, 101–102, 104–105, 123–124, 139–141
aims 4, 20, 27, 39–42, 44, 65, 67, 71, 90–91, 99, 118, 125, 128–129, 139, 141, 151–152, 155, 159, 162, 172, 184, 199, 202–203, 219, 227, 234–237, 250, 255, 263, 265
akogare 102, 181, 191
Allwright, D. 10, 17, 28, 33, 36, 46, 50, 52, 59–60, 65–68, 70–71, 91, 123, 190, 214, 216, 231–232, 235, 262

Alseweed, M.A. 23
Altbach, P.G. 223
analysis-as-data 56
assumptions 16, 46, 56, 72, 92, 119, 121, 211, 229–231, 240
Atkinson, D. 3, 10, 45, 132, 214
attendance 73, 95–96, 119, 135, 148, 152, 164, 201, 222, 224–225, 247, 253, 255
attractor state 11–12, 48, 92, 99, 142, 149, 199, 216, 224, 234
authentication 4–5, 7–8, 14, 16–18, 20, 29–30, 41, 43, 45, 47–48, 50–51, 60, 84, 142, 149, 154, 159, 217, 219–220, 226, 242, 263
authenticity; authenticity as a bridge 60, 143, 230–231; co-constructing authenticity 7, 224; continuum 10, 20–22, 48, 218, 263; debate 18–19; gap 1, 60, 83, 112, 141, 183, 228–230, 237, 265, 268; judgements 109, 115–116; authenticity as a trait 1–2, 16, 18, 25
autoethnography 5, 7, 50, 57, 61, 63–65, 68, 70–71, 75, 88, 223, 239, 263
autonomy 1, 10, 21, 28–30, 33, 36–37, 43, 56, 58–59, 91, 122, 142, 197, 213, 218, 220, 225, 227, 232

Badger, R. 200
balance 19, 34–35, 55, 77, 130, 167, 172, 181–182, 199, 211, 221, 227, 235
balanced professional 223
balanced research 53, 83
balanced teaching 53, 227
Bandura, A. 57
Banegas, D. 1, 265
Barkhuizen, G. 56, 61–63, 71, 223